World of Art

Cave Art

Bruno David

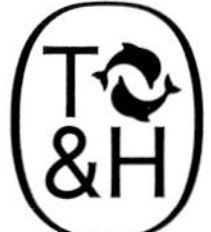

For my dear little boy Jasper, who brings joy all day long

Frontispiece:
1. Head of a rhinoceros from The Three Rhinoceroses Frieze in the cave
of Rouffignac, France. The art remains undated, but through stylistic
associations with other, dated Ice Age sites of Western Europe is thought
by some researchers to be about 15,000 years old.

First published in 2017 in the United Kingdom
by Thames & Hudson Ltd, 181A High Holborn,
London WC1V 7QX

www.thamesandhudson.com

First published in 2017 in the United States
of America by Thames & Hudson Inc.,
500 Fifth Avenue, New York, New York 10110

www.thamesandhudsonusa.com

Reprinted 2024

British Library Cataloguing-in-Publication Data
A catalogue record for this book is available from the British Library

Library of Congress Control Number 2016943097

ISBN 978-0-500-20435-1

Printed and bound in China by C&C Offset Printing Co. Ltd

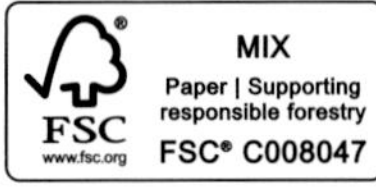

Bruno David is Associate Professor in archaeology at the Monash Indigenous Centre, Monash University, Australia. His books include *Hiri* (with Robert Skelly, 2017), the World Archaeological Congress *Handbook of Landscape Archaeology* (co-edited with Julian Thomas, 2008), *The Social Archaeology of Australian Indigenous Societies* (co-edited with Bryce Barker and Ian McNiven, 2006), *Landscapes, Rock-Art and the Dreaming* (2002), and *Inscribed Landscapes* (co-edited with Meredith Wilson, 2002). In 1994 he was awarded the inaugural Antiquity Prize for his work on the archaeology of meaning in rock art, in 2007 the Australian Archaeological Association's Bruce Veitch Award for Excellence in Indigenous Engagement, and in 2013 the Ben Cullen Prize for writings on the social construction of caves and rockshelters. His current research involves working in partnership with Indigenous communities in northern Australia and Papua New Guinea, exploring the historical connections that people have formed with places and documenting the antiquity of rock art and its meaning to local communities today.

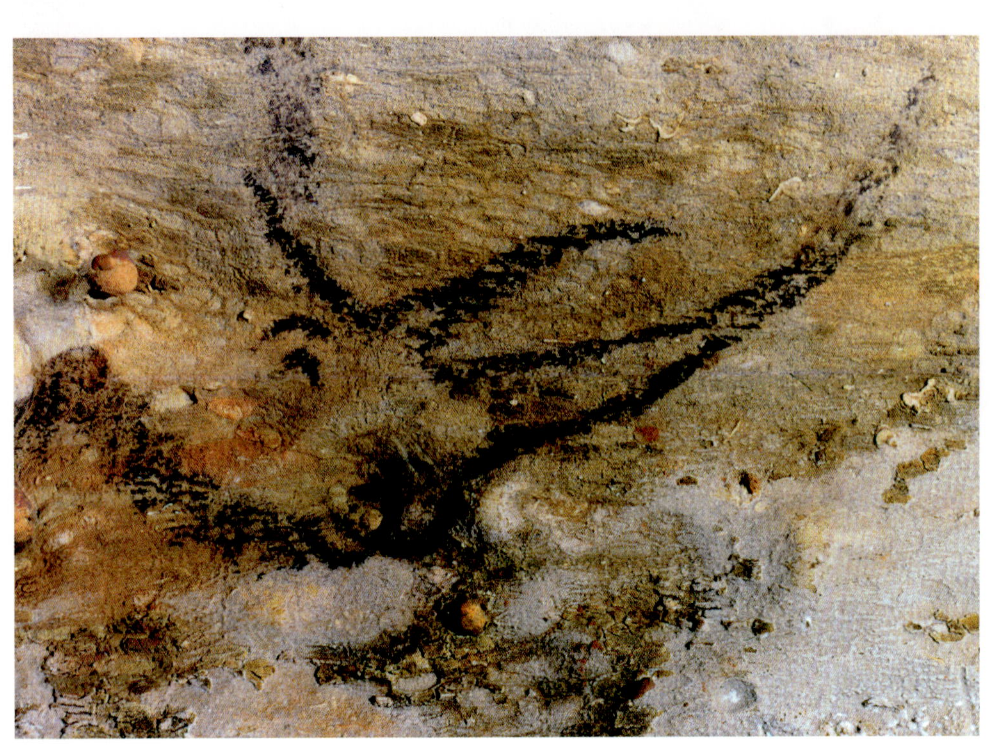

Contents

Chapter 1:   Introduction

In theory, artists can depict anything they wish, but they don't.
Claire Smith, former President of the World Archaeological
Congress[1]

In 1979 a remarkable discovery deep in the jungles of Guatemala
revealed to the world a hitherto unknown underground realm
of Maya art. The cave of Naj Tunich [2], in use during the first
millennium AD, enticed professional archaeologists and the public
alike to imagine a new kind of ancient Maya pilgrimage across
cosmic layers beneath an emerald green rainforest roof. Amid
hanging stalactites and cavernous passageways, stone altars,
smashed ceramic vessels, glyphic inscriptions and curvilinear
drawings of women, men and sacred beings in distinctive,

2. Entrance to the cave of Naj
Tunich, Guatemala, where a
previously unknown subterranean
world of Maya art and religious
performance was rediscovered
in 1979.

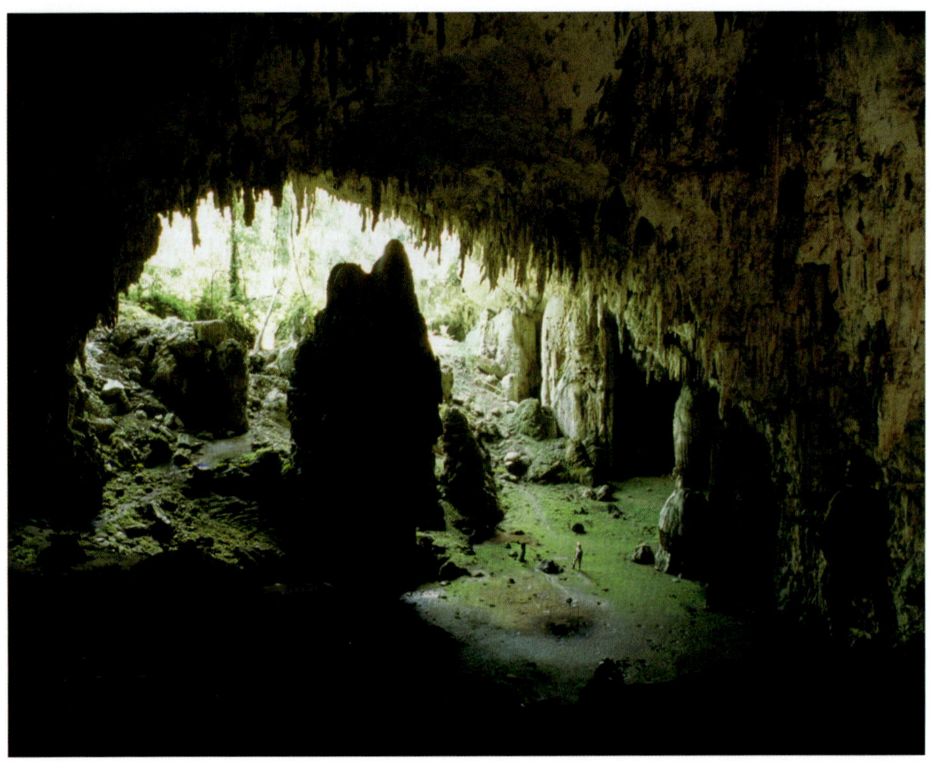

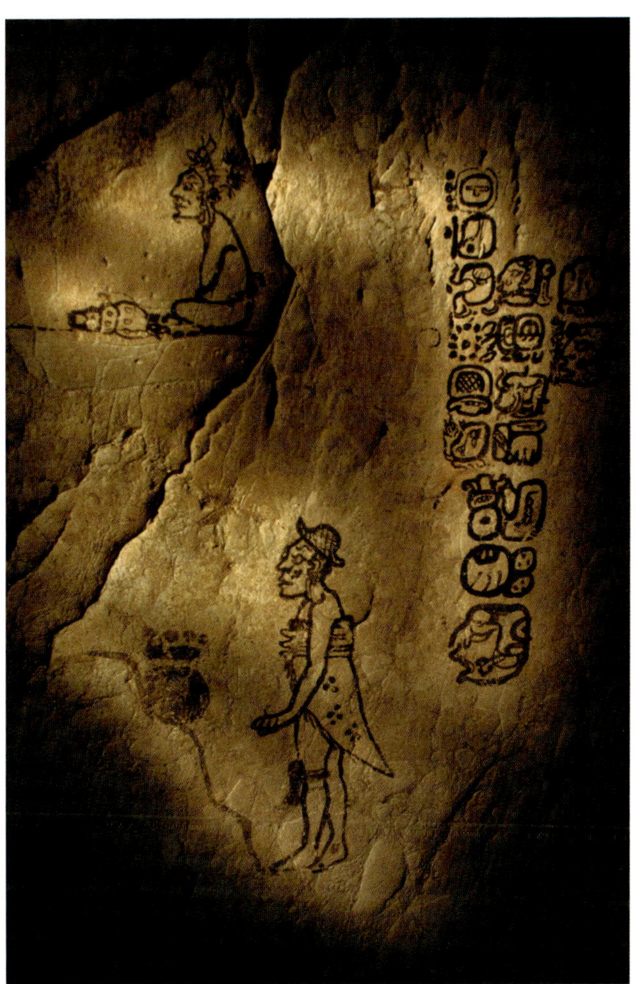

3. Maya art on the cave wall at Naj Tunich, Guatemala. Both the script and the identity of many of the personages in the art were worked out from Maya texts and ethnography (discussed in Chapter 7).

contemplative Maya pose [3] gave testimony to a sacred landscape that had remained preserved for centuries. Maya ethnography and ancient writings enabled the art and rituals to be deciphered, a knowledge to which we will return in the final chapter of this book.

In that same year, on the other side of the Atlantic, the United Nations Educational, Scientific and Cultural Organization (UNESCO) added a number of well-known French Ice Age caves richly decorated with rock art dating back some 12,000 years and more to its World Heritage List. Among these was the crowning jewel of the French Upper Palaeolithic, the cave of Lascaux with its ochre red, yellow and black pantheon of painted bulls, horses

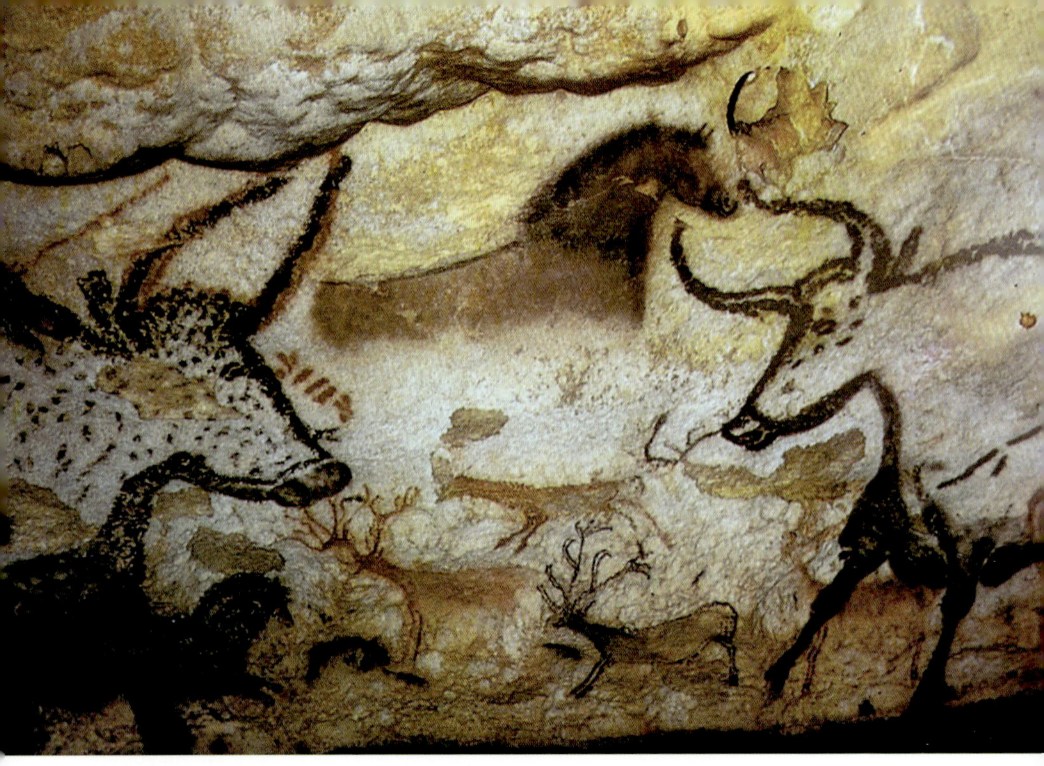

and other creatures [4]. But unlike Naj Tunich, those French sites had no ethnography of any kind, no way of making sense of what the art meant to people so many thousands of years ago.

After decades of enquiry, sometimes with considerable insights, we continue to ask: who made these fantastic paintings, deeply buried in the hollows of the earth, and why? The artists of Naj Tunich and Lascaux belonged to very different worlds and very different times, and they came from cultures utterly unlike our own. Understanding their artwork thus necessitates understanding not just the artists as individuals who painted, but also the cultures from which they came. While to some degree the works of art can be seen as the creations of individual artists, they cannot be reduced to the genius of entirely free minds, of blank slates, because how people choose to do things is to some degree conditioned by their cultural traditions. Furthermore, while an artist can decide to make or do something, the end product is rarely exactly what was anticipated at the start of the work. What we see in the art that adorns the cave walls of Naj Tunich and Lascaux, as with cave art all over the world, is as much the product of subliminal cultural forces that shaped how people once saw the world as it is the intentions of individual artists. And what *we* see in those caves also reflects how we ourselves, as observers, have been conditioned to see.

Many theories have been developed over the past 150 years to explain cave art. These have tended to be Grand Theories that tried to make sense of the art by reference to a single, overarching logic. Back in the nineteenth century, when cave art first began to be rediscovered in Spain and France, it was generally thought that the art was made for its own sake – 'art for art's sake' – as presumably ancient humans were too 'primitive' for higher kinds of reason. Then notions of totemism and 'hunting magic' became prevalent, as the world views and religious practices of living Indigenous peoples came to be documented, those new inspirations being applied to the art of Ice Age Europe. But as Indigenous communities continue to remind us today, their cultures, their artistic practices, relate to their own ways of doing things, to their own, very particular histories, not to that of others with whom they have never had any direct or even indirect contact in other parts of the world (see Chapter 7). A few decades later, these and other similar ideas were again replaced, this time by ideas of 'binary art' structured across cave walls, the assemblage of motifs signalling the unity of opposites, 'male–female' and the like. From this emerged complex notions of semiotic structure that viewed artworks as 'signs' arranged in complex but preformulated ensembles which, once understood, would reveal the meaningful 'language' of the art. More recently, there has been a swell in interest in some parts of the world, and by some researchers, in notions of 'shamanism', with all kinds of sites, cultures and artworks (other than our own!), of the past and present, being interpreted as the art of 'shamans'. These latter notions were first developed in the 1980s, in the shadow of dissatisfaction with the mechanistic interpretations of the 1970s that saw human behaviour as the product of universal laws of survival and biological reproduction, so that life (and human achievement) was usually written about in English-language science books as little more than a quest for food and survival. The 1980s rejuvenated a sense for the intangibles of life in science, reminding us that what makes existence meaningful among the world's varied cultures relates to such things as spirituality, human care, the mysteries of life and death, the emotions of everyday life, and how we make sense of and appreciate things. Interpretations of cave art thus began to search for ways to incorporate such issues, and to make them centre-stage of scientific explanations, rather than to relegate them to the edges of what really matters, more or less meaningless epiphenomena, as the 1970s had done. Yet the new explanations again came to marginalize peoples, cultures and ways of being, and as much so as the earlier Grand Theories had done, for these new explanations were also Grand Theories that paid no real attention to the reasons why particular cultures had made art in the distant past, or, in the case of most Indigenous groups across the world, why they made art recently or continue to do so today. They did not give voice to the practices and motivations of the very people who had made the art, where this was known. This is often the fate of Grand Theories that do not address or neatly fit into the ways of all.

This book takes a different tack: rather than applying an overarching explanatory framework to cave art, a Grand Theory, I am more interested in *what* happened in the past as a way of approaching *why* when dealing with decorated caves. How do we know how to make sense of such arts? I am more concerned with particularities than with overarching explanations. And I am more interested in understanding how we can be sure of our knowledge, rather than masking that knowledge with the veil of a Grand Theory. Sometimes, where artists or members of their communities can speak and explain the cultural contexts of the art for themselves, we can listen, and we can hear aspects of knowledge that we would not otherwise know about (see Chapter 7). This may not be the only story to tell – I make more of this below – but it is an important one.

Tracking history through cave art

Archaeologists are interested in understanding the past by tracking cultural practices from the depths of history: we use carbon dating to find out how old things are, space-age digital technologies to once again see colours that had, for all intents and purposes, completely disappeared from cave walls, and record traditions from Indigenous elders to try to connect artworks made by the ancestors with ideas expressed in more recent cultural perspectives (see Chapter 3). In doing so, we are also interested in understanding how the present came to be as it is today, both in our own cultures and in those of others. We do this by accessing two major sources of information: one, by understanding as much as possible the present cultures whose history we try to track, for example via discussions with community members and through the writings of anthropologists; and two, by studying the material remains of past human actions, to see what archaeological finds such as portable artifacts, ancient camp sites, artworks and the like can reveal about what people did in the past. These two sources of information allow for a 'two-way' historical investigation: tracking present cultural practices *back* in time to try to determine their origins, and following ancient practices *forward* in time to see how they have developed.[2]

Rock art specialists Paul Taçon and Christopher Chippindale have aptly pointed out that this double approach to historical research can employ two kinds of enquiry, 'informed' and 'formal'.[3] *Informed* research refers to evidence gathered from people who have first-hand knowledge about the topic of interest, for instance artists who can reveal information about their works, or community elders who can illuminate the cultural conventions under which artworks were produced. Such an approach is useful at Naj Tunich, where Maya culture and ancient texts can help us understand the art in the cave. But it is of no use for Lascaux and other Ice Age caves, so here we resort to *formal* research, where a broad spectrum of technical methods can be employed to study the paintings, such as carbon dating to determine their age, proton-induced X-ray emissions to study their elemental composition, or multivariate statistics to discover structural patterns among motif types – how different kinds of images may be associated with each other. For many images and sites, informed and formal research is done hand-in-hand, but this is only possible where the cultures that produced the art live on, or have been recorded in documents and oral traditions.

For many recently rediscovered ancient sites we must rely on formal methods, on the way that images can inspire us to think in certain ways, and on the genius of innovative researchers who find ways of shedding light on the distant past. Those researchers are readers of the art that has been left behind, those visual cues in many ways presenting themselves like graphic 'texts' made of strange, unknown signs. The images were made in the conventions of the day, and in the context of, for example, the use of particular paint recipes and colours, patterns of linework, positioning of particular images in particular locations, and associations between types of motifs. But do we really know how to 'read' those texts, given that the cultures that produced them were likely to be so different from our own? The aim of informed and formal methods is to work out elements and structures of the artworks, to try to make sense of the cultures and intentions of the people who made them. Given that they are not the products of culture-less artists, but on the contrary creations given shape by people who found meaning in their culture, can we ever make sense of the artworks?

The difficulty, as Umberto Eco has noted,[4] is that while we may know the intention of the reader, of the analyst, can we know the intention of the text, of the artworks that confront us? This is the challenge of the archaeology of cave art, explored in this book by examining how sense has been made of the cave art of other cultures, often of the distant past.

While this book focuses on the *archaeology* of cave art, there are other ways of looking at the subject. For many Indigenous peoples around the world, what is of greater interest about the cave art of their communities is how it expresses the cosmology and realities of their own world views, how it expresses a sense of their own history, and how this 'art' lives on in the present. In doing so the art connects the living with the ancestors who shaped the world in which we now live.[5] For example, the spirit *mimi*, who can be seen on the rock at Nawarla Gabarnmang in Jawoyn Aboriginal Country, northern Australia, look after 'Country' (further discussed in Chapter 7), and while they can be deeply felt as ancestral presences, other than in the art they remain unseen [5]. Here there is a focus on what the art means to the community of culture in which it is situated. These meanings express the power of the image and of the spirit-beings that the art embodies. In such cosmological understandings, artworks mediate the human world with that of the spirit world, because it is the ancestral spirits that have metamorphosized into the rock and are now visible as artworks that help maintain the health of

5. *Mimi* figure from the Jawoyn rock art site of Nawarla Gabarnmang, Arnhem Land plateau, northern Australia.

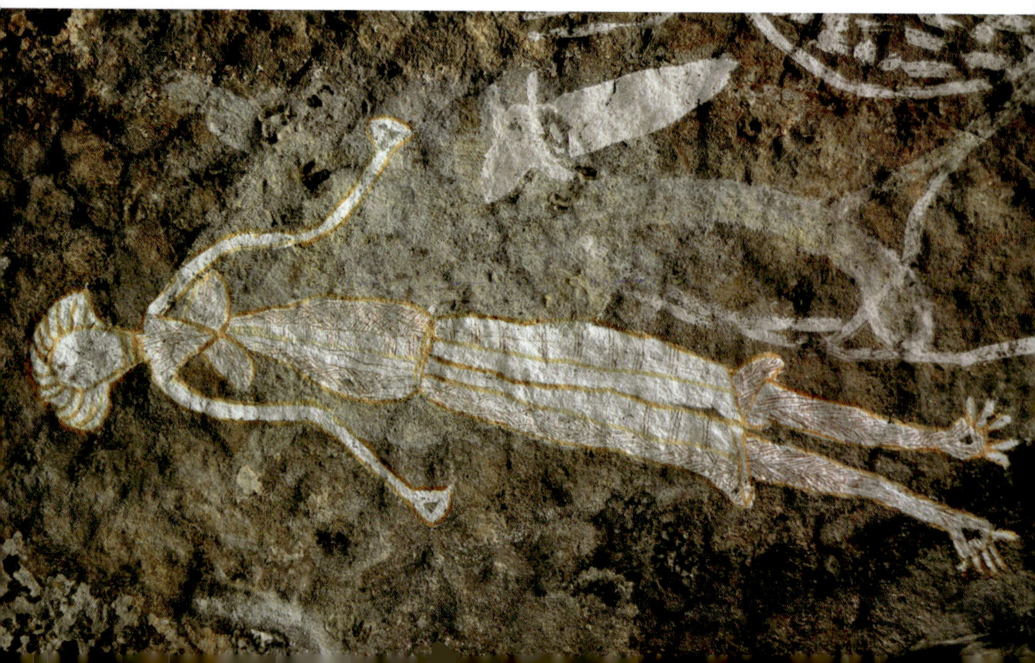

Country; it is through them that the landscape attains its present form, and it is through them that the world attains its salience and present fecundity.[6] These are understandings and concerns that can only be properly accessed through knowledgeable informants, through informed knowledge held by community members. These understandings and concerns relate to the culture of the artist, cultural perspectives that we read about in the social anthropology of art.[7] The *archaeology* of cave art is less focused on such intentions and more on structures of behaviour, geographical patterns and temporal trends, as revealed by the formal properties and distributions of artworks. In writing about cave art, the difference is about the questions that we ask of the art.

A global phenomenon

Throughout this book 'cave art' refers to artworks found in deep caves, at their entrances, and in more shallow rockshelters, rather than the art that can be found on rock pavements or at other kinds of open-air sites. Hence I refer to 'cave art' rather than to the broader concept of 'rock art' that relates to all images on rock in any setting; to do justice to both art forms would require a much longer book! In addition to the art on cave surfaces, 'cave art' also refers to buried portable art objects found in caves, such as engraved plaquettes, figurines and items of personal adornment such as jewelry.

While cave art is found around the world, it has not been recorded or studied equally everywhere. That of France and Spain has reached especially great fame over the past century, capturing the imagination of the general public as well as attracting the attention of archaeologists. Almost everywhere else, although known about for a long time, cave art only began to be taken seriously by mainstream archaeologists in the 1980s. The major reason for this late recognition is that it was only in the 1980s that we developed the technology to date it, and therefore understand the place of cave art in the historical narratives of the past. How can history be written about if we do not know *when* things happened? The development of accelerator mass spectrometry (AMS) carbon dating, a method requiring minuscule amounts of organic material to determine the age of a sample, was revolutionary for cave art research, finally enabling it to be reliably dated without degrading the art itself (see Chapter 3). The 1980s also saw an increasing interest in 'cognitive archaeology', the study of the symbolic behaviour of past peoples; was it possible to reconstruct the history of human creativity, and of the human mind? Cave art offered a perfectly rich and accessible avenue for exploring these questions, especially so given the new improvements in dating techniques. The 1970s and 1980s also saw a proliferation of cultural resource management concerns as landscape transformations associated with activities such as forestry, dams, mining and even housing developments threatened the survival of historical, non-renewable cultural sites across the world – think of the scale of China's Three Gorges Dam, or Australia's Murujuga (Burrup Peninsula) liquefied natural gas projects. With this came an increasing sense of urgency in the recording and study of vulnerable rock art sites. All these factors led to the emergence of new interest groups, rock art societies and their journals, culminating with the creation in 1988 of the International Federation of Rock Art Organizations (IFRAO), with *Rock Art Research*, established four years earlier, adopted as its official journal, in many ways uniting rock art researchers the world over.

Given this chequered history, some parts of the world boast a rich heritage of cave art research, others much less so. Our knowledge of the cave art of different regions is thus uneven. Intellectual debates relating to the cave art of certain regions have radiated far and wide, whereas those concerning less well-known artworks from marginalized areas, or advocating less popular ideas, often fall on deaf ears, despite relating what are sometimes profound insights. Some researchers have consequently resorted to announcing their points of view loudly and often, while others struggle for attention, although there is no necessary correlation between the decibels and the worthiness of the argument. Old findings have conditioned us to think in certain ways about the history of art, and new developments are sometimes challenging those preconceptions. We must be open to listening to a broad range of ideas about the art and overcoming our assumptions, however difficult. We can listen to Indigenous voices, which are teaching us of the importance of local traditions, whereas archaeologists have often been more interested in worldwide trends such as the evolution of modern humans or the origins of art itself. Such global questions have been called 'big history',[8] but who decides what makes history 'big'? For many people what is most important is specific and local, be it to ensure that the evidence is secure, one step at a time, or because the most important kind of history is that which most affects the things that are closest to our hearts.

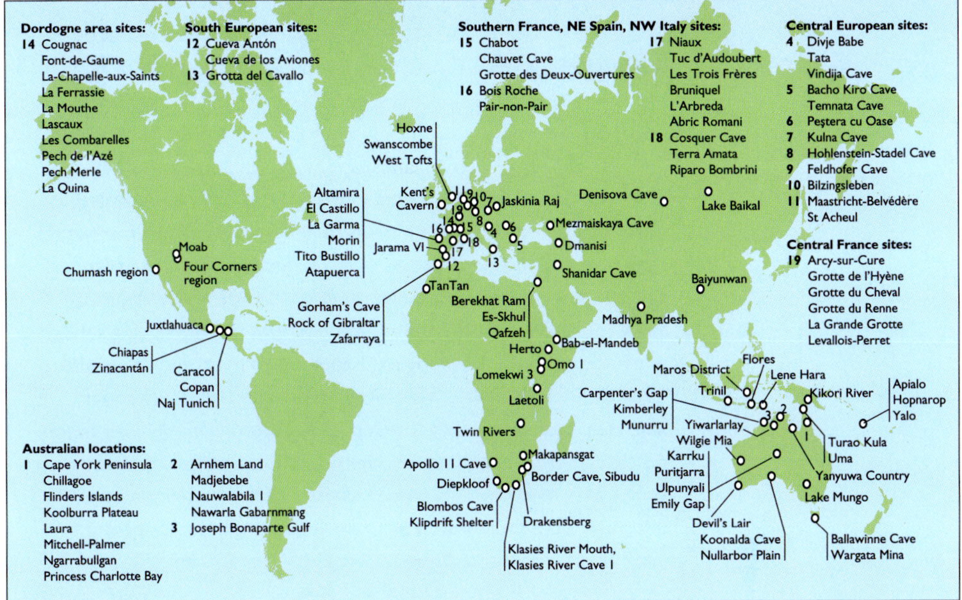

6. Map of the world showing cave art and other kinds of archaeological sites mentioned in the text.

Taking all these dimensions into account, despite wishing for equal global coverage, this book cannot, in the end, offer such balance, as the biased corpus of knowledge does not yet allow it. Rather, instructive examples from around the world give us a sense of how we each have our own, particular history: ours, that of others, and how we are all both connected to and different from each other. Celebrating that diversity in the art means that we can also celebrate a parallel diversity in our cultural differences.

Some of the examples chosen for this book are classic cases, others new findings. Some will be from our own backyards, others from distant places. In all cases, the imagery allows (hi)stories to be told, stories about the past and of the present. Western Europe continues to have more mention than elsewhere, largely because of the longer tradition of research and therefore a greater richness of available details [6]. But irrespective of the specific example, what is striking about all of these places is that the art continues to resonate with the onlooker in such a way that the site is not just a geographical location of artistic expressions, but a place that is meaningful within ourselves. It is also this sense of cave art's meaningfulness today that I wish to reflect upon in this book.[9] Though a silent reminder of distant peoples or relic of a long-gone past, cave art continues to speak to us today and to draw our imagination about how we fit in a much grander world.

Chapter 2: Discovery

Cave art occurs on all continents except Antarctica. In some parts of the world, such as northern Australia, the Four Corners region of the USA (where the states of Utah, Colorado, New Mexico and Arizona meet), the state of Madhya Pradesh in India [7], and the Drakensberg mountains of the KwaZulu-Natal province of South Africa [8], it is so abundant that hundreds and even thousands of sites have been found, and there is no doubt that much waits to be discovered in more remote regions where research has been limited or where it has not yet taken place. Some sites feature in the oral traditions of local communities, although often locations of art have been forgotten about and are only now being rediscovered. For researchers, finding sites can

7. Painted alcove at Bhimbetka, Madhya Pradesh, India.

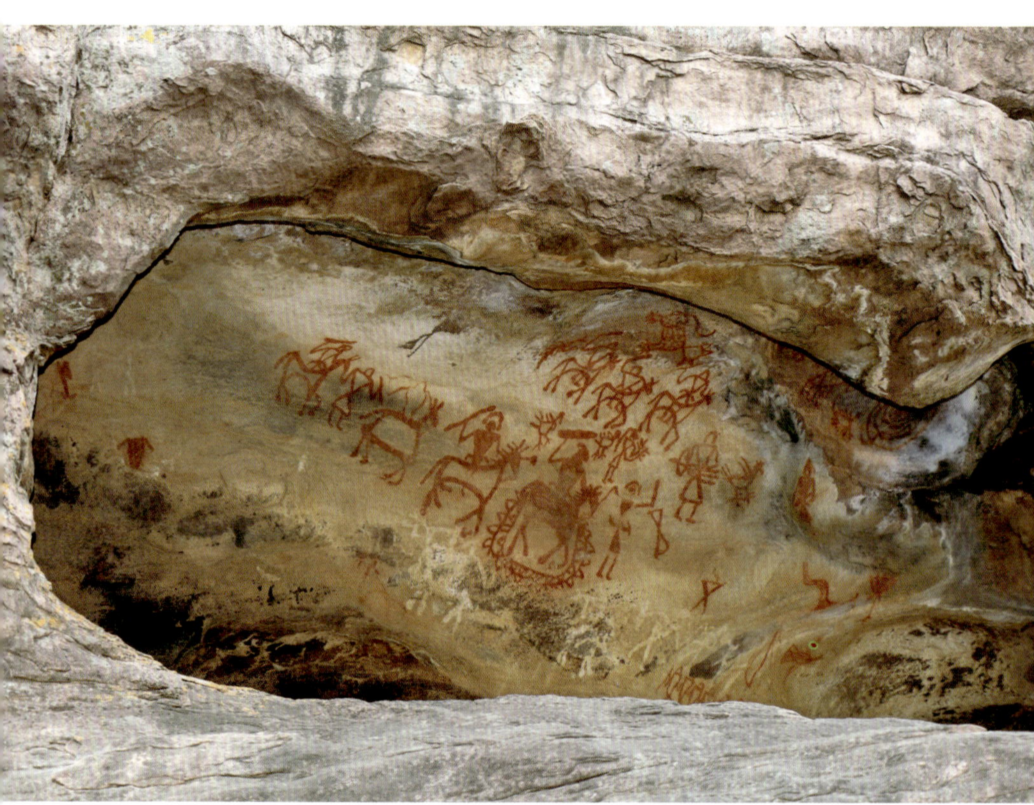

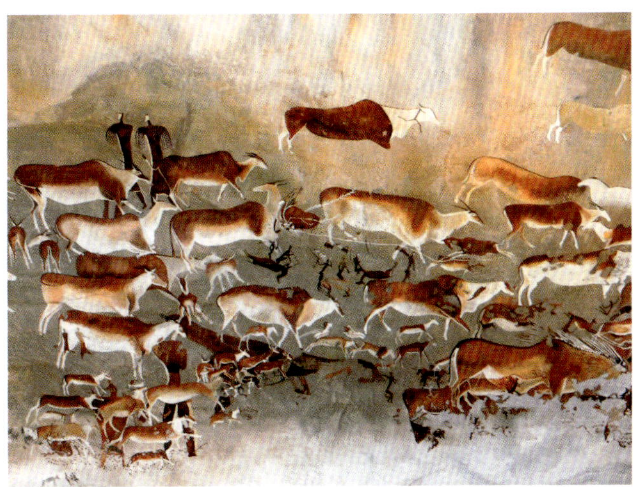

8. Paintings from Cathedral Peak in the Drakensberg, South Africa.

simply be a matter of being told about them by members of local communities, or walking past a boulder or rock outcrop during field surveys. Irrespective of the method, the act of discovery is usually part of a much bigger story, rich in human drama.

In some regions people have written about cave art for a very long time; in China those writings date back some 2,300 years.[1] Elsewhere interest in the subject is far more recent, commencing a few years ago or even awaiting first documentation. Here I discuss the discovery of four classic sites from Spain, France and Australia. Each of these will feature again in later chapters as recurring threads amid a wider geographical treatment. These sites illustrate well how the finding of cave art is not just an act of encounter, but rather one of incorporation: coming across cave art for the first time involves making meaning of that encounter, and in small or large ways those meanings come to affect how we view the world. How does a new discovery fit in with what we already know, or rather, with what we think we know? The act of discovery is entangled in a social process of meaning-making that involves many people who together make up communities of knowledge. With pre-existing knowledge the world is already understood to operate in certain ways: everything already has a place in the workings of the world, although knowledge of all things is not necessarily equally secure. The challenge is to incorporate the new encounter into that pre-existing understanding, and the pre-existing understanding into the new discovery. This is the negotiation of knowledge, and it never stops.

Altamira, Spain

The discovery of the art of Altamira in Cantabrian Spain is a now legendary encounter that forced us to rethink what we thought we knew about the history of the human mind.[2] It is a story embedded in interpersonal interactions, preconceptions and the power to wield those preconceptions onto others; Altamira brought each of these entanglements to the fore. Because of its familiar human drama, the story of Altamira is one that continues to polarize both the academic establishment and the public alike, for many emitting an emotional unease relating to the character and impact of authority and institutional power. It is a story of the pathos and injustice of how people with backing and influence can treat the less powerful, and of the abuse of establishment privileges to the detriment of individuals and novel ideas. It is also a story of social challenges and of the power of preconceptions in decision-making and in the scientific process, leading us to question the security of knowledge, and how to make sense of what we think we know. It is said that having a little knowledge about something is a dangerous thing. But when do we know that knowledge is so insufficient that it should not be brandished? When do we know that it is secure, or secure enough to transmit across society? Altamira has caused us to reflect not just on the art, but on knowledge itself.

Altamira contained the first Palaeolithic on-wall imagery to be discovered in Europe,[3] but it was years before it was recognized as such by the establishment and by the broader public. The cave has been known in modern times since 1868, when a local hunter found a narrow entrance along the side of a limestone hill near the town of Santillana del Mar. He showed the site to Marcelino Sanz de Sautuola [9], a Spanish gentleman and nobleman who lived in the nearby village of Reocín. Although he was a university law graduate, Sanz de Sautuola's passion was archaeology and the deep history of modern humans. At Altamira he saw some strange black paintings, but these were unassuming and at first he gave them no particular attention.

In 1878 Sanz de Sautuola visited the Exposition Universelle in Paris [10], a world's fair that saw France mount a cultural and trade exhibition in the wake of the draining 1870–71 Franco-Prussian war. Here he met Édouard Piette, the famed French prehistorian, and witnessed on display recently found artifacts including portable artworks that had begun to be amassed from excavations in French Palaeolithic caves [11]. Returning

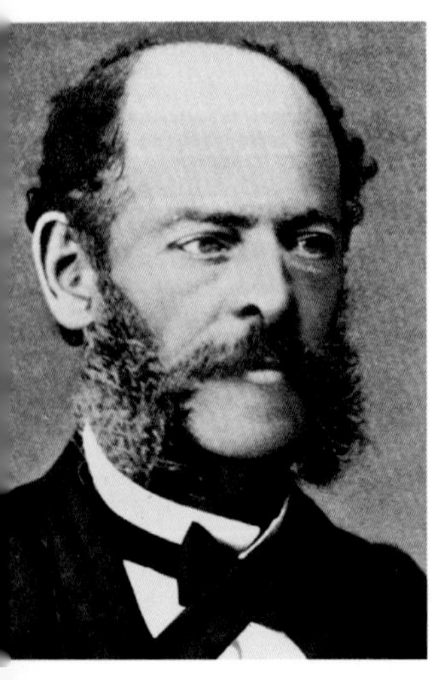

9. Marcelino Sanz de Sautuola.

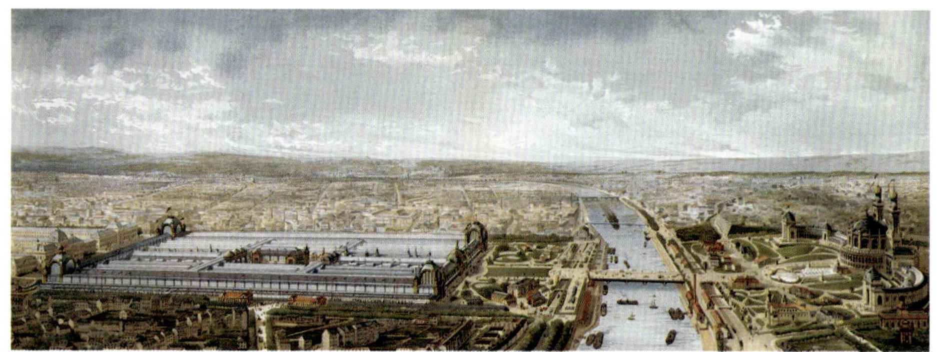

10. (above) Panoramic view of the Exposition Universelle of 1878, Paris.

11. (right) Carved antler '*bâtons de commandement*' from the Dordogne region of France, published in 1875. In 1878 Marcelino Sanz de Sautuola met Édouard Piette when he exhibited such objects at the Exposition Universelle in Paris.

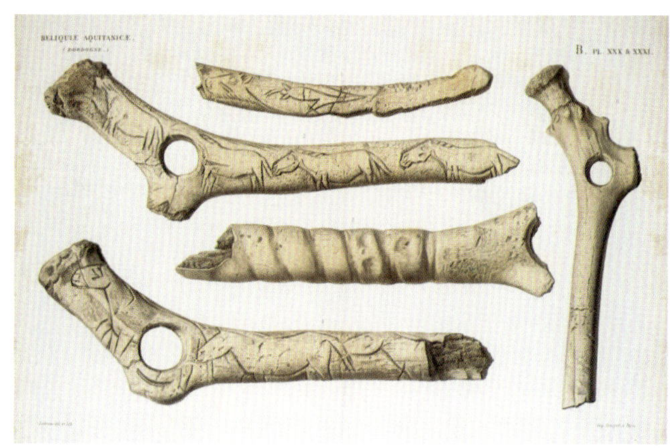

12. María Sanz de Sautuola.

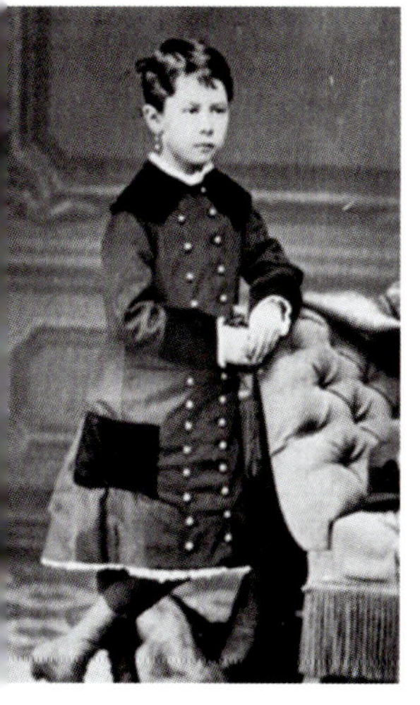

to Reocín, Sanz de Sautuola decided to undertake excavations at Altamira the following year, to see if he too could find signs of the ancients – buried artifacts and portable art objects – much as his contemporaries had done in France. Digging close to the entrance of the cave, he found numerous archaeological objects including stone tools, animal bones and fragments of ochre. But it was not these excavated artifacts that most captured his attention and that soon came to see Altamira hold centre stage in international debates, but rather the discovery of wonderful naturalistic paintings of extinct animals by his young daughter María [12], who had ventured deeper into the cave while Sanz de Sautuola was busy excavating. As legend goes, she stood in amazement in front of richly painted galleries, calling out 'Daddy, look, oxen'.[4] Her father investigated and gazed in wonder at magnificent, multicoloured depictions of bison and other animals [13].

The following year, Sanz de Sautuola published what he and his daughter had found at Altamira. *Breves Apuntes Sobre Algunos*

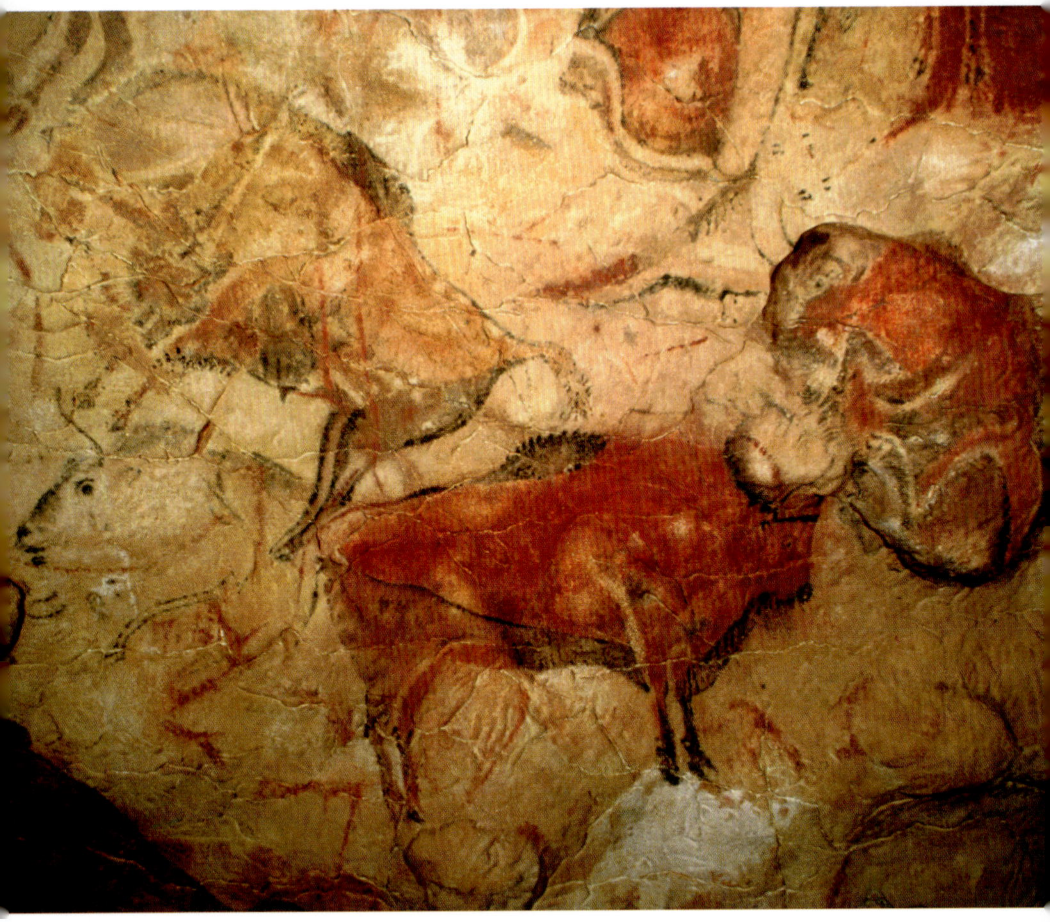

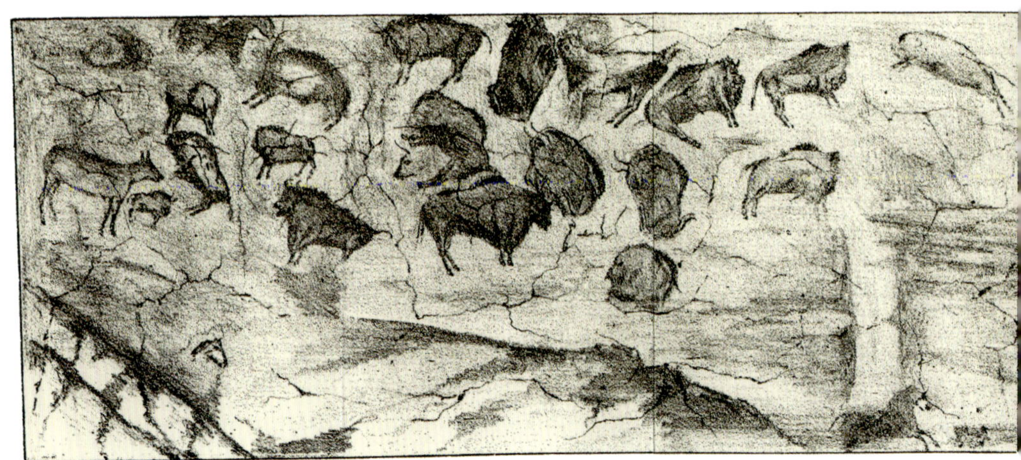

Objetos Prehistóricos de la Provincia de Santander ('Brief Notes on Some Prehistoric Objects from the Province of Santander') reported on the excavations and presented an analysis of the Altamira paintings, including what he identified as extinct bison [14]. He also compared the artworks on Altamira's ceiling with Palaeolithic portable objects carved of bone that had recently been unearthed in France, noting their formal similarities and arguing that the paintings and engravings of Altamira must be of a comparably deep antiquity. His colleague Juan Vilanova y Piera, a geologist from the University of Madrid, soon spread the word at international congresses across Western Europe. At one particularly influential meeting held at Lisbon in Portugal in 1880, the ninth International Congress of Anthropology and Prehistoric Archaeology, Vilanova y Piera presented Sanz de Sautuola's findings to some of the most influential prehistorians the world had ever seen, including Émile Cartailhac (France), Sir John Lubbock (England), Oscar Montelius (Sweden), Luigi Pigorini (Italy) and Rudolf Virchow (Germany).[5] Vilanova y Piera's commitment to the cause ensured that knowledge of Altamira's discoveries would be widely disseminated. But while some prehistorians such as Piette received the announcement of Altamira's cave paintings with cautious enthusiasm (for Piette, a Palaeolithic age for Altamira's art was entirely consistent with the Palaeolithic age of the portable art he had discovered), Sanz de Sautuola's interpretation of the Altamira paintings as made by Palaeolithic artists was met with derision and hostility by many of France's most powerful academics. This is despite Cartailhac being so impressed by the excavated archaeological findings of Portugal and Spain that soon after the Congress he coined the Iberian Peninsula 'the promised land of prehistorians'.[6]

Nothing quite like Altamira's cave paintings had been seen before, intricately carved excavated portable objects notwithstanding. And neither the general public nor the nascent science of archaeology, only newly informed by the kinds of evolutionary thought propounded by Charles Darwin in his *On the Origin of Species* (published in 1859, a mere twenty years before the discovery of Altamira's paintings), were yet prepared to recognize that artistic masterworks could have been made by Palaeolithic peoples. The portable art was conveniently airbrushed away from serious consideration when it really mattered. But Altamira quickly became a thorn in the side, so the engineer and prehistorian Édouard Harlé was commissioned by the influential pioneering French anthropologist Louis Laurent

Gabriel de Mortillet and France's pre-eminent prehistorian of the time, and the founding father of European cave art research, Émile Cartailhac, to assess Altamira's paintings, concluding in his 1881 report that they were fakes painted sometime during the 1870s, between Sanz de Sautuola's two visits. The art of Altamira could not possibly be that old, it was thought, and so was relegated to a hoax by de Mortillet, and to the work of recent Catholic priests by Cartailhac (who had only just been warned that Spanish clerics were going to try to discredit the discipline). Harlé's report was soon published in what was then one of the world's leading prehistory journals, *Matériaux pour l'Histoire Primitive et Naturelle de l'Homme*, edited by Cartailhac himself, in what was hardly an independent process of assessment and publication.[7] The result was that Sanz de Sautuola was derided for having been fooled by the paintings, and some went so far as to suggest that Altamira had been recently painted to ridicule the very prehistorians who were now attacking their discoverers. The art was simply too good and too realistic to have been made so long ago, at a time in European scholarship when evolutionary thought considered Palaeolithic peoples too primitive for refined artistic sensitivities.

In the years that followed, rich new findings in France began to align with those of Altamira, and the same prehistorians who had belittled Sanz de Sautuola came to rethink the evidence and, with this, their own position on the antiquity of Altamira's artworks. The year 1895 was key in the history of European cave art, for in that year excavations at La Mouthe [15], near the town

15. The entrance to the cave of La Mouthe, now walled off.

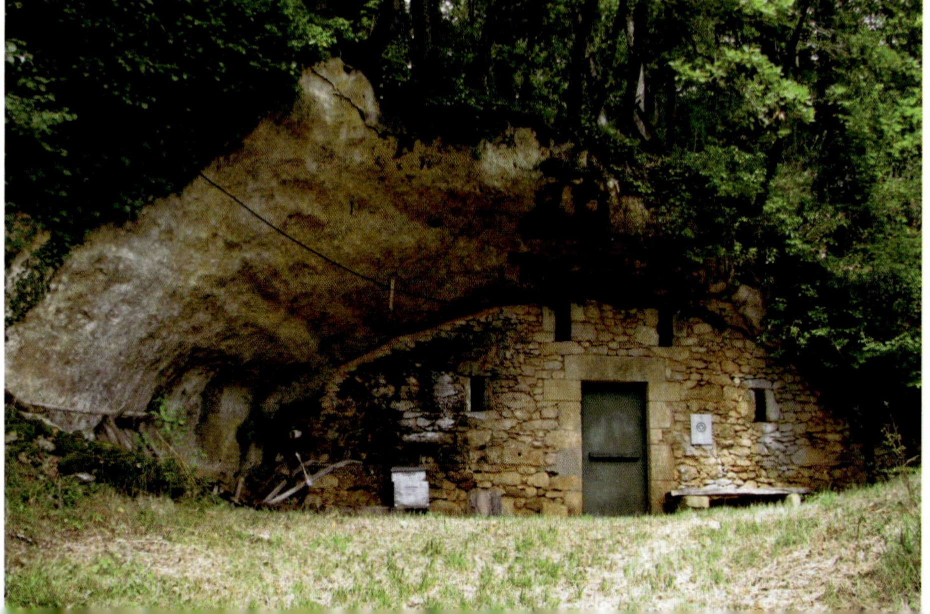

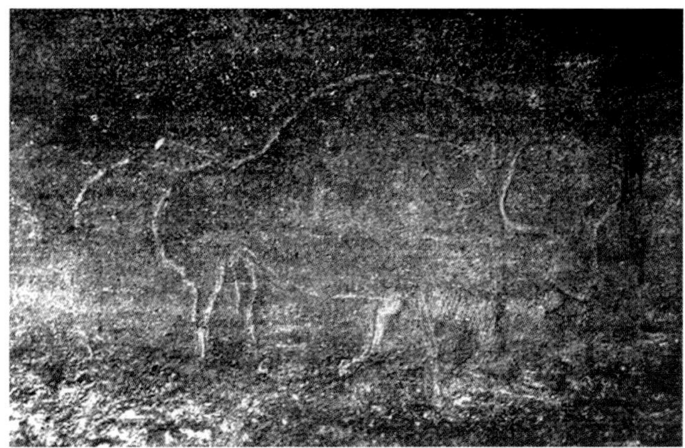

16. (right) Engraved bison deep in the cave of La Mouthe, France. This image is part of a larger set that together represent the first photographs of Ice Age cave art to be published (in 1897) anywhere in the world. It was taken by the light of 150 candles.

17. (below) Recent professional photograph of the same Ice Age engraving as shown in ill. 16.

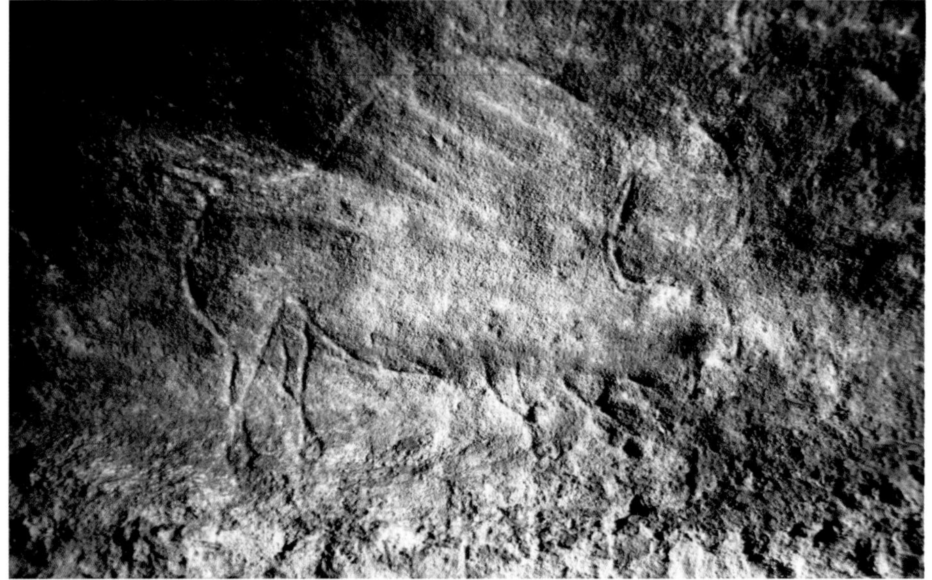

of Les Eyzies in the Dordogne region of France, revealed what would turn out to be clinching evidence for the Palaeolithic age of on-wall artworks – although it would take another seven years, when more sites yielded corroborating evidence, for virtually everyone to be entirely convinced.

At La Mouthe, the removal of rocks and soil from the rear chamber had exposed a previously unknown, deeper section of the cave. Here, along a narrow corridor some 94 m (310 ft) inside the cave, engraved bison and other artworks could now be seen [16, 17]. That same year, in 1895, Émile Rivière began

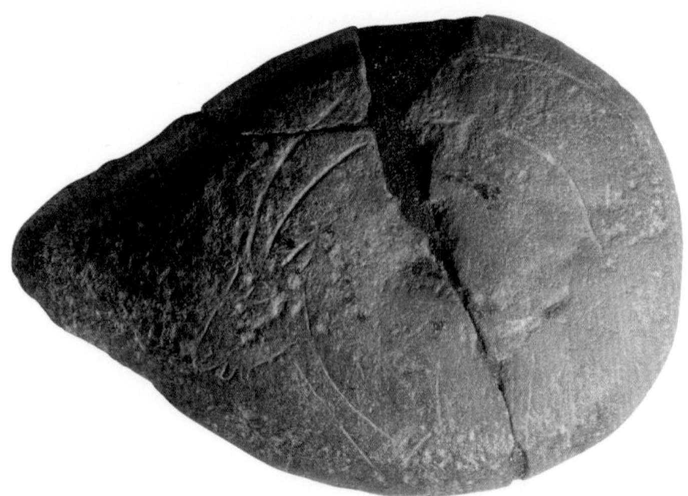

archaeological excavations at La Mouthe,[8] revealing further engravings and traces of red pigment on the walls; a Palaeolithic stone lamp was also unearthed four years later, solving the question of how the pitch black chambers could have been lit in antiquity [18]. The lower sections of some of the engravings on the walls lay buried beneath a well-defined layer of undisturbed clay that contained both Palaeolithic stone tools and the bones of extinct fauna dating to Palaeolithic times, including reindeer, hyena and cave bear. Above the clay, stalagmites had formed.[9] The art thus had to pre-date the stalagmites and be contemporaneous with or older than the Palaeolithic fauna contained in the layer of clay that partly buried it. Rivière had some of the engravings photographed by Charles Durand, illuminating the cave with the light of 150 candles; they are the first photographs ever published of any cave art in the world [16]. For Rivière the evidence had become irrefutable, as he clearly and systematically argued in his 1897 report in the *Bulletins de la Société d'Anthropologie de Paris*. Rivière was adamant: 'My mind was made up: *the engravings of La Mouthe were prehistoric*' (his italics).[10] Palaeolithic peoples did in fact make on-wall artworks that were stylistically comparable to the carvings and shallower engravings made on portable objects such as bone, antler and stone plaquettes, and deep in antiquity people had made lamps to light up the caves.[11]

Rivière had found the clinching evidence, and he wanted others to see it in all its glory. He was well aware of the scepticism that Palaeolithic cave art brought with it, so the best way to convince his contemporaries of the significance of his findings was to invite them to La Mouthe while the work was going on, so that they could make up their own minds after seeing the evidence at first hand. So it was that in 1895 he invited Louis Capitan, Maurice Féaux, Piette, Cartailhac and other pre-eminent prehistorians, geologists and specialists who had just attended the congress of the Association Française pour l'Avancement des Sciences (the French Association for the Advancement of Science) at Bordeaux, to visit La Mouthe. The guests carefully assessed the art on the walls of the cave, its stratigraphic relationship with the buried deposits that partly covered it, and its formal similarities with excavated Palaeolithic portable art and comparable engravings also covered by calcite that were just being found at the cave of Chabot. For many, the weight of the evidence was beginning to conclusively tilt in favour of Palaeolithic art.[12]

In 1896 further engravings covered by calcite were reported from Pair-non-Pair, and in 1901 from Les Combarelles in southern France. In 1901 paintings of Ice Age fauna highly reminiscent of those at Altamira were also discovered at Font-de-Gaume near Les Combarelles [19]. By the time the

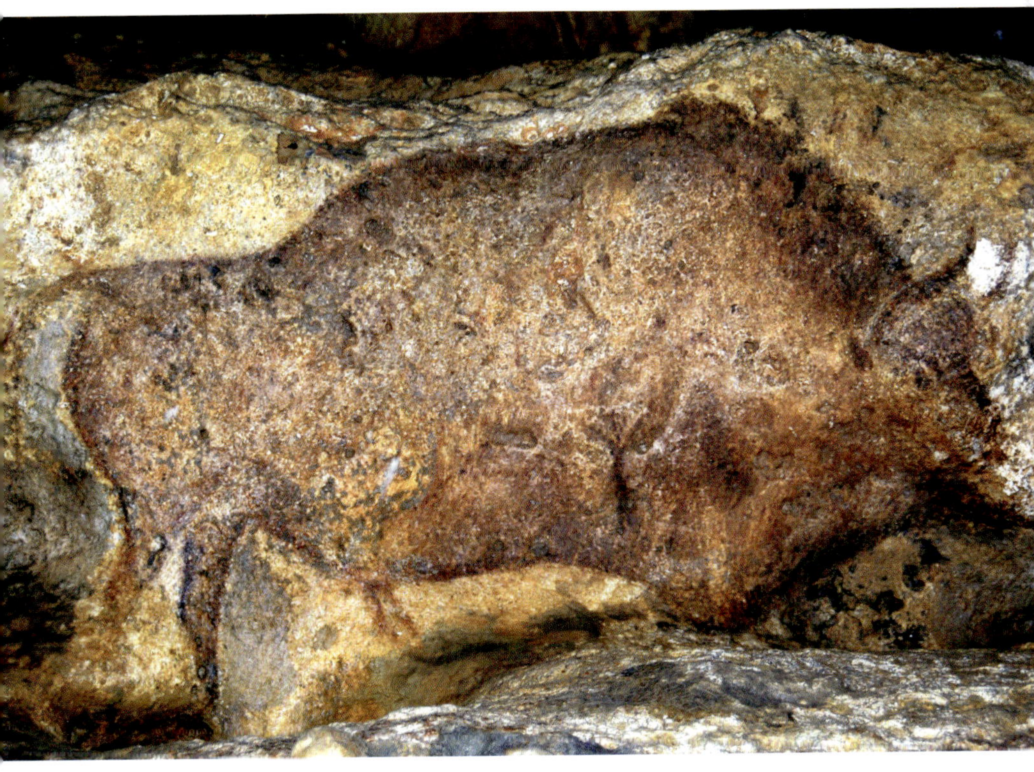

19. Painted bison at Font-de-Gaume, France.

Association Française pour l'Avancement des Sciences held its congress at Montauban in 1902, the evidence had become clear. The post-congress excursion to La Mouthe, Les Combarelles and Font-de-Gaume was well attended by senior prehistorians including Cartailhac and a number of other authorities who had previously voiced their opposition to Sanz de Sautuola's interpretations [20]. Summarizing the excursion, Rivière concluded: 'In brief, we think we can say, without being contradicted by any among them, that the Palaeolithic antiquity of all the engraved and painted images of the three caves of La Mouthe, Font-de-Gaume and Les Combarelles is no longer in doubt in the minds of our colleagues'.[13] By implication given their great formal similarities, the paintings of Altamira must also be Palaeolithic, as Sanz de Sautuola had argued in 1880.

Finally recognizing his earlier error of judgement, which he explained by an absence of precedence and a need for caution, Cartailhac formally and publically retracted his earlier stance and apologized for his attacks on Sanz de Sautuola, publishing in *L'Anthropologie*, France's leading anthropology journal, an influential paper entitled 'Les cavernes ornées de dessins, La Grotte d'Altamira (Espagne): Mea culpa d'un sceptique' ('The caves decorated with drawings, Altamira Cave (Spain): A sceptic's error of judgement'). 'From all the evidence, *we now have no reason to doubt the antiquity of Altamira's paintings*,' he wrote, 'We must bow to the truth of what lies before us, and, as for myself, make honourable amends to Mr de Sautuola' (his italics).[14] With a mix of explanation and humility he acknowledged

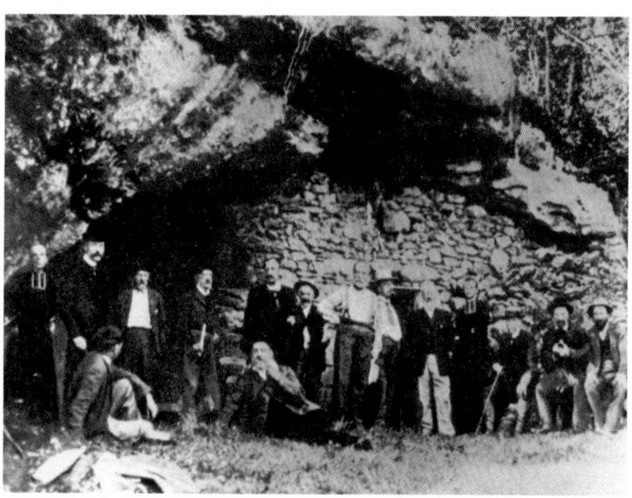

20. Delegation of the Association Française pour l'Avancement des Sciences at the entrance to the cave of La Mouthe, 14 August 1902.

that he had wronged Sanz de Sautuola, a man of integrity, and
that through his harsh attacks and intransigence he himself had
impeded the progress of knowledge. In that same year Cartailhac
visited Altamira for the first time, meeting Sanz de Sautuola's
daughter María, but, sadly, he could not apologize to her father,
who had died four years earlier.[15]

Lascaux, France

While the story of Altamira is now legendary in the global
archives of the history of archaeology, the discovery of Lascaux,
France's equally famous cave, itself began with a legend.[16] Local
oral tradition had it among long-time residents of Montignac that
a long-lost subterranean tunnel once connected the Castle of
Montignac with the Manor of Lascaux. The main tunnel, it was
said, gave way to another that led to a fabulous treasure under
the Montignac woods.[17]

On 8 September 1940, three months after the capitulation
of Paris to the Germans in World War II, seven youths were
walking through the woods with their dogs.[18] On the side of
a hill to the south of Montignac, on private land owned by the
Count of La Rochefoucauld, they came across a deep depression
in the ground, recently caused by an uprooted tree. One of the
dogs, Robot, was drawn to the hollow, sniffing at a hole between
rocks at its base. The boys began thinking about the legend of the
lost tunnel and the treasures it held, counting their luck as they
wondered if this could possibly be it. They threw pebbles into
the narrow opening, ears to the ground, carefully listening for
the sound of the rocks as they tumbled downwards.

Four days later, four of the boys – Marcel Ravidat, Jacques
Marsal, Georges Agniel and Simon Coëncas – returned to the
spot of their earlier discovery. Removing rocks to enlarge the
opening, they exposed the entrance of a shaft wide enough to
squeeze through. With a home-made oil lamp (built by Ravidat)
in hand, the four boys slid some 15 m (50 ft) down the shaft,
landing in an open chamber with a flat floor partly covered with
stalagmites and stalactites hanging from the roof. Wandering
deeper into the chamber, it was not the geological formations
that took their breath away, but a multicoloured subterranean art
gallery replete with paintings of life-sized animals that appeared
to move in the subdued, flickering light of their lamp. They had
stumbled onto the art chamber we now know as the Hall of Bulls,
one of the most celebrated cave art friezes [4]. They continued to

explore the cave until their lamp began to fade, and in haste made their way back to the entrance.

Sworn to secrecy, the next day the boys decided to return to their newly discovered underground cavern, this time equipped with a rope with which to explore deeper. Keeping their discovery from family and friends was difficult, but on that day all four boys remained silent. By the next day, 14 September, their excitement got the better of them and they told a group of friends of their discovery, inviting each to pay a small sum to enter the cave and see it for themselves. In coming days news of the discovery spread like wildfire, local villagers scrambling to see the underground artworks. The boys further enlarged the cave's opening to facilitate entrance for what quickly grew to a large crowd. On 18 September, six days after they had first entered the cave, the boys realized that things were getting out of hand, and suspecting that the art was prehistoric and of considerable importance, they told their school teacher Léon Laval, who was himself a member of the local prehistory society. Although Laval was at first reluctant to accept the boys' fantastic story, suspecting some kind of devious trick conjured by the imagination of teenagers, once he entered the cave he was immediately convinced of the art's authenticity, and of its enormous importance to prehistory. Laval instructed the boys to guard the cave and not let anyone touch the art. Marsal soon set up camp at the entrance, convinced of his need to protect the cave, as the other three boys returned to school.

On 20 September, a week and a day after the cave's discovery, Maurice Thaon, a student of Abbé Henri Breuil, then Europe's pre-eminent prehistorian specializing in rock art, visited Lascaux with Marsal acting as guide. Thaon had heard of the discovery three days earlier from the manager of the Hôtel du Soleil d'Or at Montignac, where he was then residing, and that same day had telephoned Breuil to inform him. By chance, Breuil himself was nearby at Cublac, near the town of Brive, and on 21 September, the day after his visit to Lascaux, Thaon took to his bicycle to show Breuil his sketches of the cave's artworks. Accompanied by prehistorians André Cheynier and Abbé Jean Bouyssonie, Breuil hurried to the site that same day, confirming the artworks to be Palaeolithic masterpieces as he proclaimed the site 'The Sistine Chapel of Prehistory' [21]. Within a week 1,500 visitors had entered the cave through its narrow entrance, all under the guidance of two of its original finders, Marsal and Ravidat [22]. Within eight years of its discovery, up to 1,000 visitors were entering the cave daily [23].

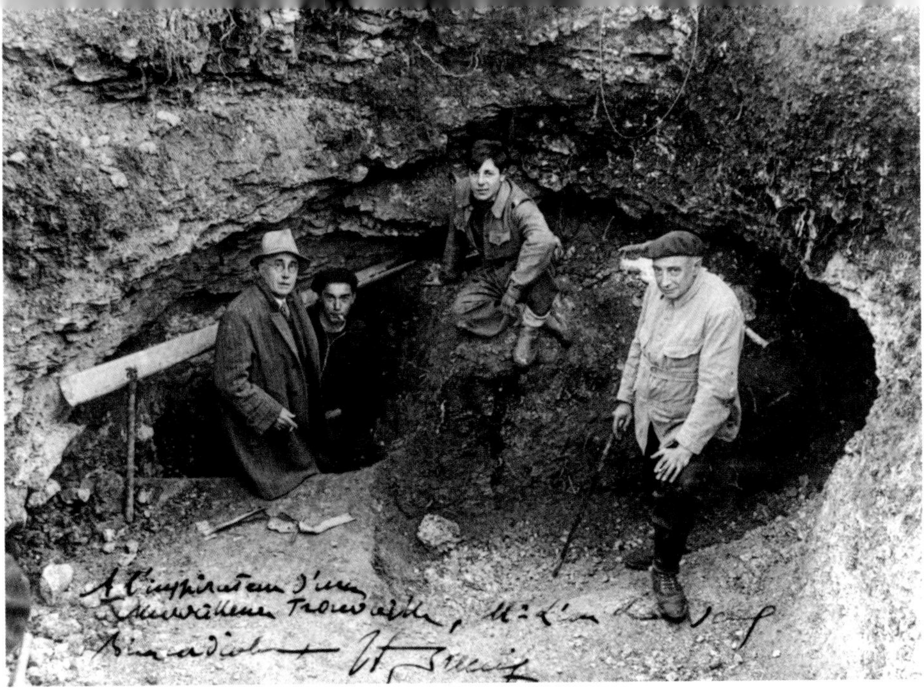

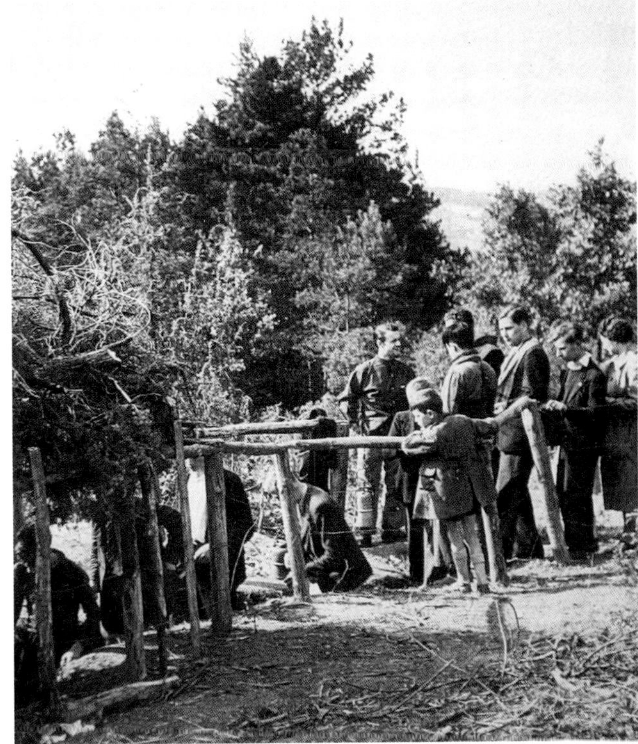

21. The enlarged entrance of
Lascaux within weeks of its
discovery in 1940. From left to
right: Léon Laval, Marcel Ravidat,
Jacques Marsal, Abbé Henri Breuil.

22 Early visitors to Lascaux soon
after its discovery in 1940.

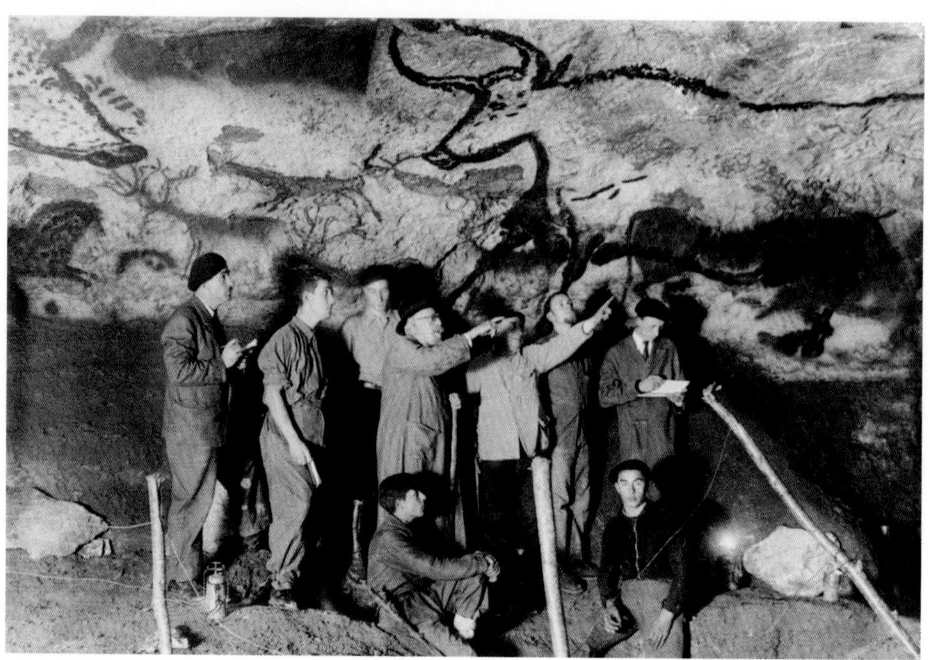

23. Hall of Bulls, Lascaux, October 1940, less than two months after the discovery of the cave. Count Bégouën and Abbé Henri Breuil are pointing to the head of the big bull; Marcel Ravidat (face to camera) and Jacques Marsal (profile) are sitting.

Lascaux's rapid rise to fame, and the high visitor numbers – over a million people visited the cave in the fifteen years between 1948 and 1963 – meant that signs of damage soon began to show on the cave's rock walls. Contaminants such as heightened levels of carbon dioxide and increased heat and humidity had been inadvertently introduced into the cave when its entrance was widened, as well as through human breath and whatever microscopic organisms people carried on them. By 1952 it was clear that the 1,200 daily visitors could not be sustained without irreversibly endangering the cave's artworks. Problems were especially evident in the growth of algae on the cave walls and on the art (the 'green sickness') followed by calcite growth (the 'white sickness'), and so in 1963 André Malraux, the French Minister of the State Charged with Cultural Affairs, permanently closed the cave, after which only a select few were permitted to enter, including those commissioned to monitor the state of the cave as conservators struggled to reverse the damage done. In the spring of 2001, new fungal growth began to appear, and in 2008 black mould spread, arguably caused by a newly installed manually switched climate control system, bright lighting and ongoing visitation by a handful of individuals. Visitation was thus further reduced as professional conservators plied their wares.

Today the cave remains closed and fungal and mould growth has ceased.[19] Despite these hazards for the art's long-term survival, Lascaux remains a cherished symbol of the origins of artistic modernity and of France's cultural heritage, and with this an icon of French national identity, in some ways much like Stonehenge is for England, the Grand Canyon for the USA, or Angkor for Cambodia.

After its discovery, Lascaux quickly grew as a symbol of French identity, known by schoolchildren and adults alike. The site and its art are held with utmost regard in the contemporary French psyche. This is unusual for a cave art site anywhere, and we may ask how this has come about. Is it the art alone that renders this particular cave of such great significance? Or rather is there something more, something subliminal perhaps, that has deeply affected the nation? There is, I think, a strong connection to make that goes beyond the site and its art, as explained below.

After a month of heavy fighting during World War II, German forces entered an undefended Paris on 14 June 1940 [24]. Eight days later France reluctantly signed an armistice with Germany that would see a puppet government installed and much of the country occupied. Lascaux's discovery in the '*zone libre*', the unoccupied part of France, exactly eighty days after the formal signing of the armistice that recognized the German occupation of the rest of the country, became a psychological respite from invasion. During and even more so after the war, in the aftermath of intense resistance to an aggressive assault that left deep and lasting physical, emotional and psychological scars and that had

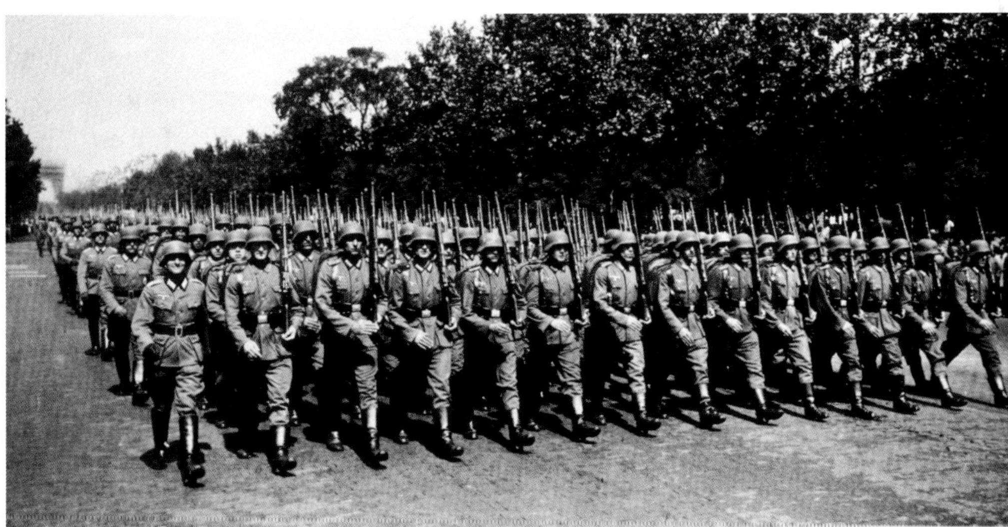

24. German troops march down the Champs-Élysées as they enter Paris during World War II, 14 June 1940.

devastated the very idea of an independent France, a resurgent
nation readily and enthusiastically adopted Lascaux as a new icon.
The discovery of cave art at the site was not only a reminder
of France's deep history, but also a cultural document visually
declaring a *French* heritage to be cherished, researched, managed
and shared by all its citizens as a unified whole. Through Lascaux
France once again rose in its own identity, its own governance.
The cave art became a symbol of French distinctiveness
and nationalism in the wake of an aggressive invasion by a
foreign power that had threatened to eradicate the nation's
independence. The significance of Lascaux's cave art is not just
in its pigments, in its designs, but in how the discovery announced
the survival and confirmation of France's own heritage. Lascaux
is a symbol of a nation that was not just ready for, but profoundly
needful of, its own continuing cultural legacy and political freedom.

It is no coincidence that in 1959 André Malraux was named
Ministre d'État Chargé des Affaires Culturelles ('Minister of the
State Charged with Cultural Affairs') by the French government.
In these post-war years, culture was explicitly and officially
recognized to lie at the heart of national identity, and Lascaux
featured prominently as an icon of history and culture. It is
under this Ministerial title, and entitlement, that Malraux closed
Lascaux from public access in 1963, to protect it from further
damage. He also featured the cave in his imaginary life story of
1967, *Antimémoires*.[20] 'Anti-memory' is how he reflected on the
way we remember the past, our own included, a melding of
actual events and experiences with conjured memories. In this
textual masterpiece, Malraux is less concerned with the nostalgia
and pain that our memories allow us to expose, as with how
those memories allow us to interrogate existence itself and the
workings of the world. Here Lascaux features as a secluded
grotto where French resistance fighters hid their weaponry
during World War II. At the very end of the book, Malraux likens
the threats to Lascaux's survival, caused by the algal and fungal
growths on the cave walls, to the threats of the war; and, like the
machinery of war, the machinery of access such as the climate
control and ladders that now penetrate deep into the recesses of
the cave threaten to strip Lascaux of its integrity as an extension
of the past that reaches to the present. Lascaux is not just a cave
of ancestral achievements, but a symbol of the combat of tyranny
and carelessness with hope and independence, and one that
requires awareness and careful management in the face of ongoing
and in many ways irreversible change.

Chauvet Cave, France

The lessons learnt from Lascaux were put to good use on the finding of another cultural masterpiece and the most recent pride of France's national heritage, Chauvet Cave. Here discovery was not made by youths, but by experienced, professional cavers looking for deep underground caves in limestone cliffs high above the spectacular Pont d'Arc in France's Ardèche region, at the junction of the Massif Central and Rhône Valley.

The approach of Christmas on 18 December 1994 will forever be inscribed in the minds of Eliette Brunel-Deschamps, Christian Hillaire and Jean-Marie Chauvet, French cavers who on that day came across what may be the most spectacular cave gallery ever discovered.

25. The spectacular cliffline on the edge of the Ardèche River, France. Here are found some of France's most celebrated decorated Ice Age caves, the most notable being Chauvet Cave.

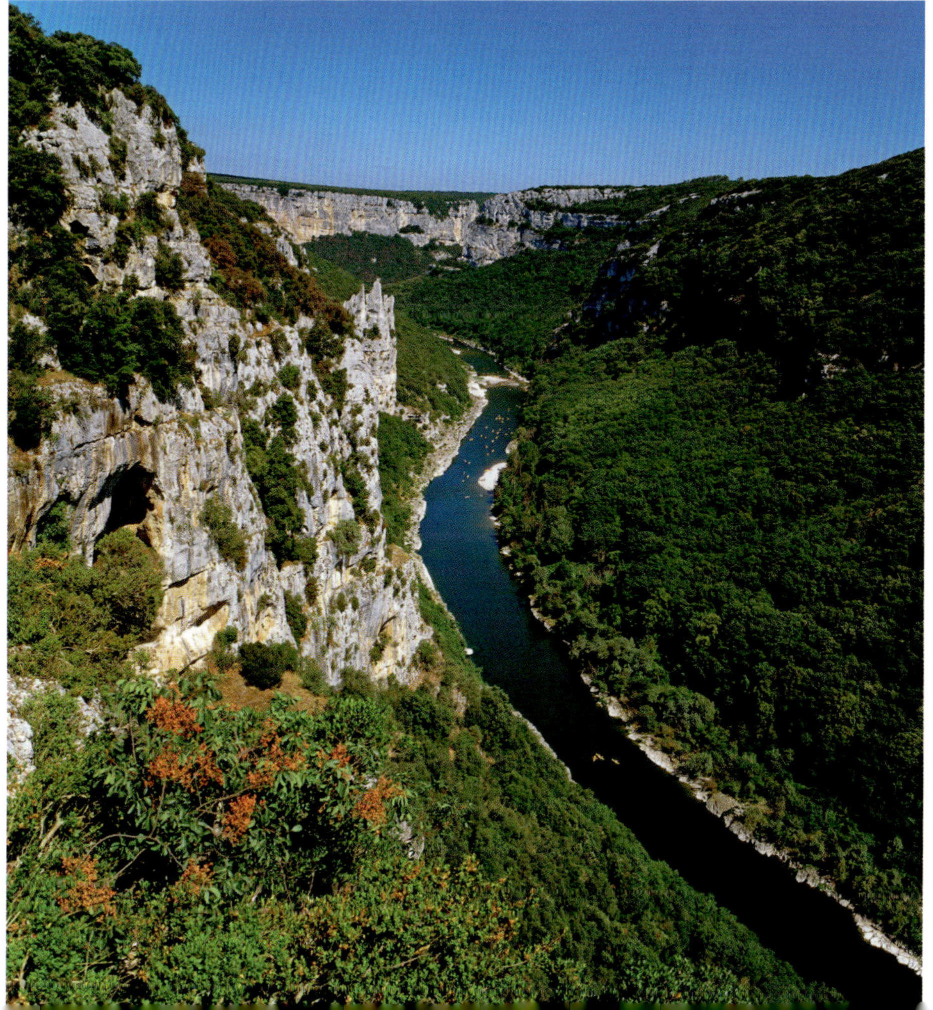

Brunel-Deschamps, Hillaire and Chauvet grew up in the wild, rugged and spectacular cliff-lined landscape of the Massif Central, where in spring the scent of wild thyme permeates underfoot. From childhood, they delighted in exploring the limestone caves that dot the rock cliffs bordering the Ardèche River and its tributaries [25]. Sometimes these are visible as gaping, arched entrances, such as the Grotte des Deux-Ouvertures, which contains many faint Palaeolithic engravings. At other times, caves could be found by the feel of drafts of air emanating from between rocks on scree slopes and ground hollows where trees had fallen or foxes dwelt, much as was also the case in the discovery of Lascaux in 1940. Once a draft of air is felt, on the back of the hand, or against the cheek, rocks and earth are manually removed, revealing the underground opening.

By 1994 the three friends had been serious cavers for more than twenty years, and the cliff lines of the Ardèche River had become a familiar backyard, albeit one of massive geographical scale. Brunel-Deschamps was particularly interested in archaeology and the ancient artworks that many caves housed. It was during a visit to the Grotte des Deux-Ouvertures, where new archaeological investigations were being undertaken, that she and Hillaire had met, and in 1988, when they were commissioned to investigate and map a previously found archaeological cave,

26. Jean-Michel Geneste, Director of the Chauvet Cave research team, on the narrow path to the cave.

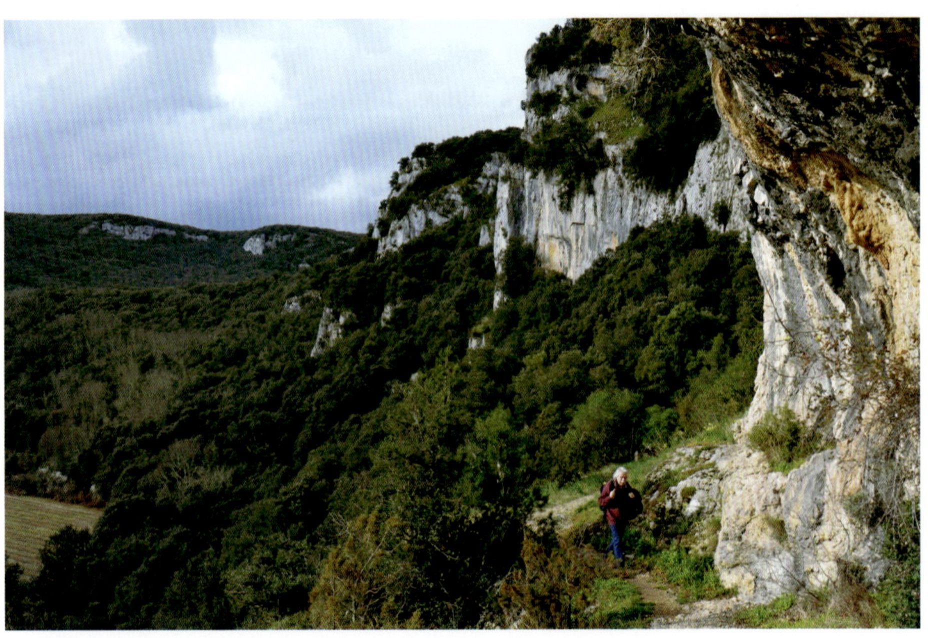

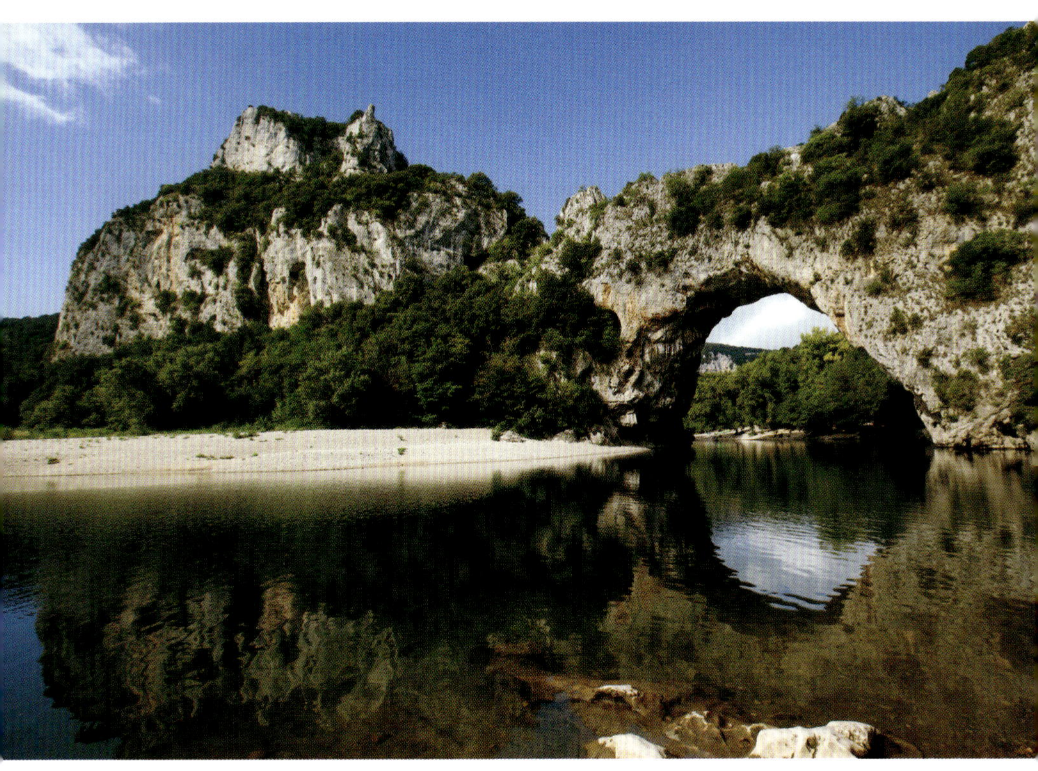

27. Pont d'Arc, a natural archway carved by the Ardèche River. Chauvet Cave is located high on the cliffline a few hundred metres away.

the three cavers began to explore together the patchily known underground world of the Ardèche. In the coming years they explored hundreds of caves, some consisting of tiny entrances that didn't really lead anywhere, others that opened up into deep and spectacular chambers. Cave art remained not entirely elusive, but it was rather sparse.

On 18 December 1994, in the mid-afternoon of a clear winter's day, the cavers followed a narrow path along a cliff face [26], from which they could enjoy magnificent views of the Pont d'Arc in the distance below [27]. They gathered in a shallow concavity in the rock, where a draft was felt. It was not a strong draft, but strong enough to cause them to expand the opening to see what lay beyond. A narrow duct some 3 m (10 ft) long was exposed. Wriggling through, the tunnel gave way to a floor 10 m (30 ft) below, confirming that this was indeed an underground cave. They shouted and an echo pierced the silence; a large void lay beyond. But descent was out of the question without appropriate equipment, so they returned to their van to fetch a cable ladder. Although it was now late in the evening, they persevered lest

others might explore the cave before they had a chance to return.
'In our impatience', they were to write some time later,

> *the descent seemed endless, especially as we could not see
> the walls…. Our hearts were thumping: a magnificent cave
> network was opening up before us. The gallery that the beams
> from our helmet lamps were lighting so feebly was immense….
> The silence was total…. We moved in single file through the
> darkness, each of us trying to follow the footprints of the one
> in front, so as to leave only one track and not damage the
> floor of the cave…. In our euphoria we gazed feverishly in all
> directions, trying to note as many details as possible. It was
> at this moment that we discovered multitudes of bear bones
> and teeth strewn over the floor…. All around us were dozens
> of depressions dug into the earth, as if the ground had been
> bombed. We recognized them as the 'nests' in which bears
> must have hibernated. Magnificent, translucent, fistulous
> stalactites hung from the ceiling like angels' hair.*[21]

Then the art came into view. At first two, short red lines.
Then a little red mammoth [28]. Mammoths had become

28. Little red mammoth painted on the hanging ceiling at the entrance of the Cactus Gallery: the first figurative image discovered at Chauvet Cave.

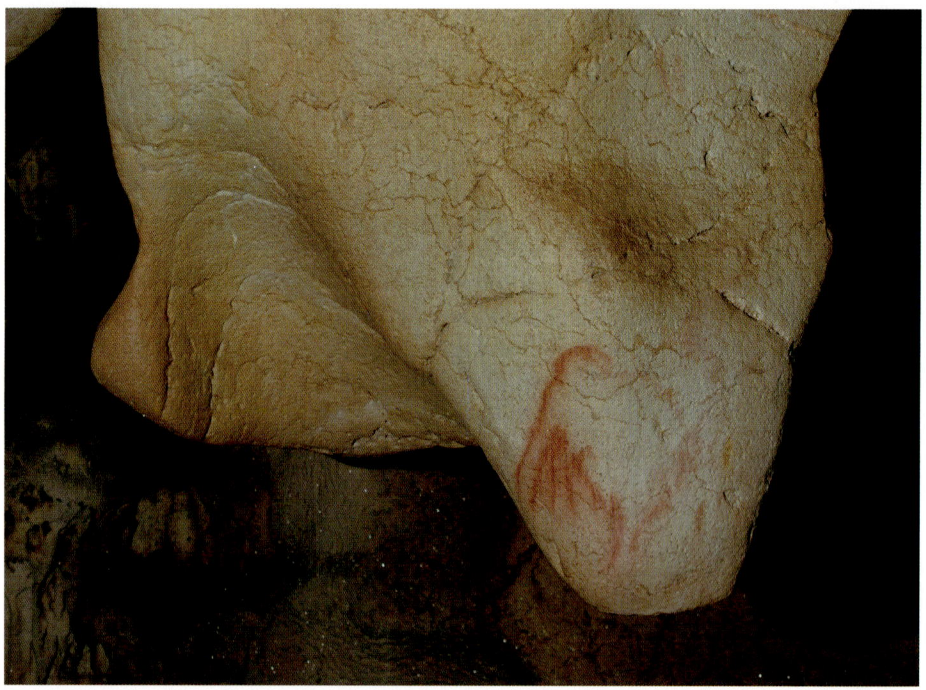

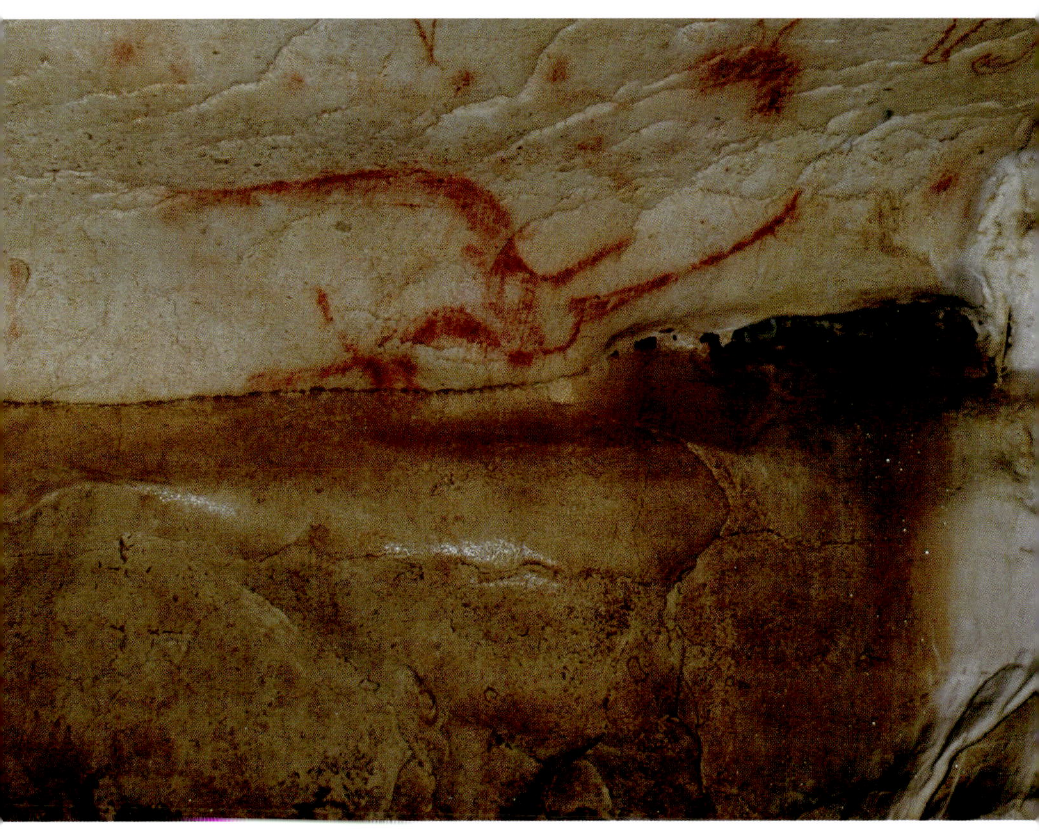

29. The first rhinoceros painting seen in the Ardèche region of France, Chauvet Cave.

extinct across mainland Europe at the end of the Ice Age more than 10,000 years ago, probably due to a combination of hunting and a warming climate. Then a large red painting of a bear. On the floor lay skulls and many other bones of cave bears, they too long extinct. Tracing back their steps, the party of three went to a second chamber. Here on the walls was more art: an enigmatic, red-winged image and a rhinoceros – the first ever to be seen in the Ardèche [29]. Another mammoth, and what appeared to be a lion. Then three more lion heads. A large frieze some 10 m (30 ft) long, covered in art. They didn't feel alone: 'the artists' souls and spirits surrounded us. We thought we could feel their presence; we were disturbing them'.[22] Then more artworks, in many ways too much to take in during a single viewing: a leopard or cheetah, an ibex, a bear [30]. On the ground were more cave bear skulls, and one from an ibex. Then a painted deer, and an animal made up of large red dots [32]. Elsewhere in the cave, an engraved owl [31].

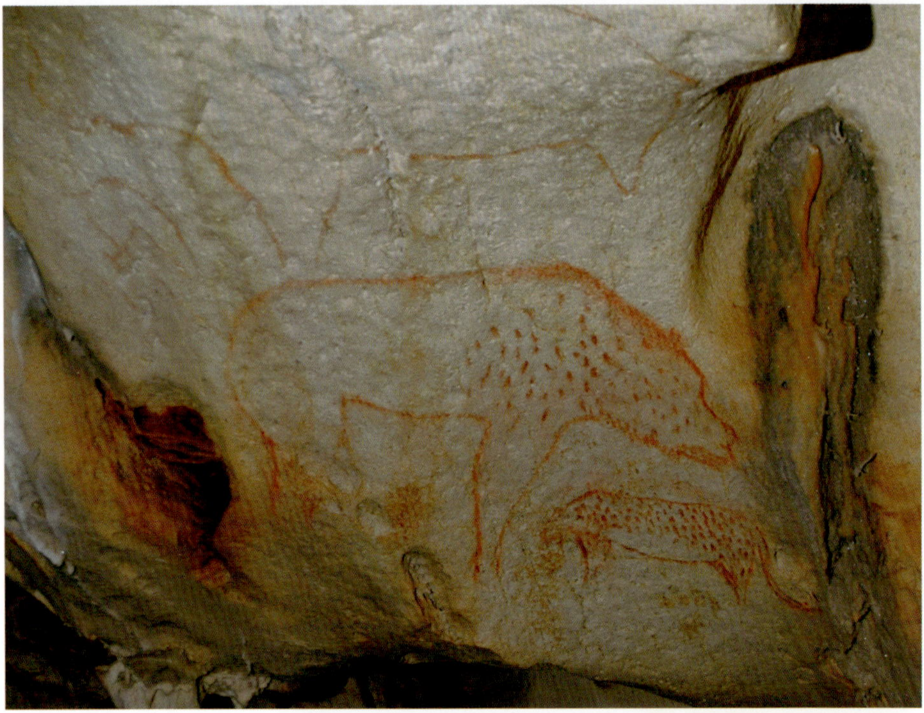

30. (above) Bear and leopard or
cheetah, Chauvet Cave.

31. (right) Owl engraved into
the hanging ceiling's soft surface,
Hillaire Chamber, Chauvet Cave.
The body is seen from the back,
the head turned front-on. It is the
earliest known depiction of an owl
anywhere in the world.

32. (opposite) Panel of large red
dots, Brunel Chamber, Chauvet
Cave. Each dot was made by
dipping the palm of the hand in
wet red ochre and pressing it onto
the rock wall. The motif is in the
shape of a rhinoceros or bison
(the form is ambiguous).

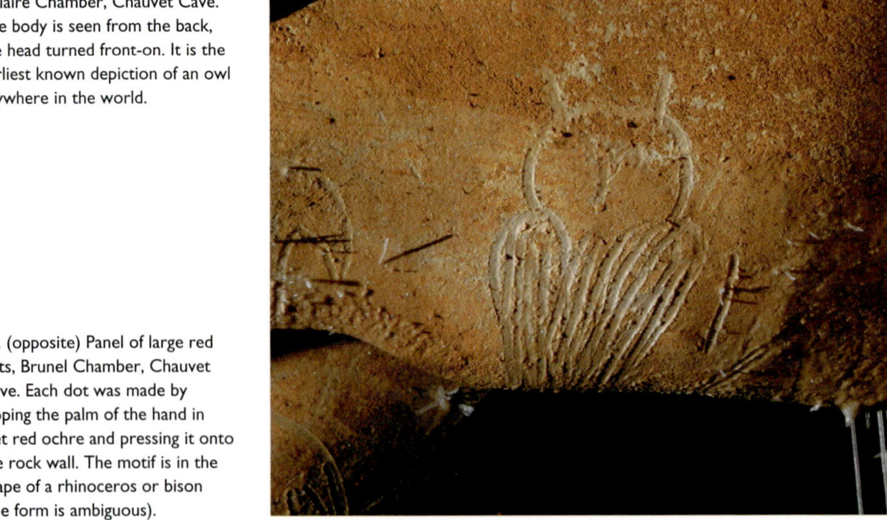

38

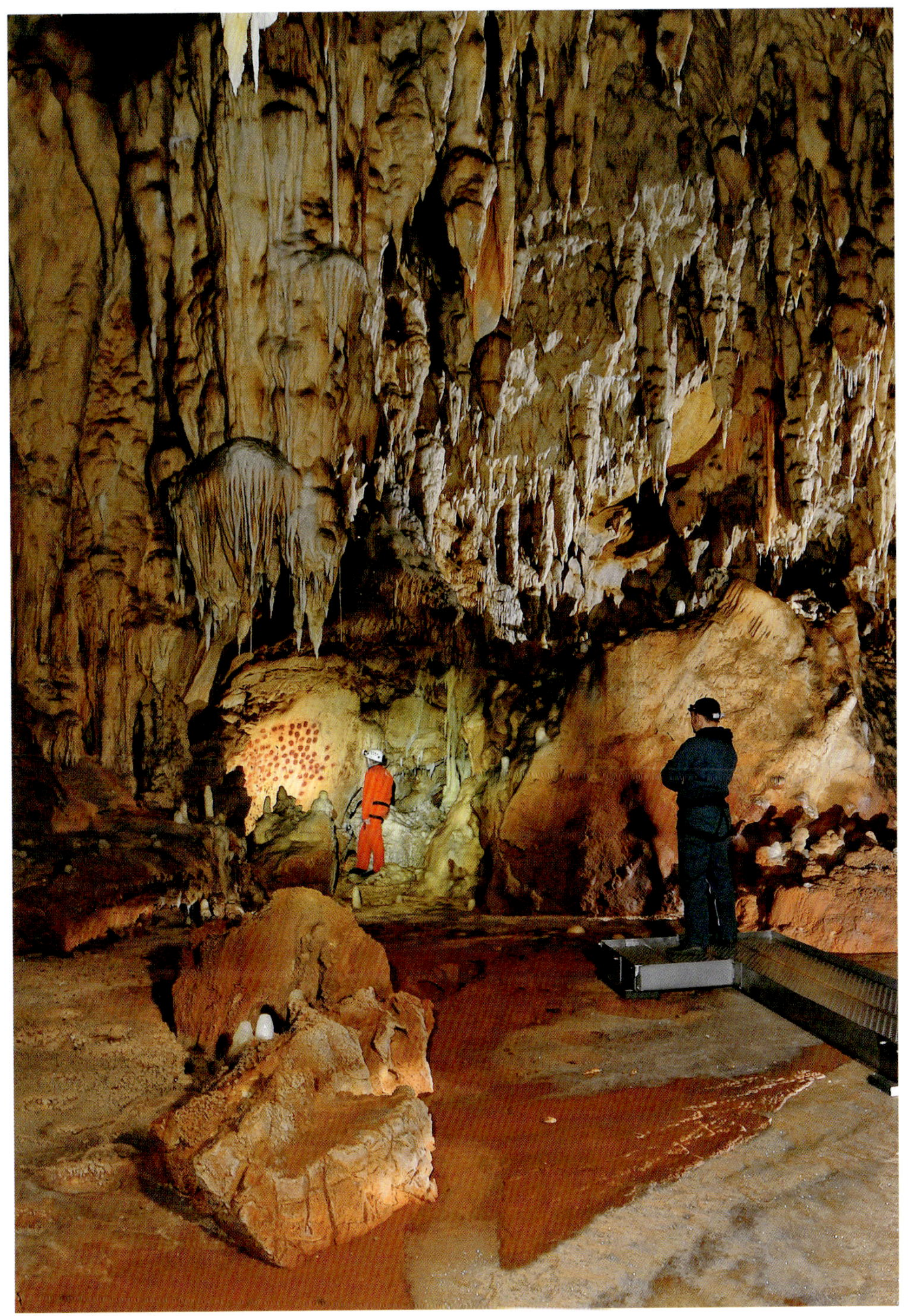

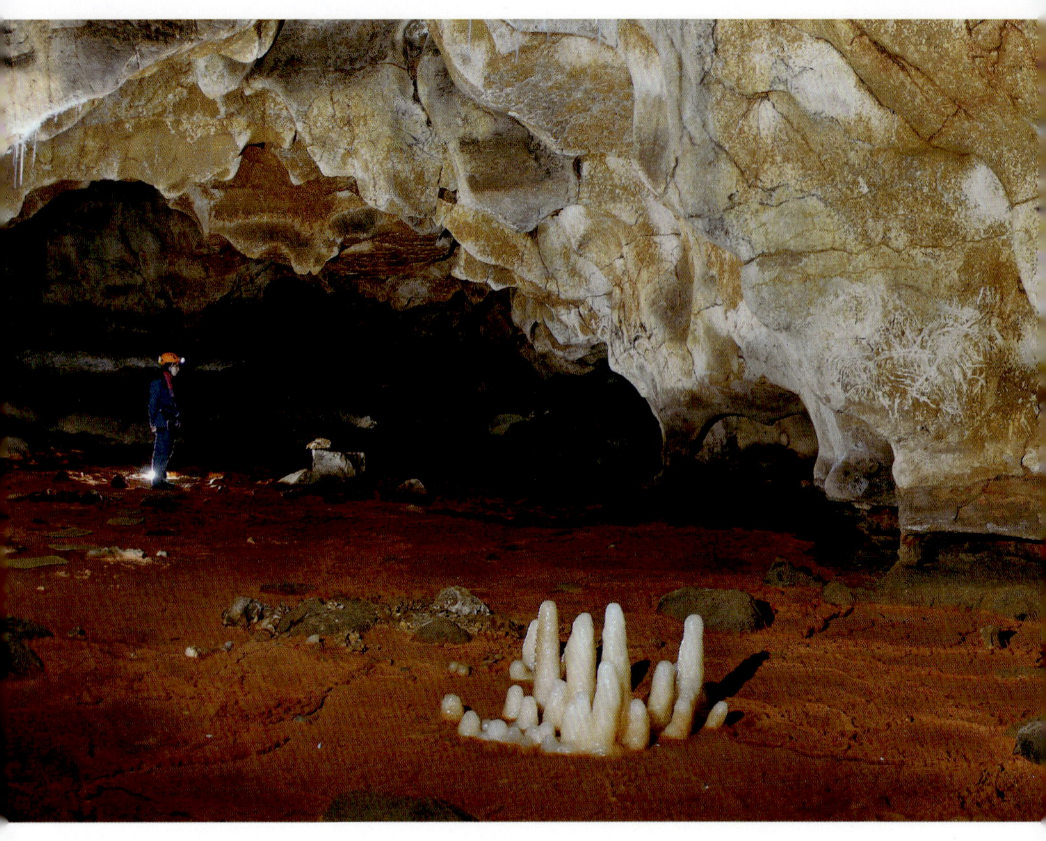

'This first visit had lasted only an hour, but we were in a state of shock'.[23] They had just discovered the largest, most decorated, most spectacular cave art site in Europe, possibly in the world.[24] The artworks would come to rock the archaeological world and fire public imagination alike, as much for their beauty [33] as for their great and unexpected antiquity (see Chapter 6).

Nawarla Gabarnmang, Australia

Great discoveries tend to astound and, with the interest they generate, opportunities for further investigation normally follow. With these extra studies and revelations, opportunities to rewrite the history books emerge. This was so of Altamira, Lascaux, Chauvet Cave and other remarkable sites elsewhere around the world, some of which will be presented in later chapters. In Australia, the spectacular Nawarla Gabarnmang

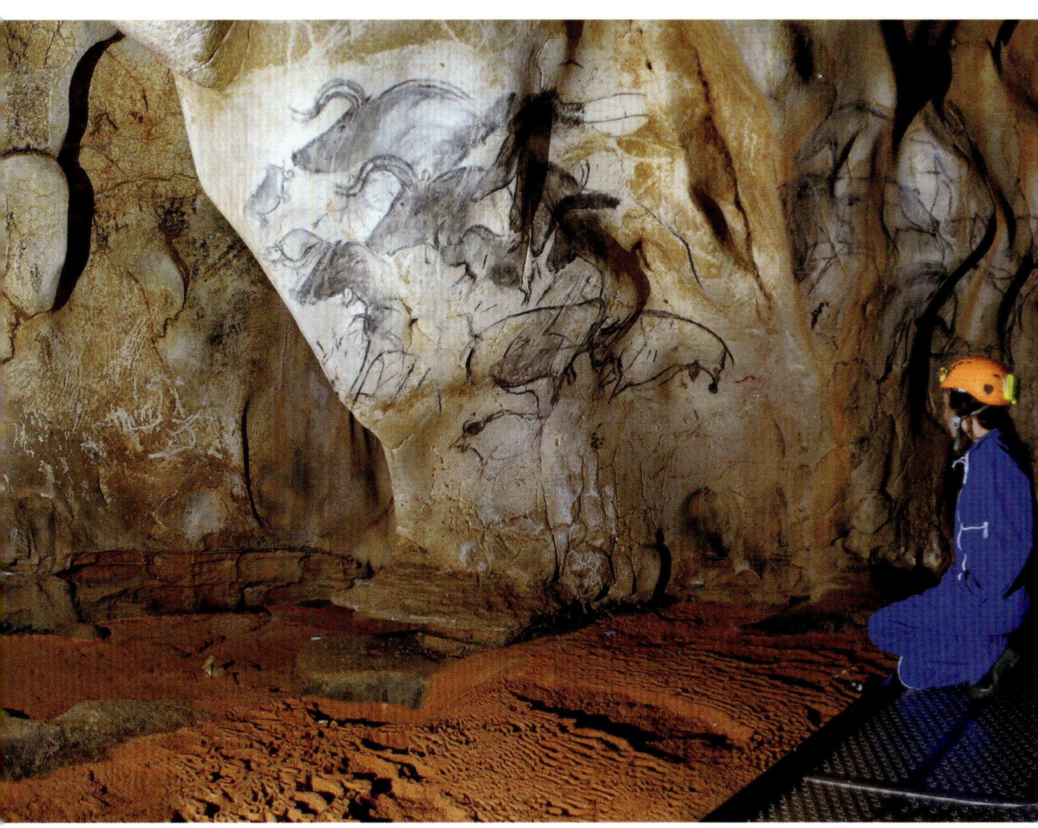

was found in June 2006 when the Jawoyn Association Aboriginal Corporation's Cultural and Environment Manager Ray Whear, together with helicopter pilot Chris Morgan, sighted the shadow of an unusually large rockshelter during a routine aerial survey of the Arnhem Land plateau [34]. They landed the helicopter, walking a short distance to find themselves in a stunning gallery with well over a thousand paintings. A search for further sites together with detailed study of Nawarla Gabarnmang followed, part of the Jawoyn Association's aspirations to rediscover and document Jawoyn ancestral places and Jawoyn history for the benefit of local youths at a time of rapid social change. This was not an abstract academic exercise, but rather a building of knowledge with community education and the health and promotion of Jawoyn culture and history in mind.

The large, double-ended rockshelter of Nawarla Gabarnmang lies on Buyhmi clan lands in Jawoyn Country. The Jawoyn words 'nawarla gabarnmang' mean 'place of hole

in the rock', a descriptive label given to the site in 2006–07
by the late Bardayal 'Lofty' Nadjamerrek, a senior and highly
respected Aboriginal 'culture man' from Arnhem Land, and that
is the name that is now generally used for it both by members
of the Jawoyn community and others. The name refers to the
rockshelter itself, but also to the area immediately around it
that spans a few tens of metres and which includes a continuous
array of shallow overhangs and rock faces, often decorated
with art, and various landscape features including a southern
'courtyard' delimited by a long, pillared rock face to its south.
Shortly after seeing the site for the first time, Ray Whear
reported his finding to senior Aboriginal elders Bardayal 'Lofty'
Nadjamerrek (who since his death is respectfully referred to as
Wamud, as is culturally appropriate), Peter Bolgay and Jimmy
Kalariya. Wamud told Whear that he not only knew of the site,
but also remembered having camped there with his father in
the 1930s as they travelled between clan lands on the Arnhem
Land plateau. The location of the site had been forgotten but
now refound, enabling Wamud to report that no new artworks
seemed to have been added since his visit in the 1930s, pointing

34. The northern entrance of
Nawarla Gabarnmang as seen
by helicopter.

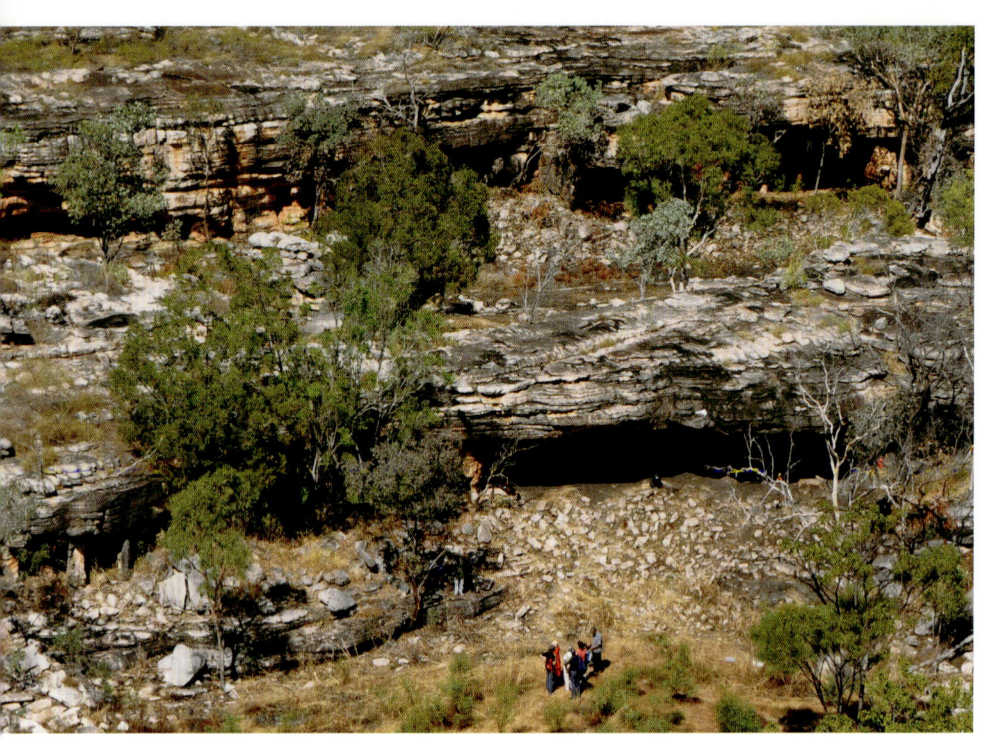

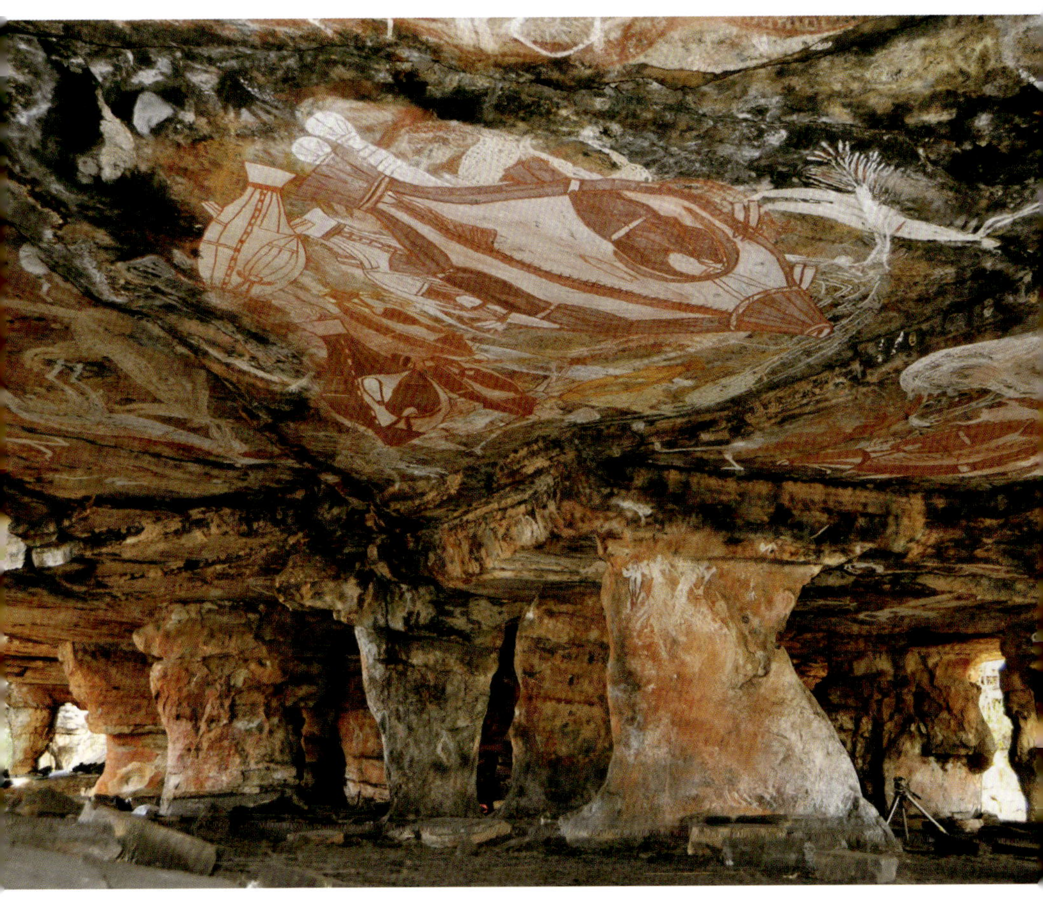

35. Nawarla Gabarnmang on the Arnhem Land plateau, one of Australia's most decorated art sites. The rock slabs on the floor were placed there by resident Aboriginal people.

out in the process also that the isolated blocks of rock that can today be seen lying flat on the ground under the sheltered area were placed there by the old people as 'pillows' on which to rest [35]. They mark the places where people slept.

Nawarla Gabarnmang is a living landscape. It is but one feature of a much larger ancestral realm that retains social currency among the Jawoyn today. The art is alive not just with the memory of the ancestors, but with their living spirits. For Jawoyn, the site and the art are imbued with the legacy of the local landscape stretching back to the beginning of time. The past remains within the present, latent but powerful as the spirit-beings continue to act in forms now less seen. Some of those spirit-beings have metamorphosized into the rock, such as the *mimi* that can be seen in the paintings [5]. But they remain alive, wandering across the landscape and wielding their spirit-force as keepers of 'Country'. The law of the land, Jawoyn law formed in the Dreaming, lives on at Nawarla Gabarnmang not as a cave richly decorated with paintings, but as Country (see Chapter 7 for discussion of the important Australian Aboriginal concepts of 'the Dreaming' and 'Country').[25]

The architecture of knowledge and discovery

None of the renowned cave art sites described above was found by archaeologists, although archaeologists do find many art sites during laborious ground walking across the regions they study. Each cave brings with it a story of discovery, and of twists and turns in knowledge. The biographies of those caves are inevitably expressions of our own lives. They help us tell the story of us as we try to make sense of things through our own relationships in places. They also alert us to the fact that there is more than one way to understand the past, and how that past sets foundations for the future.

There may well be a wide range of ways in which caves decorated with art are discovered, but all have something in common: in the wonderment of their discovery, and in the curiosity we have for their artistic hands, they reveal deep and perhaps unshakable connections with how we experience the workings of the world. From the outset, a newly found site begins to make sense as we position it into the world we already know. We approach a cave not in a detached and unconnected way. Rather, we connect with it, we bring both the site and the art into our lives by how we make them meaningful for ourselves. The locations of our thoughts and experiences are geographies of engagement, they are part of us through the meanings we give them, and in this ancient cave art sites are not simply ancient but rather ever-present as locations of our being in the here and now. They appear to us as *our* universes, our realities, because they are our own experiences, even when the sites and the art really belong to others.

Cave art makes us feel familiar, makes us feel at home. But cave art sites may not be our own ancestral places or ancestral creations: Europeans or North Americans or Africans or Asians have no claim to Nawarla Gabarnmang as an ancestral place, whereas for the Jawoyn of Arnhem Land it is very much a place of their ancestors, and those ancestral beings and spirits continue to reside within. For the rest of us Nawarla Gabarnmang retains a connection as a site we have seen in pictures, have read about in books. We experience it and thus internalize it by how we come to know about it, and in doing so it becomes a part of us. We feel some kind of connection with Nawarla Gabarnmang because it has entered the world we know, a world that we make sense of by giving it meaning. It is the same with Altamira, Lascaux and Chauvet Cave: they are all places that may or may not be genealogically ancestral, but that irrespective of such heritage for some, attain legacy for all. They enable us to locate and historicize our present through their meaningfulness, through the stories they tell and enable us to tell.

This, then, is the power of cave art, to draw us into its realm as sensual beings who recognize our own emplacement in a varied but always meaningful world. And we explore that meaning by trying to decipher the art, what it looks like, how old it is, what it means, all dimensions of attachment that begin to take shape as we come to connect.

Chapter 3:   The methods of cave art research

The discovery of cave art sometimes involves unusual techniques. So, too, does the act of giving it meaning, such as finding out how old it is, how paints were made or where pigments came from. Without such techniques, we simply would not know what to make of the art, other than perhaps to retain some personal sense of its aesthetic value. Let us take a moment therefore to consider some of the fundamental ways in which archaeologists have shaped how we see cave art today. Some of the technicalities of the science involved are critical to understanding the reliability of the things we can say about the art and our interpretations of it.

The fact that art on rock walls and ceilings is immovable means that it could not have been made elsewhere and imported to the site where it now lies. Nor could those artistic motifs on the rock have been redeposited into later settings from earlier times, as is possible with portable art that could have moved across space or been reworked from earlier deposits – hence the alternative name 'mobiliary' art for portable art. While ideas about cave art, such as stylistic conventions, would have been shared in the past between artists and communities through the course of everyday interactions, the fixity of rock art means that we can see the artistic practices as they were employed in given places at given times. Comparing the cave art of neighbouring regions and of different periods means that we can compare artistic practices across space, and through time. This empowers archaeologists to investigate changing patterns of interregional influence and interaction by studying changing distributions of style. But to do this we first need to characterize what the art looks like and how old it is, and both of these can offer unexpected challenges.

Recording cave art

There are many ways of recording cave art, but they all require the art to be seen in the first place. Some researchers create lists of motifs that they then tick off as those motifs are seen at a site. Others draw what they see onto graph paper for reproduction at a proper scale. Most researchers photograph sites and their art extensively, and many then digitally enhance those photos to make the motifs more visible. Some convert their photographs directly into three-dimensional images, for example using photogrammetry on tablets in the field. These methods are not mutually exclusive, with researchers often employing multiple methods to cross-correlate the benefits of each, and for cross-checking.

Three-dimensional laser mapping

One of the most complex but rewarding ways of documenting a site and its art is by making a high-precision three-dimensional digital model. At Chauvet Cave, the French government not only commissioned such a three-dimensional recording, but then used it to physically build a life-sized model of much of the cave [36, 37]

36. (right) Artist working on a panel for La Caverne du Pont d'Arc, France, and (below) the assembled painted frieze of the Rear Chamber nearing completion.

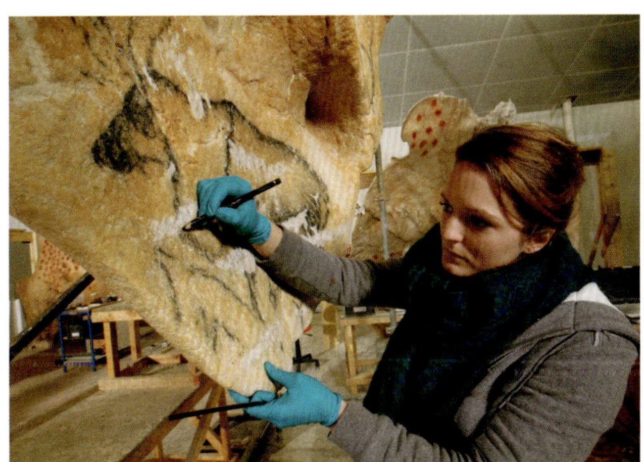

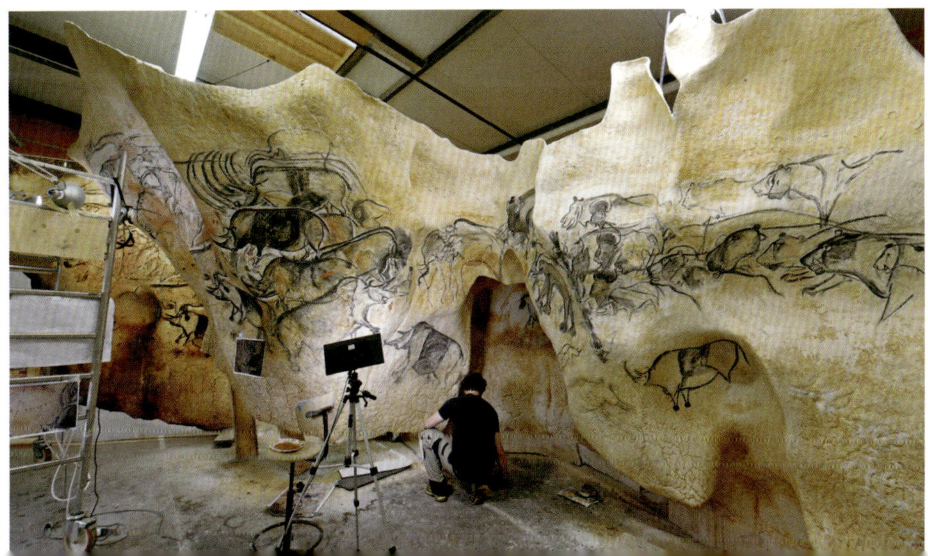

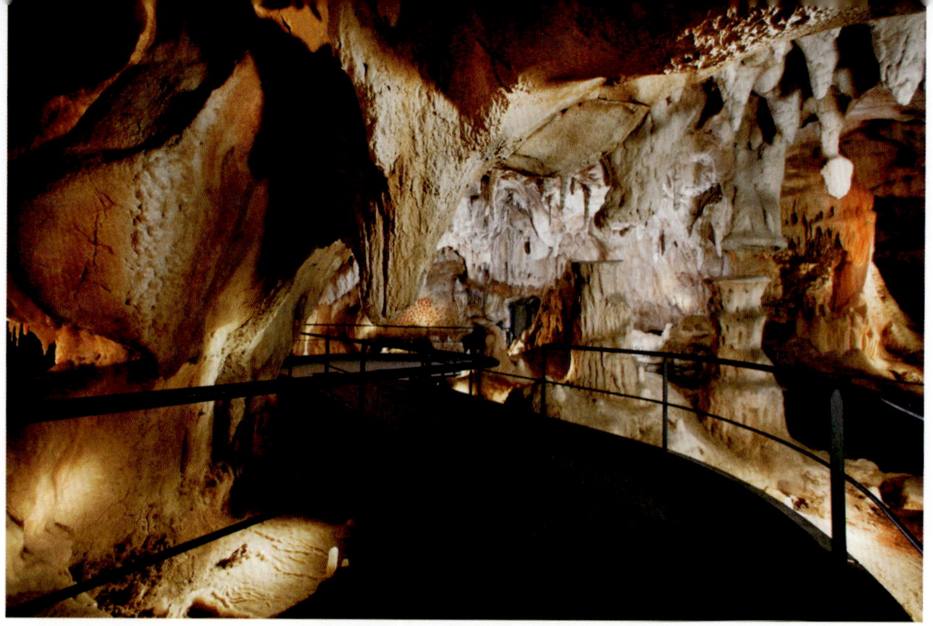

so that the public can see what the underground space looks like without detrimental effects to the original cave itself. They called it 'La Caverne du Pont d'Arc' to distinguish it from Chauvet Cave itself (called 'La Grotte Chauvet-Pont d'Arc' in France). To enhance the experience of the art in its subterranean space, experts carefully selected a range of subtle aromas to mimic the faint, earthy scent of different sections of the original cave. Over an area of 29 ha, at La Caverne du Pont d'Arc, as at Chauvet Cave, the experience of the art deep in the bowels of the earth is one that stimulates the senses.[1]

On the other side of the world, the spectacular double-ended cave of Nawarla Gabarnmang is perched on a high point above the surrounding landscape at the summit of Australia's Arnhem Land plateau [38]. Measuring 32 m long × 23 m wide × 2 m high (105 × 75 × 7 ft), the sheltered space is held aloft by over fifty natural rock pillars supporting a large protective roof over a flat floor [35]. The long, wide ceiling is made up of flat, but staggered, sections of layered rock, offering its artworks and accumulated sediments underneath good protection from the elements. On the ceiling alone 1,391 paintings and stencils adorn the rock, with hundreds more on the walls of the pillars. The extensively painted pillarscape of Nawarla Gabarnmang makes it one of the most decorated Aboriginal art sites in all of Australia.[2]

Recording Nawarla Gabarnmang's art is no simple task, partly because of its many layers of superimposition, and partly because the site is structurally complex. This complexity has developed over many thousands of years of pillar collapse and roof fall. To properly record and understand the art, we need to understand the evolution of the cave as a structure, and here three-dimensional mapping has been of great service.

At Nawarla Gabarnmang the rock matrix was formed when sand was laid down in littoral (near-shore) conditions some 1,700 million years ago. The sand layers metamorphosed into rock through strong underground compaction. While still underground, vertical hair fractures developed at regular intervals as a result of the weight of the overlying rock mantle. Over many millions of years, groundwater then slowly ate away at the rock along those hair fractures, and much later, as the rock became exposed to the elements, flowing water emptied out the decomposed ('ghost') rock that had accumulated around the fractures, creating empty spaces around remnant pillars. Then, around 50,000 years ago, Aboriginal people arrived in Australia and began to occupy the northern and southern entrances of the cave, for initially its inner spaces were too densely packed with pillars to allow penetration further in. Sometime after 35,000 years ago – and probably only after 23,000 years ago, the exact timing is uncertain as research is ongoing – people began to knock down pillars to expand the space under shelter. We know this because in some parts of the site, pillars were left half-broken where people abandoned their activities unfinished: the tell-tale traces can still be seen today in the form of extensive flaking and removal of sections of pillars

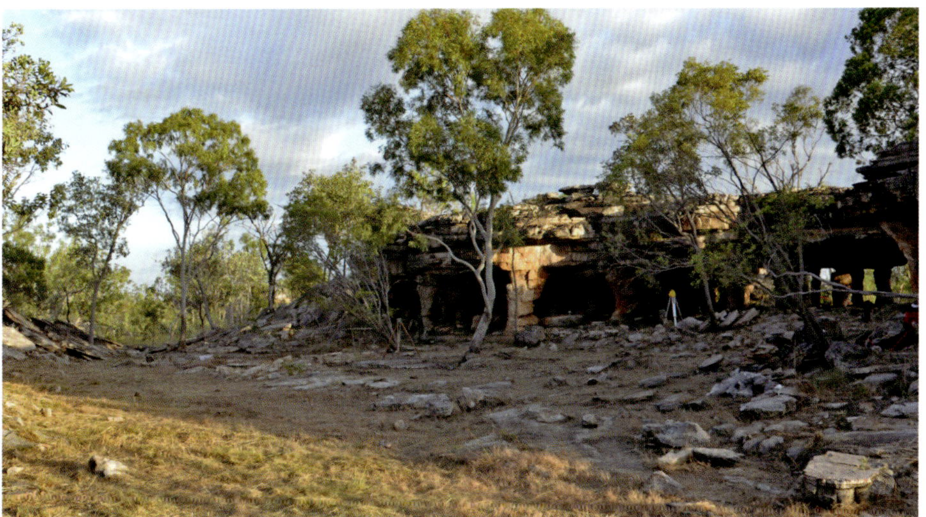

38. The southern, courtyard entrance of Nawarla Gabarnmang on the Arnhem Land plateau, Jawoyn Country, Australia. The double-ended art site Is perched above the surrounding landscape.

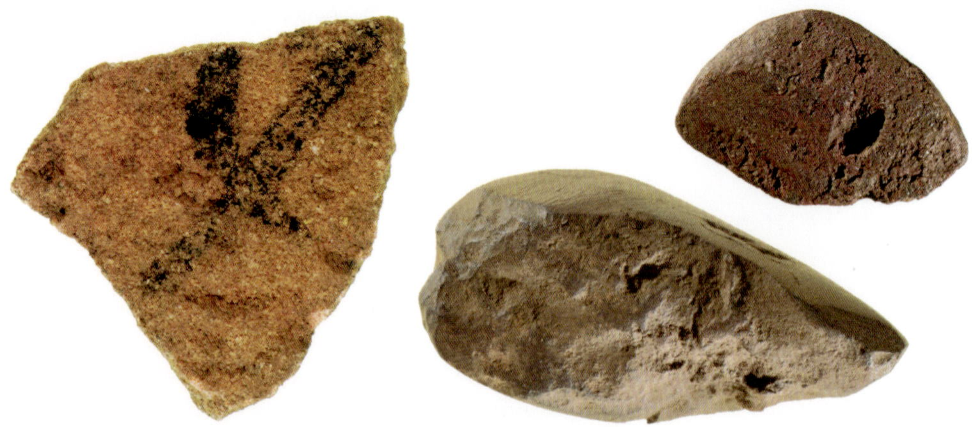

towards the outer reaches of the cave as people carried away and then threw aside fragmented rock. As pillars were removed individual layers of ceiling rock began to fall down, for they now lacked support, each newly exposed ceiling surface potentially creating a new canvas for artworks.[3]

As the physical shape of the internal structure of Nawarla Gabarnmang changed, so too did the placement of the art on the rock: broken layers of ceiling rock and pillars left behind partial fragments of ancient paintings, as the fallen rock carried with it other parts of those same paintings. A small piece of one of these fallen painted ceiling layers dating back to 27,000 years ago has been excavated, proof that paintings were made around that time [39].[4] We also know that people began painting at Nawarla Gabarnmang tens of thousands of years ago because used ochre

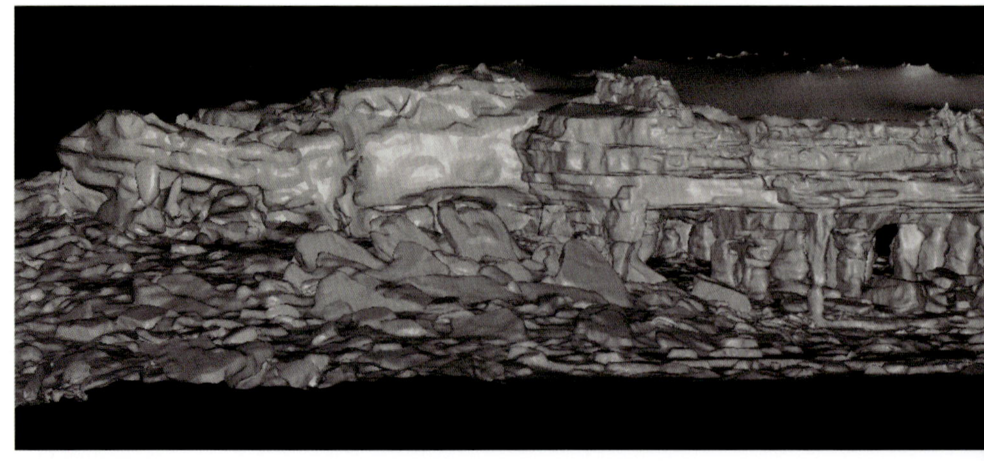

crayons were recovered from the archaeological excavations [40], although we do not know what images people then created, nor how much art they made. How, then, are we to make sense of the remnant artworks in this three-dimensional space, a space that can only be properly understood by taking into account a fourth dimension, the evolution of the cave's material fabric through time.

This is where three-dimensional laser mapping comes into its own. To record the art, geomorphologist Jean-Jacques Delannoy and digital mapping specialist Benjamin Sadier, both of the Université de Savoie Mont Blanc in France, began by making a high-definition three-dimensional laser model of the structure of the cave [41]. The art panels could now be individually investigated and interrelated in their proper spatial contexts [42]. Positioning the art in its appropriate location within this pillar landscape is important because Aboriginal people had systematically knocked down pillars and removed layers of rock ceiling at various times in the past, meaning that each extant surface has a different age: some rock surfaces are many thousands of years old, going back to the Ice Age, others are much more recent, going back a few hundred years only. While the age of a rock surface does not tell us the age of the art itself, it does set a maximum age for the paintings on it. So intensive was the activity of opening up the cave by removing pillars that in the central section of the site standing pillars are now 8 m (26 ft) or more apart, rather than the original 1 to 2 m (3 to 7 ft) for the period prior to human modification [41]. Then, 11,000 years ago, it all suddenly stopped, although people continued to paint. Why they ceased to open up the site's internal space we do not know, although the ruins of an adjacent, collapsed

41. Three-dimensional model of Nawarla Gabarnmang as seen from its southern entrance. The wide space between the pillars was created when Aboriginal people knocked down individual pillars more than 11,000 years ago.

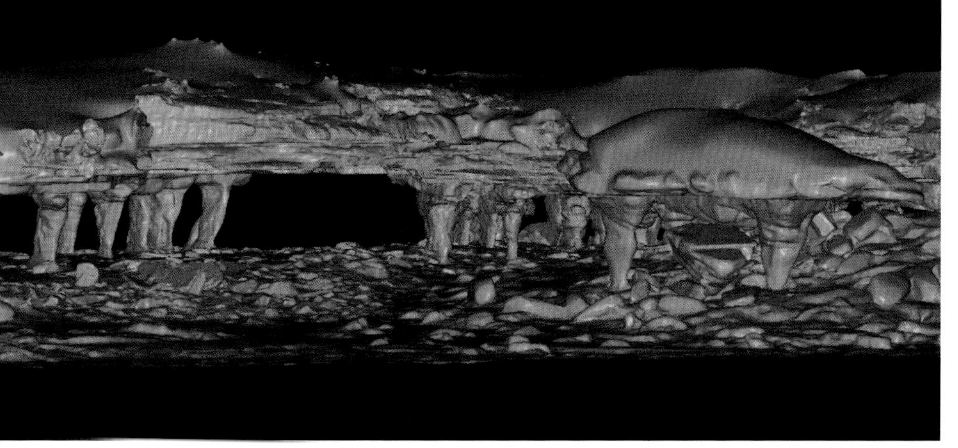

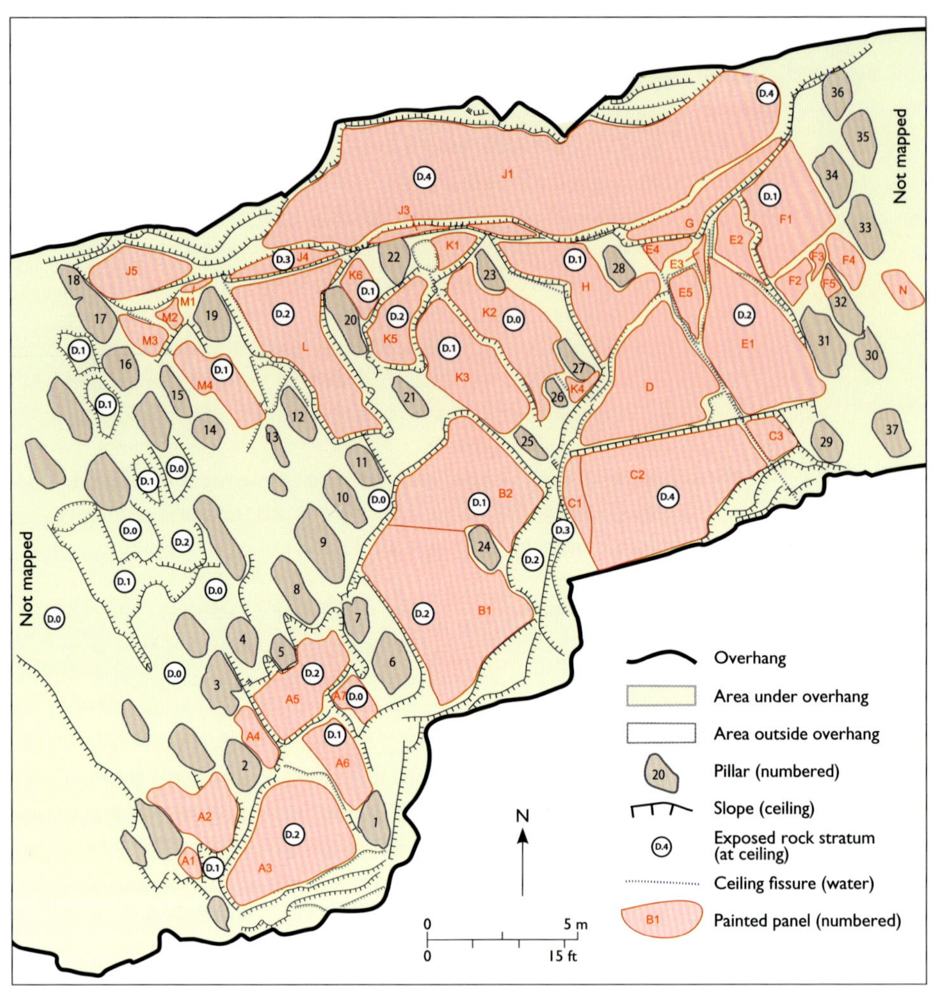

42. Map of Nawarla Gabarnmang's ceiling, showing the locations of individual art panels.

cave with removed pillars testifies to the complete destruction of a nearby site some time in the past [43]. We suspect that that calamity is contemporaneous with the cessation of pillar removals at Nawarla Gabarnmang, but the collapse in the twin cave has not yet been dated, so we cannot be certain of the relationship between the two events. Irrespective of the cause, Nawarla Gabarnmang cannot simply be conceived of as a natural cave in which people lived and painted, but rather a grand, architectural monument that was also a complex, three-dimensional artistic canvas, one whose shape was altered by people over the course of time. This is not how we usually think of Australian Aboriginal culture or of Aboriginal art sites. Nawarla Gabarnmang is

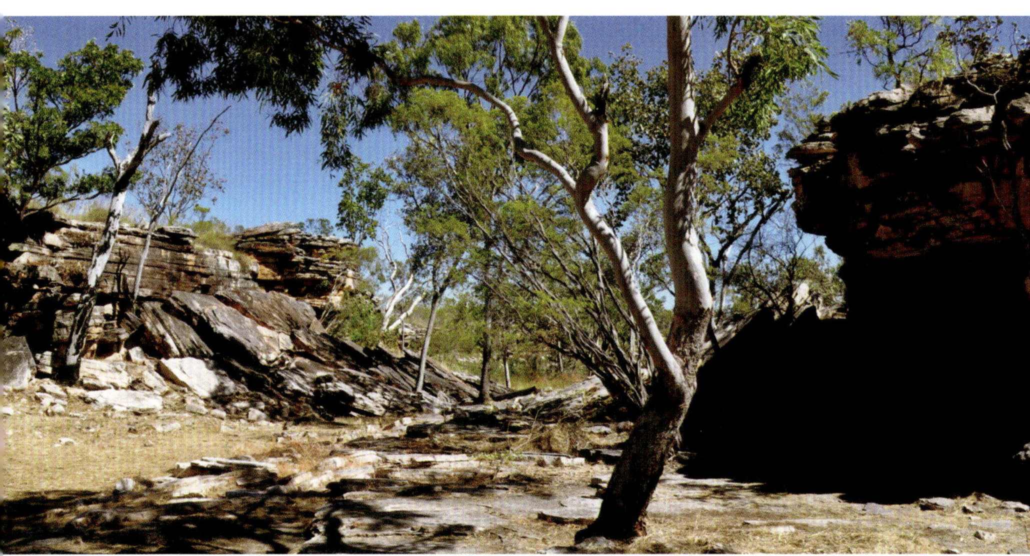

instructive in showing us that once people enter the scene, they become active agents in constructing their landscapes, rather than being passive pawns on an environmental stage. The making of rock canvasses upon which to create cave art is one dimension of that active agency, and the general principle of actively inscribing one's landscape with architectural and artistic designs applies to all peoples of the world, albeit they each did so in different ways.

Seeing the invisible

Cave art researchers are faced with a problem common to all archaeologists: the object of their study begins to break down over time. Issues that particularly affect cave art include granular disintegration of rock surfaces; biological activity such as algal, fungal or lichen growth (such as encountered at Lascaux, as discussed in Chapter 2), insect nests and the rubbing of animals against rock walls; water damage; graffiti; and the accumulation of thin grime and dust mantles that end up forming mineral crusts on walls. The result is a worsening visual appearance of the art through time. These problems are so acute that typically one-tenth to half the paintings in many art sites have faded beyond recognition, although the very oldest artworks are often long gone and do not feature in these statistics. But new computer techniques have emerged that enable us to see many of these disappearing ancient artworks again.[5]

Digital image enhancement has been around since the 1960s, when it was used to better recognize details in photographs taken by secret spy satellites and by space missions such as the Ranger lunar program, or to enhance the profiles of distant aircraft during the Cold War. Since the 1980s, computer vision specialists such as John Brayer of the University of New Mexico adapted and further developed and applied such technologies to the study of rock art around the globe.[6] Now, thanks to commercially available software such as Adobe Photoshop or DStretch, for example, digital image enhancement is available to anyone with a home computer and a camera.

How does it work? Visible light consists of a 'rainbow' or spectrum of electromagnetic waves of different wavelengths. The colours of an object – such as a rock background or a painting – differ when the light that reflects off the surface has different amounts of intensity in different parts of the electromagnetic spectrum. A digital camera records this light on a sensor consisting of a rectangular array of pixels, or picture elements. In addition to the individual colours themselves, there are shades of grey from black to white, which emerge from a combination of colours. The less grey is contained within a colour, or the 'purer' it is, the more that colour is said to be 'saturated'.

As cave art fades through the slow accumulation of dust on paintings, formation of thin translucent mineral films, or loss of paint, for example, the differences between the paintings and rock reduce. At the same time the colour values move closer to one another, and closer to grey, so that differences – contrast – may eventually disappear. The task of the digital enhancer is to increase the noticeable difference between the colour of the background rock and the colour of the rock art. One way of doing this is to instruct the computer to increase the distinctiveness of the rock by recolouring the grey or brown pixels (mostly background) of a photograph. Likewise, where there are red paintings, for example, intensifying the reddish colour of all pixels will affect the foreground more than the background and bring out the contrast of all coloured pixels and thus coloured regions on the rock surface. And as saturation represents how much grey is mixed with a 'pure' colour, increasing the saturation of colours would remove the impact of greys, further increasing the colour contrasts.[7]

Let us apply this technology to a rock surface on the remote island of Mua in Torres Strait, midway between the northern tip of Australia and the island of New Guinea in the western Pacific

Ocean, much as took place in 2001. The local Mualgal Indigenous community at the coastal village of Kubin had asked a team of archaeologists to record cultural sites across the island as part of an awareness programme aimed at ensuring the education of Mualgal youths on cultural matters relating to their own historical traditions, but here the art had faded beyond recognition, to the point that no one knew it even existed, let alone what it had looked like.[8]

Early in the dry season of 2001, archaeologists Ian McNiven, Joe Crouch and I were taken by Mualgal elder John Manas, his daughter Louise Manas and Guy Neliman to a place called Uma where twin springs flow. Here lay a pile of rocks marking the grave of a man who in around the 1870s had been killed by a party of headhunters from the neighbouring island of Badu. To this day, the story of that event continues to be commemorated by the Mualgal, not so much for the death of the man, but for the survival of his young son Goba who, according to oral tradition, had hidden up a tree at the urging of his father to escape the warring party.

Some 100 m (330 ft) from the grave at Uma is a small, low hill on top of which sits a large granite boulder locally known as Turao Kula (*tura* = spy, *ao* = past tense, *kula* = rock), a natural lookout point onto which Mua Islanders once climbed to survey their surroundings [44]. On the ground under the overhang at

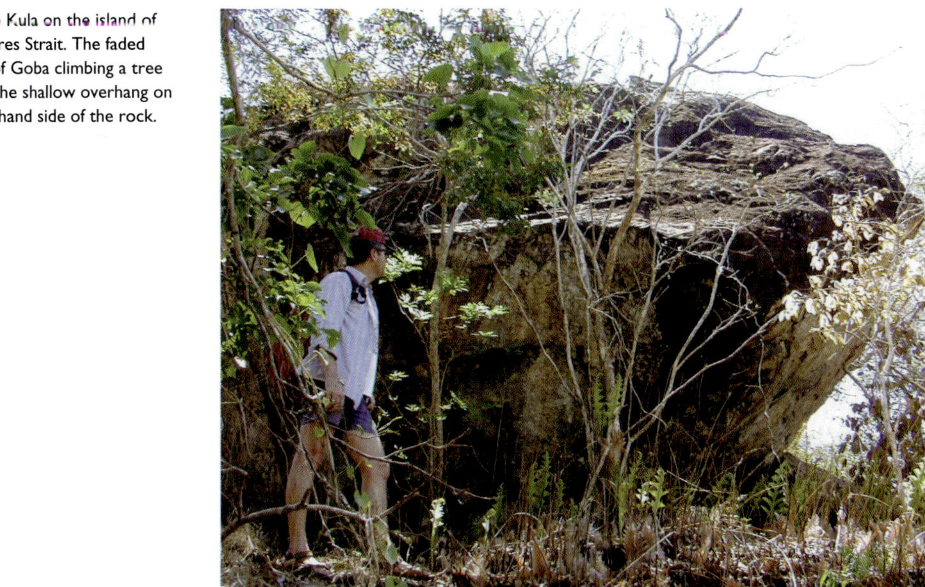

11. Turao Kula on the island of Mua, Torres Strait. The faded painting of Goba climbing a tree is under the shallow overhang on the right-hand side of the rock.

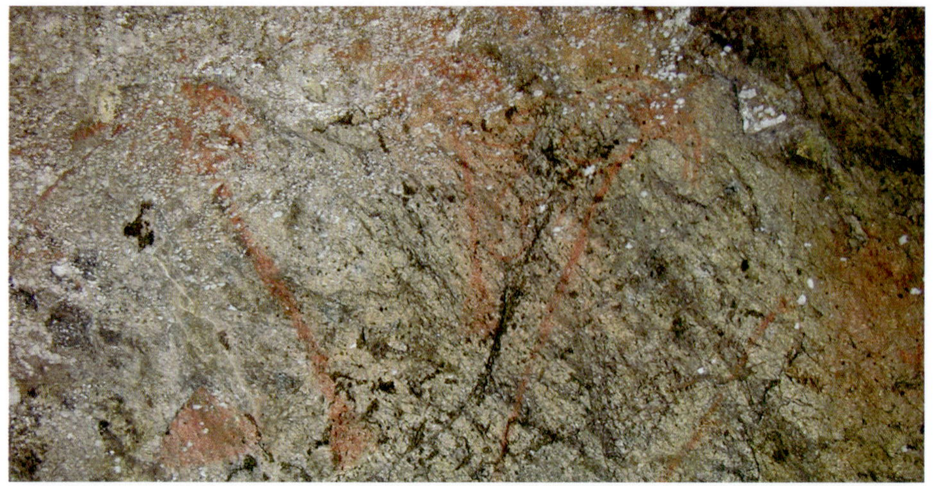

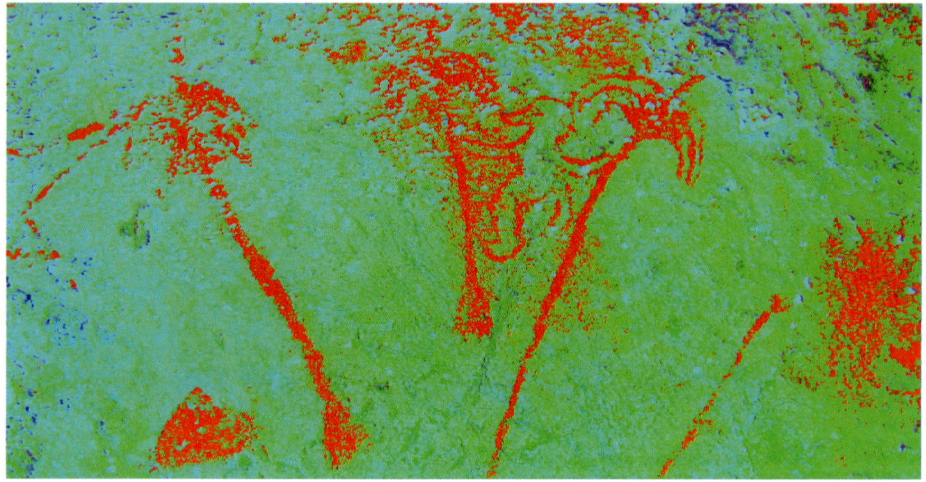

Turao Kula are many stone artifacts, marine shells, bones, pieces
of use-worn ochre, charcoal and some glass and metal from
more recent times. Faint traces of red could be seen on the
rock wall, but these were too faded to make out the shapes
of the paintings [45].

So we took pictures with a digital camera and transferred
them to our laptop. Then we adjusted the photographs'
brightness and contrast to get the best picture (this is like
adjusting the 'brightness' and 'contrast' controls on a TV).
Next we adjusted the image saturation, intensifying the colours
and making them look more distinct (like the TV 'colour' control).

All the time we were making these adjustments, we looked at the results and tried, by repeating previous steps, to get the best results.

We then adjusted the hue in the image, because the human eye can distinguish some colour (hue) differences better than others (this is like adjusting the 'tint' control on a TV). Next we tried to expand the contrast between the average colours of the different regions of the spectrum. This is something we can't do on a TV, but can do in some image-processing programs. We continued to experiment with these tools until we reached results that produced the best contrast between the background rock and the foreground paintings.

On the computer screen, from a mass of grey with faint tinges of red emerged a clear image of a person climbing a tree [46], akin to the tale of Goba as retold in oral traditions, a story referring to an event that had taken place precisely in this location close to 150 years ago. Digital enhancement had revealed a painting done long ago about an actual event that has to this day been retained in social memory. The following year, the Mualgal community began what would become annual celebrations to remember and honour local culture and local history; these are held at Uma and feature prominently the Goba story and the rediscovered paintings on the rock at Turao Kula [47]. The archaeological work at Uma, and the associated digital enhancement of the art under the granite

47. Customary Mualgal dances celebrating culture and the rediscovery of the painting of Goba at Turao Kula, October 2002.

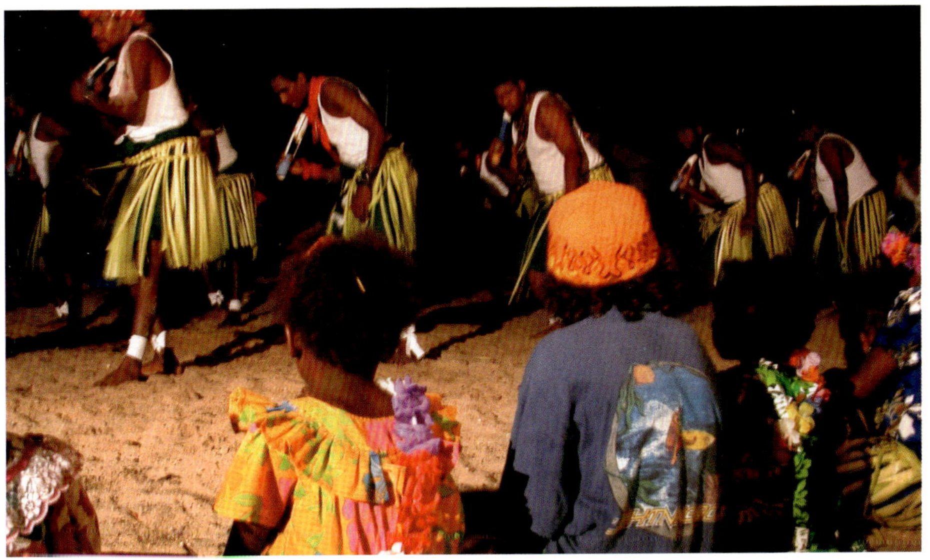

rock's overhang, were undertaken as a community programme with cultural survival and educational aspirations in mind.[9] The newly discovered artworks at Turao Kula were not just about the past, but also about present social concerns for the cultural well-being of an Indigenous island community.

Dating cave art

Being able to see the art is one thing, but finding out how old it is brings an entirely new set of challenges. The age of cave art is something we will return to repeatedly throughout this book. But accurately assessing how old it really is requires some knowledge of the science underlying the various available dating techniques.

Let us begin by differentiating between two kinds of chronologies: relative and absolute. Relative dating refers to the ordering of artworks in a relative temporal sequence, absolute dating to obtaining actual ages for the art. Various kinds of information can help us understand the relative age of artworks: more or less weathered or exfoliated rock surfaces are usually signs that longer or shorter periods of time have passed since artworks were created, although rates of weathering and erosion can differ across surfaces. Evidence that water flow has shifted across a rock surface can tell us that environmental conditions have changed, for example that rainfall levels once caused water to flow in a particular way across a particular rock wall, but the situation changed as rainfall regimes changed. Changes in the physical structure of a rock can tell us that enough time has passed for the rock itself to have witnessed major movements, or that earth forces (such as earthquakes) have disrupted the earlier shape of the rock. In the limestone cave of Yalo on the island of Malekula in Vanuatu, an earthquake in 1965 caused a massive rock fall in a part of the cave (see Chapter 7 for a more detailed discussion of Yalo). The rock wall that was newly exposed must date to after the time of the earthquake in 1965, as must any art on it.[10] Conversely, older rock art may be present on collapsed blocks at the foot of the wall.

The main method of relative dating documents how artworks are layered on top of each other on a rock wall: a painting that has any part of it covered by another means that the underlying one must be older than the one on top. However, we do not know from this information alone how much older the underlying art is: it could have been done immediately before the overlying image during a single artistic event, or it could have been done thousands of years before.

A good example of superimpositions again comes from the site of Nawarla Gabarnmang. Robert Gunn of Monash University in Australia has been studying the rich artworks at the site, photographically recording the rock surfaces and then digitally enhancing the artworks using DStretch, an automated digital enhancement program specifically designed for rock art. This has enabled Gunn to more clearly distinguish the paintings and the relative order of their superimpositions. Once the individual paintings were clearly distinguished from each other, the superimposed layers could be separated out one at a time on the computer. A series of progressively underlying artworks were thus identified, representing a series of increasingly older paintings [48]. With this, a sequence of changing artistic styles became evident. The pattern of superimpositions in one panel

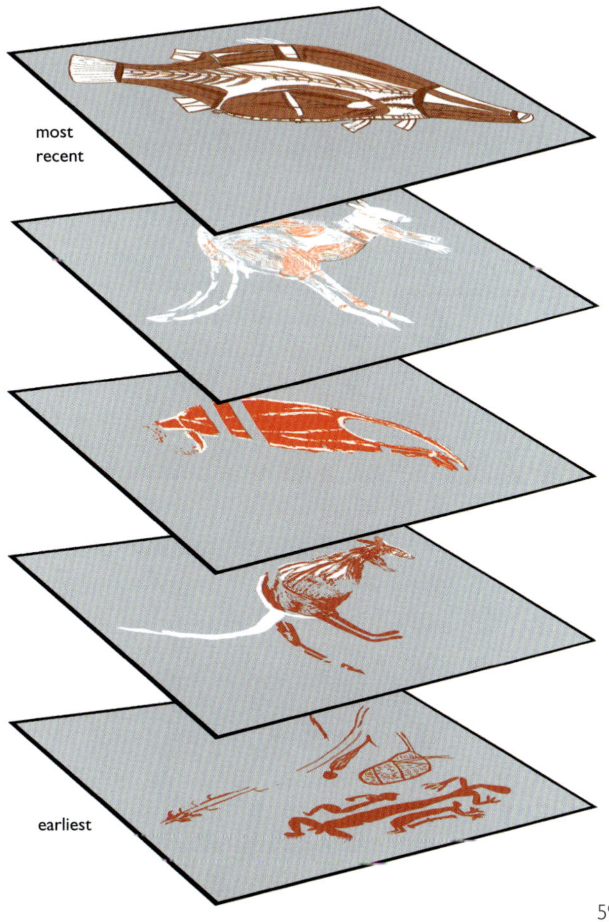

48. Part of the layered sequence of rock art styles painted on the ceiling at Nawarla Gabarnmang.

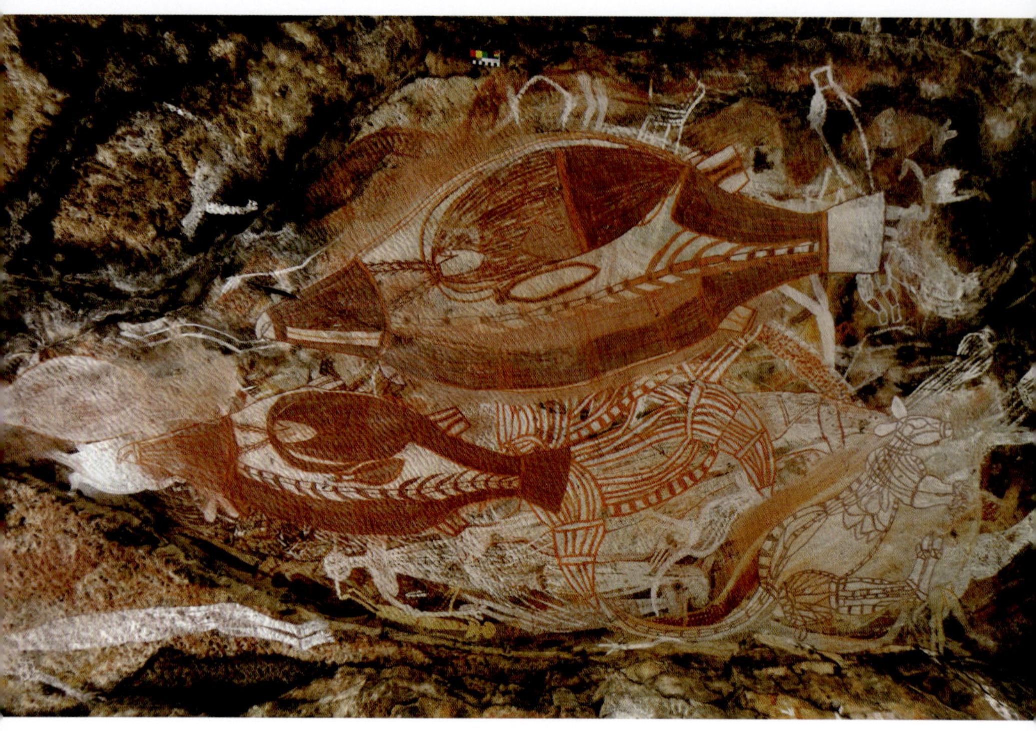

49. Dense pattern of overlying paintings on Panel E1 at Nawarla Gabarnmang. Only the uppermost layers have complex X-ray animal designs.

shows well the evolution of so-called 'X-ray' art, but it was only by separating out the individual layers that this could be worked out. Hence, art Panels D, E1, F1 and H on the Nawarla Gabarnmang ceiling contain 406 paintings between them, but only a few of these have complex X-ray designs of a kind practised in Arnhem Land during the ethnographic period of the 1800s and 1900s (this is the early period of European contact during which writings, photographs and anthropological studies recorded local cultural practices) [49]. Archaeologists had long theorized that such X-ray art is probably no greater than 3,000 years old across the region, but no actual carbon dates had been obtained for the style, so its real age was not known. At Nawarla Gabarnmang, Gunn worked out that all the complex X-ray paintings of fish and other fauna lie exclusively in the uppermost layers of painted panels, some of which had up to forty-three layers of artwork. Complex X-ray art at Nawarla Gabarnmang, the southernmost site with such art ever found in Arnhem Land, is therefore relatively recent in the broader artistic sequence, but exactly how recent required the addition of further information relating to the absolute age of the various art layers.

This was done by obtaining absolute ages on non-X-ray art from other layers on the panels. The art above the dated layers would be younger, that underneath older. Hence in Panels F1, H, J1 and K4, five pieces of beeswax that had been pressed onto the rock surface as elements of larger paintings were each carbon dated to the past *c.* 400 years (see below for an explanation of how carbon dating works). Furthermore, Panel D has a large painting of a horse [50], with many other paintings lying under or over it. As horses first arrived in this part of Australia when the explorer Ludwig Leichhardt passed through in 1845, all the overlying paintings must be younger than this date. While some of the underlying layers older than the dated beeswax contain paintings of animals with rudimentary X-ray features [51], the more complex X-ray art only occurs above the layers dated to the past *c.* 400 years, and most of it – and possibly all of it, as the evidence is somewhat ambiguous on this point – occurs above the layer of the horse. Here, therefore, complex X-ray art dates not to the past 3,000 years as previously thought for this style, but to the past *c.* 400 years only, and it may even all date to the period after the arrival of Europeans with horses in 1845. There seems, then, to have been a southward expansion of a more northern X-ray art style either shortly before or during the early

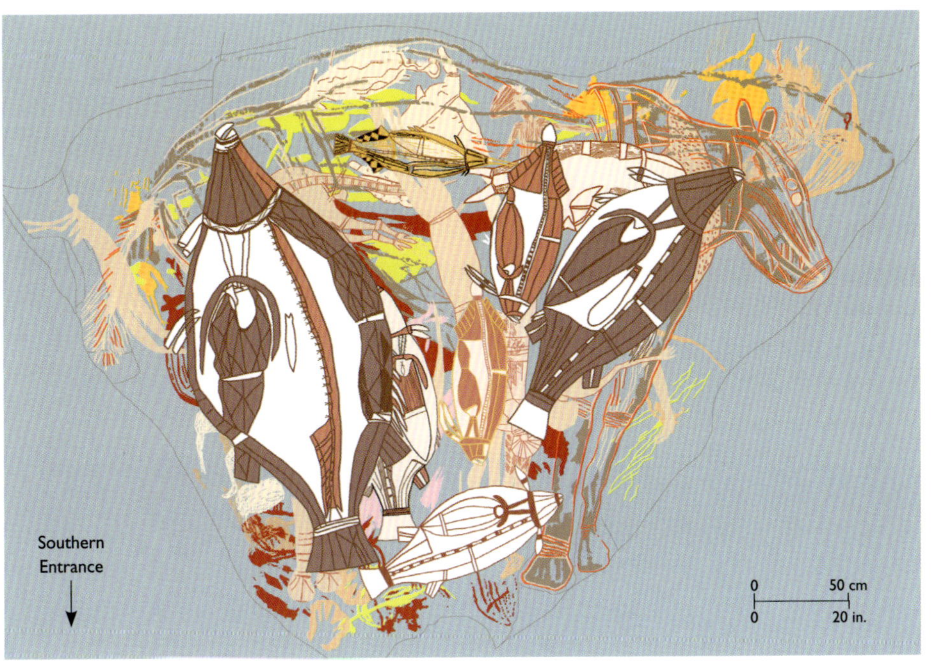

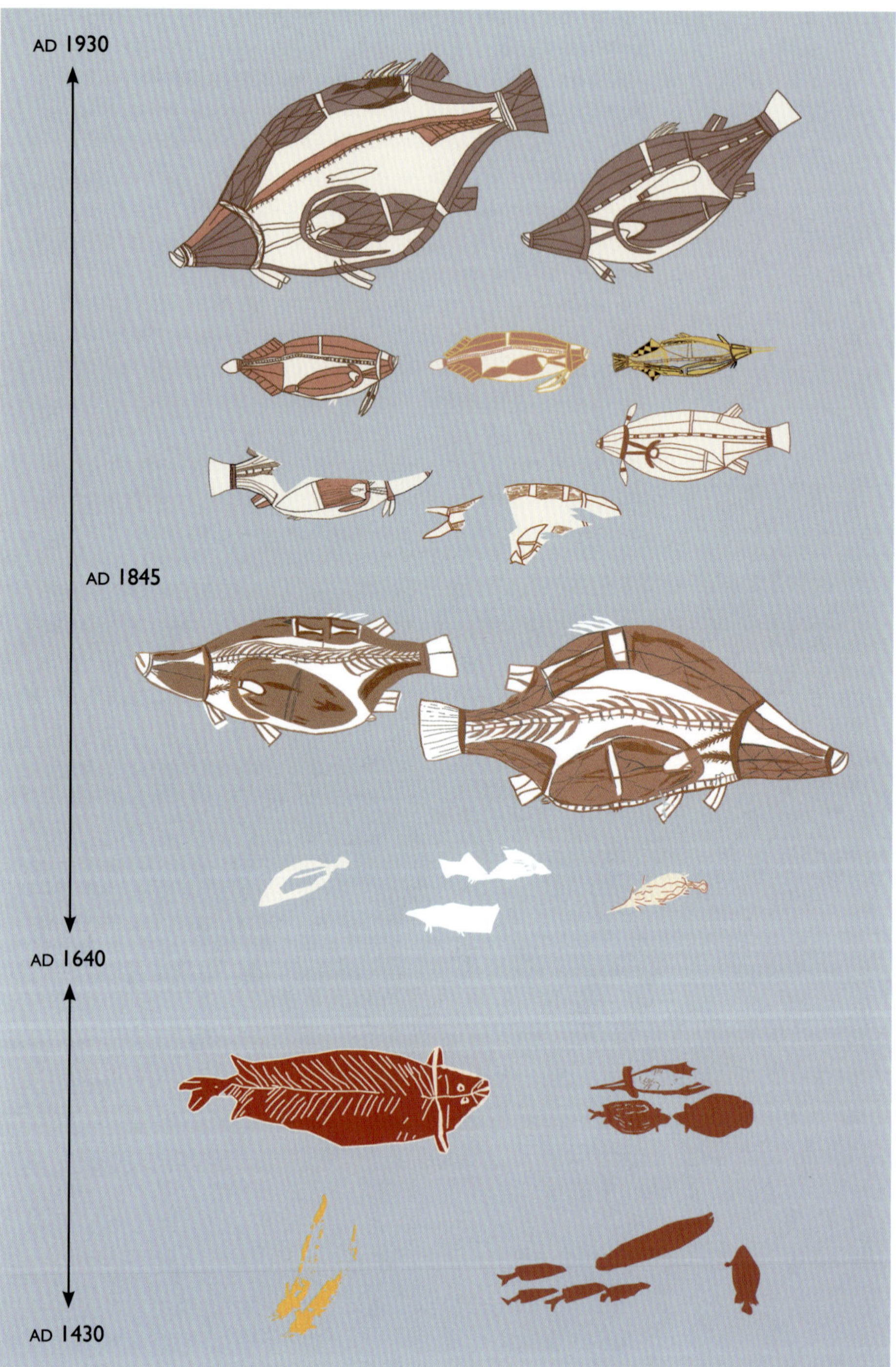

AD 1930
AD 1845
AD 1640
AD 1430

period of European intrusion. At Nawarla Gabarnmang it was by clarifying the pattern of superimpositions through on-site examination and digital enhancement, and then dating individual paintings within that clarified sequence, that Gunn was able to work out how the art had changed in relation to the region's known social history.[11]

The number of paintings found in superimposed layers is considerable at Nawarla Gabarnmang, and this is made more complex by the fact that the artworks are unevenly scattered on panels across a very large site with uneven rock surfaces. Archaeologists sometimes employ a useful graphic method to show the temporal relationship between images in such complex configurations, as did Gunn at this site. The graphic, known as a Harris Matrix, was originally designed to keep track of the relationship between soil layers in archaeological excavations.[12] There is a basic rule in archaeology: layers of soil get progressively older the deeper you go. It is easy to work out the patterning of sub-surface layers when they lie neatly on top of each other. But the situation is not always so simple: layers are spatially discontinuous, they sometimes lie side-by-side without all of them overlapping, post-holes and other features such as animal burrows intrude into layers from one or other ancient surface, mixing and sometimes even inverting the redeposited soil, and so on. At large excavations, or large sites where there is considerable variability in the clarity of details between layers across space, it is critical to keep track of the vertical relationship (pattern of superimposition) between all layers, and the Harris Matrix allows archaeologists to do this in a systematic way.

We can think of artworks on rock surfaces in the same way as layers of soil underground, albeit at a micro-scale. While layers of soil are usually centimetres or tens of centimetres thick, layers of paint are typically fractions of millimetres thick, but the principle is the same. Hence at Nawarla Gabarnmang, each panel can contain many dozens of paintings, some of which overlap, some of which do not, but on the whole most or all of the paintings within a given panel touch another painting. That means that a relative temporal sequence of artworks can be worked out for each panel, taking each instance of overlap into account, as described for the emergence of complex X-ray art on Panels D, F1, H, J1 and K4. But the overall pattern is too complex to work out by eye, so Gunn instead used computerized Harris Matrices [52],[13] which became a

51. Evolution of the X-ray style on fish designs at Nawarla Gabarnmang.

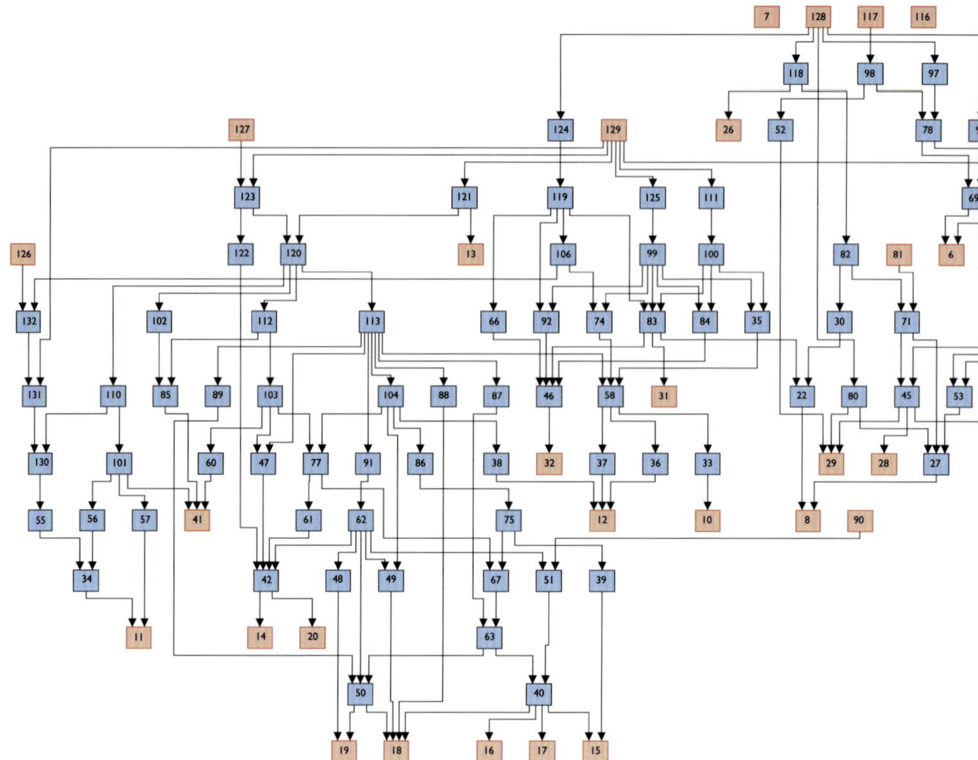

52. Pattern of superimpositions detailing the relative chronology of individual artworks, as revealed by the Harris Matrix for Panel H at Nawarla Gabarnmang. Each square represents an individual, numbered painting or stencil. The red squares represent artworks that have other paintings or stencils either below or above them (but not both), or are not involved in any superimposition. The blue squares represent artworks that have other artworks both above and below them. The lines indicate superimpositions between individual artworks; the squares not connected by lines represent paintings or stencils that are not involved in any superimposition with other artworks.

fundamental tool by which to then further explore patterns of superimposition not just within single panels, but across panels as well in ever-expanding spatial scales and, with this, in increasingly complex networks of spatial data.

Carbon dating

It is through carbon dating that archaeologists first realized in the 1990s that the oldest paintings on the walls of Western European caves date to more than 35,000 years ago. Yet despite obtaining clear results, controversy erupted over the dating of the oldest Ice Age art as soon as the first series of carbon dates began to be published (see Chapter 6 for a discussion of these controversies). To understand these debates, and what the carbon dates really mean, we need to understand carbon dating itself.

The basic principle of carbon (or radiocarbon) dating is that radioactive carbon atoms change at a known rate over time. There are three types of carbon atoms (called isotopes) in nature, ^{12}C, ^{13}C and ^{14}C, the 'C' being the chemical symbol for 'carbon'

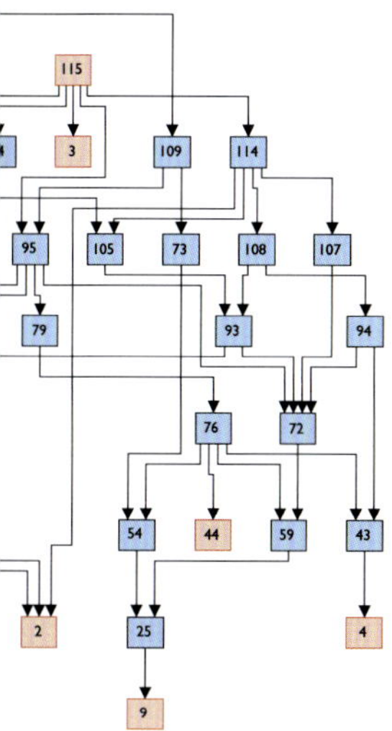

and the superscript number to the left of it (called the 'isotopic mass') representing the total number of neutrons and protons in the nucleus of the atom. When in the stratosphere – the upper parts of the earth's atmosphere – atoms get bombarded by powerful cosmic rays. When this happens, ^{14}N atoms – the stable nitrogen isotope and most abundant component of the atmosphere – are changed so that they form radioactive ^{14}C atoms, which are unstable, and through time revert back to stable nitrogen, ^{14}N. Over many years of research, physicists have worked out that ^{14}C atoms decay at a steady rate: half of the ^{14}C atoms revert back to ^{14}N approximately every 5730 ± 40 years. This is known as the 'half-life' of ^{14}C. This rate is critical for our ability to reliably determine the age of cave art by carbon dating.

All living organisms are carbon-based, meaning that carbon is an important component of living tissue. When an animal or plant is alive, it consumes carbon through nutrients from the environment that include radioactive ^{14}C from the atmosphere. But when the organism dies, the radioactive carbon ceases to be replenished, and thus the amount of ^{14}C in the decaying plant or animal remains, including charcoal and bones, slowly reverts back to ^{14}N. But the amount of ^{13}C and ^{12}C remains the same, as these are not radioactive but stable. Because scientists know how much ^{12}C, ^{13}C and ^{14}C there is in nature, and because they know the decay rate of ^{14}C, the ratio of remaining ^{14}C to the other two carbon isotopes effectively becomes a formula for working out when an organism died. If exactly half the proportion of modern ^{14}C is found in an animal bone or piece of charcoal, then we know that that animal or tree died 5730 ± 40 years ago. If only a quarter remains, then the sample would be 11,460 ± 80 years old, and so forth. Carbon dating only works up to about 55,000 years ago, because by that point the amount of ^{14}C left in a sample is too small to measure reliably (although beyond about 35,000 years ago, determinations get considerably less accurate as contamination by more recent sources of carbon – such as atoms carried by infiltrating water – becomes increasingly problematic).

The ± value, or error, is extremely important and indicates that the true age is likely to lie within this range. In the example above the error limits are based only on the uncertainty in the measured half-life. However, no measurement can be made perfectly, so additional uncertainties from the measurement of the carbon isotopes will further increase the calculated error limits. Errors are usually expressed as one standard deviation, which indicates a 68.3 per cent probability of the age lying within the quoted ± limits; doubling the standard deviation would increase confidence to 95.4 per cent, and tripling it to 99.7 per cent.

A carbon date should always be interpreted within its quoted confidence interval, so it is important to remember that the true age of a painting will usually be slightly different to the carbon date itself, the number before the ± sign. Carbon dates are reported as 'BP', before present, with 'present' being 1950 (because carbon dating was first invented in the late 1940s, so 1950 became a convenient standard for reporting purposes). An important assumption in the carbon dating method is that the level of ^{14}C in the atmosphere has always been the same as it is today. However, slight variations in cosmic radiation and therefore the production of ^{14}C through time mean that 'carbon years' do not exactly correspond with calendar years. Those slight variations have been measured by carbon dating objects that can be independently dated, such as individual rings on species of trees that clearly build up annual rings or coral growth bands and by other methods. This enables archaeologists to convert or 'calibrate' carbon years to more useful calendar years.[14]

Carbon dating is the most commonly used method of absolute dating in cave art research, because some artworks contain organic carbon in such materials as charcoal or beeswax that can be reliably dated. There are different methods of sample preparation and measurement that can be used in carbon dating. The one most suitable for cave art involves the chemical preparation of a sample to eliminate dust and other contaminants and to reduce the sample to pure carbon, then converting that carbon to graphite to make a target that is then placed in an accelerator mass spectrometer where the number of ^{12}C, ^{13}C and ^{14}C atoms are counted. Accelerator mass spectrometry (AMS) carbon dating is ideal for rock art because only a tiny amount of carbon is required, as little as 0.001 g. The AMS counting reveals the ratios of ^{14}C to ^{12}C and ^{13}C, and a carbon date is worked out. It is important to stress that carbon dating only applies to organic material, formerly living things, because these are the organisms that once continuously replenished the carbon in their bodies in equilibrium with that in their environment (people have tried carbon dating non-organic materials such as redeposited calcium carbonate that re-absorbs environmental carbon when forming, with limited success). Other, non-organic materials such as stone tools, mineral paints and the like can only be indirectly dated by ^{14}C, for example by carbon dating charcoal found in the same buried layer as a stone tool.

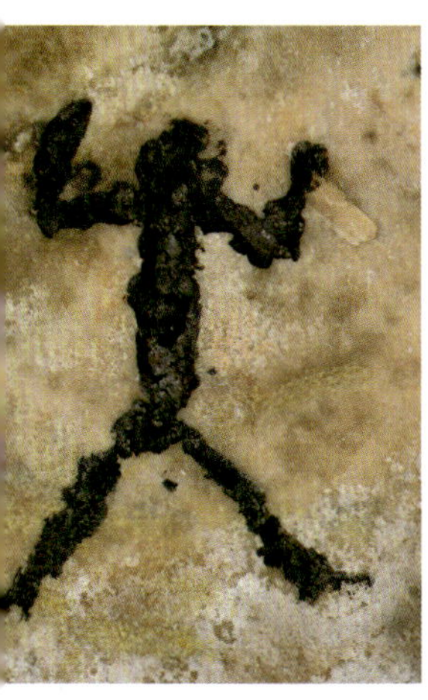

53. Beeswax applied to the rock wall to form a human shape on Panel K4 at Nawarla Gabarnmang. A tiny piece of the beeswax was carbon dated. The result indicates that the design was made sometime between AD 1633 and AD 1953.

For cave art, what is dated in carbon dating is the time when the radioactive ^{14}C contained in organic material relating to the artworks stopped being replenished by new ^{14}C, not the paintings themselves, so in reality while carbon dating gives us an absolute age, the age refers to when the organism that gave the carbon atoms died, rather than when the painting itself was made. We can usually assume that those two events – the death of the organism and the creation of the artwork – took place at about the same time, within an archaeological timeframe. But caution is needed, as black charcoal drawings, for example, could have been done with old pieces of charcoal that had lain on the ground surface for long periods of time, what is known as the 'old charcoal' problem. Or, because the trunk and limbs of a tree have their oldest, dead wood nearer their central cores, with the more recent, living wood (called the 'cambium') in their outer layers close to the bark, the burning of very old trees will make the charcoal from the inner wood as old as the tree when it began to grow, and the charcoal from the outer wood as young as the time of its death. This is the 'old wood' problem (there is another kind of 'old wood' problem also: the dating of charcoal that was made by burning parts of long-dead trees picked up from, say, swamps). Luckily this is not a significant issue for those parts of the world where trees only grow for a few decades and where dead wood quickly disintegrates in the environment, but to be certain archaeologists like to analyse the charcoal to determine the tree species at stake, to make sure that they don't unknowingly introduce carbon dates with ancient inbuilt ages into the mix. The dates obtained on beeswax from Nawarla Gabarnmang [53] do not have this problem, as beeswax does not tend to have an inbuilt age: old beeswax loses its plasticity, becoming friable within a few years of its production, and thus rapidly losing its suitability as a medium for plying into artworks on rock surfaces.

In the tropical islands of Vanuatu, Meredith Wilson and her co-researchers used carbon dating in a different and rather unusual way to date art on cave walls.[15] Wilson was doing a systematic study of the cave art of the archipelago. On the island of Malekula, near the northwestern coastline in an area known as the 'dog's head' (because a plan view of the island resembles the profile of a dog), she was taken to the site of Hopnarop by the local village chief. Here in 1996 Wilson set about systematically recording the art, documenting in detail the range of motifs present. The artworks were varied and included thirteen black linear paintings or drawings, thirty-three black hand stencils, and traces of thirteen indeterminate black paintings, drawings or stencils. She returned to the site the following year to collect samples of mud-dauber wasp nests that lay sometimes under, sometimes over the art, and tiny scrapings of the black charcoal artworks, to work out how old the art was by carbon dating those samples. Her aim was to see how art styles had changed through time since the initial occupation of the island by Lapita settlers close to 3,000 years ago.[16] Rock art is a good way to explore changing cultural expressions, because, as previously noted, the art is fixed on the rock and thus can be confidently shown to relate to that location, so that the spatial patterning of stylistic conventions can often indicate geographical connections and even places of origin for founder populations. Because artistic conventions are amenable to change with the times, it also informs on the creative hand of the artists and their cultural mores.

During her second, 1997 trip, Wilson rephotographed the art and set about collecting samples for carbon dating, each carefully chosen to date specific motif types by which she could then work out the age and sequence of styles for this site and for the region. Comparing her 1996 photographs with those of 1997, however, she noticed that something had changed: on a wall close to the outer edge of the cave two new, freshly created black hand stencils stood out against the weathered background of the limestone rock [54, 55]. Hopnarop was not simply a cultural site of times past, but a living cultural landscape with which local people continued to engage and to make art. This was an opportunity to test the reliability of carbon dating on cave art by dating artworks of a precisely known age, something that had surprisingly hardly

54. The cave wall at Hopnarop, Vanuatu, in 1996. No artworks are present in the area outlined by the rectangle.

55. By the time Meredith Wilson returned to Hopnarop in 1997, two black charcoal hand stencils had been blown onto the cave wall.

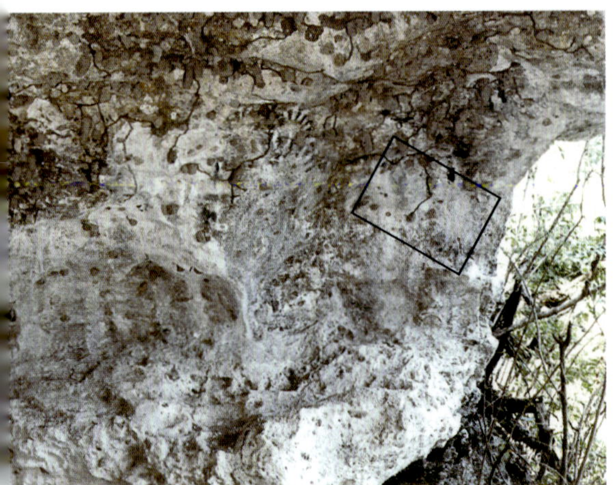

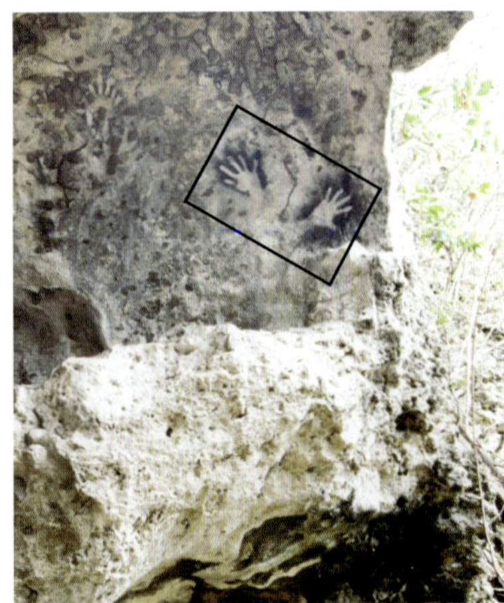

happened before in rock art research. There was need for testing, because once on a cave wall an artwork's thin charcoal layer can be bombarded by all kinds of contaminants, such as dust, redeposited calcium carbonate, the oil from human hands that may have touched the art subsequent to its creation and, even more critically, by micro-organisms introducing fresh carbon on the rock surface.

Wilson obtained twelve carbon dates from five charcoal hand stencils and from pollen or insects drawn from three mud-dauber wasp nests, many of these samples lying in superimposition. Charcoal from one of the hand stencils created between 1996 and 1997 was divided into two samples, dated twice. They gave near-identical ages, as discussed below. That from the other hand stencil done between 1996 and 1997 gave a similar age. Pollen and an insect in a wasp nest lying immediately under one of the 1996–97 stencils was slightly older, consistent with the order of superimposition. Charcoal samples from two other hand stencils located under wasp nests were both slightly older than the nests themselves, again consistent with the pattern of superimpositions. 'The radiocarbon determinations are in all cases in accordance with the relative stratigraphic positioning of samples', Wilson and her colleagues concluded.[17]

What is of particular interest in Wilson's study is that most of the wasp nests and hand stencils she dated were made during the twentieth century, sometime after atmospheric testing of atomic bombs had commenced in the 1950s and 1960s. This is significant because atomic testing caused a massive increase in the production of ^{14}C in the atmosphere, altering the composition of the air we breathe, and with this the ratio of carbon isotopes in all living matter. In 1963, the Nuclear Test Ban Treaty saw a cessation of atmospheric testing of atomic bombs, and since then the amount of ^{14}C has slowly been decreasing towards its previous levels, but even today there is still considerably more ^{14}C in the air than previously. Because of those heightened levels of ^{14}C, scientists can determine whether the animal or plant responsible for a sample of bone or charcoal died before or after the period of heightened atomic testing beginning in the 1950s. If a sample has more than 100 per cent of the ^{14}C levels of 1950, it is said to have evidence of the 'bomb pulse', and because of the rapid rise of ^{14}C levels, followed by a steep decrease after 1963, we can determine within about six months' precision when an organism died – although often a sample will have two alternative ages, one on the rise of the bomb pulse curve, one on its downturn. Wilson and her colleagues were able to put this knowledge to good use in dating the art of Hopnarop, as most of the hand stencils, including the two undertaken between 1996 and 1997 that were dated to check on the method, had evidence of the bomb pulse. Much of the dated art at Hopnarop was shown to date to the latter half of the twentieth century, confirming that the site had probably never ceased to hold significance for local communities after the social changes that began to take place following the arrival of Europeans about 400 years ago, and certainly that over the past few decades local peoples continued to practise their cultural ways through rock art in this remote limestone cave on a Pacific island in Vanuatu.

At Nawarla Gabarnmang and Hopnarop, as with dozens of other sites around the world, archaeologists have successfully determined the age of paintings and stencils by carbon dating their organic components. These are additive kinds of art, where images are created by adding pigment onto rock walls. In some cases, plant fibres from the binders used to make the paint or from the brushes used to apply it onto the wall have even been preserved in the art, and these can be picked out one by one and carbon dated.[18] But there are other kinds of art, engravings where the image is made by removing parts of the wall surface to make a mark. How, then, can we obtain absolute ages on images not made by the addition of datable materials, but rather by the deletion of parts of the rock surface? For a long time there appeared to be no answer to this dilemma, until in 2000 geochemist Alan Watchman offered an ingenious solution.

At the Wardaman Dreaming site of Yiwarlarlay, to the southwest of Arnhem Land in northern Australia, there are numerous engravings, some made by rubbing the edge of a rock against the soft sandstone wall and thereby making abraded grooves, others made by pounding a rock onto the wall until a depressed shape was formed. Here a row of kangaroo or wallaby tracks was pounded onto the wall sometime in the past [56], but the rock surrounding those tracks has remained intact. Across this part of the wall the rock surface has built up microscopic layers of mineral accretions, a cortex skin that covers both the engraved tracks and the untouched rock next to them. That rock skin both within and abutting the kangaroo or wallaby tracks was sampled with a scalpel blade. Watchman then looked at the mineral cortex in cross section by turning the samples sideways, literally micro-excavating, sometimes with hand tools and sometimes with a laser, a sequence of laminated micro-layers of cemented mineral crust one at a time and capturing the emitted laser-ablated gas in glass phials.[19]

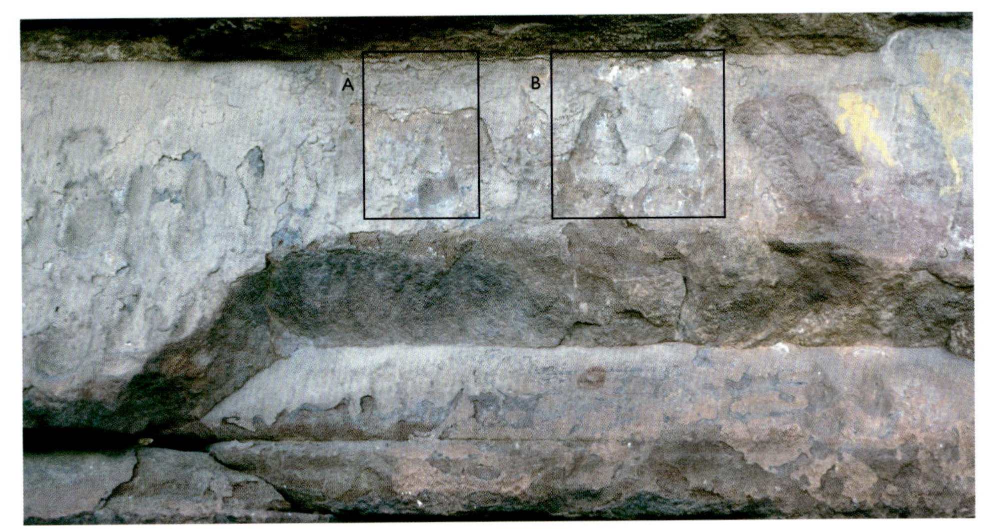

A
B

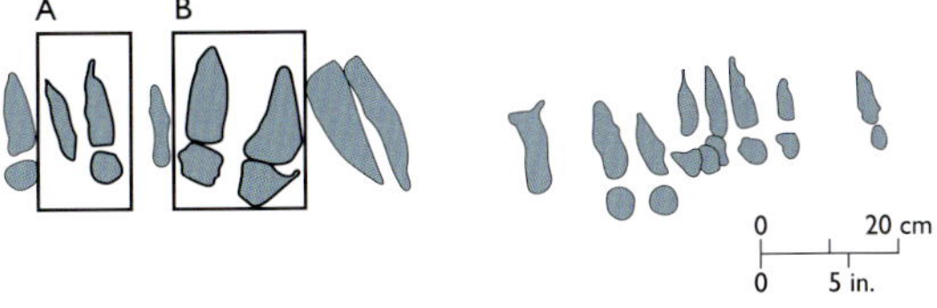

A
B
0   20 cm
0   5 in.

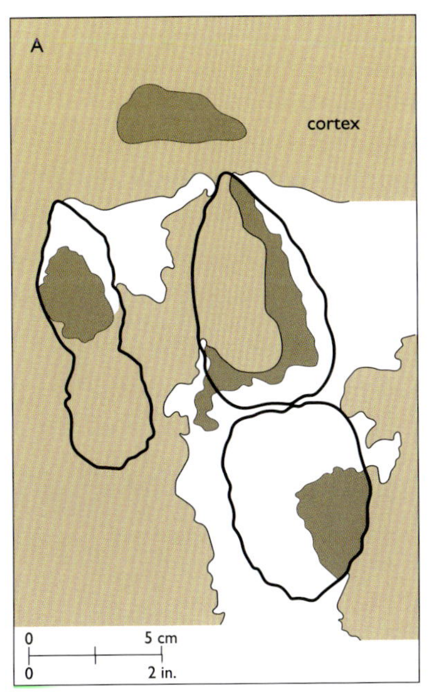

A
cortex
0   5 cm
0   2 in.

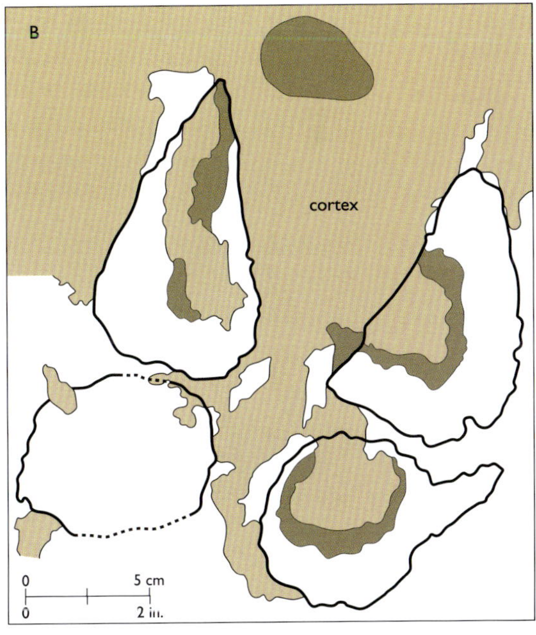

B
cortex
0   5 cm
0   2 in.

Through time, accumulated salts, dust from the surrounding landscape, ash from landscape fires and organic compounds laid down by insects had repeatedly built up on the rock surface, much like dust today builds up on furniture and house walls. Buried within those micro-laminae of variably cemented minerals, clear micro-layers of white, red and yellow pigment could be seen in the cross-sections, evidence of ancient paints that cannot now be seen on the present rock surface. At Yiwarlarlay some of the individual layers of mineral crust contained the calcium oxalate mineral whewellite, a mineral salt of organic origin and containing enough carbon for dating. By dating the carbon trapped in micro-layers below and above buried layers of paint (and released into Watchman's phials), maximum and minimum ages could be obtained for those painting events.[20]

As for the engravings, at some time in the past a 'hammerstone' was used to hit through the surface of the rock, thereby creating the animal tracks. The sequence of micro-layers of cemented crust on and immediately off the art showed that the engravings were made by removing a thin layer of silica immediately overlying the bedrock. At the time of their creation, that thin layer was partly covered with red paintings. Through time, salts and dust particles accumulated both on the newly created rock surface of the engraved tracks, and on the surrounding untouched areas. Red and black paintings were then added. Further dust, oxalate and gypsum salts continued to accumulate on the surface, along with microscopic specks of charcoal probably originating from the smoke of surrounding grass fires. More black, yellow and red paintings were added, and then oxalate and gypsum salts, dust and charcoal specks again built up across the entire rock surface. White and red paintings were once more added. The developing mineral crust then began to fracture, possibly as a result of environmental drying, some pieces falling off the wall. Finally, oxalate and gypsum salts and dust particles again accumulated onto the wall.

Carbon extracted from strategically selected micro-laminae of the accumulated rock crust allowed Watchman and his team to determine how old the engraved tracks were: around 3160 ± 60 BP, equivalent to a calibrated age of c. 3,400 years ago. This was worked out by dating the first (lowermost) layer of crust that had built up inside the concavity of the engravings after they had been made; the engravings have to have been created some time before that. A carbon date of 4080 ± 50 BP, equivalent to about 4,700 years ago, was obtained for the base layer immediately adjacent to the art, the layer that the artist had pounded through. That layer already existed when the engravings were made, and so the engravings must be more recent than 4,700 years ago. Those two ages, 4,700 and 3,400 years old, bookend the period within which the kangaroo or wallaby tracks were done, but the younger of the two dates is closer to the mark, because of the proximity of the base of the track to that dated layer. By looking at the relationship between the engravings and the micro-layers of mineral crust in cross-section – by looking through the rock – Watchman was able to give an envelope of time, a maximum and a minimum age, for the engravings. Although other researchers had obtained dates for rock crusts before, Watchman had invented a new method to date rock engravings.

Optically stimulated luminescence

We have already seen how the organic contents of mud-dauber wasp nests can be dated by carbon dating, but occasionally those same nests can also be dated in another way. Mud-dauber wasps gather mud, often from creek banks, to build nests on rock surfaces. The gathered mud usually contains large quantities of sand grains made of quartz (silica). Over time, electrons in the silicon and oxygen atoms making up the quartz may be knocked out of their stable orbits by exposure to background radiation from the radioactive decay of uranium, thorium (and their 'offspring' isotopes), and potassium present in the local materials surrounding the sand grains, and to a small degree from cosmic radiation from outer space. The emitted electrons may be trapped in defects within the crystalline structure of the quartz where they will progressively accumulate over long periods of time, up to hundreds of thousands of years, provided they are not exposed to strong sunlight. The energy from sunlight allows the trapped electrons to return to their original state accompanied by the emission of light (luminescence), so that it is only when the grains become hidden or buried from light that the trapped energy begins to accumulate at a regular rate.[21] By measuring both the amount of luminescence emitted from quartz grains in the laboratory and the rate at which radiation is being absorbed from the local environment, a luminescence age can be calculated. The quartz grains effectively act as minuscule time clocks.

Mud-dauber wasp nests may be large enough to contain sand grains hidden from sunlight at their cores. In cave and rockshelter sites across northern Australia and other parts of the world, mud-dauber wasp nests abound on rock walls – sometimes in their thousands – and artworks can occur either under or over the nests. Single-grain optically stimulated luminescence (OSL) dating is a technique that causes the trapped electrons to be released from individual sand grains. Under controlled, laboratory conditions the amount of released energy is measured as photons using sensitive instruments, as the emitted light is much too dim to see with the naked eye. That measurement is then converted to an age that represents the time elapsed since the energy started to accumulate inside the grain; that is, when the sand grains began to be hidden from sunlight. For mud-dauber wasp nests, those measurements date the creation of the nest.

In a secluded sandstone rockshelter in the Kimberley region of northern Australia, Richard Roberts of the University of Wollongong applied OSL dating to quartz sand grains embedded in three mud-dauber wasp nests superimposed over red Wandjina anthropomorphs [57, 58].[22] During the ethnographic period of the 1800s and 1900s, powerful Wandjina spirit-beings were painted and retouched as part of a pact between local clan representatives and spirit-beings to 'look after Country', to ensure that the law and well-being of the land was appropriately maintained (see Chapter 7). Wandjina paintings are thought to be relatively 'recent' in the sequence of art styles in the region, although exactly how ancient the oldest ones are remains a mystery. Roberts's results indicate that two of the wasp nests he dated are 100 to 150 years old; the third is 600 years old. Therefore, the underlying Wandjina paintings must be older, but how much older we do not know.

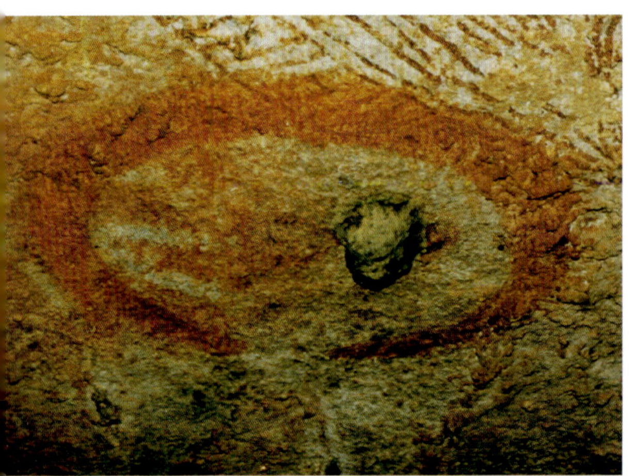

57. Wasp nest over a Wandjina painting near the Drysdale River, Kimberley region of northern Australia. The nest was dated to 600 years ago, and therefore the underlying painting must be older.

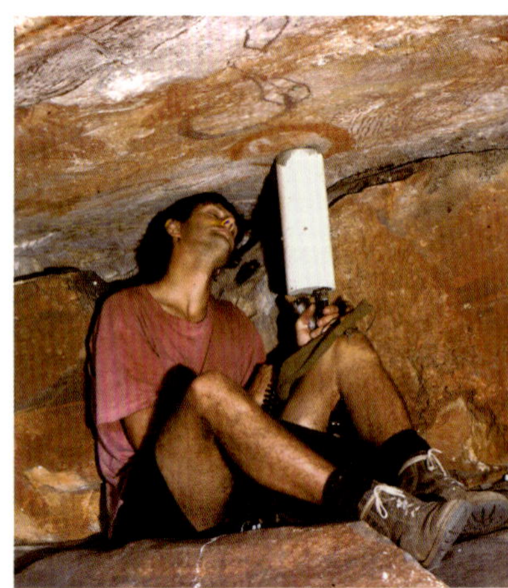

58. After removing the wasp nest shown in ill. 57, Richard Roberts recorded with a gamma ray spectrometer the ambient radiation in the area of the nest. The reading was then used to calculate the dosage rate and, with further measurements made in the laboratory, the age of the nest.

Uranium-series dating

Another approach is uranium-series (U-series) dating of calcium carbonate deposits bracketing paint layers on cave walls (this is often undertaken in association with carbon dating), as applied for example in Timor Leste (East Timor),[23] China,[24] Spain[25] and Sulawesi.[26] U-series dating is based on the complex series of decay steps that occurs as [238]U decays through a sequence of intermediate isotopes to its ultimate stable product [206]Pb, with an overall half-life of *c.* 4.5 billion years. After about 500,000 years the relative proportions of all the intermediate decay products reaches an equilibrium that does not change further and the intermediate steps can be ignored. However, before this time the amounts of the intermediate decay products progressively build up towards their equilibrium values and can be used as independent dating systems applicable to shorter time scales. Most of the intermediate decay steps have very short half-lives ranging from seconds to years, but two isotopes have much longer half-lives, [234]U (half-life = 245,250 ± 490 years at two standard deviations) and the insoluble thorium isotope [230]Th (half-life = 75,690 ± 230 years at two standard deviations).

Calcite in limestone cave deposits can incorporate soluble uranium isotopes into its structure when it is precipitated and it is usually assumed that these crystals will not contain any [230]Th (because it is insoluble),[27] Through time, [234]U decays to [230]Th The measured concentration of [230]Th is thus assumed to be derived through radioactive decay from precipitated [234]U (and parent [238]U) in redeposited layers. However, it is also generally recognized that redeposited speleothems (cave features such as stalagmites, stalactites, columns and flowstone, formed by precipitated carbonates) may contain relict materials and detritus from both bedrock and extraneous sources such as aeolian dust. These contaminants may contain U-series isotopes contributing to the overall age of the sample, thus leading to age overestimates. This possible contamination may be difficult to identify but can sometimes be corrected for (especially when the level of contamination is minimal). Results obtained from redeposited calcium carbonate thus typically indicate maximum ages due to the possible inclusion of initial [230]Th and geologically ancient carbon, although the variably porous nature of speleothems implies more or less open systems that allow transfer of more recent carbon through water action, and the leaching of inbuilt isotopes.[28] This latter problem can be largely

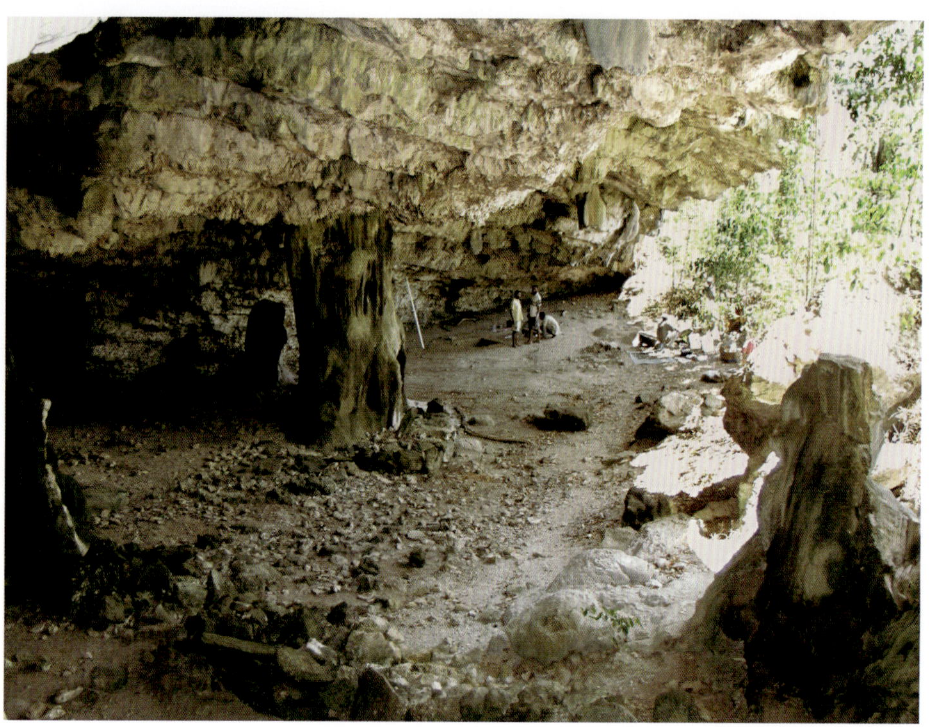

resolved by obtaining a series of measurements within a sample, to ensure the sample profile behaves as it should (i.e. that it gets older progressively deeper into the sample).

At the Pleistocene archaeological site of Lene Hara in Timor Leste [59], redeposited calcite covers the cave wall. Multicoloured paintings, mostly thought to belong to Neolithic times when pottery was in use, decorate the walls, including anthropomorphs carrying weapons, boats, star-shapes, circles, scrolls and fauna, some in an X-ray style [60]. Here Griffith University geochemist Maxime Aubert, Australian National University archaeologist Sue O'Connor and their co-researchers sampled a redeposited thick, laminated calcite coating over limestone bedrock.[29] Inside the carbonate crust, about halfway into the cross section, a finely laminated layer of red could be seen [61]. U-series dating of laminae revealed that a near-surface painting nearby must be less than 6,300 years old, consistent with the Austronesian (a cultural phase of the region) interpretation for the painting based on its style, but the older pigment actually seen in the cross-section is bracketed by ages of 30,500 and 22,500 years ago on fine, 1 mm-thin micro-layers of calcite below and above the

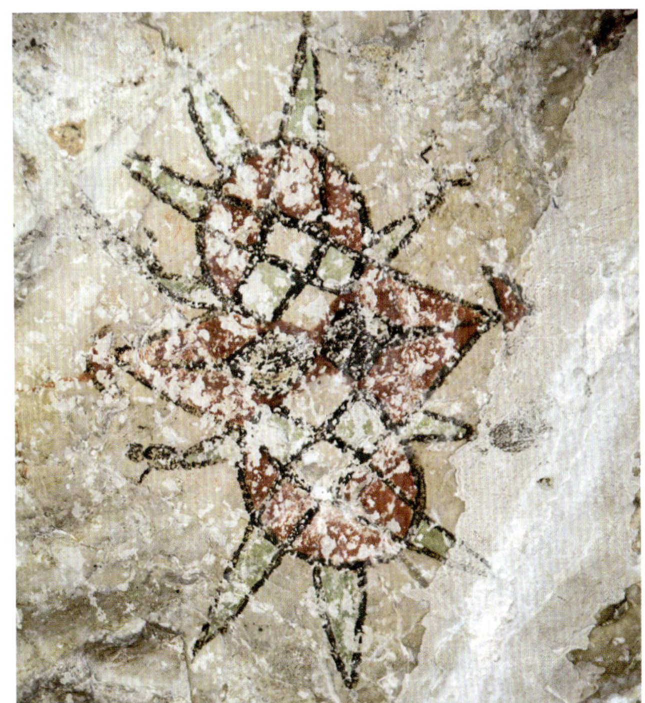

60. Black, red and green painting at Lene Hara. This painting is thought to have been made during Neolithic times.

61. Thin layer of red pigment embedded in a finely laminated calcite crust over the rock wall at Lene Hara. U-series dating on either side of the red layer indicates that it is between 30,500 and 22,500 years old.

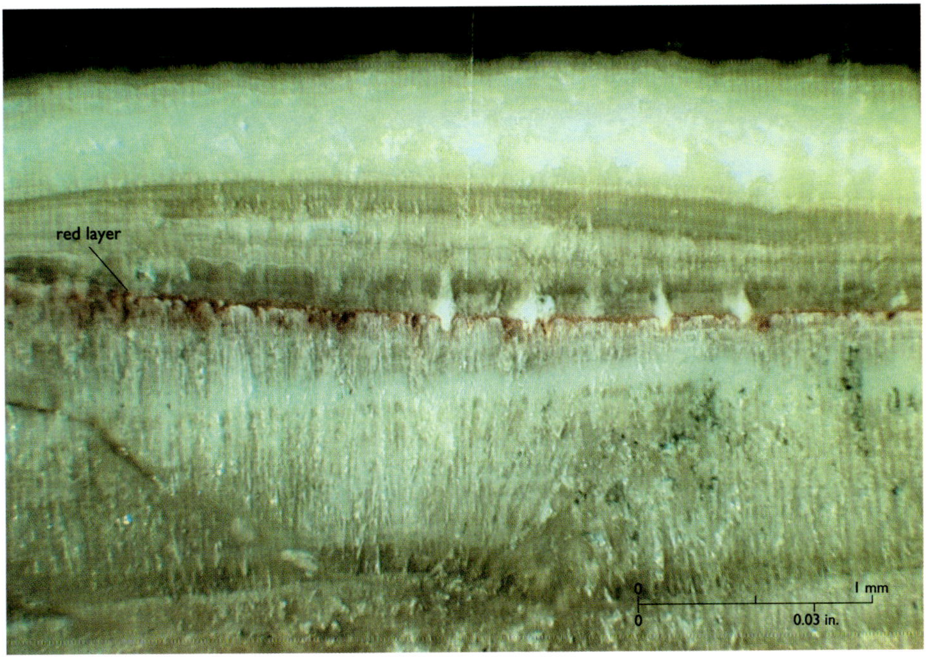

art, respectively. The shape of that latter artwork could not be determined, because the red could only be seen in the sampled cross section, but its age is contemporaneous with evidence of people in the cave, as determined by archaeological excavations. No outcrops of red ochre occur within the site, but pellets of the substance were found in the excavated Pleistocene deposits, indicating that people must have brought in colourants from some distance away. This innovative study showed that redeposited calcite under and above art could be used to obtain U-series dates by which to bracket the age of paintings in caves.

Aubert and his team followed up their work at Timor Leste by obtaining the first U-series dates for cave art in China.[30] Here, at the Baiyunwan art site in the Jinsha River area, Yunnan Province [62], U-series dates were used to bracket the age of red paint layers trapped in calcite. Because one of the motifs – a large deer head – occurred only a short distance below the surface of the redeposited limestone, it could be seen after digital enhancement by Photoshop and DStretch, as described above. Both U-series and carbon dates were obtained from laminae below and above the deer head, bracketing the age of that painting to sometime between 5,738 and 2,050 years ago. Traces of a deeper and older red layer, possibly a painting whose shape could not be determined, were also observed in the sample's cross-section; that red layer was at least 3,400 years old. This was only the third time that rock art had been dated anywhere in China.

In 2014 Aubert and his co-researchers dated rock art in the spectacular limestone karst towers of the Maros district of

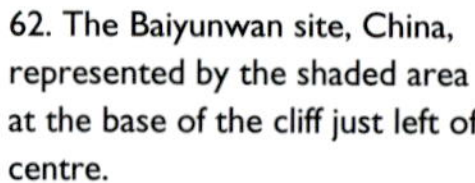

62. The Baiyunwan site, China, represented by the shaded area at the base of the cliff just left of centre.

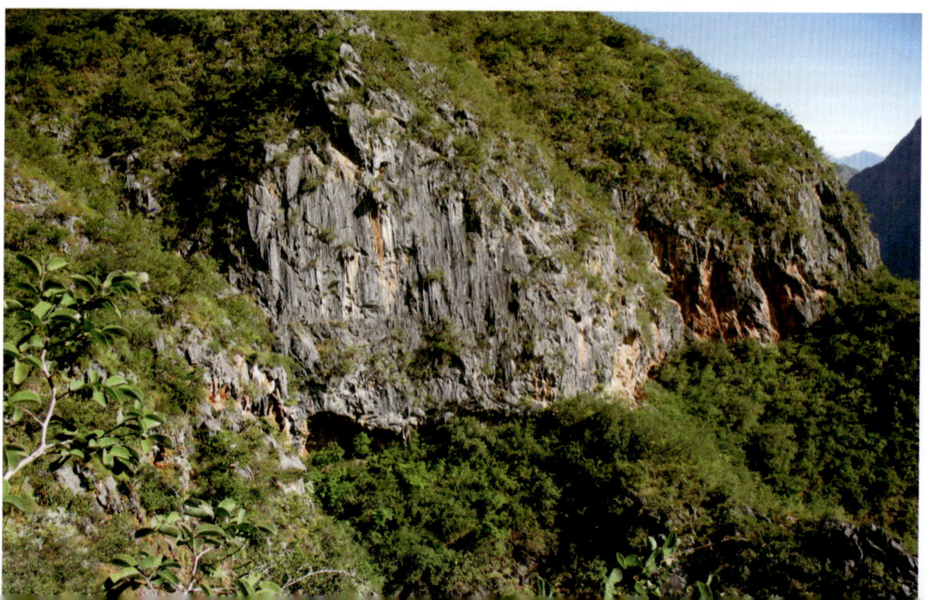

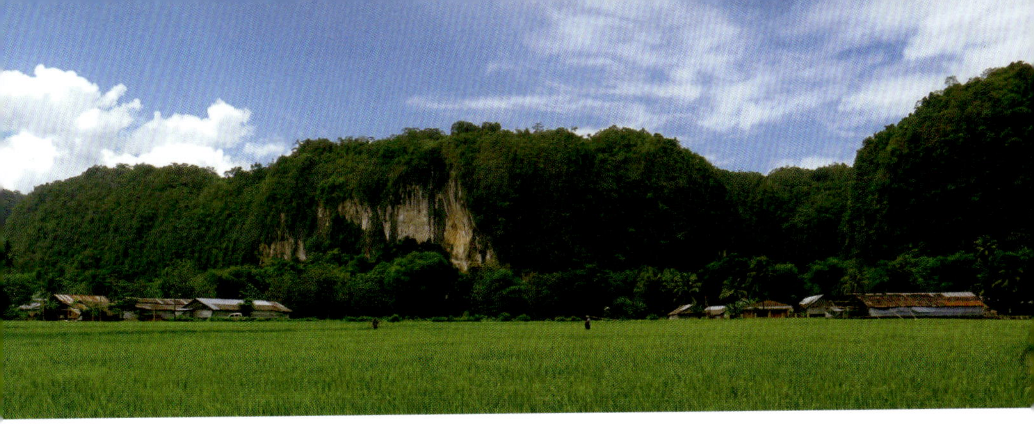

63. Limestone karst landscape of the Maros district in Sulawesi, where a cave stencil dating to more than 39,900 years has been found.

Sulawesi in island Southeast Asia [63].[31] Here they used U-series dating on calcite nodules accumulated over the art to obtain minimum ages on twelve hand stencils and two naturalistic paintings of animals from seven caves. One of those hand stencils is at least 39,900 years old, and a naturalistic painting of a babirusa 'pig-deer' is more than 35,400 years old [64], comparable in age to the oldest known of Europe's famed Ice Age art (see Chapter 6). We will return to these sites in later chapters.

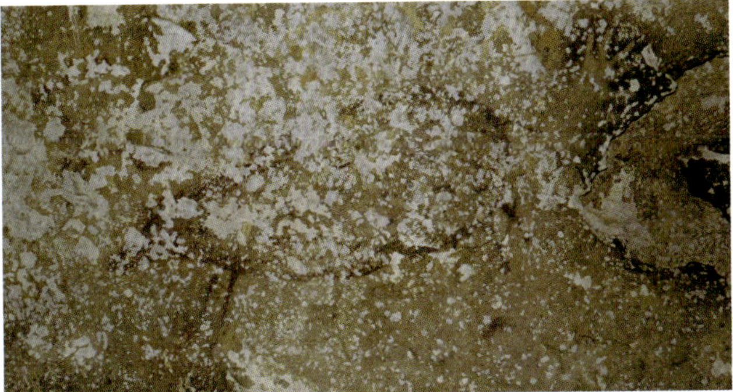

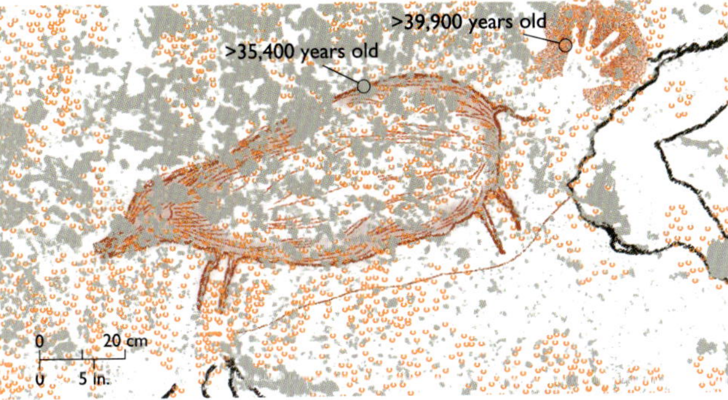

64. Photograph and photo-tracing of a painted babirusa 'pig-deer' and hand stencil dated to more than 35,400 and 39,900 years ago respectively, from a cave in the Maros district, Sulawesi, Indonesia. The detail above shows the sample taken from the babirusa, with the pigment clearly sandwiched between U-series-dated layers.

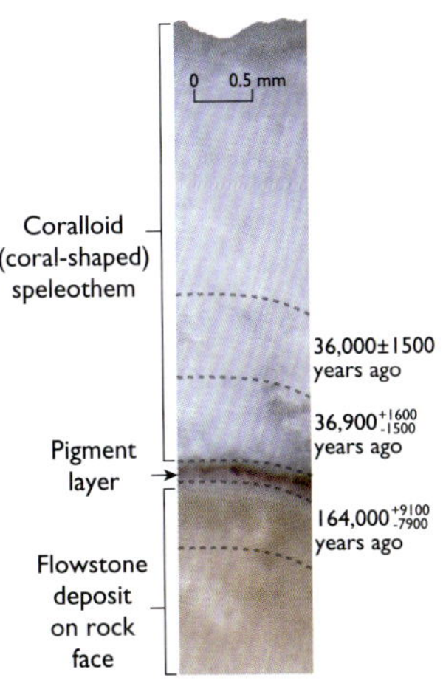

Where did the pigments come from?

There are various ways of obtaining information on the pigments used to make art in caves. Some of these will be discussed for Ice Age Europe in Chapter 6. At the archaeological site of Puritjarra in the heart of the Australian desert [65], Mike Smith excavated large numbers of imported ochre pieces covering some 35,000 years of Aboriginal occupation.[32] With specialist colleagues, he studied ochre mines across the landscape [66], covering many hundreds of kilometres of desert in all directions around Puritjarra. Smith's research team utilized a broad range of established mineralogical and elemental techniques to 'fingerprint' source ochres, developing some new methods along the way. One innovative technique involves identifying the ratio of oxygen isotopes in the fine-grained quartz particles of ochre, each source area having its own isotopic 'fingerprint'.[33] Another involves working out the magnetic properties of ochres from individual quarries.[34] Other researchers around the world have also engaged chemists and related specialists to work out where excavated and on-wall pigments originally came from by studying their chemical properties.

At Puritjarra, Smith found that red ochre from Karrku, a subterranean ochre mine located 125 km (80 miles) to the north of the site and still used by Warlpiri Aboriginal people today, began to be used as far back as 35,000 years ago, declining after 15,000 years ago during a period of peak aridity at the height of the Ice Age. This decreasing use of Karrku ochre at Puritjarra indicates

65. Puritjarra, a 35,000-year-old rockshelter in the heart of the Australian desert, where Mike Smith excavated quantities of imported ochre.

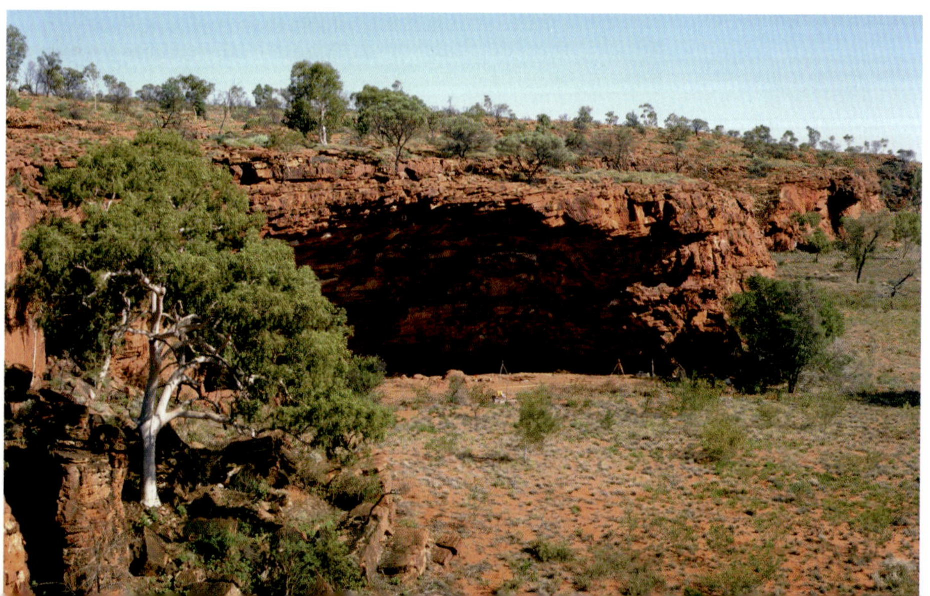

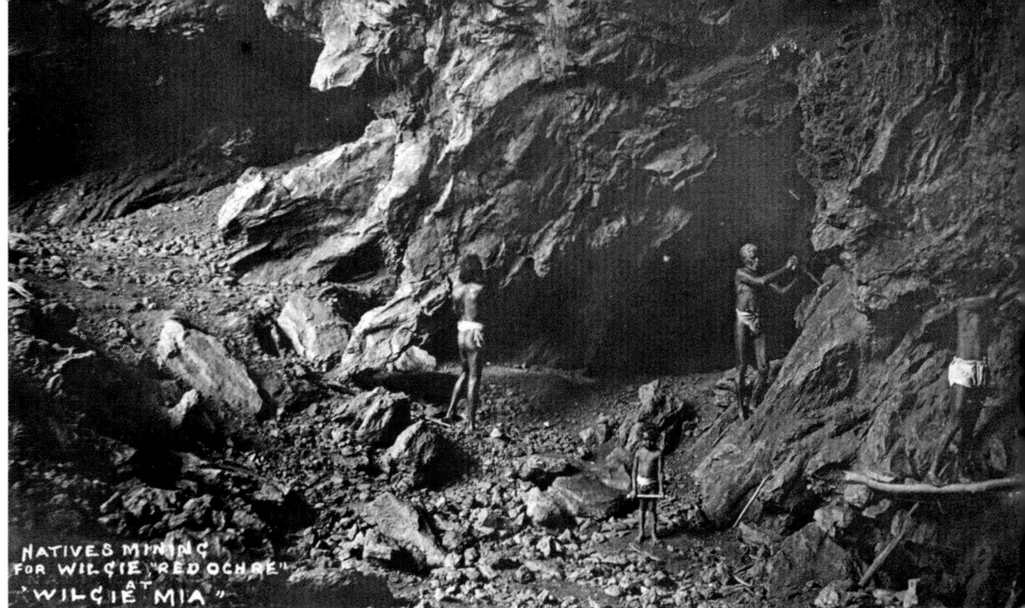

66. The red ochre mine of Wilgie Mia in the Weld Ranges in the arid west of Australia, 1910. Aboriginal people have mined and traded the ochre from this source for thousands of years.

that the size and shape of the territory, and social connections across the landscape, changed during the Ice Age. But Karrku ochre again became predominant during the last millennium. Other ochre quarries variably distant from Puritjarra came in and out of favour during this whole period, signalling changes in access to, and perhaps preference for, high-quality red pigments coming from different quarries to the north, south, east and west of the site. Greasy, purplish-red ochre from Ulpunyali, 65 km (40 miles) to the southeast, began to be used in large amounts 15,000 years ago at Puritjarra, precisely when use of the northern Karrku quarry was on the wane. A constriction of the range of sources and increasingly southward focus of Puritjarra's imported ochre catchment thus took place during the period of peak aridity associated with the Ice Age, indicating a changing configuration of resource use and landscape engagements.

The geographical distribution of pigments from variably distant sources, first from Karrku then from Ulpunyali, suggests that the Aboriginal desert dwellers of central Australia modified the way they organized themselves and engaged with their landscapes through time. Like the geographical distribution of artistic styles that testifies to social influences across space, exploring how access to pigments from varied sources changed through time helps us understand past social networks, how some areas and their resources came into the purview of social territories, and how cultural restrictions waned or disappeared altogether.

Chapter 4: The beginnings of art

Ours is the only species to make and use representational imagery in its natural environment, although experiments with non-human primates such as chimpanzees and gorillas show that under laboratory conditions they, too, have some sense of recognition of and appreciation for coded visual symbols and an ability to communicate extrasomatically (other than through the body). So how has our ability to engage with art come about?

If we track our ancestry back far enough in the depths of time, we would reach an era when such faculties did not exist. Did our species' apparently singular capacity for complex expression and communication through language, visual symbols and culture emerge suddenly at a defining moment in the past – what archaeologist Paul Mellars and palaeoanthropologist Chris Stringer have called a cognitive or 'human revolution'[1] – or rather was it more gradual, a slower evolution without a defining moment, what Sally McBrearty and Alison Brooks refer to as 'the revolution that wasn't'?[2] To better understand the difference between these two stances, we need to have a sense of how we have evolved as a species.

In the past decade huge strides have been made in mapping out the human evolutionary tree [67]. Two main kinds of evidence have helped illuminate this topic in different ways. Fossils are the absolute hard evidence of human evolution. Important new fossil discoveries of early humans are announced nearly every year, and improvements in dating methods have provided ages for both recently discovered and classic examples. Different ways of studying fossils are also shedding light on some aspects of lifestyle, such as the diet and behaviour of early humans. So, while there are still many gaps in the fossil record, the timing and order of key anatomical developments along the path towards fully modern humans is now quite well known.

The second kind of evidence is contained in the complex molecule called DNA that is held in almost every cell in our bodies and which may also survive, albeit in a degraded condition, in ancient human remains such as bones and hair, including some that date back tens of thousands of years. DNA is best known as the double-stranded helix that contains the 'instructions'

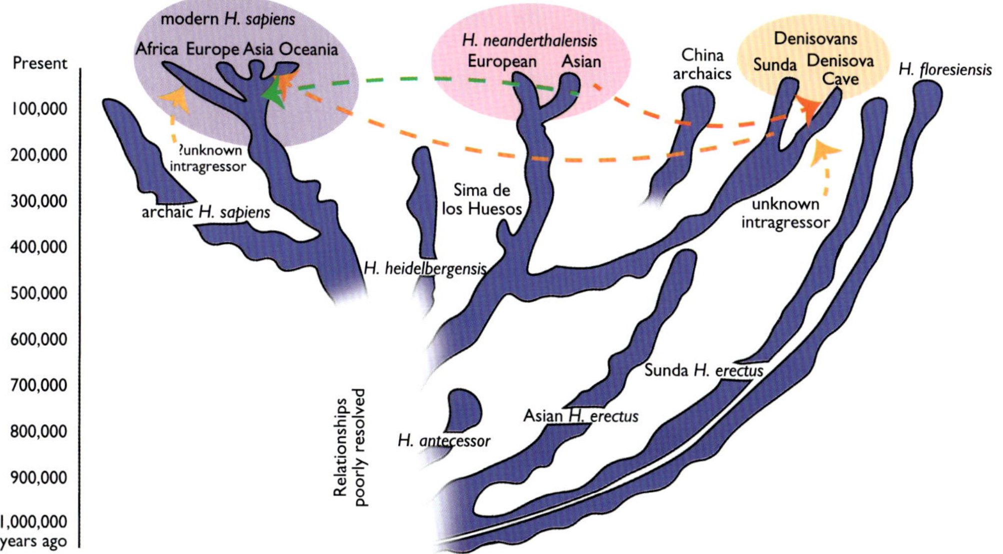

67. Palaeoanthropologists have long debated how hominid fossil remains are best classified and related to each other, so that the evolutionary trees created often vary between researchers. The one shown here for the last million years, by Chris Stringer, takes into account both the latest skeletal and DNA evidence. The dashed lines represent interlineage gene flow, as determined by the DNA.

(including the elements called 'genes') that allow each of us to develop following the union of a sperm cell from the male and an egg from the female to produce one complete, new 'genome'. Less widely known is the extraordinary usefulness of the same genetic material for investigating the evolutionary history of all organisms, including humans.

The cells in our bodies contain two kinds of DNA – nuclear and mitochondrial. Nuclear DNA resides in the cell nucleus while mitochondrial DNA is found only in the mitochondrion, a discrete organelle that exists outside the nucleus and which produces energy for cellular function. Mitochondria are required in most cell types, and our bodies thus contain large quantities of mitochondrial DNA, but nuclear DNA makes up the vast bulk of the total genome. Most of the latter is inherited in two copies – one copy contributed by the sperm and the other by the egg (this material is technically called 'autosomal' DNA, but we will use the simpler label 'nuclear'). At the time of conception, the two copies interact in a complex way that results in the exchange of blocks of DNA, so that each final strand is different from either of the original versions. This process is known as 'recombination' and is one of the two main ways in which genetic variation is produced. Mitochondrial DNA is provided by a mitochondrion that is present in the egg and thus derives exclusively from the mother. Males alone carry additional DNA that they inherit exclusively from their fathers – a small parcel of nuclear DNA that is bundled together on the Y-chromosome and which causes the embryo to develop as a male rather than a female. Because mitochondrial and Y-chromosome DNA are only inherited as single copies (they are 'uniparental'), they are not subject to recombination like biparentally inherited nuclear (autosomal) DNA.

Mutation is the second process that produces variation in DNA. Mutation occurs whenever double-stranded DNA is unwound and a new copy is made. Across the whole genome copying is never perfect, and each new copy will differ from the original. When this occurs in a normal body cell, it may affect cellular function but the mutation cannot be inherited. However, when it occurs in a cell that is destined to become a sperm cell or an egg, the mutation is heritable. Mutation, unlike recombination, affects every kind of DNA – nuclear (autosomal), mitochondrial and Y-chromosomal.

Any genetic changes that are transmitted down through successive generations are cumulative over time, hence a pair of closely related organisms will generally show fewer differences than a more distantly related pair. When such comparisons are made between members of different populations or even different species, the resulting pattern of similarities and differences can be used to reconstruct the sequence in which genetic changes have occurred, and from this, the evolutionary tree of the organisms being compared. Moreover, if certain assumptions are made about the rate at which mutation or recombination events occur in a particular group of organisms, the evolutionary tree can be given a timescale. Geneticists call this kind of inference a 'molecular clock', and many attempts have been made to apply this dating method to human evolution.

Early attempts to study human evolution with genetic information used mitochondrial and Y-chromosome DNA because of their simpler, uniparental mode of inheritance, in which all changes can be attributed to mutation rather than the more complex process of recombination. However, rapid advances in technology since about the year 2000 have made it possible to sequence entire genomes from many individuals representing all of the major living human populations, as well as examples of each of our closest relatives among the great apes. Powerful new methods have also made it possible to reconstruct the entire genomes of certain, particularly well-preserved fossils, including early examples of our own species and of close relatives including the enigmatic Neanderthals. Comparisons of entire genomes rather than just small portions allow far more sophisticated inferences to be drawn, not only about the structure of the human evolutionary tree but also about the timing and extent of gene flow between populations and between species (through hybridization), and the nature of selective pressures that have operated at different times and places. The resulting 'explosion' of genetic information has produced startling new insights into the pattern and process of human evolution, and given entirely new meaning to what it means to be a 'modern human'. Some of the new insights from the study of DNA will be explored later in this chapter, for they have implications for understanding who made the first cave art. However, genetic and fossil evidence relates to biology, and may in itself not reveal much about cultural practices such as the ability to make art. For that we must turn to another field of study: archaeology, the investigation of artifacts and other material traces of past human behaviour.

Cave art, both as buried portable objects such as personal adornments and as designs on rock walls, plays a key role in scientific debates concerning the degree to which cognitive modernism evolved with, or independently of, biological modernism. One reason for this is that artistic expressions are 'proxies' for aesthetically loaded forms of representational behaviour, for the ability to simulate and think in abstract ways that also tap into senses of appeal. By definition, artworks are objects of aesthetic attraction (what makes an object a work of 'art' may be in the eye of the beholder, but senses of beauty are at least in part socially and culturally learnt). Graphic arts visually express senses of balance, beauty and emotion.

As creations that tap into senses of appreciation, artworks also signal an ability to express and communicate through visual codes; those codes have the ability to be socially recognized and to have social appeal. Artworks simultaneously imply aesthetic appreciation and cultural messaging, and they engineer decision-making in the process. Artistic cultural messaging takes place through symbols that represent things other than themselves. In doing so, artworks more than *represent* objects or ideas: they set up how we come to socially and culturally perceive, or 'know', things, and therefore how we come to act on those things. Images establish reference points, *our* reference points that orchestrate how we come to see the world, how we give meaning to it. For example, an image of a pig signals how we think about and communicate the idea of 'pig', not through the animal itself but through culturally appropriate notions of the beast.

The image establishes relationships between pigs and people, for the artist expresses the order of things (take, for example, the very different attitudes towards pigs in different cultures; we would not see among Muslim or Judaistic societies, where the consumption of pork is prohibited, an image of a dissected pig such as we see in 'Christian' butcher's shops, and in New Guinea Highlands societies pigs are a sign of wealth, communal feasts and, with this, the ability to muster social support). The anthropologist Claude Lévi-Strauss influentially wrote that 'Species are chosen not as good to eat, but as good to think with',[3] and those thoughts are mediated through cultural symbols. The animal does not have to be there for us to communicate meaningfully about it; rather, the idea of a chosen taxon takes on meaning through its symbol. The artist becomes a communicator of knowledge acquired through culture and social interaction. Artworks help us give meaning to the world we live in, to make sense of it, and to communicate that sense, and cave art needs to be understood in that context.

The evolutionary tree before Homo sapiens

At what point did our ancestors first attain the ability to make pictures and create a sense of order through symbols? Before we can address this question, it is necessary to briefly define some terminology.

We will use the term 'anatomically modern' (others sometimes use 'biologically modern') to refer to humans that were anatomically indistinguishable from contemporary *Homo sapiens*, other than in minor features of the kind that distinguish modern geographic variations among our species. We will also refer to 'cognitively modern' humans that behaved in modern ways and had essentially the same abilities to think, communicate, make and use symbols and engage in culture as we do. The term 'fully modern' is used for human populations that have developed both anatomical and cognitive modernism. A key question remains whether anatomical and cognitive modernism evolved in tandem with the emergence of *Homo sapiens*, or whether the two developed at different times in the past.

Some other useful terms to remember are 'hominid', 'hominine' and 'hominin'. Hominids are members of the family Hominidae – in modern taxonomy this is now often defined as the group that includes modern humans and the various species of great ape (the two species of orangutan, the chimpanzee, the bonobo, and the gorilla). It also includes the common ancestor of all of these living species and any other extinct lineages that were also descended from that common ancestor. Hominines are members of the subfamily Homininae – the more restricted group that excludes the earliest branching lineage that lead to the orangutans (that branch of the hominid tree is the subfamily Ponginae). Hominins (the Hominini) are an even more restricted taxonomic unit that contains only one living species, *Homo sapiens*. There is much debate as to which fossil species should be included in this group and the decision is thus arbitrary to a significant degree. One view is that the Hominini should be restricted to members of the genus *Homo*, with other early human-like creatures who are not our evolutionary ancestors but rather our cousins (such as the genera *Australopithecus* and *Paranthropus*) being placed elsewhere in the evolutionary tree.

We can possibly trace the evolutionary origin of the genus *Homo* (our evolutionary lineage) as far back as 2.7 million years ago, although we are still unsure which species the earliest, fragmentary fossils belong to. Dating to soon after that time are *Homo habilis* fossil remains from eastern and possibly also southern Africa. The name *Homo habilis* means 'Handy Man' and it is likely that many of the earliest known stone tools were made by this species (although recent discoveries of 3.3 million-year-old stone tools from the site of Lomekwi 3 in Kenya suggest that an earlier and perhaps pre-human species was actually the first to make stone tools).[4]

Other fossils dating to around 1.9 million years ago from eastern Africa and classified as *Homo rudolfensis* show a significant increase in brain size and a few other anatomical changes towards modernity. However, there is no evidence of real cultural advance until we meet the next species to evolve, *Homo erectus*.

Homo erectus appears to have evolved in Africa by about 1.9 million years ago, with fossils found throughout much of the continent, except in the west where few fossil sites of this age are known. Significantly, it was probably the first species of *Homo* to move out of Africa – its skeletal remains have been found in western Asia (the oldest dated at 1.8 million years ago from Dmanisi in Georgia [68]), China and Indonesia. The spread of *Homo erectus* into new kinds of habitats was accompanied by anatomical changes, and regional populations existed in East Asia, where the earliest remains date to about 1.6 million years ago, while the probable descendant species *Homo antecessor* ('Pioneer Man') is represented by well-preserved remains from Atapuerca

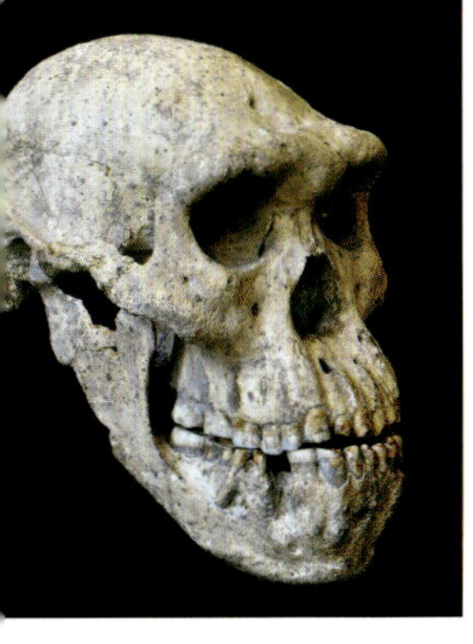

68. 1.8 million-year-old *Homo erectus* Skull 5 from Dmanisi, Georgia.

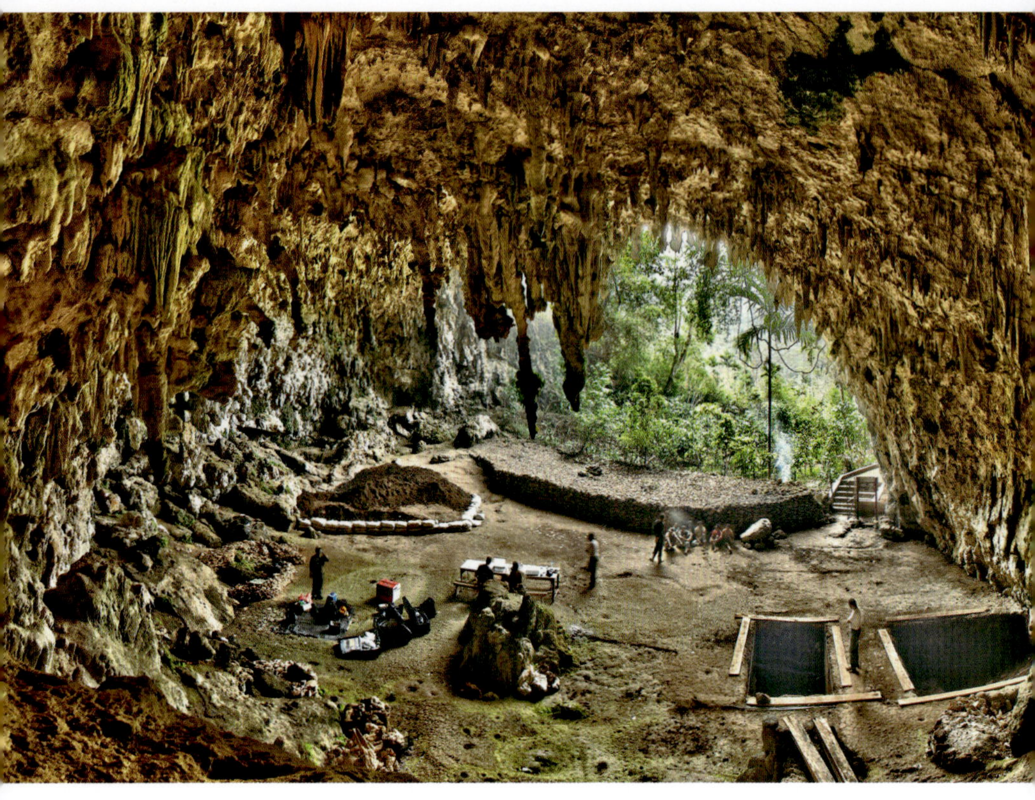

69. Cave of Liang Bua in Flores, Indonesia, where skeletal remains of 'the hobbit' have been found buried deep underground.

70. (opposite) Reconstruction of 400,000-year-old hut structure at Terra Amata, southern France, based on archaeological evidence.

in Spain dating to about 850,000 years ago.[5] A population that became isolated on the small island of Flores in eastern Indonesia went through a process of dwarfing (this is common among animal populations on small islands) and also developed other unique traits. This species is called *Homo floresiensis*, but it is better known by its popular name 'the hobbit', and many fossil remains have been found in the spectacular, cathedral-like cave of Liang Bua near the centre-west of the island [69].[6] It survived on Flores until sometime between 100,000 and 50,000 years ago (the latest dating suggests that it died out around the time that *Homo sapiens* arrived in the broader region – although modern human remains of that age have not yet been found at Liang Bua itself – leading us to wonder if the latter had anything to do with their demise).[7]

The trend towards modernity resulted in the emergence of a new species called *Homo heidelbergensis*. Like *Homo erectus* before it, this species also expanded widely, and by 600,000 years ago populations were established in Africa, Europe and Asia [67].

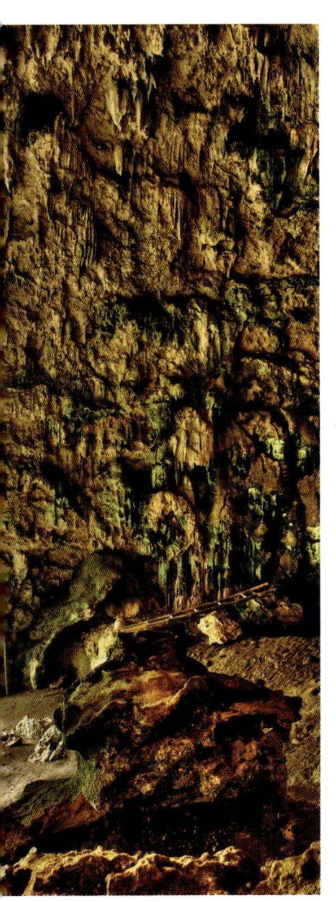

Homo heidelbergensis may have been the first species to construct artificial shelters, as indicated by what some archaeologists have interpreted as 400,000-year-old hearths, post-holes and associated low stone walls at the beach-side archaeological site of Terra Amata in southern France [70].

By about 400,000 years ago, populations living in western Eurasia had developed a number of unusual characteristics that set them apart from all other prior populations – these represent the beginning of the lineage known as Neanderthals (*Homo neanderthalensis*), the archetypal 'caveman' of popular imagination (the term is a double misnomer: although Neanderthals, like *Homo sapiens*, sometimes frequented caves, they were by no means just a cave-dwelling species, mostly living in more open landscapes; and there were both females and males!). Neanderthals survived for nearly 400,000 years, persisting until *c.* 40,000 years ago, as evidenced by skeletal remains from a number of caves in Spain such as Jarama VI, Zafarraya, L'Arbreda and Abric Romaní, in France at sites such as La Quina, and in Italy at Riparo Bombrini (other Neanderthal sites from the Iberian peninsula, such as Gorham's Cave at the southeastern edge of the Rock of Gibraltar, have more recent carbon dates, but the quality of these dates is currently under debate and they cannot therefore be used as evidence for the later survival of Neanderthals).[8]

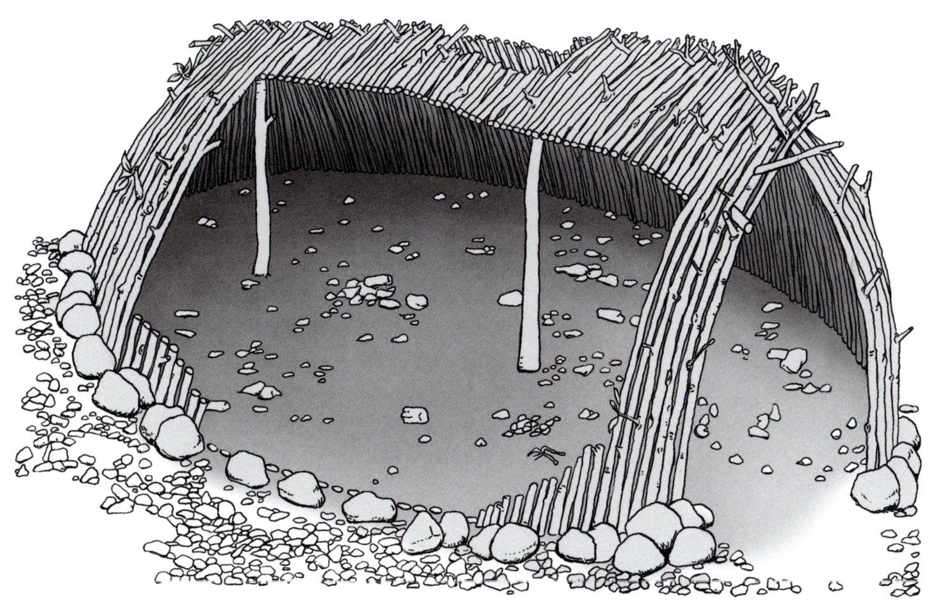

The earliest fossils showing the characteristic anatomical features of extant *Homo sapiens* come from Africa and date from around 200,000 years ago. Elsewhere around the world, fossils with the same features are present in more recent contexts. When the ages of these finds are plotted on a map they appear to document a third dispersal out of Africa, perhaps starting around 120,000 years ago. By 55,000 years ago, and perhaps earlier, this dispersal had resulted in the colonization of eastern and Southeast Asia, followed shortly thereafter by significant water crossings to the Australian continent and islands of Melanesia, regions that had never before been occupied by any species of hominid. With migration of *Homo sapiens* into Europe around 43,000 years ago (based on the earliest known skeletal remains), and around 16,000 years ago into the Americas (this date is hotly disputed),[9] the colonization of the world by our species was effectively complete, leaving only the Antarctic continent and the more remote island realms of the Indian and Pacific Oceans for later discovery.

Across large areas of western Asia and Europe, dispersing bands of *Homo sapiens* are likely to have encountered resident populations of Neanderthals. The question of what happened during this crucial period remains one of the greatest mysteries of human history. How different were the two species in terms of abilities and cultural sophistication? How did they interact? Were encounters ever harmonious or were they more likely to start or end in open aggression? And if *Homo sapiens* ever intermingled with Neanderthals, could the two species interbreed? Were any offspring infertile – like a mule, the result of crossing between a horse and a donkey? If Neanderthals became extinct rather than being assimilated, did *Homo sapiens* adopt any cultural practices from Neanderthals, and vice versa? Do we still carry any legacy of this profound interaction between the two species? How can cave art research help us better understand such questions?

Neanderthal remains were an obvious target for scientists experimenting with methods for recovering ancient DNA from fossils. Initial successes included the extraction and sequencing of short segments of mitochondrial DNA from several Neanderthal fossils;[10] these early results indicated that *Homo neanderthalensis* was genetically very distinct from the *Homo sapiens* lineage, with the most recent common ancestor probably living about 500,000 years ago. The mitochondrial DNA results were also interpreted as strong evidence that the two species of humans did not interbreed to any extent during their period of contact, either because they were biologically incapable of doing so or for cultural reasons. A 500,000-year-old divergence would be consistent with the common ancestor of *Homo neanderthalensis* and *Homo sapiens* being *Homo heidelbergensis*, but nuclear DNA suggests a somewhat earlier divergence, perhaps more consistent with derivation from *Homo antecessor*.

It is often said in science that too much data can spoil a good story. In this case the initial version of history started to wobble under the weight of data that came from whole genome sequencing of contemporary human populations. As more and more human genomes were mapped from around the world, it became increasingly clear that there was genetic material present in human populations living outside of Africa that could not have originated in Africa and, furthermore, it was too different to be explained by the usual processes of recombination or mutation. However, the full implications of this unexplained genetic material did not become clear until scientists working with Neanderthal remains from Vindija Cave in Croatia were able to sequence large parts of the Neanderthal nuclear genome as well as Neanderthal mitochondrial DNA.[11] There, finally, were the missing genetic components: the evidence that we did interbreed with Neanderthals, at least occasionally, and produce offspring who were themselves capable of breeding,[12] thus allowing fragments of the Neanderthal genome to transfer across into our own through the process of recombination and, thereby, survive through to the present day.[13]

In 2016, a further dimension was added to the story when Fernando Mendez, David Poznik, Sergi Castellano and Carlos Bustamante, from Stanford University and the Max Planck Institute for Evolutionary Anthropology, managed to extract Y-chromosome DNA from a *c.* 49,000-year-old Neanderthal skeleton from El Sidrón in Spain. As had been found earlier for the mitochondrial DNA of Neanderthal bones from Spain, Germany, Croatia and Russia, the Neanderthal Y-chromosome DNA from El Sidrón was strongly divergent from all of the variation found among fossil or living modern humans.[14] How can we reconcile this with the seemingly strong evidence for interbreeding from the nuclear DNA?

The absence of one or other of the uniparental Neanderthal genetic components in the modern human population might be explained by a strong sexual bias in ancient interbreeding (e.g. only male Neanderthals bred with female modern humans, which could explain the absence of Neanderthal mitochondrial DNA). However, the absence of both uniparental components points instead at different kinds of explanations, one possibility being that the Neanderthal mitochondrial or Y-chromosome DNA was selected against because they didn't function as well in the context of the modern human genome (and therefore individuals with both Neanderthal and modern human ancestry had lower chances of survival over the long term). Another possibility is that the interbreeding events were not very common and the shared genetic components simply dropped out of the modern human genome by chance. Persistence of some parts of the Neanderthal nuclear DNA under either circumstance is intrinsically more likely when both sexes contribute equally to the genome of their offspring, when some shared components are neutral or selectively advantageous over the long term, and when the mixing that occurs through recombination (as happens in nuclear DNA but not in mitochondrial or Y-chromosome DNA) further increases the chances that at least some parts of a 'foreign' genome will be carried through into future generations.

Although the incorporation of Neanderthal nuclear DNA into the genome of non-African *Homo sapiens* explained much of the previously mysterious variation, it still did not explain all the anomalous components, especially some that are found in the highest proportion among populations in Asia and Melanesia. Where this other DNA had come from was revealed when genomes were extracted from fragmentary human remains dating from more than 50,000 years ago from Denisova Cave in Siberia. These remains turned out to represent a third kind of hominin that was somewhat closer to *Homo neanderthalensis* than to *Homo sapiens* – presumably another regional derivative of *Homo heidelbergensis* or *Homo antecessor*.[15] Exactly what these 'Denisovan' people looked like is not clear because only a few small pieces of bone and teeth have been discovered so far. But what is clear is that at some point during the migration of *Homo sapiens* across Eurasia, contact and interbreeding occurred between these people and one or more populations of Denisovans. Because this population of *Homo sapiens* was already carrying genetic components derived from earlier interbreeding with Neanderthals, the result was an even more complex genome made up of three genetic components – *sapiens*, Neanderthal and Denisovan. At its maximum degree, the non-*sapiens* genetic components amount to around 7–8 per cent of the total genome of some living humans, a not inconsiderable legacy from the history of interactions between different species of hominins in prehistoric times.

Early artistic expressions

So far this chapter has told the story of the emergence of modern humans as assembled from a rapidly growing body of fossil and genetic evidence. But what about the emergence of cognitively modern humans? Archaeologists think that *Homo erectus*/*Homo heidelbergensis* were not capable of the kinds of complex symbolic behaviours that modern humans exhibit, because there is no evidence of fully blown symbolism or complex artworks prior to the evolution of *Homo sapiens*. There are, nevertheless, signs that *Homo erectus*/*Homo heidelbergensis* had some form of aesthetic appreciation.

In Africa, western to central Asia and Europe, we find beautifully symmetrical teardrop-shaped stone artifacts – Acheulean 'hand axes' – dating from about 1.7 million to 100,000 years ago (the term 'Acheulean' is the name given to the artifacts made by, and cultural practices of, *Homo erectus*/*Homo heidelbergensis* and early *Homo neanderthalensis*). Many of these are cores from which implements were struck off, rather than tools themselves, but they are beautifully crafted nonetheless. A striking example from 250,000 years ago – late Acheulean times – comes from West Tofts in Norfolk, England [71]. It has a centrally positioned fossil shell embedded in the rock, as do a few other stone artifacts from this period. That shell was part of the original rock; the fact that it was left intact and prominently displayed at the centre of the artifact implies recognition and appreciation of symmetry, an expression of aesthetics among its *Homo erectus*/*Homo heidelbergensis* crafters. From Hoxne in Suffolk, England, comes a particularly elegant cordate (heart-shaped) 'hand axe', dated to about 400,000 years ago. Of similar age are the pointed

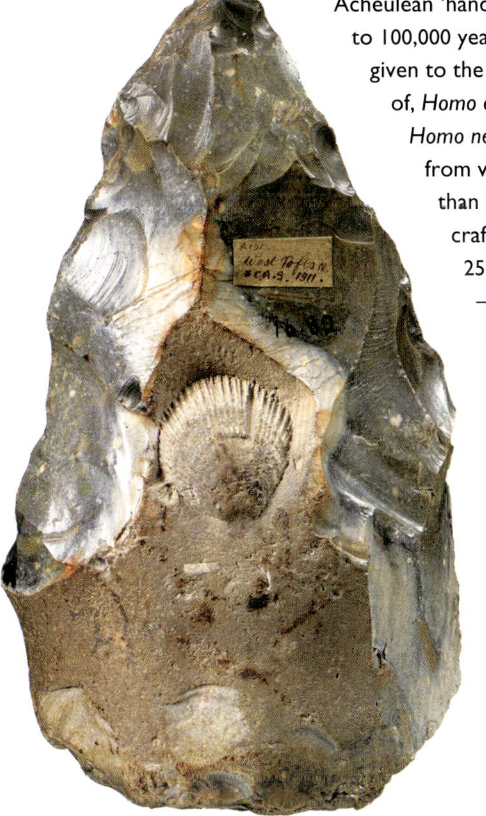

71. 250,000-year-old Acheulean 'hand axe' from West Tofts in Norfolk, England. The stone artifact was shaped in such a way that the naturally embedded shell remained central to the finished object.

72. Beautifully crafted
c. 300,000-year-old geometric
almond-shaped stone artifact
from St Acheul in France.

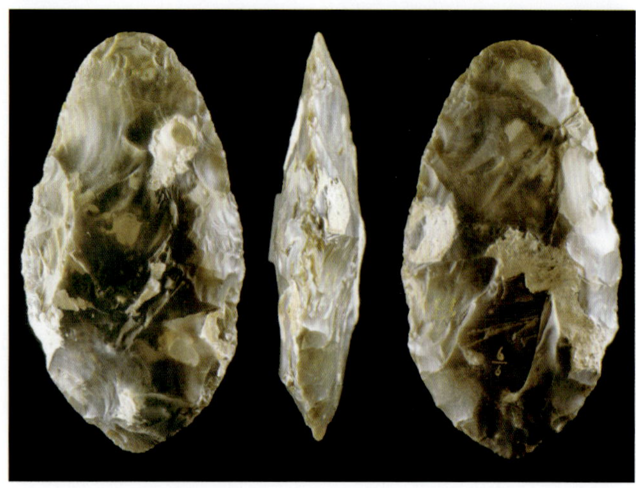

'hand axes' from Swanscombe in Kent. From St Acheul in France
we have *c.* 300,000–100,000-year-old almond-shaped stone
artifacts [72].[16] These and many other examples of beautifully
crafted stone tools all signal an exquisite sense of symmetry and
perhaps a targeting of the rock's rich colours. These artifacts are
more than functional cores or tools – they also embody a strong
sense of design and aesthetic appreciation.

Early beads?

The fashioning of stone artifacts into fine, symmetrical
shapes continues into the Mousterian period, the era of the
Neanderthals, and is even further developed in the material
culture of the earliest *Homo sapiens*. But there are no clear
signs in the archaeological record that either *Homo erectus*
or *Homo heidelbergensis* practised other forms of complex
symbolism. It was once widely thought by archaeologists that
Homo erectus/Homo heidelbergensis strung beads for personal
decoration, and some still claim that they collected naturally
shaped anthropomorphic objects – perhaps adornments or
talismans indicating at least recognition and perhaps extension
of the self to an outer expression. Jewelry and other body arts
beautify a person in a way that enhances their ability to position
themselves and be appreciated as a social being. As a form
of jewelry, beads are distinctively aesthetic expressions that
symbolize and communicate a sense of social order and beauty,
and are thus of special interest to the question of the origins

of art among humans (remembering that other animals also socially present and beautify themselves, for example through grooming, plumage and dances to attract mates; in some cases, for example bowerbirds and Japanese pufferfish, they carefully prepare their surroundings also).

In all cases, the evidence for the use of beads by *Homo erectus*/*Homo heidelbergensis* is controversial. Hundreds of *Porosphaera globularis* 'beads' have been reported from Acheulean sites in northern France and England [73]. *Porosphaera globularis* are spherical fossil sponges, typically 5–20 mm in diameter, and they date back to the time of the dinosaurs some 100 to 62 million years ago. Some of the fossils contain natural tunnels bored by the sipunculan (meaning 'small tube') worm species *Trypanites mobilis* to create a protective, mobile home from the hard, fossil sponges. Although *Trypanites mobilis* are not known to have made tunnels that penetrated entirely through the sponge, subsequent natural erosion can sometimes break through into the blind end of the tunnel, thereby creating a natural object that resembles an artificially perforated bead.

Rock art specialist Robert Bednarik, and then in a separate study archaeologists Solange Rigaud, Francesco d'Errico, Marian

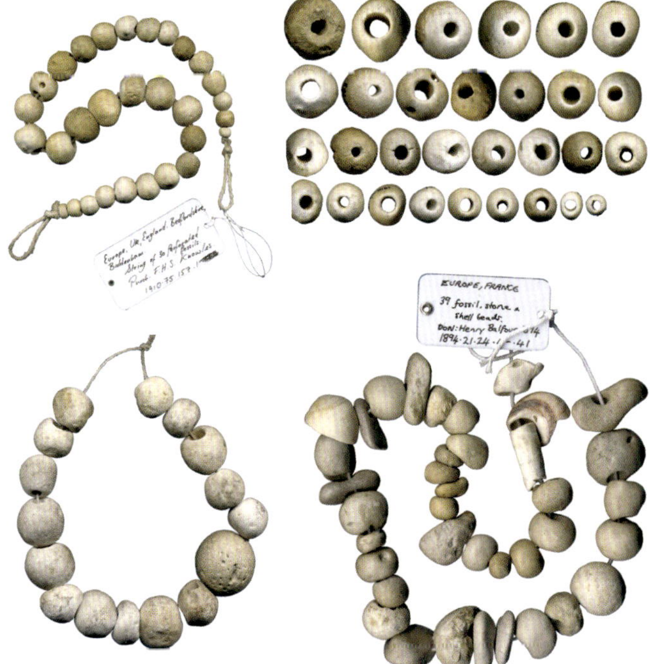

73. *Porosphaera globularis* 'beads' from Acheulean sites in northern France and England. These so-called 'beads' are naturally perforated fossil sponges that have been held (and strung) in museum collections for decades, in some cases for over 150 years. They were previously thought to be cultural beads, but now are thought by most researchers to be purely natural objects, and therefore cannot be taken as evidence of body art.

Vanhaeren and palaeontologist Christian Neumann, re-examined
349 *Porosphaera globularis* 'beads' from thirteen museum
archaeology collections that had first been reported between
1847 – by Boucher de Perthes, the first person to identify their
archaeological significance as 'grains de colliers' ('necklace beads')
– and 2005.[17] While both studies concurred that the 'beads', and
the perforations, were natural, Bednarik argued that damage to
the entrance of the perforations was due to human modification
and wear caused by the strings that connected them when worn.
Rigaud and her colleagues, however, leave the door open for a
very different explanation:

1. The beads were excavated from gravel deposits that
    contain an abundance of naturally occurring fossils
    (i.e. they were not brought to the site by people).
2. Having eroded from nearby fossil beds, the beads would
    have suffered knocks with surrounding sediments including
    pebbles and other particles (i.e. potentially suffering
    micro-flaking of edges in the process).
3. They were excavated during the nineteenth century under
    coarse handling conditions (i.e. some could have been
    damaged during excavation).
4. There are no records of exactly where they came from
    within a deposit (i.e. we do not know if they are really
    associated with the cultural, Acheulean horizons at the
    sites in question).
5. Excavations at those same sites undertaken in the last
    few years have failed to reveal any new examples of such
    'beads' specifically from the cultural layers (i.e. those that
    were collected in the nineteenth century probably came
    from non-cultural layers, and are thus natural inclusions).
6. The studied 'beads' have long been strung together for
    storage and display in museum collections (i.e. over a
    hundred years of handling may have caused perforations
    and perforated edges to be abraded from rubbing against
    the strings).

While the evidence is not conclusive, we therefore cannot
say with any sense of certainty that *Homo erectus/Homo
heidelbergensis* used *Porosphaera globularis* beads, and given
the lack of positive evidence for having been modified during
Acheulean times, it is more likely that they are natural inclusions
in ancient sediments.

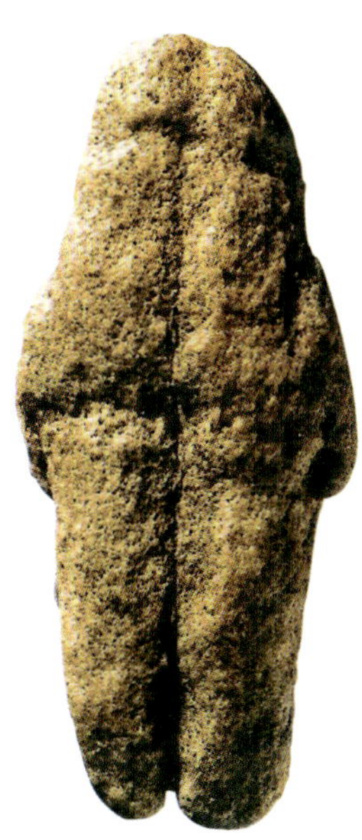

74. The Tan-Tan 'figurine' from Morocco.

Pre-modern human figurines?

The presence of enigmatic but naturally shaped objects in cultural deposits might prove significant nonetheless. While it may not be wise to run too far with the idea of cultural significance for naturally formed artifacts when the evidence for their cultural selection and retention is insecure, still we should keep an open mind, at least until more reliable evidence one way or the other comes to light (let us not forget the scepticism and downright rejection that once surrounded Altamira – see Chapter 2).

The Tan-Tan 'figurine' is a case in point [74]. This 6-cm-long (2.4 in.) piece of quartzite was found by German archaeologist Lutz Fiedler. It came from a depth of 15 m (50 ft) on the north bank of the Draa River in Morocco. While the deposit from which it was found has not been dated, the presence of nearby Acheulean 'hand axes' indicates that it probably dates to between 500,000 and 300,000 years ago. While all researchers agree that the general shape of the stone is natural, there is disagreement about the origins of some of its grooved lines. Robert Bednarik argues that five grooves were enhanced by impact marks caused by human flaking,[18] whereas University of Illinois archaeologist Stanley Ambrose disagrees, suggesting that the 'figurine' may have been entirely formed by 'fortuitous natural weathering'.[19] There are no clearly agreed signs that the Tan-Tan 'figurine' was entirely fashioned by hand: it appears to be a rock that naturally weathered into a human shape, and debate continues as to whether or not that natural shape was further enhanced by human hand. Additionally, a small number of microscopic red particles occur in tiny surface pits in the rock; Bednarik has argued that these are remnant traces of pigment that had once been applied to the object, but others are not so sure, wondering if it is merely soil from the local burial environment. If the Tan-Tan rock held significance to its *Homo erectus* or *Homo heidelbergensis* contemporaries – irrespective of whether or not they modified it to enhance its shape and colour – it would be the oldest culturally meaningful human-shaped object in the world.

We are faced with a similar situation with the 300,000–200,000-year-old Berekhat Ram 'figurine' from the Golan Heights in Israel [75]. This human-shaped rock was excavated in 1981 by archaeologist Naama Goren-Inbar, and it came from an archaeological horizon containing more than 6,800 worked stone artifacts. The Berekhat Ram 'figurine' is made from volcanic tuff, the only such volcanic 'artifact' found in the excavation, although

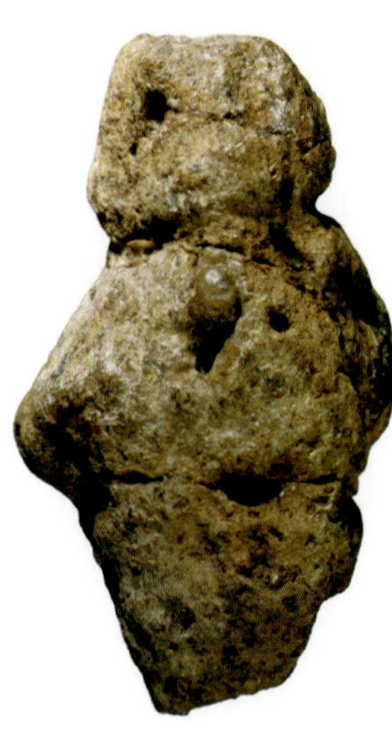

75. The Berekhat Ram 'figurine' from the Golan Heights, Israel. It is very small, about the length of a human finger bone.

76. The Makapansgat cobble from South Africa.

natural volcanic gravels and pebbles were found aplenty.[20] The object is small, only 3.5 cm (1.4 in.) long, with heavily weathered, pock-marked surfaces shaped by deep grooves for the 'neck' and 'arms' and with a pronounced 'chest'. After several hundred thousand years buried deep in sediments on the edge of an extinct volcanic crater, now a lake, subsurface humidity and contact with surrounding sediments have worn the pebble's surfaces, without removing its principal distinguishing features or overall anthropomorphic three-dimensional shape.

The Berekhat Ram 'figurine' was carefully examined microscopically by Alexander Marshack in 1997, to determine whether the remnant surfaces and grooves were made by rubbing or cutting with tools, or whether the object is an entirely natural pebble that by chance is reminiscent of a human shape.[21] Francesco d'Errico and April Nowell re-examined the 'figurine' three years later, applying new techniques of microscopic analysis and comparing the pebble's surface texture and groove characteristics with experimental cut marks and natural surface features on other volcanic pebbles from the site.[22] Both sets of researchers concluded emphatically that the grooves were artificial, having been made by hand with tools: the pebble was purposefully modified to give it a human shape. But the question as to who made it is unresolved, for it dates to a time when *Homo sapiens* was just beginning to evolve in Africa.

There is also the curious case of the Makapansgat cobble [76]. This is a much older object, close to three million years old, and it is associated with Australopithecines that precede the genus *Homo* on the evolutionary tree. It was found in 1925 by Wilfred Eitzman, a local school teacher, at the cave site of Makapansgat in the Makapan Valley in South Africa [77]. The cobble was soon shown to anatomist-come-palaeoanthropologist Raymond Dart, but it was three decades later that he first wrote about it, and not until 1974 that he pointed out that two 'faces' could be seen, and others further imagined from minor protrusions and the shadows they create, depending on the angle of view.[23] In 1997, Bednarik examined the cobble microscopically, conclusively showing that it was naturally formed.[24]

The cobble is 8.3 cm (3.3 in.) long and made of jasperite, a hard, red rock the closest source of which is 4.8 km (3 miles) to the north-northeast of the cave.

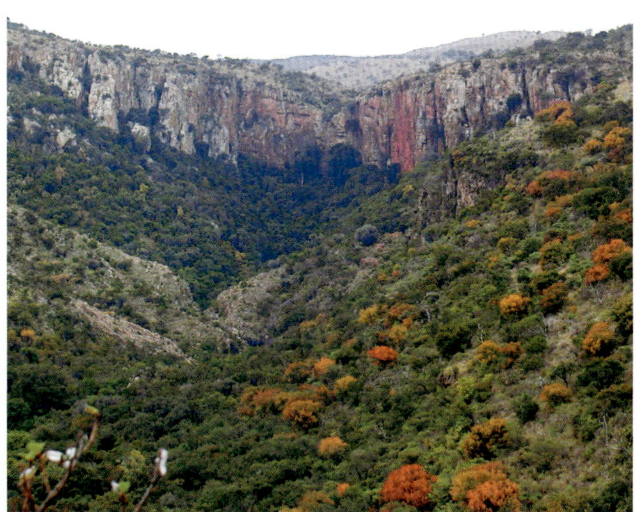

77. The Makapan Valley, South Africa, where the Makapansgat cobble was found.

Bednarik points out that the cave from which it came does not contain sediments transported by water, as would be necessary for natural sediments with jasperite cobbles to reach the cave, and the cobble is too large to be a bird gastrolith (many birds and reptiles ingest pebbles to help digest food in their guts, carrying those pebbles with them from place to place until they are regurgitated or the animal dies). It seems like it could have only been carried into the cave by hominids, but there is no proof of this.

The Makapansgat cobble is thus wholly natural, without any signs of manual modification, yet its curious resemblance to a face keeps it re-appearing in specialist and popular discussions on the origins of art. This is one case that we can do little with other than to keep it in mind, for we do not even know the exact spot from which it came in the cave, nor do we know if hominids actually lived in the cave or whether their fragmentary skeletal remains were brought there by scavengers. Nor can we be sure which species of hominid the Makapansgat cobble may have been associated with. All we know is that it appears to have come from a layer that also contains Australopithecine bones, that it is in the vicinity of three million years old, and that it is entirely natural but looks like a hominid face. Again, while we cannot make too much of this given the uncertainties, we also cannot dismiss the possibility that the pebble was picked up and retained by an early hominid, either an archaic ancestor along the direct evolutionary line of modern humans, or an ancient cousin from a deviating lineage. The implication of the Makapansgat cobble having been brought to the cave by hominids would seem to be, at the very least, a sense of self-recognition and value, but the 'ifs' are loud and clear.

The Trinil shell

More convincing than the examples above is the making of a geometric pattern on the back of a *Pseudodon vondembuschianus trinilensis* shell valve at Trinil on the island of Java, Indonesia, as far back as *c.* 500,000 years ago [78].[25] Given the antiquity of the shell, it must have been made by *Homo erectus*. In 2015, Josephine Joordens, Francesco d'Errico and a team of scientists restudied

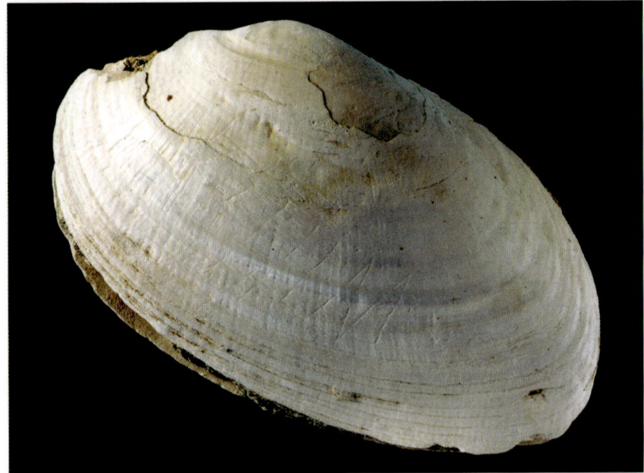

78. The *c.* 500,000-year-old engraved shell valve from Trinil on the island of Java, Indonesia, with a close-up view of the linear incisions.

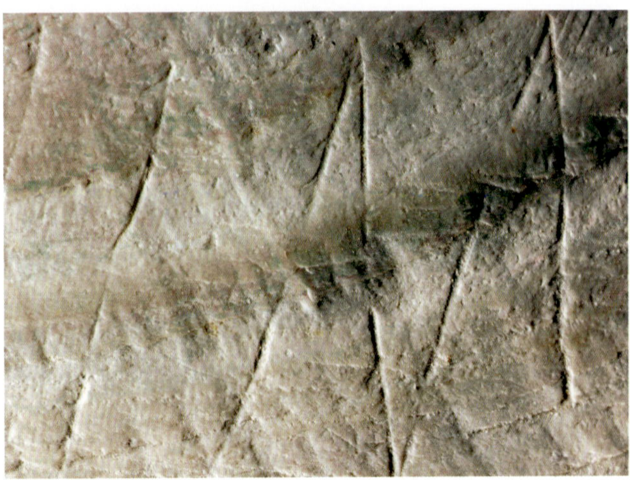

shells that had been excavated by Eugène Dubois in 1891.
The collection had been stored away in what is now called the
Naturalis Biodiversity Center in Leiden, in the Netherlands, for
more than 120 years. Dubois was a Dutch palaeoanthropologist
who had travelled to Indonesia in 1887, convinced that the secret
to human origins was held in the tropics. He thus enlisted in the
army so that he could be posted to Indonesia and, once there,
began excavations in Java where four years later he found the
first skeletal remains of 'Java Man', *Homo erectus*.

The engraved shell from Trinil features zigzagging lines made
with good manual dexterity, suggesting an ability to execute fine
linear geometric designs. Exactly how far we can go with this
remains uncertain, however, as the shell is the only example of
its kind dating this far back in time. At the very least, it signals
that *Homo erectus* created rudimentary geometric lineworks.
Further evidence from this period is required to determine the
degree to which such imagery indicates social symbolism towards
information exchange between individuals and groups.

Early use of earth pigments

Earth pigments (often popularly called 'ochre', although that term
technically refers only to earth pigments containing hydrated iron
oxide) are often found in archaeological sites, and are particularly
useful in determining whether or not people painted in the past,
because ochre crayons survive well even in ancient archaeological
sites. Ochres occur in a broad variety of colours ranging from
yellow to orange, red, purple and brown. White also occurs as
a natural earth pigment, as does black (which can also be made
from charcoal). The presence of ochre in the ground does not
necessarily imply the making of rock paintings: ochre could have
been used in body painting, for example, or as part of burial
practices (human bones and burial pits are often covered by red
ochre), or to decorate objects such as spears or bags. Red ochre
is also known to have been consumed in small quantities, and
used as an antiseptic and as an ingredient in the tanning of animal
hides. But normally we can reasonably assume that the finding
of ochre in an archaeological deposit signals that something was
decorated with colour.

There is evidence for the extraction and use of earth pigments
around 300,000 to 200,000 years ago in Africa, presumably by
Homo heidelbergensis or an early form of *Homo sapiens*. At the
Twin Rivers site in Zambia, for instance, archaeologists found

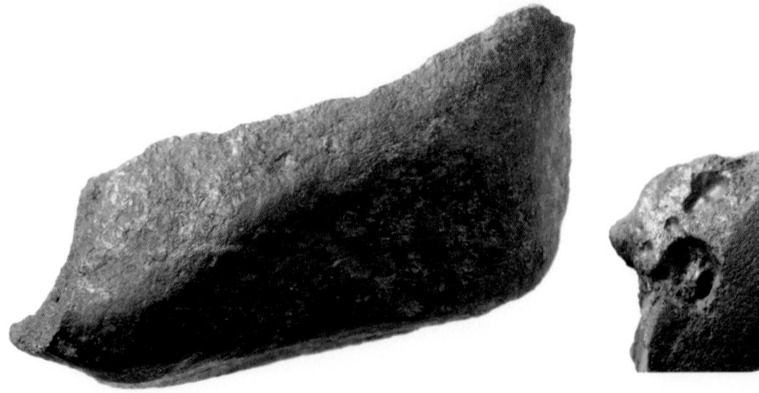
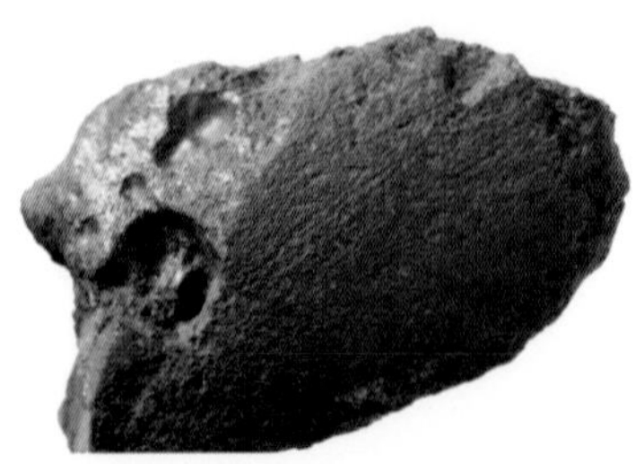

79. 300,000- to 200,000-year-old abraded ochre fragments from the Twin Rivers site, Zambia.

302 pieces of limonite (yellowish green), haematite (earthy red), ferruginous sandstone (reddish), manganese dioxide (black) and specularite (dark, sparkling purplish red), the latter imported from outcrops located 5 km (3 miles) to the north and west of the site. Ten of the pieces of specularite and one of the haematite have fine striations or facetted surfaces indicating abrasion, proof that the pieces of pigment were rubbed or ground to make colourants [79]. Additionally, an imported quartzite cobble – quartzite does not occur naturally at the site – is pockmarked from contact against another hard object such as a rock or piece of ochre, and has yellow ochre all around it. That yellow pigment is different to the soil from which it came, and suggests that the cobble was used to grind or pound pieces of mineral pigment. Archaeologist Lawrence Barham from the University of Liverpool estimates that more than 60 kg (130 lb) of pigment was brought to the cave between 300,000 and 200,000 years ago.[26]

Did Neanderthals make art?

In the Near East and Europe, the rise of the Neanderthals beginning some 400,000 years ago brought with it a new material culture that archaeologists call the Mousterian. During its early stages, the kinds of 'hand axes' that already existed from the Acheulean continued to be made, along with a range of stone tools involving a new kind of technology: the preparation of a stone core so that a large, central flake could then be removed and from which new tool types such as knives and projectile points could be shaped [80]. We call this way of shaping stone tools the Levallois technique, after the site of Levallois-Perret in Paris where it was first identified.

Making a stone tool using this multi-stage technique requires preparation and forethought, a sense of what the intermediary stages to the finished product will look like. Unlike the preceding Acheulean technologies, where stone artifacts were flaked off a core, with that core often taking shape in the process, the Mousterian Levallois technology practised by Neanderthals involved preparing the core in order to remove a large flat to convex flake that would itself then serve as a preform, replete with the scars from earlier episodes of flaking, making sharp edges, that could then be further shaped towards a final tool. Neanderthal tool-making involved a more complex mental process than shown by earlier species.

Complex, multi-stage tool-making implies complex cognitive functions including the ability to anticipate morphologies in the making, many of these geometrically shaped. It also implies a sense of perfection and aesthetic appreciation, for many of the resulting artifacts attained geometric morphologies beyond those required for efficiency of tool use. Simply put, some of the Mousterian stone tools, such as triangular or cordate 'hand axes', have aesthetic properties that imply an incipient artistic appreciation, much as the earlier Acheulean 'hand axes' had done but now produced with more complex technological forethought. What, then, is the evidence for Neanderthal art other than that evident in beautifully shaped functional tools?

80. Using the Levallois technique, a large stone flake (right) could be removed from a prepared core (left). The artifacts shown here were found at the turn of the nineteenth century at Baker's Hole in Kent, England.

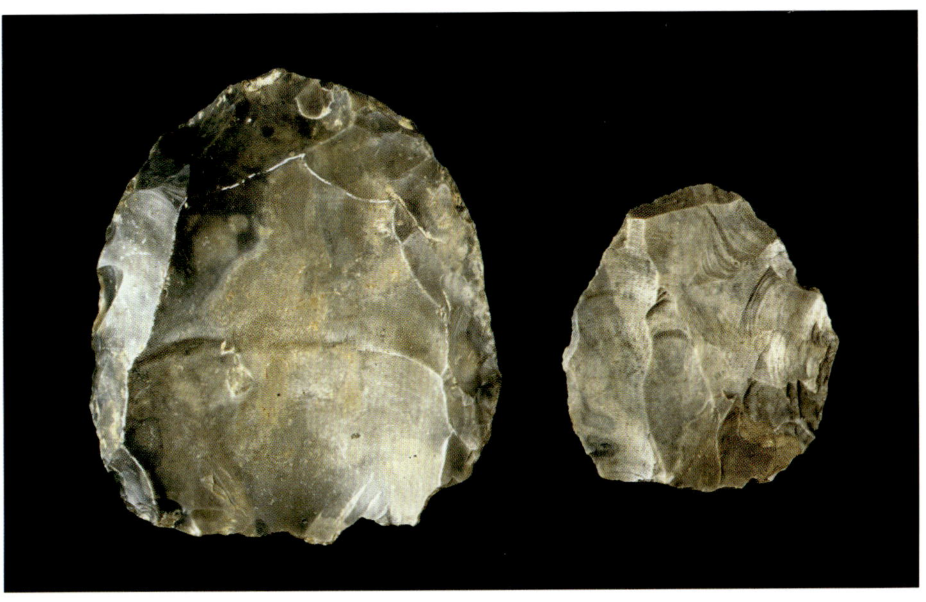

The material culture of early Neanderthals is essentially a continuation of that of their predecessors. In time, however, they developed a number of cultural practices that saw them bury their dead, obtain and use earth pigments ('ochres') from distant quarries, and obtain and carry marine shells inland for reasons other than food. Some archaeologists argue that once Neanderthals came in contact with modern humans, initially in the Levant region of western Asia and then across Europe, they also began to fashion artworks from bone and stone (see below and Chapter 6 for further discussion of this). We thus find Neanderthal burials dating back to 80,000–70,000 years ago at the site of Shanidar Cave in northern Iraq [81]. Here the skeleton of a 30–45-year-old man appears to have been buried with care and ceremony. The pollen of bachelor's button, hollyhock, St Barnaby's thistle, yarrow and other kinds of flowers with medicinal properties have been found in the soil surrounding the skeleton, suggesting compassion and ritual commemoration of the dead as flowers were deposited with the body during burial (the Shanidar Cave skeletal remains inspired some of the lead characters in Jean Auel's best-selling novel *Clan of the Cave Bear*).

However, a number of archaeologists, such as Robert Gargett, then of the University of California, Berkeley, and Paul Pettitt from Durham University have questioned this

81. Shanidar Cave, Iraq.

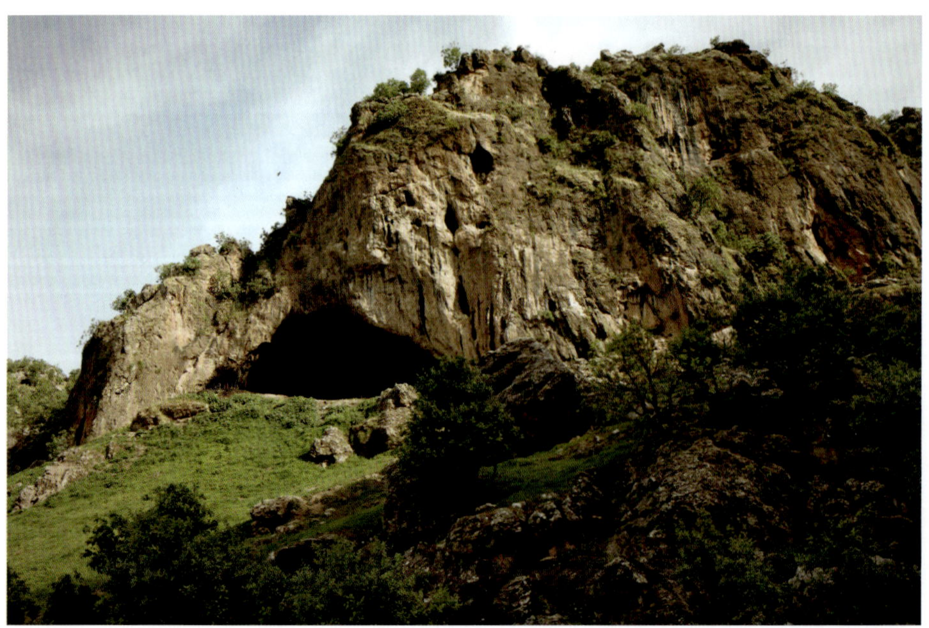

interpretation, pointing out that local villagers brought flowers
into the cave during the archaeological excavations in the
late 1950s and early 1960s, so that twentieth-century pollen
effectively contaminated the 80,000–70,000-year-old Neanderthal
burial.[27] The Persian jird (*Meriones persicus*), a burrowing rodent
that hoards seeds and flowers underground, is also known
to have tunnelled into this site, potentially contaminating the
sediments surrounding the Neanderthal burial.[28] The latest
suggestion involves bees bringing the pollen to the site![29]
To this day specialists still debate whether or not the Shanidar
Cave Neanderthal was buried with offerings of flowers.[30]

There are about twenty other examples of Neanderthal
burials in the Levant and Europe. At La Chapelle-aux-Saints
in France, a less than 60,000-year-old Neanderthal skeleton
was carefully buried in a shallow but well-defined grave.[31]
Also in France, the site of La Ferrassie has revealed numerous
Neanderthal skeletons. One of these, of a young child, was found
in a shallow grave known as 'burial 6'. The grave pit was covered
during late Mousterian times by a large limestone slab containing
eighteen hollows ('cupules'), apparently made by pounding with
stone tools. Both the burial and the cupules seem to have been
made sometime between 70,000 and 40,000 years ago, and the
cupules are the oldest dated artificial marks on a broad rock
surface in Europe.[32]

A major indication for the appreciation and creation of
decoration through colouration among Neanderthals is the
archaeological evidence for red and black pigments in Mousterian
deposits. There are occasional claims for red ochre use by earlier
species, such as the microscopic traces of red powder on the
Tan-Tan 'figurine' dated between 500,000 and 300,000 years ago,
but these are controversial, with some researchers arguing that
they may be natural earth staining from surrounding sediments.
The major exceptions are the 300,000–200,000-year-old use-worn
colourants from Twin Cave in Zambia, discussed above (there are
also ochre pieces with rub marks and unpatterned incisions dating
to more than 180,000 years ago from Wonderwerk Cave in South
Africa).[33] In the Levant and Europe, it is during late Mousterian
times that red ochre begins to be commonly found, sometimes
in the form of nodules of haematite and other kinds of earth
colourants, sometimes as powder within the soil – indicating that
ochre was sprinkled to render surfaces red – and sometimes as
red coatings on artifacts. There are thus some seventy late Lower
to Middle Palaeolithic horizons – excavated layers dating to

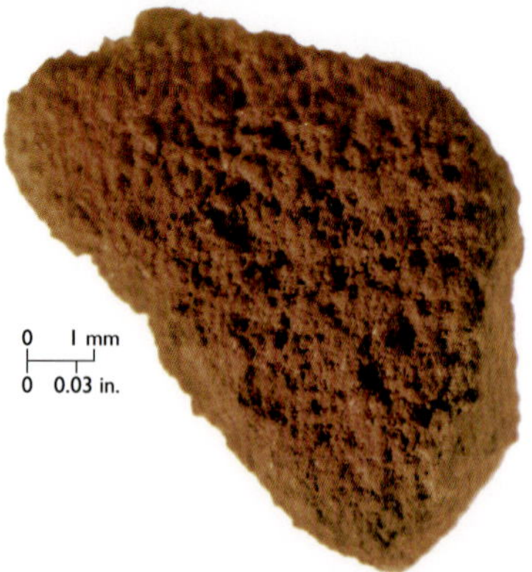

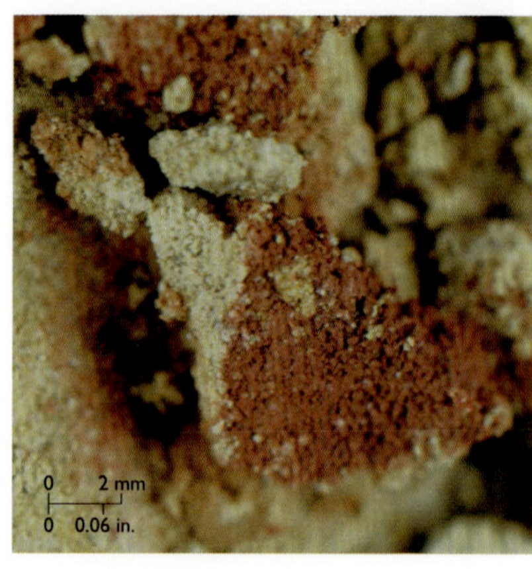

82. Concentrates of red haematite excavated from a *c.* 250,000-year-old level at Maastricht-Belvédère site C.

between 300,000 and 40,000 years ago – with earth pigments or tools evidencing the grinding of such pigments.

Almost all the archaeological evidence for the use of ochre by Neanderthals dates to between 60,000 and 40,000 years ago, but there are some earlier examples. The earliest comes from Maastricht-Belvédère in the Netherlands, where eighteen small 'concentrates' of red haematite ochre and numerous Mousterian artifacts were excavated from *c.* 250,000-year-old riverine deposits [82].[34] The small patches of ochre are not hard nodules with marks of grinding, but concentrates of haematite that were originally dissolved in water; they have been interpreted as preserved drops of red ochre paint that spilled onto the ground and subsequently dried. There are no other patches of red ochre anywhere else in the vicinity, and the closest source of ochre is 40 km (25 miles) away in the Ardennes and Eifel regions. At Maastricht-Belvédère the ochre is only found in two areas, termed 'site C' and 'site F', where there are concentrations of Mousterian stone artifacts manufactured from Levallois technology. Also found at site C were 162 flint flakes that could all be refitted into a large nodule of stone [83], evidence that Neanderthals used it as a camp and that to this day the site has remained largely intact. Concentrations of charcoal also indicate the presence of at least one fireplace, and possibly more, and the ochre concentrates all occur either near the fireplace or near the concentration of flint flakes where a Neanderthal once sat to make stone tools.

The vast majority of earth pigments, mainly manganese dioxide and red and yellow ochres, are found towards the end of the era of the Neanderthals. At Jaskinia Raj ('Paradise Cave'), a Neanderthal cave site in Poland, quartzite and granite

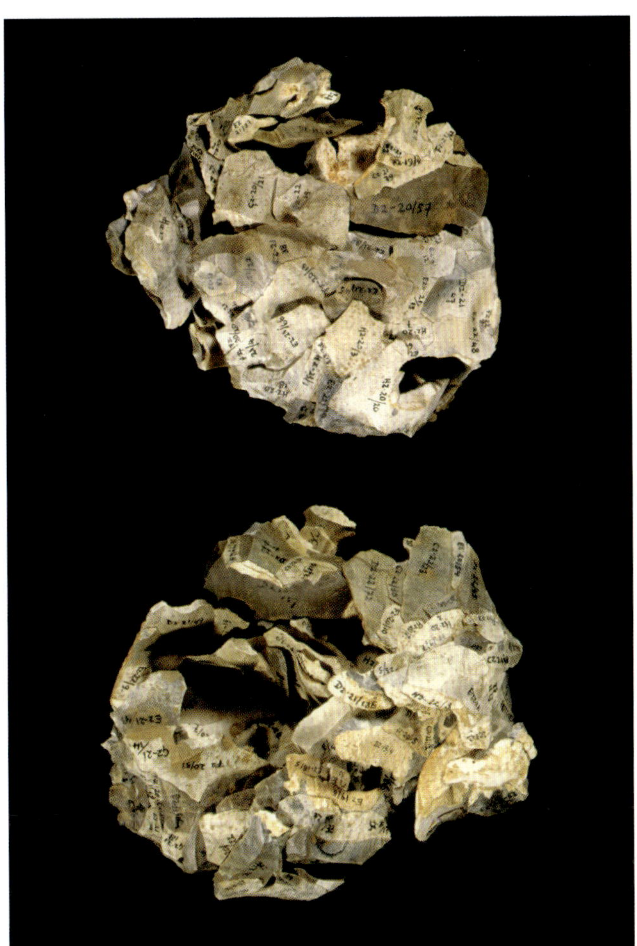

83. Reassembled set of 162 conjoining Mousterian flint artifacts from Maastricht-Belvédère site C.

cobbles with surface coverings of red ochre have been found in 60,000–50,000-year-old deposits. At Pech de l'Azé I in France, over 500 fragments of manganese dioxide and red and yellow ochre have been excavated from Mousterian levels dating to around 43,000 years ago, more than 250 of the black manganese dioxide pieces exhibiting striations from grinding. Some 80 m (260 ft) away at the site of Pech de l'Azé IV, twenty-six pieces of a similar age were found, fifteen with evidence of use wear in the form of striations. At both sites the characteristics of the striated surfaces indicate that the crayons were ground down with fine-grained sandstone tools to make black powder. While none of the red or yellow ochre fragments have signs of grinding, the black crayons suggest that Neanderthals made black pigment here.[35]

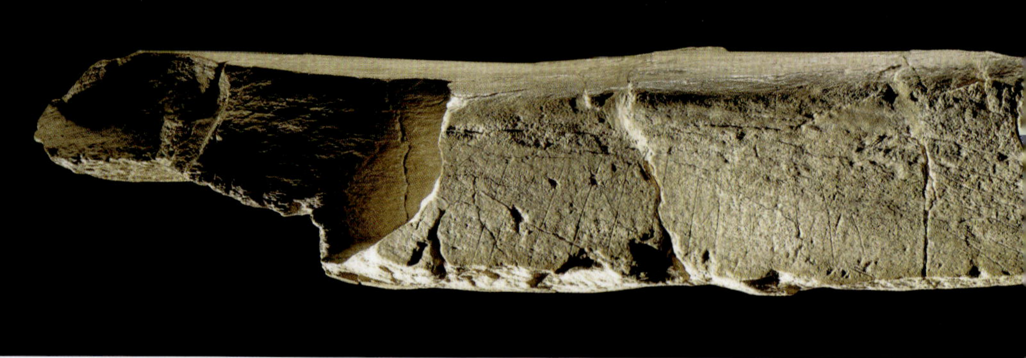

A number of bones and stones with faint scratches and more
or less vaguely patterned cut marks on their surfaces are known,
including from the *c.* 350,000-year-old Bilzingsleben site in Germany
[84], the 50,000–40,000-year-old cultural horizons at Bacho Kiro
Cave and Temnata Cave in Bulgaria, and the *c.* 100,000-year-old
site at Tata near the Danube River in Hungary. It is unclear,
however, whether the cut marks on bones were the by-products
of defleshing, whether the pebbles were simply water-worn,
or whether both were early attempts at marking objects with
basic lineworks, representing symbolic behaviour.[36] We cannot,
therefore, take these artifacts as clear-cut traces of symbolic
behaviour evidencing advanced cognition among Neanderthals.
Similarly, what were once thought to be Neanderthal perforated
beads from Bois Roche and Pech de l'Azé II in France and Kulna
Cave in the Czech Republic, and remnants of a 'flute' replete
with perforated finger holes from Divje Babe in Slovenia, have
now been shown to be puncture marks made by the teeth of
carnivores, in many instances cave bears or hyenas. As Marie
Soressi and Francesco d'Errico stress, we do not have any evidence
whatsoever that Neanderthals wore any of these naturally
perforated bead-like objects; all we can say is that they are natural
objects that have accumulated in animal dens or lairs.[37]

As was the case with *Homo erectus/Homo heidelbergensis*, there
continues to be no reliable evidence for the manufacture or use
of perforated beads by Neanderthals: the notion of drilling holes
to string decorative objects, and perhaps the ability to do so,
remains entirely unknown from the Mousterian (until the time
when early *Homo sapiens* was also present). There are, however,
both naturally perforated and unperforated marine shells dating
back to the period of the last surviving Neanderthals, such as the

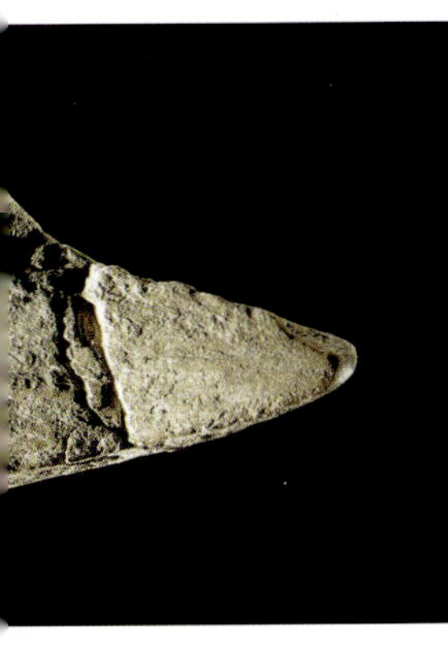

c. 43,500–37,400-year-old perforated *Pecten maximus* shell from Cueva Antón in southeastern Spain (which contains traces of orange pigment, a mixture of red haematite and yellow goethite) and the probably naturally perforated *Acanthocardia tuberculata* and *Glycymeris insubrica* shell valves from the *c.* 50,000-year-old cultural horizon at the cave site of Cueva de los Aviones, also in southeastern Spain [85]. Here one of the *Glycymeris insubrica* valves contains faint traces of red haematite pigment. Also from this latter site come three *Spondylus gaederopus* shells, each exhibiting traces of a mixture of earth pigments such as red lepidocrocite, dolomite, haematite, pyrite and charcoal, suggesting that the shell may have been a paint palette or container for carrying pigments. These controversial findings suggest that Neanderthals of this period had not only brought back marine shells from coastal environments somewhere between 1.5 to 7 km (1 to 4 miles) away to inland settings before modern humans were around in Europe, but also that they may have used pigments and known how to use and probably mix raw materials to make paints of varying colours.

85. *Acanthocardia tuberculata* and *Glycymeris insubrica* shell valves from Cueva de los Aviones, Spain.

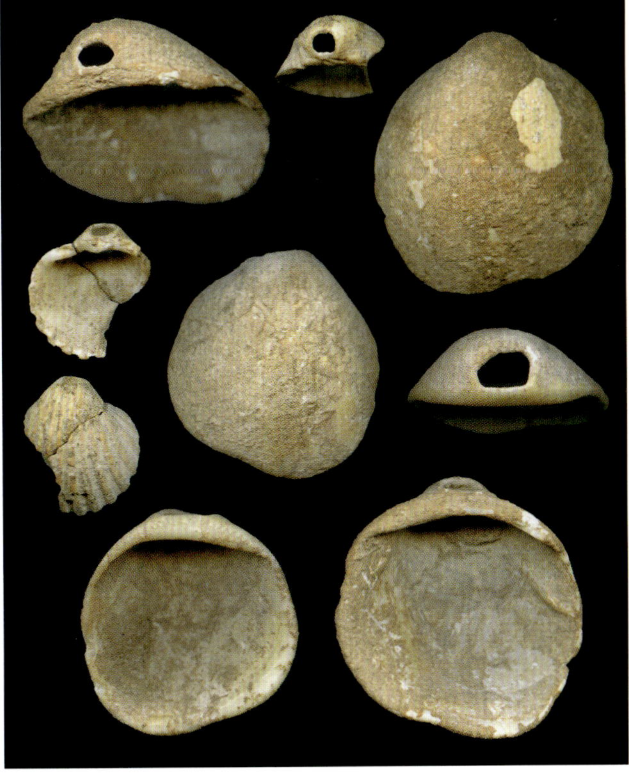

Arranged stalagmites and eagle wings: shedding new light on the Neanderthal mind

86. 176,000-year-old Neanderthal stalagmitic structures deep in the cave of Bruniquel, France. The vertical stalagmites post-date the Neanderthal construction.

87. Three-dimensional model of the stalagmitic structures made by Neanderthals at Bruniquel (the model excludes speleothems that have naturally grown over them in more recent times).

One of the more remarkable cave discoveries of recent years concerns the stalagmites that grow naturally on the floors of caves. It is not their growth that is of interest here, but rather why they stopped growing, and what happened to them afterwards. Deep in the cave of Bruniquel, in southwestern France, archaeologist François Rouzaud had been investigating enigmatic circular arrangements [86, 87] and accumulated piles of artificially broken stalagmites some 336 m (1,100 ft) into the cave.[38] Among

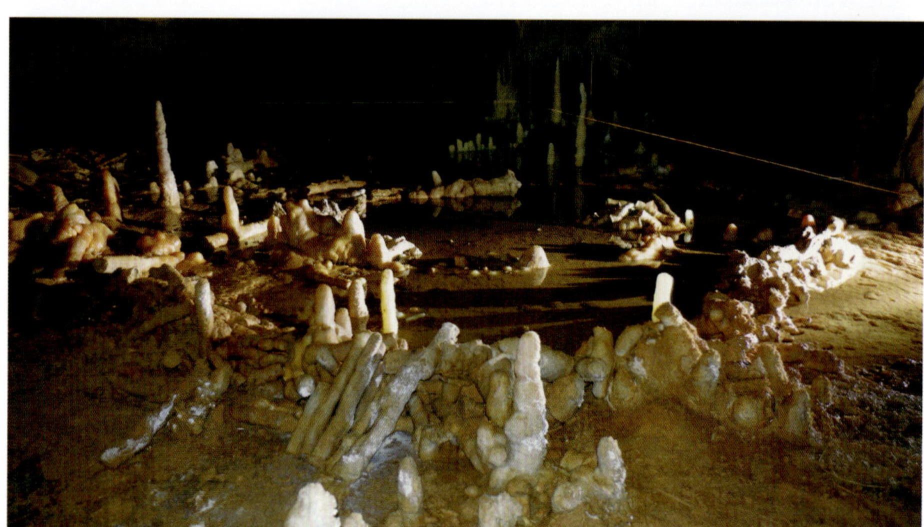

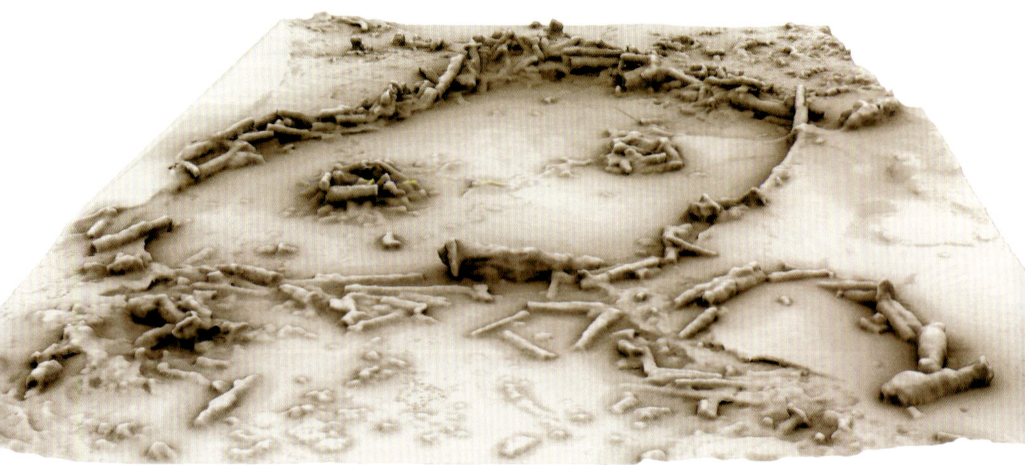

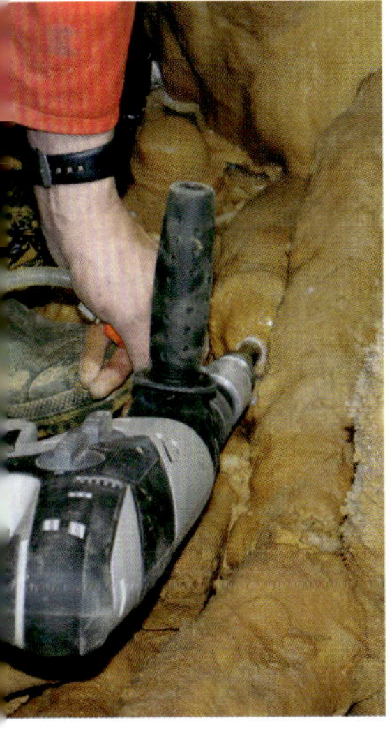

88. Burnt broken stalagmites indicating the main fireplace in the large circular structure at Bruniquel. The two white stalagmites in the centre-left of the photograph began growing on top of the structure many thousands of years after it was built.

89. Extracting a calcite core for U-series dating from the tip of a horizontal stalagmite in the main Neanderthal structure at Bruniquel.

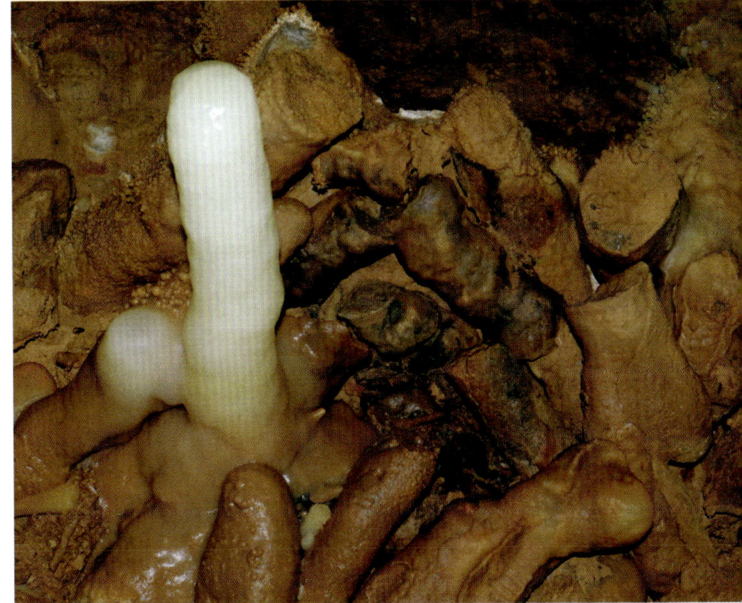

these structures 57 reddened and 66 blackened areas were in due course detected on the floor and among the stalagmites, signs of ancient fires that had been built within, or on, each of the six structures [88]. The structures, the largest of which is 6.7 m long by 4.5 m wide (22 by 15 ft), and contains between one and four layers of superimposed horizontal stalagmites, had been built so far into the cave that here the tunnel was pitch black, too far from the sunlit entrance to receive any light.

At first it was assumed that those structures deep in the belly of the cave had been built by modern humans during Upper Palaeolithic times, but a carbon date on a piece of burnt bone gave a minimum age of 47,600 years (the bone was so old that there was not enough ^{14}C left in it to give an actual date, only that it must be older than this). How could this be, if modern humans had arrived in Western Europe no earlier than 45,000 to 43,000 years ago?

Sadly Rouzaud passed away in 1999. After his death, work largely ceased at Bruniquel, the cave remaining closed and the research dormant. Then, in 2013, after twenty years of mounting curiosity, Jacques Jaubert of the Université de Bordeaux 1, along with a team of researchers, re-opened the study of the cave. By then both mapping and dating techniques had improved, allowing Jaubert's team to undertake three-dimensional laser mapping of the cave structures, magnetic surveys of the floors (to determine where fires had been lit), and to date their formation using the U-series method [89]. One group of dates came from the extreme ends of the stalagmites, those parts that were last to grow before they broke; these would give a *maximum* age for the structures, for they could only have been built after the stalagmites had stopped growing (irrespective of whether their growth had ceased when they were snapped or beforehand). Another group of dates derived from the calcite flowstone that had built up on the floor, including over the structures after they had been built; these would give a *minimum* age for the structures, because they must have already been built before the flowstone grew on the floor over them.

The results, announced in 2016 in the world's leading scientific journal, *Nature*, were unlike anything previously seen: they indicate that the stalagmitic structures were built around 176,000 years ago, and that as a result of humid conditions, calcite flowstone had started to slowly form over the structures very soon afterwards. What these dates show is that it could

90. Archaeological excavations in progress at Grotta di Fumane, Italy.

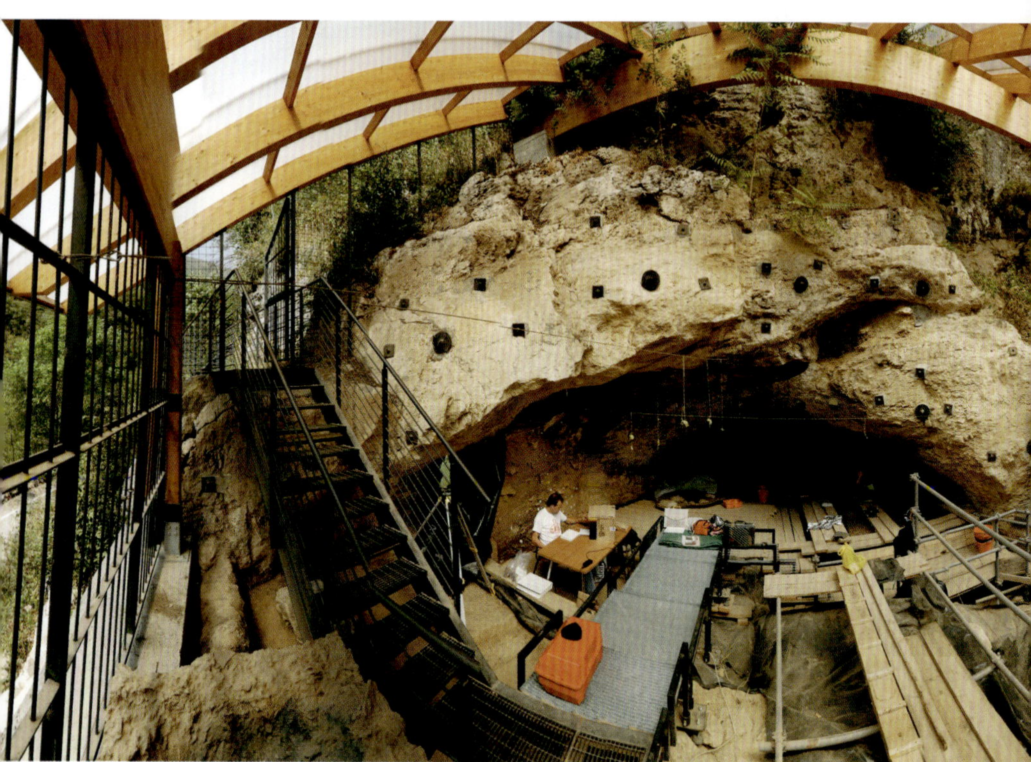

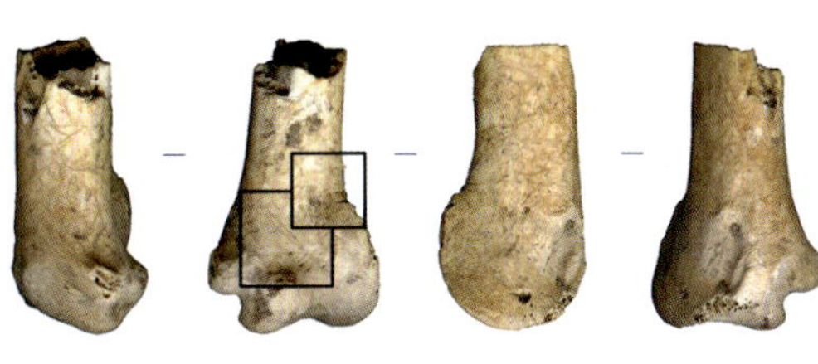

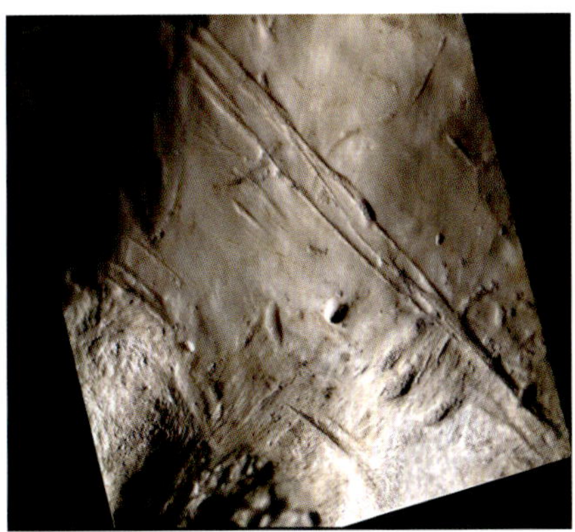

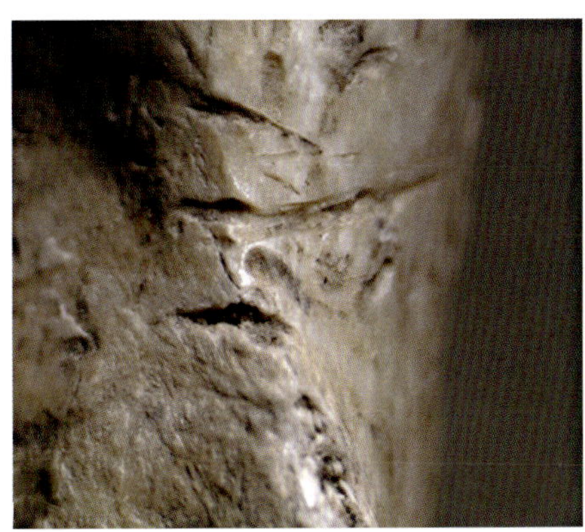

91. Example of *c.* 44,000-year-old cut marks on the wingbone of a bearded vulture (*Gypaetus barbatus*) from Grotta di Fumane, Italy.

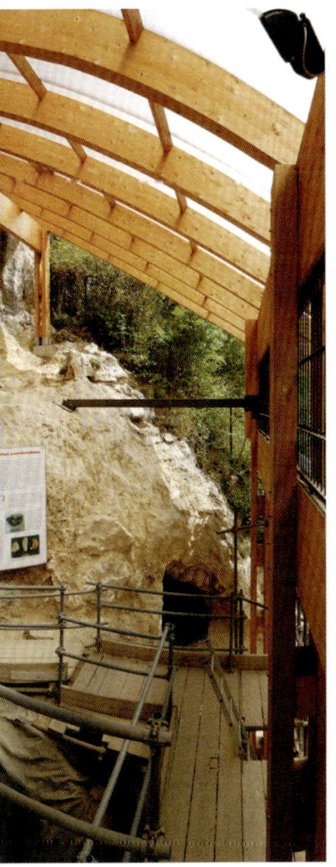

not have been modern humans who had built the structures, but only Neanderthals, for no other hominin species lived in Europe at that time. Here at Bruniquel, for the first time we find unequivocal evidence for the building of complex structures – evidence of complex spatial organization – along with the mastery of fire and the occupation of deep cave passages by Neanderthals. Even if no evidence of Neanderthal artworks has yet been found, they were able to bring light deep into caves, and undertake elaborate social activities requiring the careful preparation and orchestration of space.

Another curious recent discovery is the finding of bird wingbones and talons with cut and scrape marks at a number of Neanderthal sites, such as Grotta di Fumane in Italy [90] and Krapina in Croatia. The presence of cut marks on animal bones is not unusual, as this would normally merely signal the butchering of animal parts for consumption and possibly the sharing of cuts of meat. But here the animals are birds of prey not known to have been eaten by hominins: bearded vulture, Eurasian black vulture, golden eagle and red-footed falcon, among other species [91]. At Grotta di Fumane, it is only the wingbones that have traces of cutting, indicating that during late Neanderthal times, sometime between 44,800 and 42,200 years ago, wings or feathers were removed for purposes not relating

113

to food procurement but rather for decorative or symbolic purposes.[39] This is an enigmatic period in Europe, for it overlaps with the timing of the first arrival of *Homo sapiens*, and so while the Grotta di Fumane cut bones are stratigraphically associated with Neanderthal levels, including stone tools made by Levallois technology, there is no guarantee that modern humans were not also present at this time.

However, the Krapina cut-marked white-tailed eagle talons are much older. There are eight such cut claw bones, all excavated from a single layer dating to *c.* 130,000 years ago, a time well before the arrival of modern humans (there is broad agreement as to their antiquity, despite the fact that they were excavated more than 100 years ago when excavation methods were much coarser than they are today). All the talons have cut marks in the same region at the base of the claw. They have been interpreted as evidence of the making of jewelry by Neanderthals.[40]

It is during the period of overlap between the earliest *Homo sapiens* in Europe and the last Neanderthals that we find the greatest range and density of artistic productions relating to Neanderthals. What are we to make, then, of the fact that Neanderthal sites begin to exhibit material evidence of complex art objects in many ways akin to early Upper Palaeolithic ones made by modern humans (see Chapter 6)? Is this an indication that late in their evolution, perhaps beginning around 60,000 years ago and ending with their final demise in most places around 40,000 years ago, Neanderthals in Europe evolved cognitive abilities akin to those already evolved by *Homo sapiens* in Africa and the Levant? Or is this evidence that late Neanderthals copied the arts of *Homo sapiens* once they arrived in Europe, around 45,000 to 43,000 years ago (with the exact dating of that initial arrival still unsure given the uncertainties associated with carbon dating and also considering that the earliest sites are unlikely to have yet been found or studied)? Or, rather, does it signal that what we think of as Neanderthal artifacts of that age were really not made by Neanderthals at all, but rather by modern humans who used the same sites during this general period?

Neanderthals and *Homo sapiens* coexisted in the Levant at eastern Europe's doorstep only between 100,000 and 40,000 years ago, but *Homo sapiens* first entered Europe from Africa by at least 45,000 to 43,000 years ago, as indicated by the earliest *Homo sapiens* skeletal remains from Grotta del Cavallo in Italy, Peștera cu Oase in Romania and Kent's Cavern in England. This means that, as far as the current archaeological evidence is concerned, the two species lived together in Europe only between *c.* 45,000 and 40,000 years ago, perhaps for slightly longer in Spain and Portugal where the most recent Neanderthals still need to be reliably dated. Is it possible that modern humans had arrived in Europe a bit earlier, but that we have not yet found their skeletal remains and therefore are not in a position to identify material culture items of that age as belonging to that species, attributing them to Neanderthals instead? For researchers such as palaeoanthropologist Erik Trinkaus of Washington University in St Louis and archaeologist João Zilhão of the University of Barcelona, the question needs to be conceived differently, as Neanderthals did not quite go extinct, but rather in western Asia and Europe were to some degree absorbed into early *Homo sapiens* populations (as evidenced by the presence of Neanderthal DNA among many present-day humans), so that during the key period of cohabitation, the cultural, artistic abilities of one also merged with those of the other.

An intriguing answer is broadly, but not unanimously, entertained in Western Europe: the Châtelperronian. This is said to be a phase of cultural and, with that, cognitive abilities and practices which relates to that period of time when Neanderthals and *Homo sapiens* co-inhabited Western Europe, between 45,000 and 40,000 years ago. The Châtelperronian marks the start of the Upper Palaeolithic, and its stone artifacts are at a cultural interface between those of the Mousterian – they include production using Levallois technology – and those of early modern humans in Europe, such as pressure-flaked, toothed blades. But the Châtelperronian includes more than this, for now we find artistic objects shaped in ivory and other raw materials. Some archaeologists treat the artifacts as the products of Neanderthals who had to some degree acculturated to *Homo sapiens* ways of doing things. For them, Châtelperronian artifacts, such as six perforated teeth from the Grotte du Renne at Arcy-sur-Cure and perforated marine shells from Italy and Greece [92], were made and used by Neanderthals who had been in contact with *Homo sapiens*, learning or copying skills practised by them. These are sites where skeletal remains of Neanderthals have been found, but they date to the terminal phase of their survival, either immediately before or potentially overlapping with the presence of *Homo sapiens* in the regional landscape. Prior to the arrival of *Homo sapiens*, Neanderthals did not make such artifacts, but many researchers believe that they

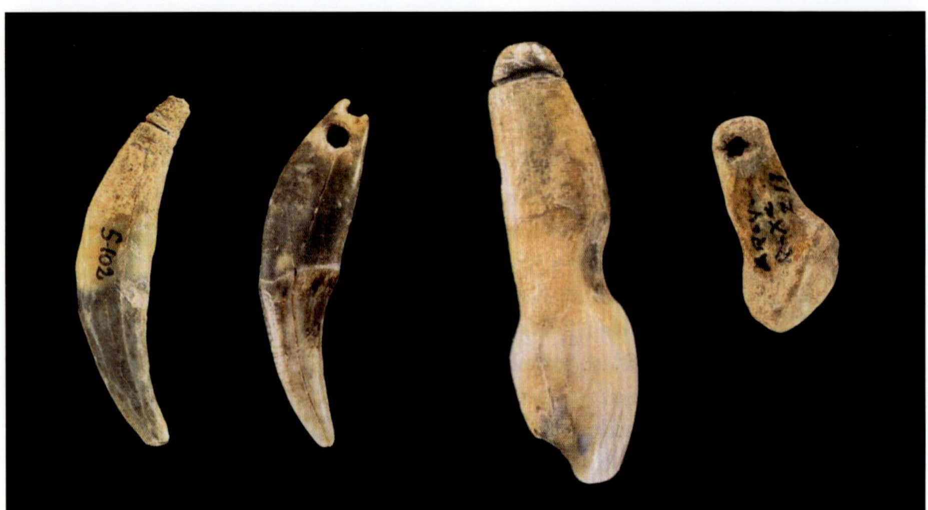

92. Worked teeth from Châtelperronian levels at the Grotte du Renne, Arcy-sur-Cure, France. They come from a buried level that straddles the period of late Neanderthals and early modern humans, with carbon dates ranging from as old as 49,000 years ago (when Neanderthals were still around) to as young as 21,000 years ago (by which time Neanderthals had long been extinct as a species of their own).

had already evolved the capacity to do so, and therefore the arrival of modern humans was all it took for Neanderthals to adopt at least some of the former's complex symbolic practices. The Châtelperronian thus explains why it is only during the period of overlap that we see the material culture of Neanderthals exhibit complex symbolism of a kind akin to that of contemporaneous *Homo sapiens*.

Yet there is another possibility, one that we normally don't think about when trying to explain sites with a combination of late Mousterian technologies and novel symbolic expressions. Rather than indicating evidence of late Neanderthals becoming acculturated to newly arrived *Homo sapiens*, could we alternatively, or also, think the other way round: newly arrived modern humans copying Neanderthal technologies (such as in the making of large triangular Levallois flakes) anywhere along the route where the two species came into contact? Such possibilities are only beginning to be aired by archaeologists trying to make sense of mixed cultural deposits at the interface of the last Neanderthals and first *Homo sapiens*, especially in Europe.

A third possibility is favoured by some archaeologists, including Paul Mellars, who argue that at key sites such as the Grotte du Renne at Arcy-sur-Cure, where Neanderthal levels are superseded by later soil levels with *Homo sapiens* artifacts, the Châtelperronian consists of mixed Neanderthal–*Homo sapiens* levels (and their artifacts), with the *Homo sapiens* artifacts of the overlying level having intruded down into the old floor levels, thereby getting interwoven with the underlying Neanderthal material. For these archaeologists, therefore, artistic objects from this period of overlap known as the Châtelperronian do not relate to Neanderthals at all, but rather to *Homo sapiens*, having become mingled with earlier or contemporaneous deposits in the ground (more will be made of the notion of 'Châtelperronian' in Chapter 6). That critical interface between the time of the last Neanderthals and the arrival of the first *Homo sapiens* remains one of the most enthusiastically researched and contentious topics of Palaeolithic archaeology today. What is clear is that once modern humans arrived in the land of the Neanderthals close to 45,000 years ago, they came with an artistic package that was already in full bloom.

Chapter 5:   The earliest art of modern humans

Two hundred thousand years ago, during the age when the Neanderthals dominated Europe and central Asia, *Homo heidelbergensis* had begun to evolve into a new species in Africa. Skeletal remains of archaic members of the species *Homo sapiens* (to which all peoples of the earth today belong) have been found at two Ethiopian sites: Omo 1, dating to 195,000 years ago, and Herto, 160,000 years ago. By 120,000 years ago these early modern humans had made their way to Tanzania (as evidenced by a skull from Laetoli, known as LH18, and fossil footprints along the shores of Lake Natron, one set of prints coming from a band of eighteen individuals walking together). By between 115,000 and 90,000 years ago they had travelled as far south as Border Cave and Klasies River Mouth in South Africa, and northwards to Es-Skhul and Qafzeh in Israel.[1] Our species was steadily spreading out of its East African homeland, in streams of migration[2] following a number of routes. *Homo sapiens* had begun its long, slow march out of Africa and would in due course come to occupy all the corners of the earth.

Early Homo sapiens *art*

The dispersal of early modern humans out of Africa is an exciting episode in the story of human creativity, for we can now start to track how the development of new forms of artistic expression developed as people spread across the globe over tens of thousands of years. Did the earliest members of our species leave Africa already equipped with an aesthetic sense, an ability to create and read symbols, and the capacity to hold abstract thought and religious beliefs to explain the mysteries of life, much as we do today? Or did these new kinds of behaviour – that we recognize as distinctively modern in ourselves – emerge slowly, as people spread across the globe? In other words, did people develop fully modern cognition with, or after, the evolution of full biological modernism?

Remarkable recent discoveries in South Africa help us to answer these questions.[3] Perched 35 m (115 ft) high in a limestone cliff close to where the Indian Ocean meets the eastern Atlantic seaboard, Blombos Cave offers magnificent views across a distant skyline [93]. What lies inside is well protected under a high sheltering roof that arches 7 m (23 ft) across the cave's entrance [94, 95]. Beneath the present floor of the cave, deeply buried under alternating layers of yellow, brown and khaki sands interspersed with black, hearthy layers, lay an entire workshop for the processing of paint pigments. Archaeologists have unearthed two paint-mixing palettes made of shell, mineral ochres that had been rubbed to produce powders for the making of paint pastes, and tools used to process those pigments. Even more exceptionally, these individual items were found still neatly arranged together, as if they had been left behind after use only yesterday, though in fact they were abandoned 100,000 years ago.

At Blombos Cave, the highest (and therefore youngest) Middle Stone Age layers are 70,000 years old; lower levels have been dated to 73,000, 77,000, 82,000, 85,000, 94,000 and 97,000 years old. It is deeper still in this layer-cake of sand, at a clearly undisturbed level dating to sometime between 105,000 and 97,000 years ago – the best scientific results indicating somewhere in between, around 101,000 years ago – that the paint-making workshop lay buried.

93. Sea-bordering cliff that contains Blombos Cave, visible about half-way up the rise.

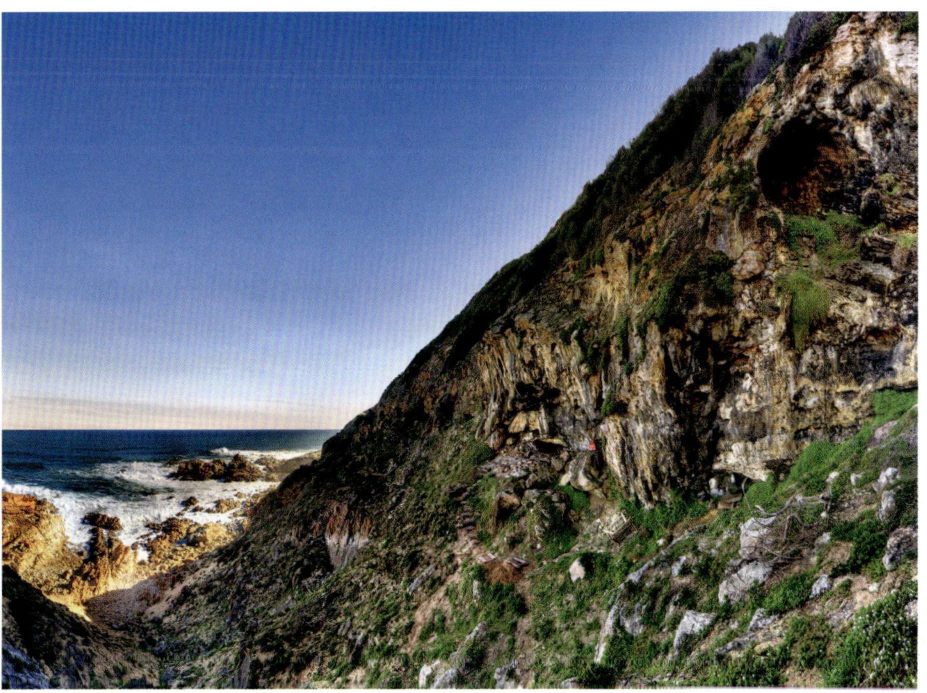

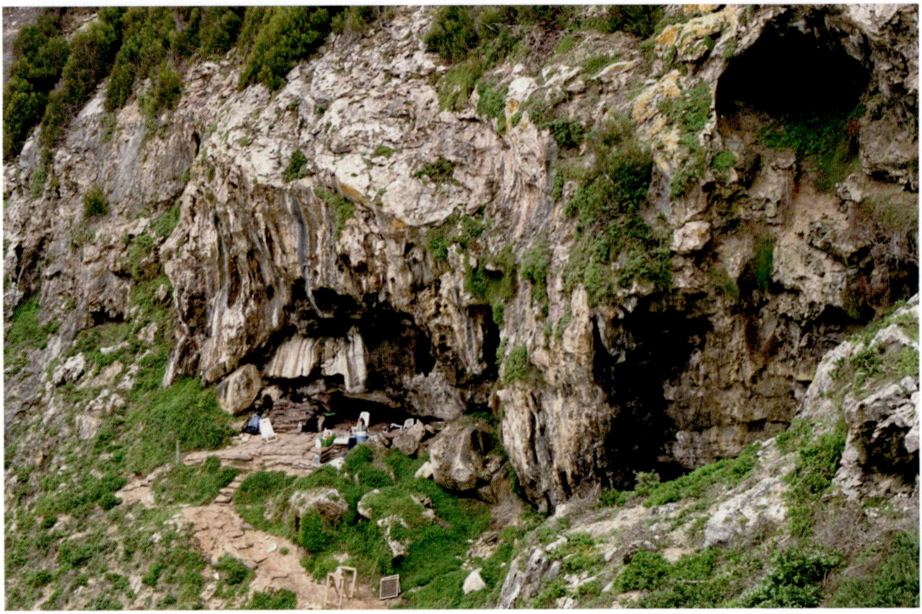

The discovery of the Blombos Cave workshop rocked the scientific world when it was announced. The palettes were not fragmented into small pieces, as often happens once objects become gradually buried beneath hundreds of kilograms of soil over the course of tens of thousands of years. Nor were the individual items dispersed across the site, as could easily have happened, for example, if an animal had wandered by and, through curiosity or by chance, disturbed the stacked items as they lay exposed on the cave floor. Instead, archaeologist Christopher

94. Blombos Cave from the outside, excavations in progress.

95. The interior of Blombos Cave.

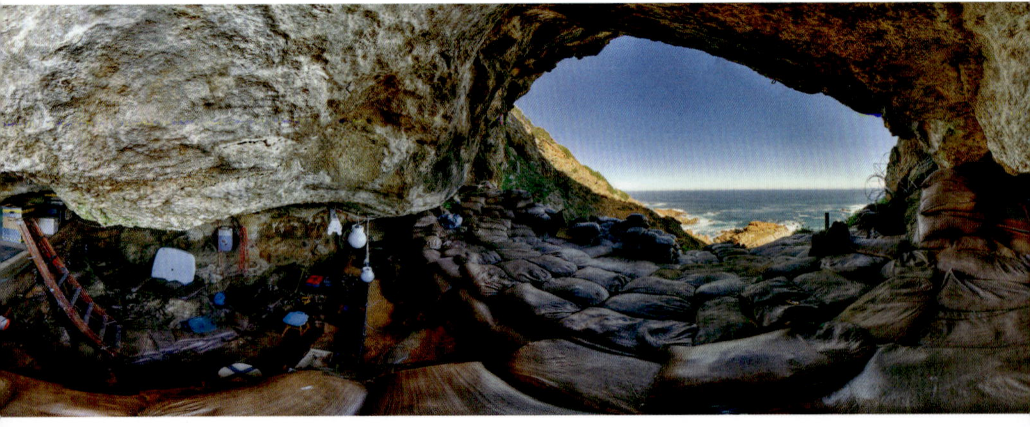

Henshilwood and his team from the University of Witwatersrand, South Africa, and University of Bergen, Norway, found the workshop virtually intact. The two sets of paint-making toolkits were found neatly stacked just 16 cm (6.3 in.) apart, both in the same layer and therefore of the same great age [96].

A quartzite cobble sat snugly inside the shiny, nacreous bowl-like inner aperture of an abalone shell used for one of the paint palettes, known as TK1 [97]. The cobble has marks on its surface that show it had served to hammer and grind red ochre and porous bone tissue of a kind typically found at the ends of long bones or inside flatter bones, such as the pelvis. When the archaeologists removed the cobble, they found thick red paint still adhered to the shell [98]. Analysis of the paint revealed that it had been made by mixing two kinds of red ochre with a binder derived from the marrow- and fat-rich spongy bone to make a more usable paint paste that would stick when applied to a 'canvas'. The bone had been burnt before crushing, helping to better release the fatty juices into the paste. Rare fragments of wood charcoal held in the shell suggest that it, too, was probably

96. Christopher Henshilwood (at the rear overseeing the excavation) and his team excavating at Blombos Cave. The layer-cake sand layers can be seen on the right-hand side of the excavation pit.

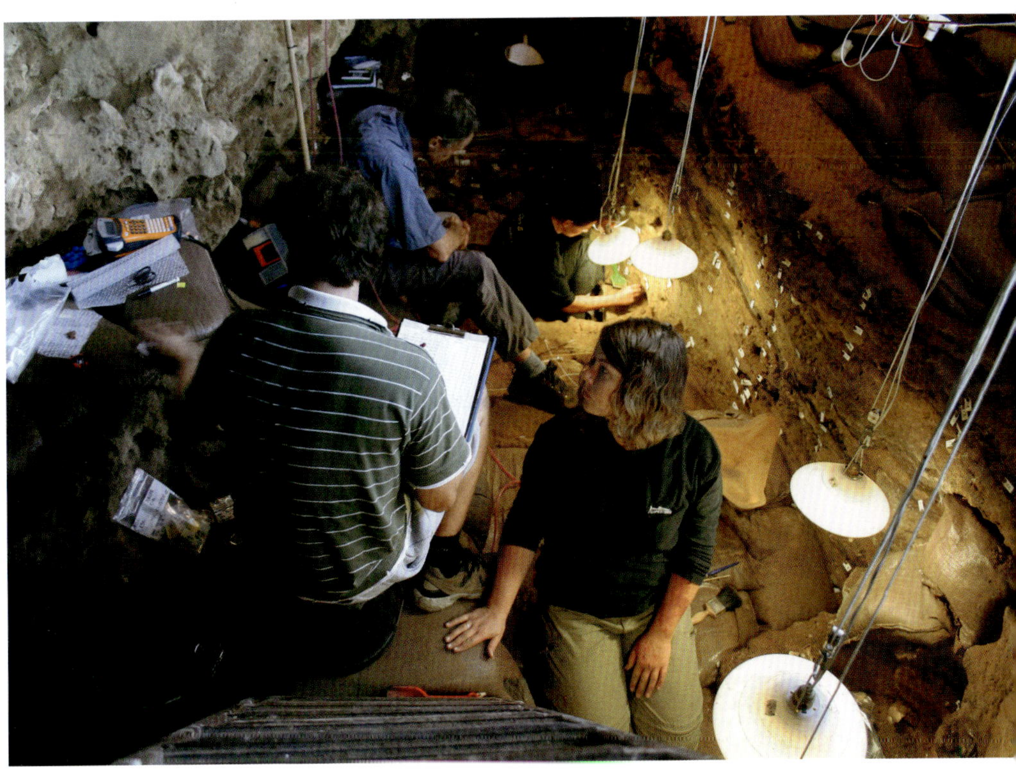

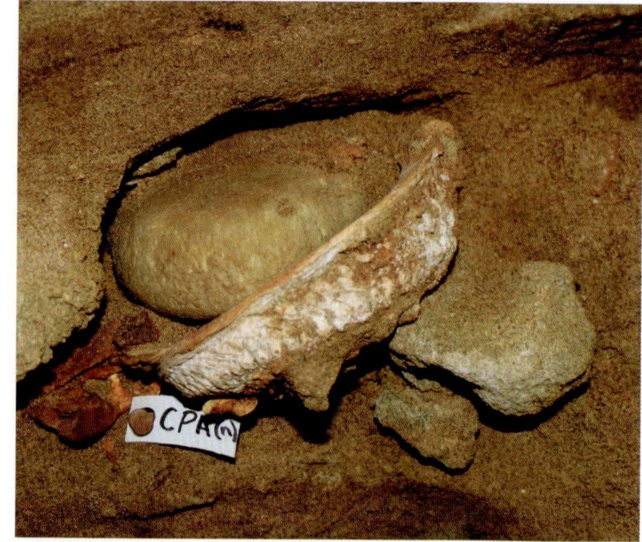

98. (below) The stone cobble separated from the abalone shell as it is being excavated, paint-making toolkit TK1 from Blombos Cave, South Africa. Under the accumulated sediment, the inside of the shell reveals thick red paint.

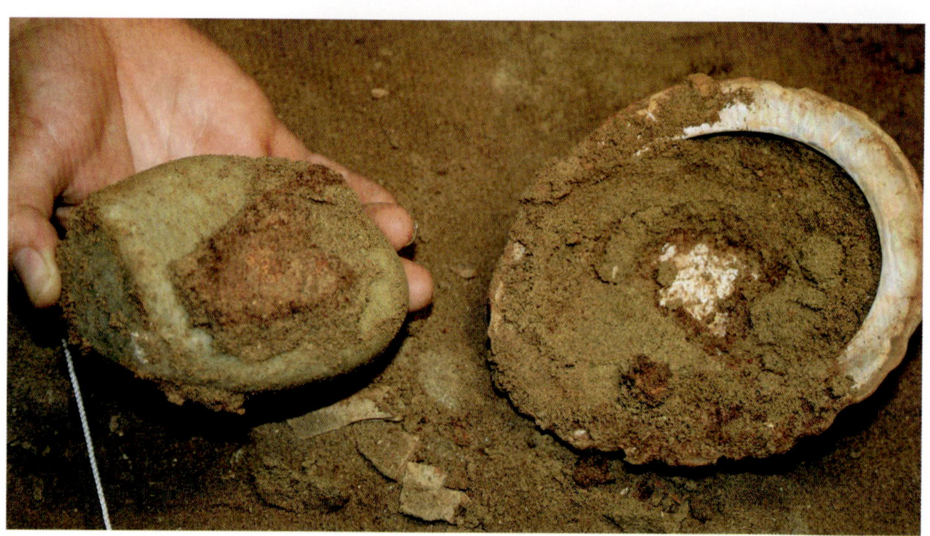

part of the recipe. Pieces of ochre were also found in the shell container, as were small stone tools that had ochre smeared along various edges and surfaces, including one slab of quartzite stained with pigment indicating that, like the cobble, it had been used to grind ochre. Underneath the shell was the foreleg bone of a carnivore, perhaps a fox, and the shoulder bone of a seal, both stained with ochre along their edges. A bone of a cloven-hoofed animal, possibly an antelope, two other quartzite grinding

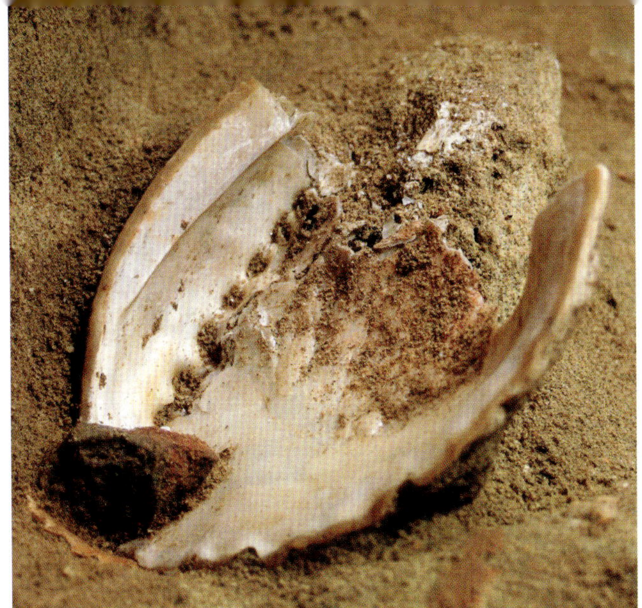

99. Paint-making toolkit TK2, at Blombos Cave as it is being excavated.

tools stained with ochre, and another, unstained stone tool were all neatly stored with the abalone shell and its contents.

The second toolkit, TK2, was also tightly packed around an abalone shell with red paint in its inner concave surface [99]. That red paint was constituted of exactly the same mix of ochre and bone found in the first palette. The inner surface of the shell, near its outer lip, had been stained red as the paint paste was mixed. A stone tool that had been used to grind crayons of ochre into powder lay against the shell. An ochre crayon lay 5 cm (2 in.) away; small pieces had been flaked off for grinding, and it had also been rubbed to make more powder. The ochre found in the two toolkits does not occur locally: it had to have come from at least a few kilometres away, as did a silcrete stone tool that had been used to flake or grind the ochre. This is important as it implies that people had come to Blombos Cave with a well thought-out plan to make pigment with imported ingredients and tools. The making of paint had come with careful preparation and forethought 100,000 years ago.

We do not know if well-delineated images were created with the paints manufactured at Blombos Cave (or were they just aimed at covering something in red?); nor do we know where such paintings would have been made. The 'canvas' could have been a rock surface, a person's body or an object that people carried around. It appears though that two people may have been working side-by-side, each toolkit more or less identical and containing pigment made using a single formula consisting of multiple ingredients. The fact that both toolkits had been stored so close together, a mere handspan apart, suggests that these two individuals were either kin or close friends, and certainly that they were familiar enough with each other to closely work together and then store their toolkits alongside each other. As we reflect on these ideas, the very fact that we can even begin to realistically imagine not just an evolving species, but such details for individuals so far back in time, is mind-boggling. Some 100,000 years ago, our ancestors took part in creative endeavours that we now take for granted, as for instance when we buy and use paints and crayons. Deep in the recesses of Blombos Cave, the manufacture and use of paint signals something much grander: the beginnings of an active, creative mind, and of what we have come to know as 'art'.

Artistic activity during the Middle Stone Age of southern Africa

The Blombos Cave paint-making toolkits were used during a period that archaeologists call the Middle Stone Age, which began around 280,000 years ago in East Africa.[4] This period began with archaic human behaviour gradually emerging with the onset of biologically modern *Homo sapiens* around 200,000 years ago. It was during the Middle Stone Age that early modern humans first began to spread across, and then out of, Africa. These humans invented new kinds of stone tools, including long, narrow blades that required greater mastery of knapping techniques; stone and bone points that were hafted onto wooden shafts to make projectiles such as spears and perhaps even arrows; and bone needles to work animal hides [100]. At the rockshelter of Sibudu in South Africa, there is evidence that humans were making bedding out of aromatic and insecticidal plants by 77,000 years ago.[5] And, as we have seen at Blombos Cave, for the first time in human evolution there are unmistakable signs of things being decorated by painting with complex paint recipes.

The paint-making toolkits of Blombos Cave, at the very southern tip of Africa, provide the first unambiguous evidence for planned art-making and human thought processes that begin to resemble our own (with more elementary abilities shown by *Homo erectus* in eastern Asia and *Homo heidelbergensis* in Africa, as indicated by the Trinil engraved shell, use-worn ochres from Twin Rivers, and perhaps the Berekhat Ram 'figurine' from the Golan Heights, for example). There is thus a period of around

100. Bifacial stone points and bone tools from *c*. 75,000-year-old Middle Stone Age levels at Blombos Cave, relating to a cultural phase known as 'Still Bay'.

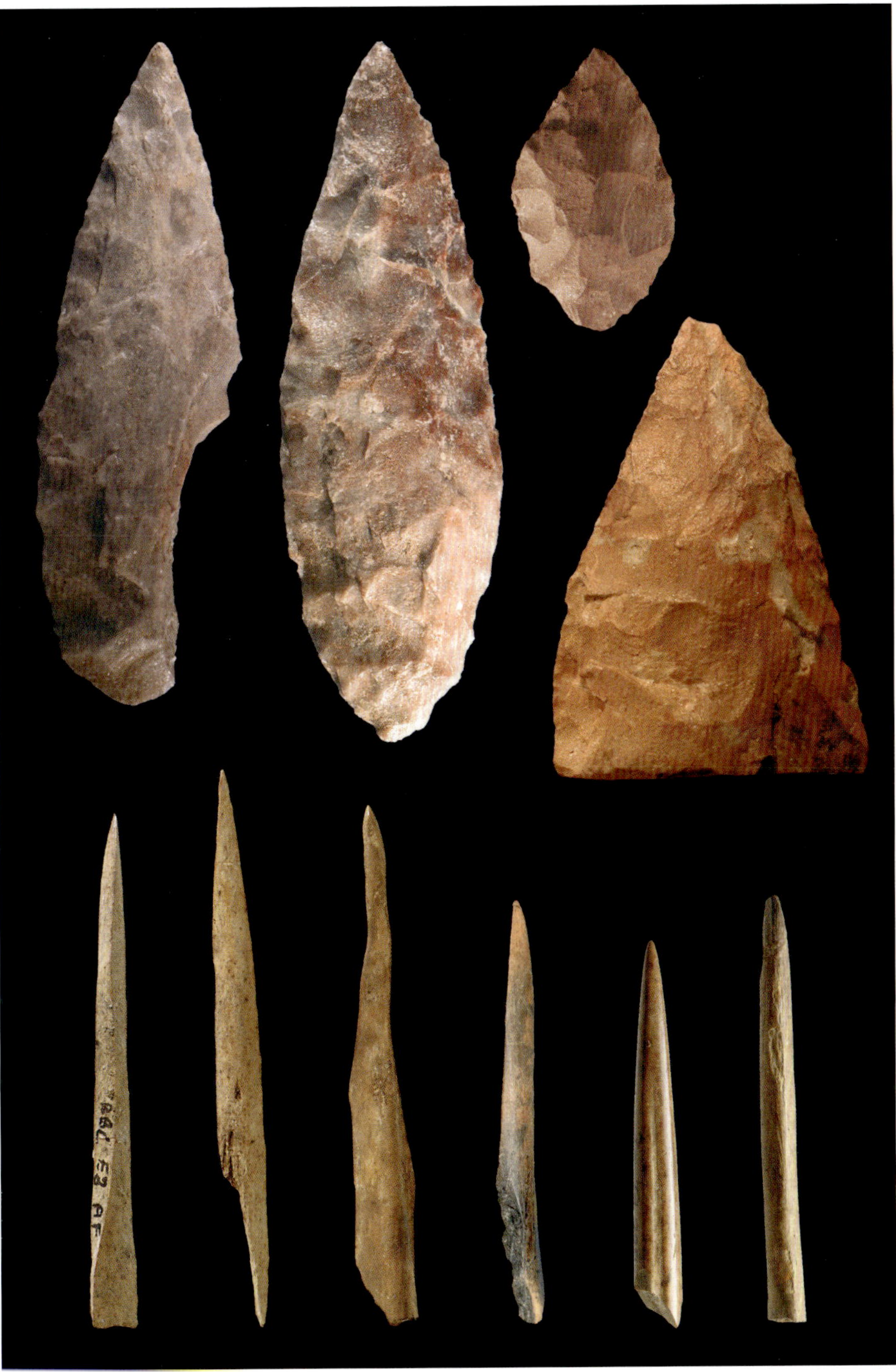

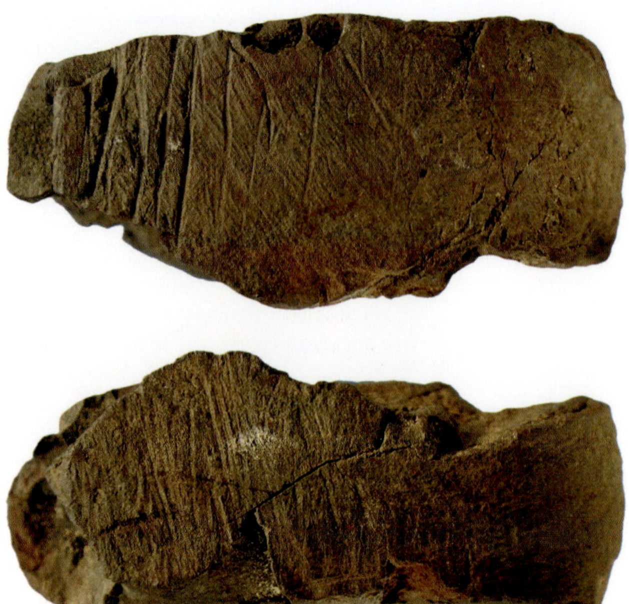

100,000 years between the earliest fossil traces of biologically
modern humans *c.* 200,000 years ago and the first clear traces
of an ability to prepare and cache multiple ingredients and
toolkits for artistic purposes.

The idea that the use of ochre represents symbolically
mediated behaviour takes a curious twist at Blombos Cave and a
site some 350 km (220 miles) to the east of it, Klasies River Cave 1,
also on the southern African coast. We would normally associate
red ochre with the production of red pigment for painting and the
making of imagery. But what about when the ochre crayons are
themselves the artworks: when they are themselves decorated
with symbols? This is the case at both sites. At Klasies River Cave 1,
six ochre crayons were extensively ground between 101,000 and
85,000 years ago, but one is particularly interesting because of
the engraved geometric design it carries on its smooth-ground
surface [101].[6] The engraved lines are pronounced, exhibiting a
combination of parallel and angled lines. They had been made with
a pointed stone tool, and were not accidentally produced in the act
of grinding. The engraved piece is broken, representing a fragment
of an originally larger piece, so the full design is not clear.

Similar engravings on ochre were found by Henshilwood and
his team at Blombos Cave, where fifteen pieces lay buried in layers
above (and therefore more recent than) the two paint-making

toolkits already described.[7] These were dated between 100,000 and 75,000 years ago and had surfaces smoothed flat and incised with geometric lines. Sometimes the incised lines are rather faint and weathered, making no clear pattern that we could unambiguously identify as image-making. But in two cases, both dated to 75,000 years ago, the pattern and the intent to create a design are unmistakable. One of these, a 5.4-cm-long (2.1 in.) lustrous pink siltstone and fine sandstone, was flaked, ground smooth and then incised with a cross-hatched pattern consisting of two sets of superimposed parallel lines overlaid by a further angled line [102]. The second piece is even more impressive. Measuring 7.6 cm (3 in.) in length, this angular reddish-brown siltstone was first shaped by grinding, after which three sets of parallel lines were incised one over the other to form a cross-hatched pattern on one face [103]. Many of the lines are not clean strokes, but rather were made by repeatedly cutting into the moderately soft rock, exposing a determination to execute a preconceived design. The overall arrangement is clear and clean nonetheless: depending on one's point of view, we can choose to see it either as a broad pattern of criss-crossing lines, or of abutting diamond shapes framed above, below and across the middle by a latticework of long incised lines.

Whether we see the patterns on the incised ochres from Klasies River Cave 1 and Blombos Cave as the products of

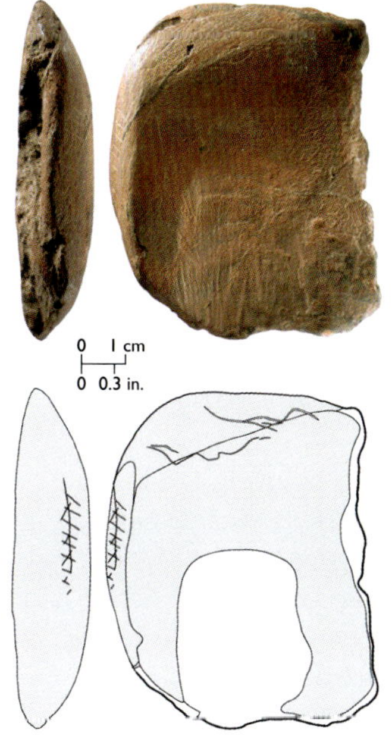

102. 75,000-year-old engraved ochre piece from Blombos Cave.

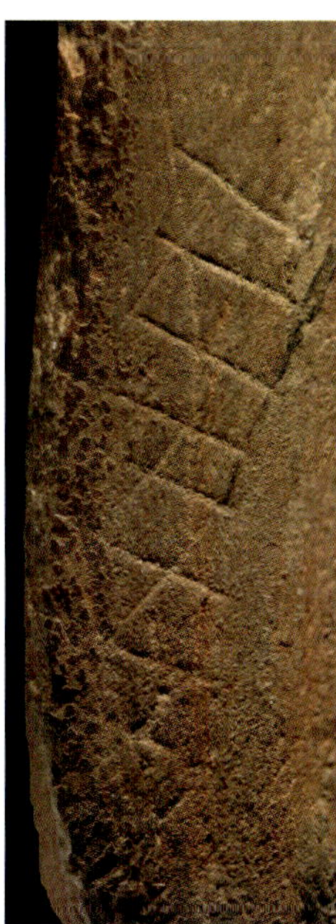

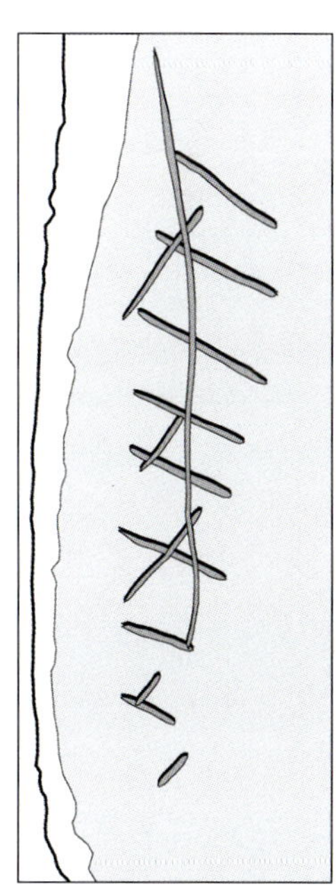

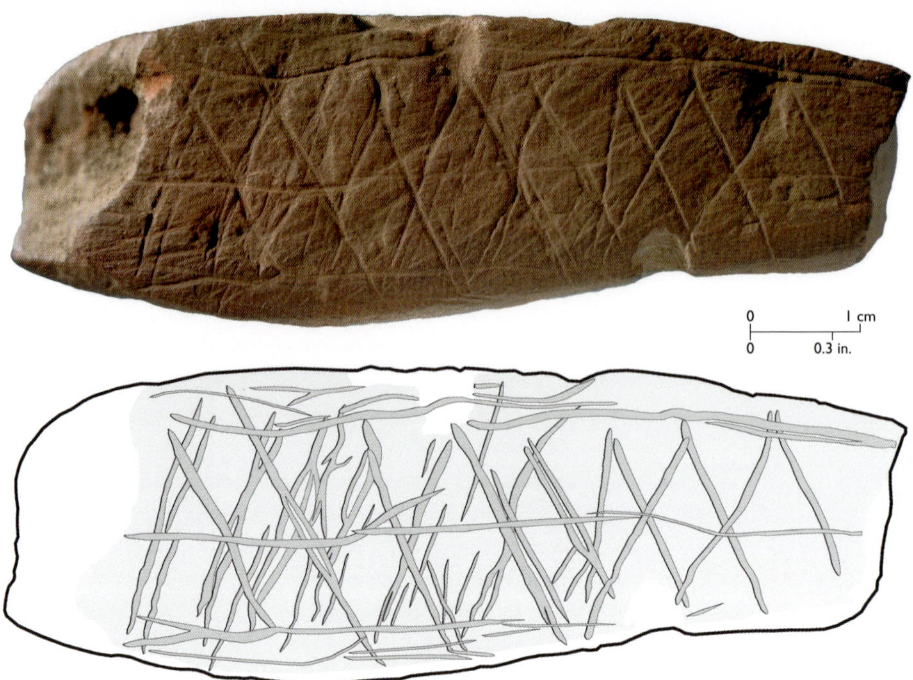

103. 75,000-year-old ochre piece from Blombos Cave, showing the engraved latticework pattern.

imaginative doodling or as designs that were consciously conceived to depict and communicate a particular idea, they signal the creation of a mental template. That template is shaped and controlled. The geometry of the whole was not made accidentally; it was not made by an unthinking and uncultured mind, but rather indicates a way of doing things through symbols and aesthetic balance. The engraved ochres of Blombos Cave are signs of people expressing themselves creatively. This is the stuff of symbolic behaviour and of art. The paint-making toolkits recovered from Blombos Cave announce that art was already being made in South Africa by the Middle Stone Age some 100,000 years ago, and through these incised ochres we see for the first time what some of that imagery looked like by 85,000 to 75,000 years ago.

The use of linear incisions to create aesthetically balanced, geometric designs is repeated at two other sites in South Africa: Diepkloof Rock Shelter, some 17 km (11 miles) inland of the Atlantic coastline, and Klipdrift Shelter, a mere 50 km (30 miles) west of Blombos Cave, this time on ostrich eggshells [104].[8] Originally excavated in 1973 by John Parkington and Cedric Poggenpoel from the University of Cape Town, and more

recently researched by Pierre-Jean Texier and his team from the
Université de Bordeaux 1, some 408 fragments of eggshell, dated
to 65,000–55,000 years ago, were recovered from Diepkloof Rock
Shelter, each decorated with geometric incisions [105]. A variety
of patterns were inscribed onto the eggshells, together giving a
sense of the range of cultural expression (much as the sum of
Scottish tartan patterns gives a sense of the overarching graphic

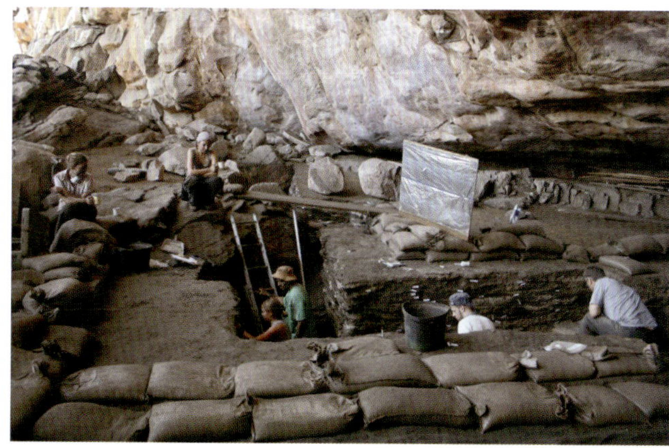

104. (right) Excavations in
progress at Diepkloof Rock
Shelter, South Africa, where
65,000- to 55,000-year-old
geometrically incised ostrich
eggshell fragments have been
found.

105. (below) Examples of 65,000-
to 55,000-year-old incised ostrich
eggshell fragments excavated from
Diepkloof Rock Shelter.

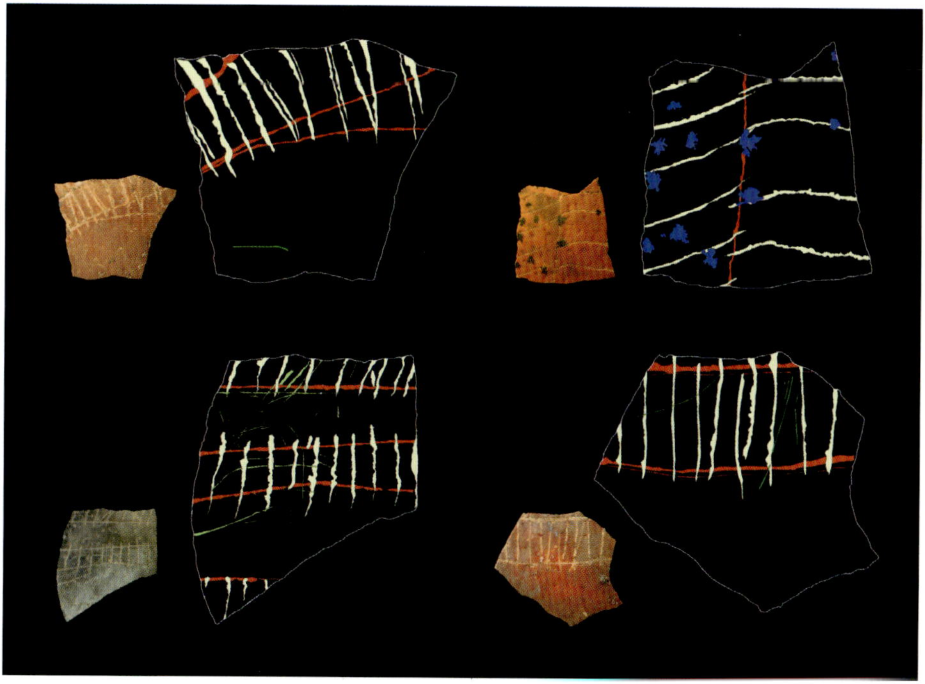

leitmotif). We can therefore recognize a symbol-making and aesthetic mindset in the manufacturing process, even if we can't interpret the original meanings of the motifs.

Klipdrift Shelter is part of a cave complex situated in the De Hoop Nature Reserve, again at the southern tip of South Africa. The shelter has been excavated by Christopher Henshilwood and Karen van Niekerk (the latter from the University of Bergen, Norway) since 2011. Here, in layers dating to between c. 66,000 and 59,000 years ago and associated with an innovative stone artifact assemblage (of a tradition called 'Howiesons Poort' that is geographically confined to southern Africa), more than seventy fragments of clearly and deliberately engraved ostrich eggshell were recovered. The designs entail recurring themes, variations of cross-hatching or sub-parallel lines, and most are similar to those reported from layers of a similar age at Diepkloof, and also from Apollo 11 Cave in Namibia.[9] The exceptions are several fragments from the upper (most recent) layers that exhibit a finely engraved diamond-shaped cross-hatched pattern, distinctly different to those from layers below, and from the 'cross-hatched grid motif' at Diepkloof.

The Diepkloof eggshells are decorated with one of five designs: hatched bands; cross-hatched grids; sub-parallel intersecting lines; reversed curvature; and sub-parallel rectilinear or curved lines. None of the fragments of shell possesses more than a single one of these patterns, indicating that each whole eggshell – or at least each discrete region of eggshell, given that most of the recovered fragments are fairly small – was probably decorated with a single pattern. Some large pieces, up to 8 cm (3 in.) long, allow us to make out the overall design, and support this idea.

There is no doubt that the decorated Diepkloof eggshells (like those from Klipdrift Shelter) are artistic creations produced by a creative mind. As Texier and his team have noted, the repeated patterns signal that rules for composing designs existed, but there was room within the rules for individuals or groups to exercise creative freedom. The ostrich eggs were not simply eaten then discarded, or reused functionally, as receptacles to hold water or the like, but rather, or additionally, were used as a medium by early modern humans to express themselves to the world through symbols that they associated with and that they could carry around in their travels. Those symbols allowed people to portray themselves not just as cultural beings, but as particular kinds of people who belonged to socially organized groups. The symbols that people identified with allowed others to understand something of their identity. The Diepkloof eggshells are signatures of creative minds that enabled people to represent and organize themselves as groups and to interact together through their shared symbols.

Shell beads

Along with its painting paraphernalia, Blombos Cave yielded a number of ancient shell beads from its deeper levels (not quite the oldest in the world, but ancient nonetheless). An assemblage of forty-one perforated *Nassarius kraussianus* 'tick' shells was discovered, like the incised ochres dating to around 75,000 years ago [106]. These marine shells could not have come into the cave by themselves; they were brought there by people, who

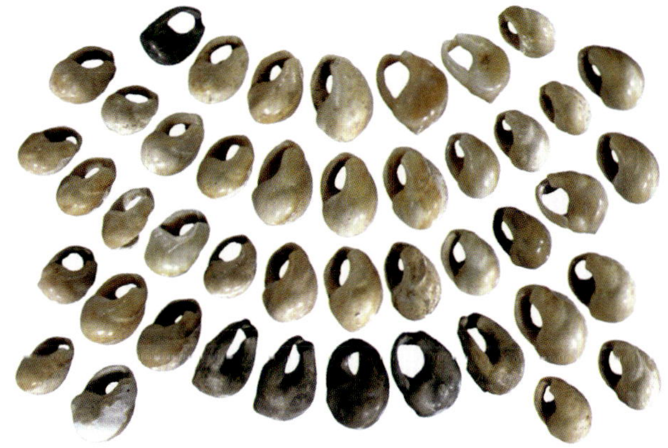

106. 75,000-year-old perforated *Nassarius kraussianus* shells from Blombos Cave, South Africa.

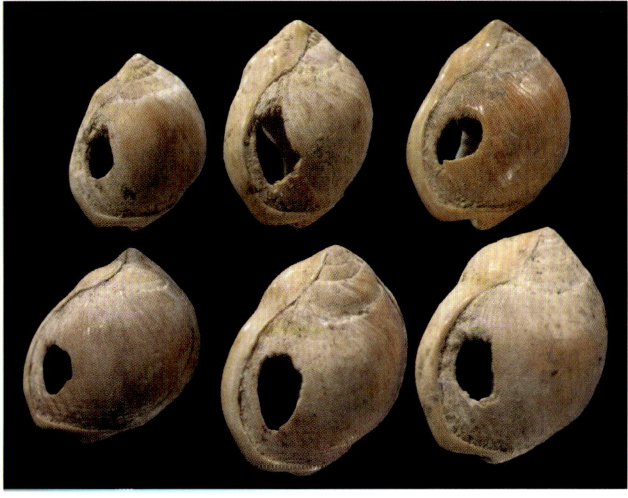

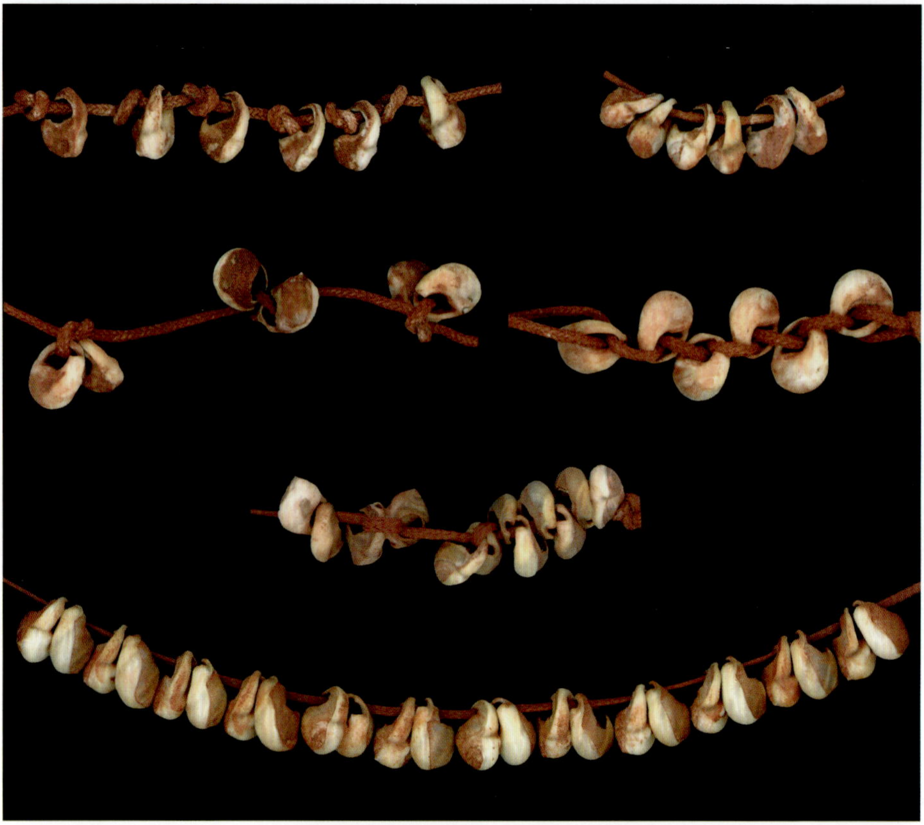

107. (above) Six hypothetical ways (using modern shells) that the *c.* 75,000-year-old *Nassarius kraussianus* beads from Blombos Cave may have been strung. (right) Experiments with modern *Nassarius kraussianus* shells show how strung shells would result in polishing along their edges and surfaces.

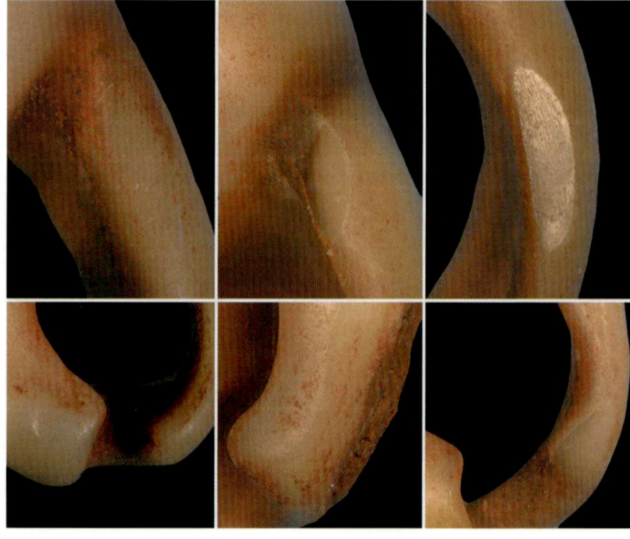

perforated them with bone points. When examined under a microscope, the edges of the perforated shell walls show that they had been polished round as a result of having been strung [107]. The shells had likely been worn as beads for personal adornment, indicating that people had enhanced how they presented themselves to society through culturally prescribed forms of artificial beautification. This again indicates a modern human mind, reflected in behaviour, that is concerned not just with finding water, food, shelter and a mate, but with how individuals and groups present themselves socially via culture and status in communities of people. As previously mentioned, for rock art specialist Robert Bednarik, beads are important for tracing the origins of modern human behaviour, as simply by being worn they imply a sense of personal style and thus self-awareness.[10] Personal adornments, as forms of body art, speak of symbolic expression in a modern fashion.

Beyond Africa

As anatomically modern people left the African continent, we begin to find evidence for symbolic behaviour along the dispersal routes eastwards across southern Asia into Australia, and north and westwards into Europe and northern Asia. At first the evidence is patchy, in part because of the test of time, and especially for those areas where research has been limited. It is in Israel, at the doorstep between northeastern Africa and southwestern Asia, that we find the earliest evidence of early modern humans outside Africa. Here, at the rockshelter site of Es-Skhul on Mount Carmel, two perforated *Nassarius gibbosulus* shell beads were recovered from layers dating to between 135,000 and 100,000 years ago [108]. The shells were gathered from the shore of the Mediterranean

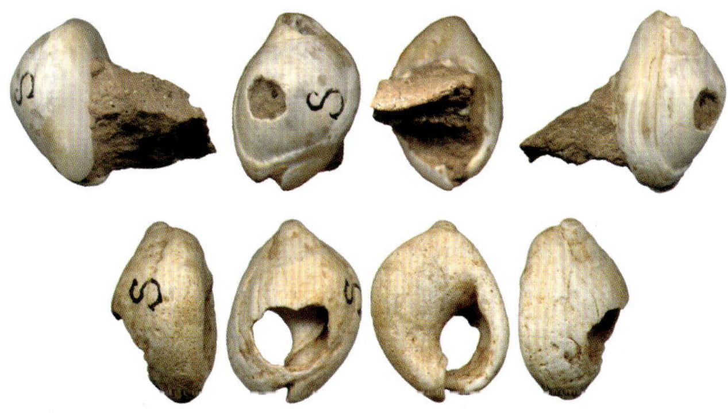

108. Multiple views of two 135,000- to 100,000-year-old perforated *Nassarius gibbosulus* shell beads from Es-Skhul in Israel.

some 3.5 km (2 miles) to the north and carried into the cave.
They are associated with early modern human remains and are
the oldest known shell beads in the world. In the cave of Qafzeh
in the Lower Galilee region, 30 km (20 miles) away, human burials
dating to around 92,000 years ago have been found, along with
a stone flake incised with short parallel lines,[11] ochre used for
painting[12] and perforated *Glycymeris insubrica* beads made from
shells carried 35 km (22 miles) from the Mediterranean – some
painted with red ochre – and used as strung ornaments, probably
for personal adornment such as necklaces or on garments [109].

Little is currently known of developments in artistic
capabilities as humans journeyed further eastwards into Asia.
What is of great interest, however, is the arrival of people
in Australia beyond the far southeastern edge of the Asian
continent sometime between 60,000 and 50,000 years ago, for
the cultural package that arrived with the earliest Australians
would presumably have already developed by the time people
crossed from the Southeast Asian seaboard. Hence we find red
ochre crayons with facetted edges made when they were rubbed
to create pigment as far back as $61,000 \pm 13,000$ to $45,000 \pm$
9000 years ago at Madjebebe (aka Malakunanja II), and $53,400 \pm$
5400 years ago at Nauwalabila I, both rockshelters in northern
Australia's Arnhem Land region [110].[13] At Carpenter's Gap
in the Kimberley region of northwest Australia, archaeologist
Sue O'Connor found a slab of limestone rock stained with red
ochre, signalling the making of artwork sometime between 50,000

109. *Glycymeris insubrica* shell
beads, *c.* 92,000 years old, from
Qafzeh, Israel.

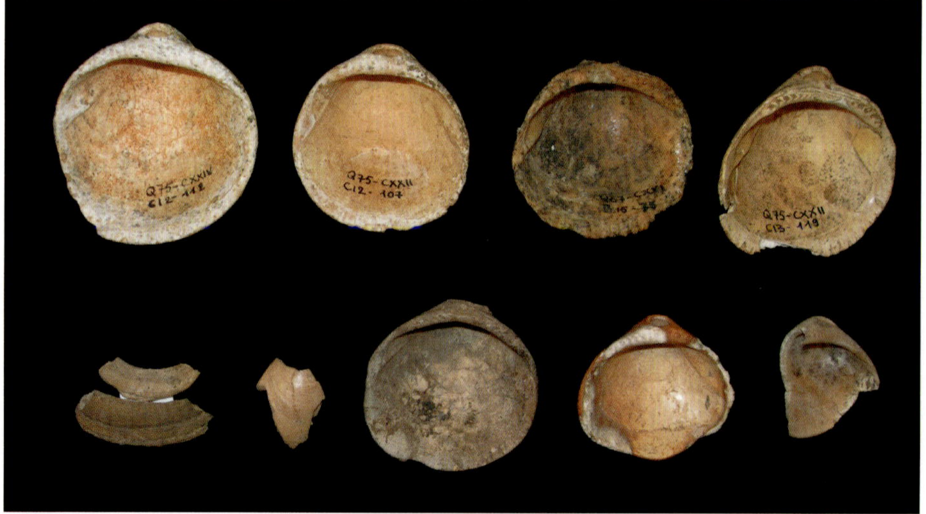

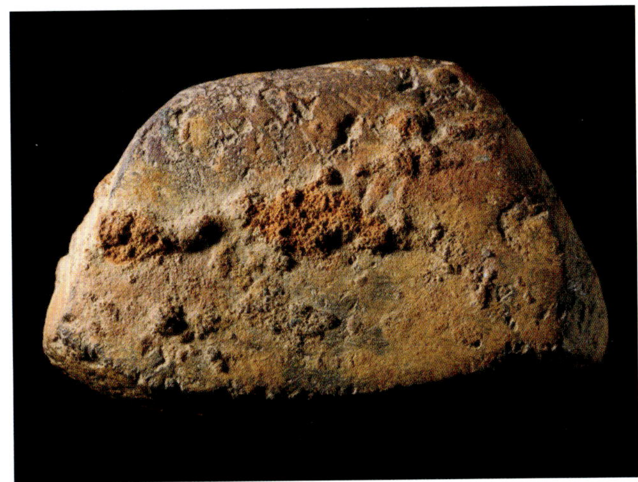

110. Piece of use-worn ochre crayon from Madjebebe (Malakunanja II), northern Australia.

and 37,000 years ago.[14] It is uncertain whether the pigment on that rock slab represents a faded image or the result of ochre being ground to make paint for use elsewhere; the traces are too faded to tell for sure. Either way, the processing and use of pigment to make imagery is implied. These Australian findings, dating to around 50,000 years ago and therefore approximately contemporaneous with the earliest Australians, strongly suggest that by the time people arrived in Australia the art of painting was already well established. We will explore exactly what this means for the development of early art in the next two chapters.

Chapter 6:   The art of the Ice Age in Western Europe

Everyone has heard of the 'Ice Age', but there were in fact many ice ages, with those occurring during the history of species of *Homo* spanning a geological period of the earth's history that scientists call the Pleistocene. It begins 2.6 million and ends 11,700 years ago, and refers to a long era of alternating cycles of colder ice ages (also called glacials) divided by warmer interglacials. During each ice age, the earth's high northern and southern latitudes became covered with extensive ice sheets that stretched far beyond their current reaches, only to contract during the warmer phases as the ice melted. So too were mountain tops blanketed with ice, even those in tropical regions such as the highest mountains of New Guinea where little or no snow falls today [111].[1]

There are a number of reasons behind these fluctuating conditions. Predominant among them are the so-called Milankovitch cycles, which see three interacting factors affect conditions across the earth's entire surface. First there is the amount of radiation that reaches the globe as a result of changes in the shape of the earth's rotation around the sun. When the orbit is more elongated, the earth gets colder the further it gets from

111. Extent of ice cover over the northern hemisphere 20,000 years ago, during the Last Glacial Maximum.

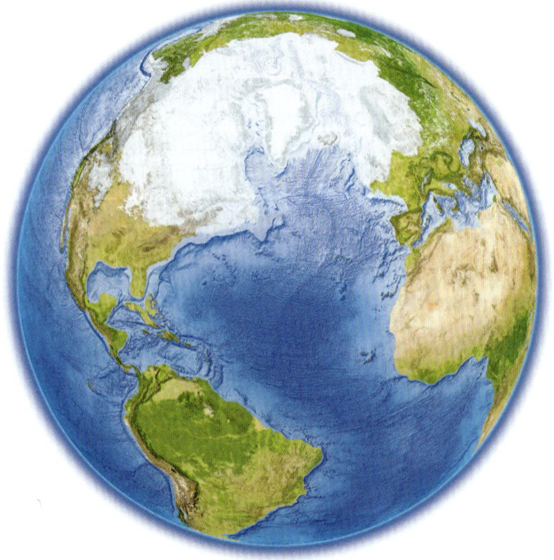

the sun; when it is more circular, less ice accumulates because solar radiation is more constant and evenly spread. Second is the tilt of the earth along its central axis. This affects the timing and duration of the seasons. Third is the way that the earth wobbles as it spins around its axis, affecting how temperatures sway from season to season. The three cycles are of different lengths, each running into tens of thousands of years, and while there are considerable complicating factors, when the cycles align together at their coldest they give rise to a glacial period.

During each ice age, heightened amounts of the earth's waters were trapped in ice sheets at the expanded northern and southern poles and in mountain glaciers. The last ice age, which we will capitalize as the Ice Age, was one of the coldest. So much seawater was trapped as ice that at its peak – a period we know of as the Last Glacial Maximum – global sea levels had dropped by 120 m (400 ft), exposing vast coastal plains that had previously been submerged beneath ocean waters. This last Ice Age began about 110,000 years ago as the earth slowly started to cool, with the most extreme part beginning around 50,000 and ending about 12,000 years ago after rapid global warming. During the Last Glacial Maximum, between about 27,000 and 14,500 years ago, the average annual temperature of the earth's surface had lowered by about 4°C (7°F) relative to today, although across the globe the exact timing and degree of temperature lowering varied.

As a result of the lower sea levels, land bridges became exposed: Siberia and Alaska were connected by 'Beringia', which spanned the exposed Bering Strait, Bering Sea and Chukchi Sea; the British Isles were joined with continental Europe; much of the Red Sea and Persian Gulf was exposed as dry land, forming a continuous land bridge across the Bab-el-Mandeb from northeastern Africa to southwestern Asia via Sinai; many of the islands of Southeast Asia connected together into a single landmass known as Sunda; and Australia and New Guinea formed the giant island of Sahul.

It is soon after the start of the coldest phase of the Ice Age that we find the first cave paintings anywhere in the world, although the degree to which cooling conditions affected people's decisions to make art remains the subject of archaeological debate. Some argue, for example, that artworks enabled people to create for themselves an enhanced notion of style that facilitated alliances and interactions between social groups and, with this, access to resources at times of environmental stress. But most researchers think that there is older art out there waiting to be

found or dated, and certainly that artworks were being made long
before the earliest examples we know about, as shown by the
100,000-year-old Blombos Cave paint-making toolkits that testify
to a much more ancient ability to make paintings.

The earliest cave paintings of Europe

In this chapter we will examine the Ice Age art of Europe, for it
forms the best-studied geographical entity in the world. From
this corpus, general themes – some positive, some highlighting
the problems – can be brought out, with broader implications
for cave art more globally.

In the late 1800s and into much of the 1900s, humanity's
artistic origins were widely thought to lie in continental Western
Europe, particularly in France and Spain, because this was then
the only place in the world where Ice Age art could be seen in
all its glory. It was also in Western Europe that great attention
had been given to unearthing evidence of what were then called
'Cro-Magnons', the earliest modern humans known, and
therefore it was from here that information about our species'
earliest activities disproportionately grew, fortifying the idea
of Western Europe as the cradle of humanity's creative genius.
Today we now refer to those ancient modern humans as early
European *Homo sapiens* rather than 'Cro-Magnon', and we know
that they first arrived in Europe around 45,000 years ago, well
after the evolution of modern humans in Africa or their expansion
across much of Asia and into New Guinea and Australia. But
the legacy of that early research focus, and of the associated
preconceptions of Europe as the source of our artistic abilities,
still pervades, only beginning to be broken down in recent years.

Ice ages may have come and gone during the Pleistocene, but
artworks first and foremost relate to the actions of people, not
to changing environmental conditions. Archaeologists have thus
designated terms of their own to refer to what people did in the
distant past, relating to the archaeology rather than geology or
climate change, and this is particularly so in Europe. The term
'Palaeolithic' was coined in 1865 by the English archaeologist
and First Baron of Avebury, John Lubbock – a friend and close
neighbour of Charles Darwin – to refer to the 'Old Stone Age',
a prolonged period of time when stone tools were fashioned by
flaking prior to the Mesolithic, Neolithic (when stone tools also
began to be made by grinding, such as to make axes) and the Metal
Ages. The Palaeolithic was later subdivided into a sequence of

finer-grained eras, each identifying a particular set of stone tool types going back to the very first European stone toolmakers. We have already seen how the Acheulean refers to the cultural practices of *Homo erectus*/*Homo heidelbergensis*, and the Mousterian to those of Neanderthals. In Europe, the Upper Palaeolithic is the time of *Homo sapiens*, and it begins with the first signs of modern humans some 45,000 years ago, during the Ice Age.

The Upper Palaeolithic was chronologically further subdivided into a sequence of stone industries by which to better characterize technological innovations, each represented by its own types of stone tools and stone technologies. Later, these same chronological subdivisions were (and still are) applied to other kinds of cultural products, such as portable art and cave paintings, but as we shall see below, we now realize that the art does not neatly fit into the same scheme as the stone artifacts. As discussed in Chapter 4, the first phase of the Upper Palaeolithic has been called the Châtelperronian, a much-debated period beginning around 45,000 and ending 40,000 years ago, which overlaps the period of the last Neanderthals with that of the earliest modern humans. The Châtelperronian consists of a blend of late Mousterian (Neanderthal) and new kinds of (*Homo sapiens*) tools – in particular stone scrapers and 'backed blades' blunted along their back edges [112], as well as shell, bone and ivory artifacts (including items of personal adornment such as beads) not previously seen in the toolkits of Neanderthals.

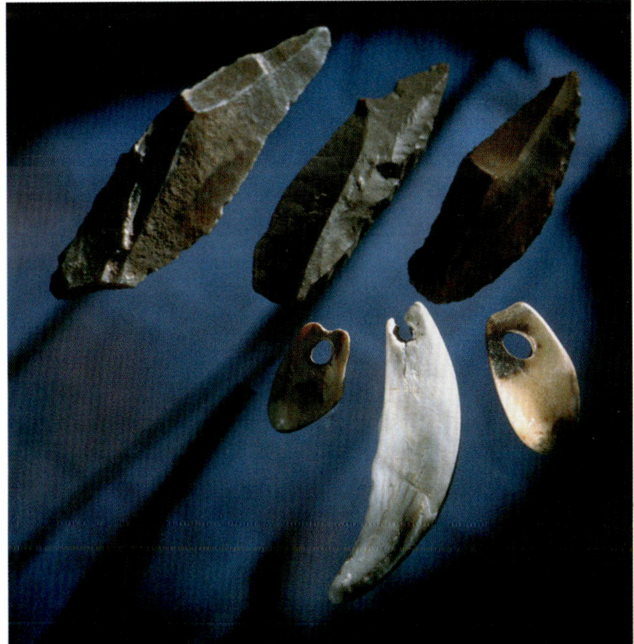

112. Characteristic stone artifacts and perforated teeth from the Châtelperronian, France.

113. Aurignacian split-base antler points excavated by Édouard Lartet and Henry Christy in 1863 from l'Abri Lartet, Dordogne region of southwestern France.

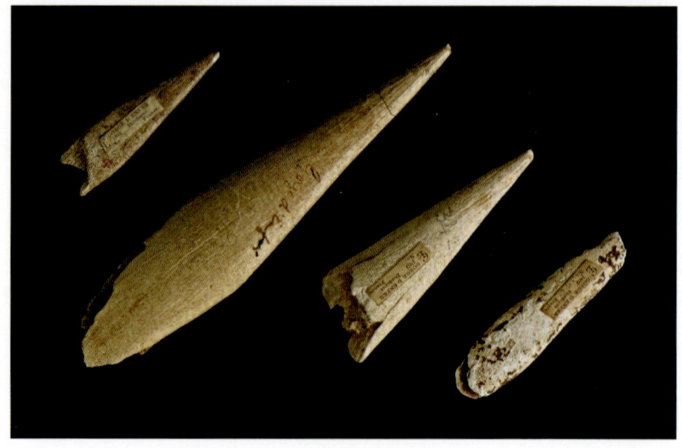

The Aurignacian (*c.* 45,000–30,000 years ago) was a period of many innovations, such as the first use of prismatic cores for the making of fine, long stone blades, and the shaping of bone and antler into points and awls [113]. It is during this time that we begin to see the first unambiguous signs of Ice Age art, such as the earliest paintings at Chauvet Cave in France, and the oldest stone and ivory figurines, such as those of Hohlenstein-Stadel Cave in Germany [114] where the first part-animal/part-human depiction in the world has been found [115].

114. Hohlenstein-Stadel Cave, Germany.

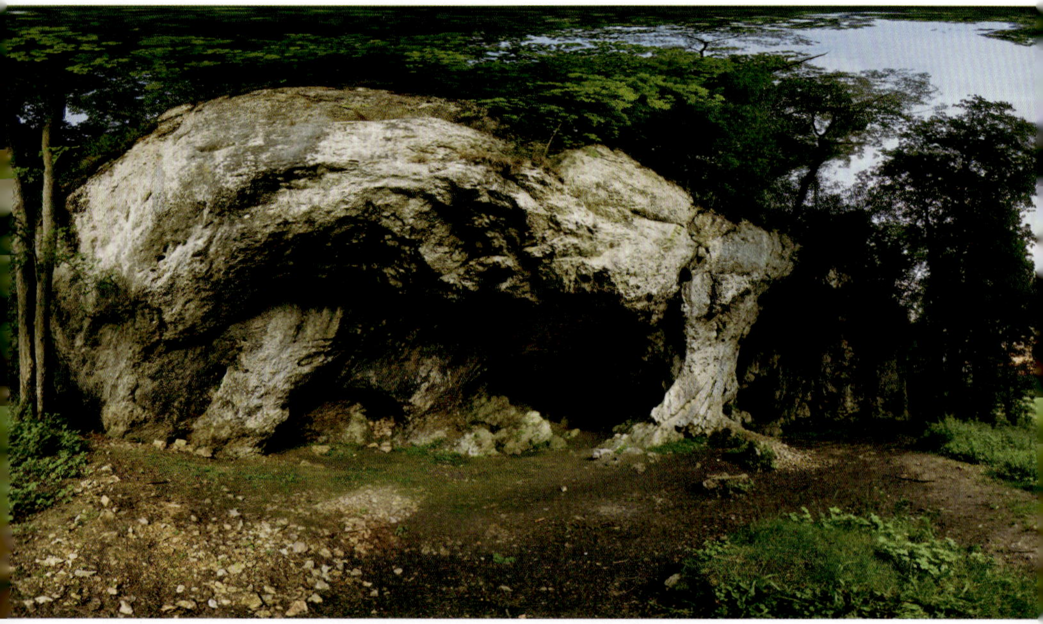

115. Oldest known compound
animal-human depiction in the
world, combining a lion's head with
a human body, carved in woolly
mammoth ivory. The figurine was
excavated in 1939, just one week
before the outbreak of World
War II. The excavation pit was
hastily filled with the soil of the
original excavation, and from the
1960s to 2013 new excavations
of the fill and in situ deposits
recovered further conjoining
pieces, allowing the figurine to
be more accurately reconstructed
and its stratigraphic context
better dated. Aurignacian period
(c. 40,000 years old), Hohlenstein-
Stadel Cave, Germany.

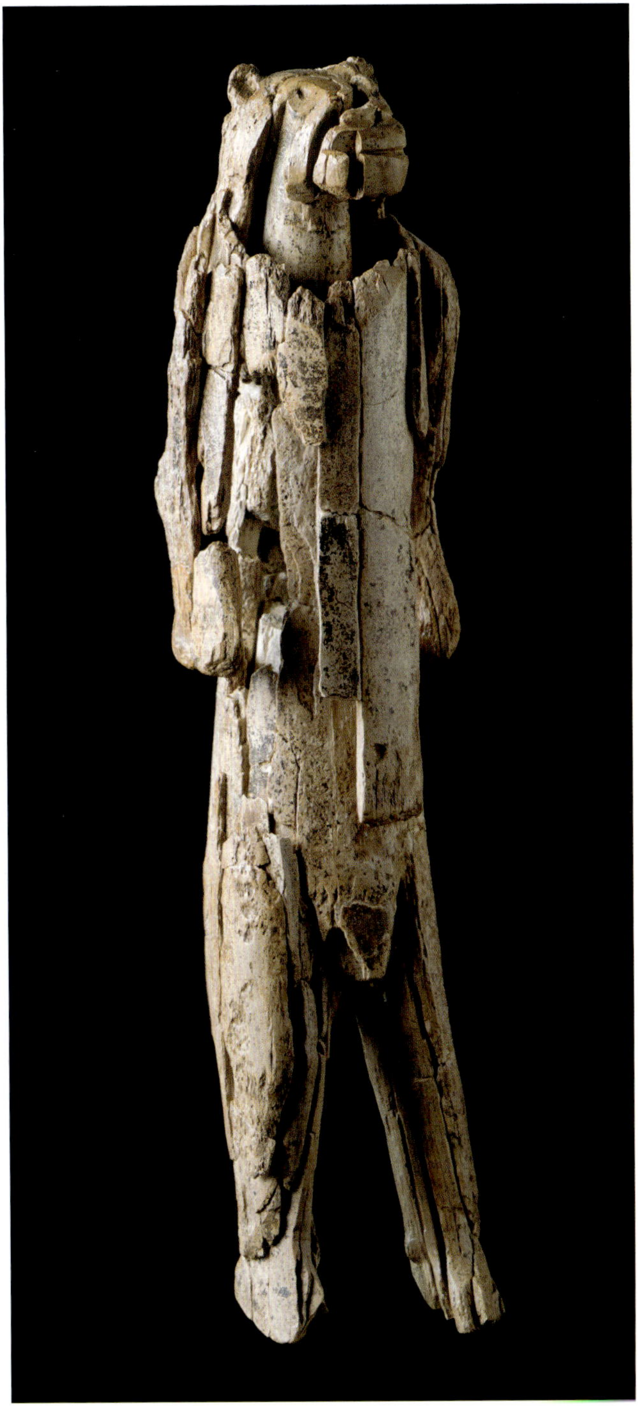

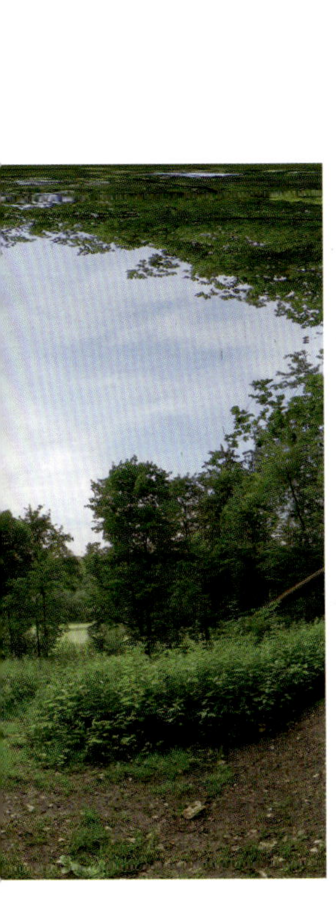

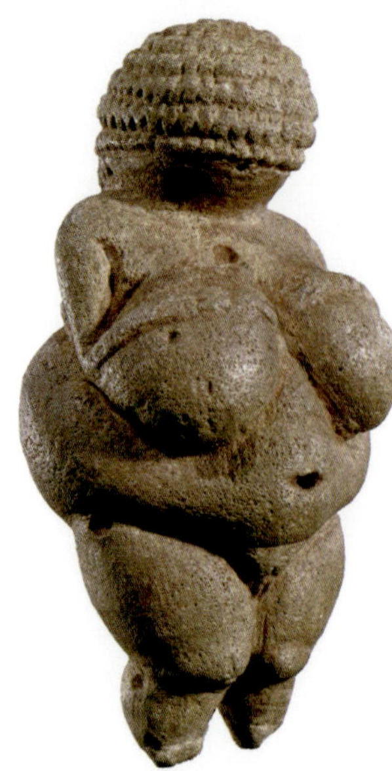

The Gravettian (30,000–22,000 years ago) then saw a proliferation of stone burins, small engraving tools made from blades that were further struck to produce a narrow ridge at the tip, much like the edge of a modern narrow chisel. The Gravettian also saw the production of so-called 'Venus figurines', a kind of anthropomorphic carving usually shaped from ivory, bone or soft stone that was widely spread from the Pyrenees in Western Europe to as far east as Lake Baikal in Siberia [116]. While the popular term Venus figurine has traditionally been given only to female figurines with more or less curvaceous attributes – in particular the stomach, breasts and buttocks – with a tapering small head at the top and narrow lower legs devoid of feet at the bottom, in reality Gravettian figurines exhibit a broad range of body shapes [117], although these have tended to not feature in popular discussions on the

116. The 'Venus of Willendorf', 11 cm (4.4 in.) tall and carved from oolitic limestone between *c.* 28,000 and 24,000 years ago. It was excavated from a river terrace overlooking the Danube near Willendorf, Austria in 1908.

117. (right) Upper Palaeolithic figurine from Kostenki in Russia.

118. (below) Mammoth ivory figurine from Dolní Věstonice, Czechoslovakia, *c.* 26,000 years old.

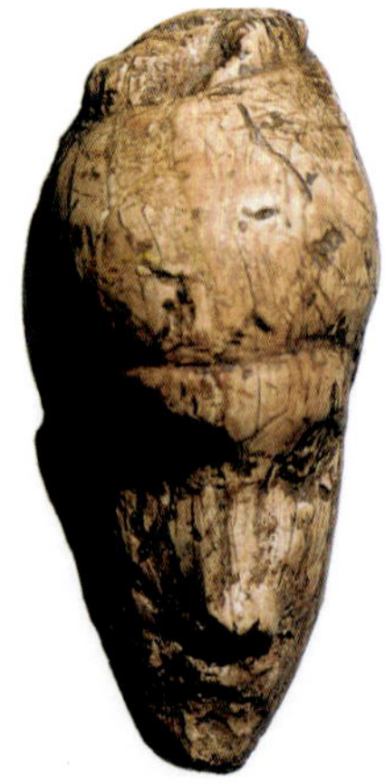

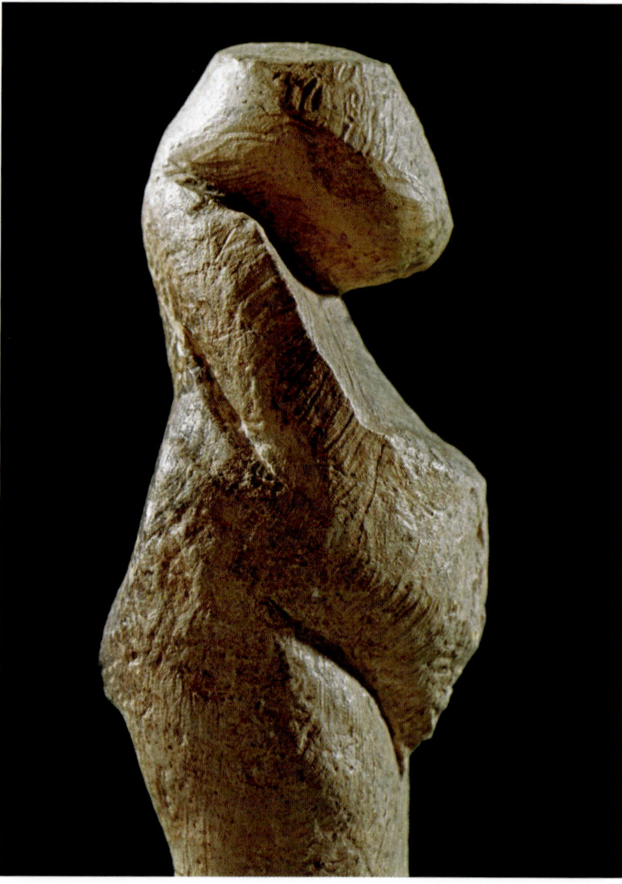

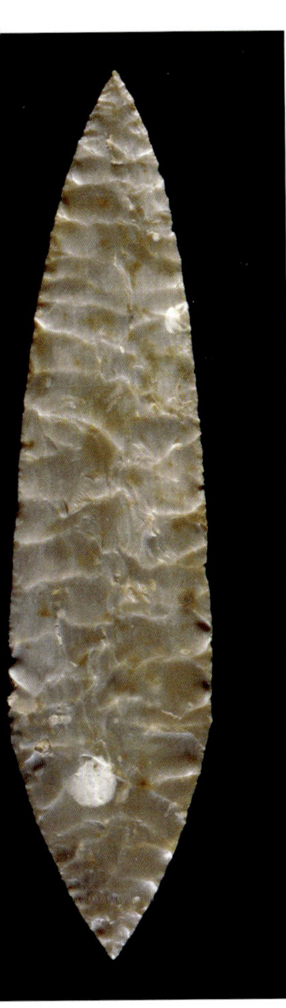

119. Bifacially flaked Solutrean 'laurel leaf' point excavated in 1874 from Volgu, Saône-et-Loire region, central-eastern France.

subject [118]. They tend to be small, mainly 4–25 cm (1.5–10 in.) in height, and have provoked many different interpretations ranging from children's dolls to 'mother goddesses'. They have been thought by some commentators to have acted as symbols of fertility in a harsh Ice Age environment where fecundity was highly valued, by others as images of women's bodies by and for men, and by others again as self-representations by women, or as obstetric devices to monitor the growth of the foetus and to aid with childbirth, or as a standardized way of stylized depiction to facilitate information exchange between communities. But in truth, and despite the tabling of many, at times ingenious, ideas, we don't really know what these Upper Palaeolithic figurines meant to their creators, nor how they were used. The interpretations that have been attributed to them seem to reflect more the culture and preconceptions of those doing the interpreting over the past 150 years than the Upper Palaeolithic cultures from which they came. From male-dominated viewpoints in the first part of the twentieth century to more self-reflective approaches that focused on the social construction of gender and calls for self-determination following the 1960s, to the symbolic power of information exchange in the 1980s, Venus figurines have become a useful way of exposing the sociology of our own Western biases. By examining how we interpret and write about the past through the archaeological objects of that past, we can come to know better ourselves in contemporary society.[2]

After the Gravettian came the Solutrean (22,000–17,000 years ago), which saw the invention of beautifully made, sharp-edged stone points with teardrop shapes. These delicate tools were extensively flaked along both faces, resulting in very thin artifacts that were of more than functional value: as spear points, a single impact against a hard surface would have shattered the fragile point, suggesting that they were at least as important for show as symbols of manufacturing know-how and embedded social value than as functional tools or weapons [119]. The Solutrean also saw a proliferation of types, raw materials, and technological approaches to the manufacture of carved antler batons, beads, bone pins and numerous different kinds of elaborate arrowheads. Along with the ensuing Magdalenian, for many commentators the Solutrean represents the apogee of Upper Palaeolithic artistic achievements.

The Magdalenian (17,000–12,000 years ago) continues the trend of exquisite bone, ivory and antler art that had begun in the Solutrean, with even more elaborate decorations of harpoon

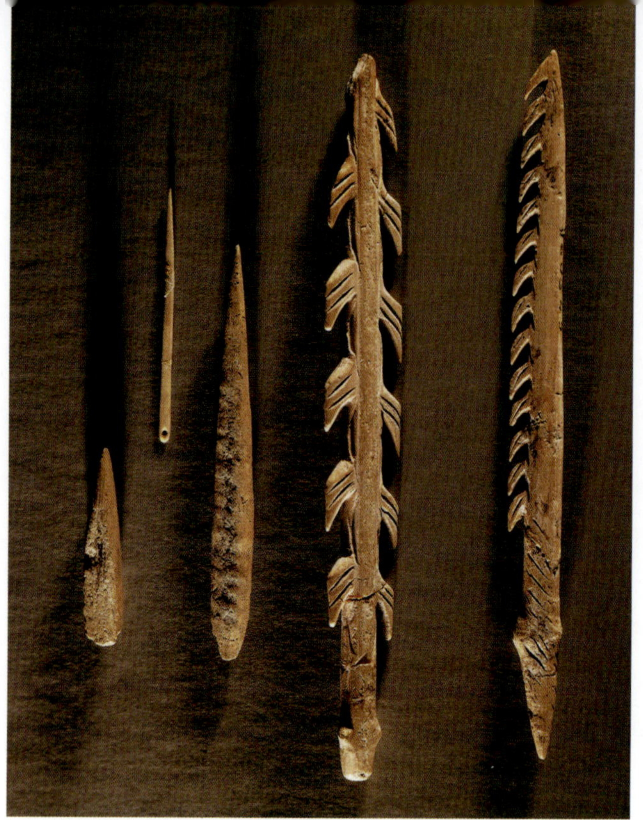

120. Magdalenian antler and bone harpoon heads, points and needle, France.

heads being relatively common [120]. The Magdalenian coincided with the peak of the Ice Age, at a time when reindeer hunting became particularly important.

The sequence of archaeological 'cultures' from the Aurignacian to the Magdalenian is sometimes taken as indicative of a sequence of distinct cultural groups, such as 'the Gravettian people', 'the Solutrean people' and so on, but in reality these are just ways that archaeologists have divided the archaeological evidence rather than real cultural groups. Over the course of many thousands of years, early modern humans in Europe invented new ways of doing things while also continuing some old practices and dropping others, and it is this pattern of continuity and innovation that caused the sometimes subtly shifting archaeological record (including both portable and fixed artworks). And as the Magdalenian ended, so too did the Ice Age, although people continued to live and develop new ways of doing things in response to social and environmental stimuli. Global temperatures increased, glaciers melted and sea levels rose, and Western Europe's Ice Age art came to an end.

The oldest European cave art

As the Ice Age began to bite around 40,000 years ago, we begin
to see the first signs of artworks on cave walls in Western
Europe. It is only very recently that we have truly begun to
understand just how old those early artworks really are. From
eleven limestone caves in Asturias and Cantabria in northwestern
Spain, Alistair Pike and his co-researchers carefully collected
fifty small samples of calcite that lay over, and sometimes under,
Upper Palaeolithic paintings, hand stencils and engravings.[3]
Altamira, El Castillo and Tito Bustillo, three of the studied caves,
are spectacular subterranean formations in their own right, today
showcased as UNESCO World Heritage Sites [121]. It was at
Altamira that the first Palaeolithic cave art had been identified
by Sanz de Sautuola back in 1879 (see Chapter 2 for details of
the controversies surrounding the discovery of its art). But until
Pike's work, none of the art had been dated; all estimates of its
antiquity had been made by comparing the art styles with those
of other, also largely undated sites along with those of excavated
and dated portable art objects.

Pike and his team knew well that they would likely obtain
old ages for the art if they could date the calcite deposits that had
formed over it, using the U-series method. Yet the results they

121. El Castillo in Cantabrian
Spain, showing the Corredor de
los Puntos, where U-series ages
on calcite under and over two of
the red circles indicate that they
date between 36,000 and 34,100
years ago. The homogeneity of
design and preservation probably
indicates that the entire panel of
red circles is of that age.

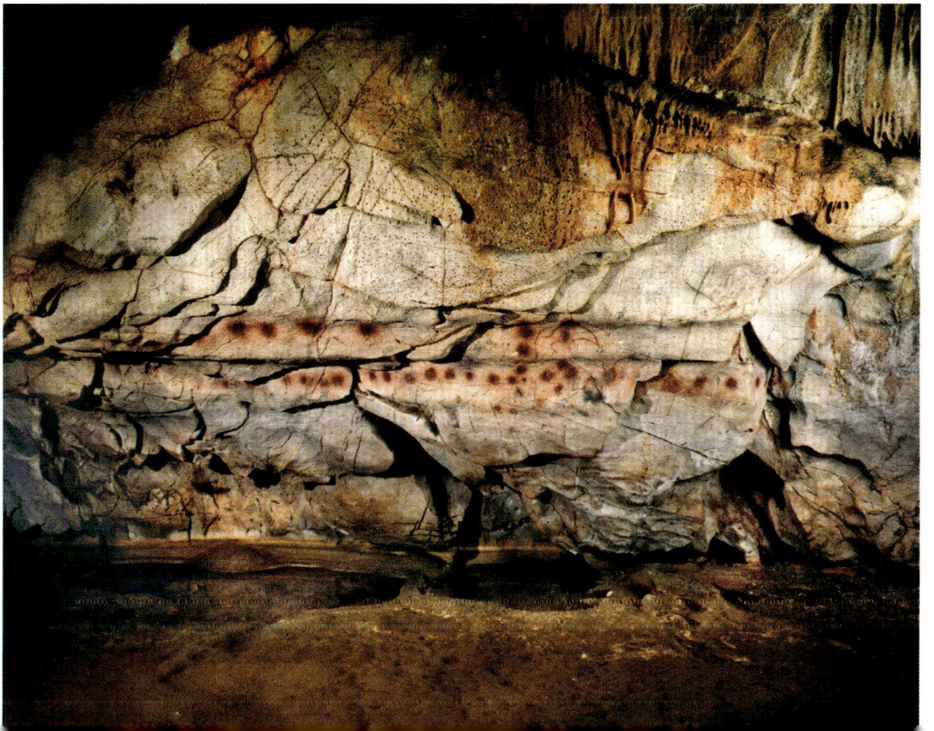

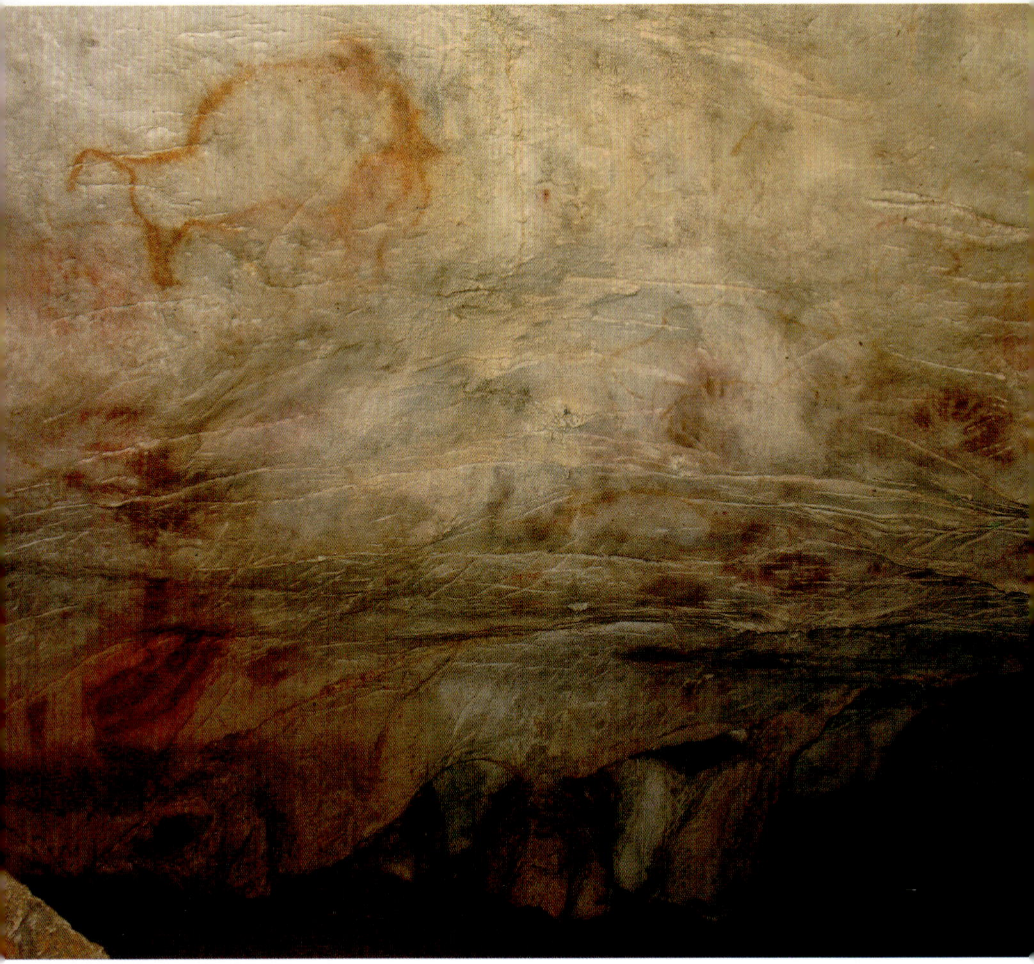

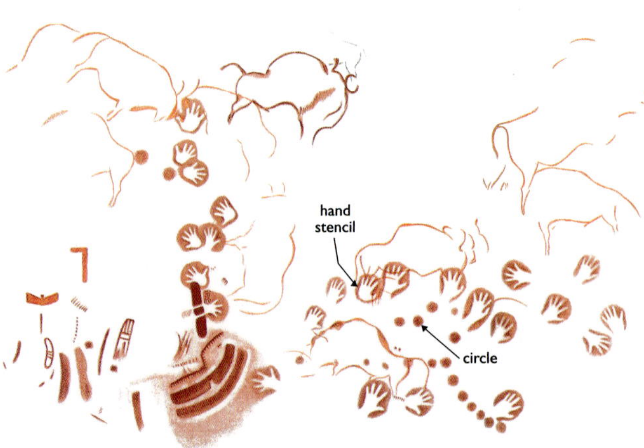

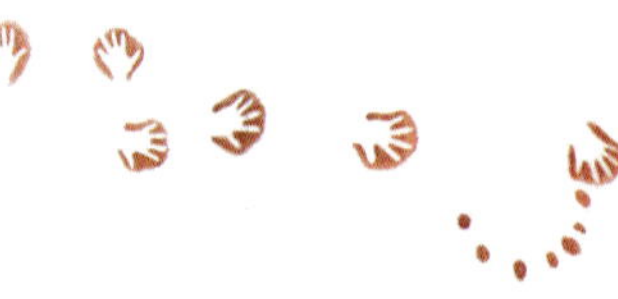

122. (above and left) The Panel de las Manos at El Castillo, Cantabrian Spain. U-series dates from calcite over a red hand stencil revealed an age of *c.* 37,300 years, and over a red circle an age of *c.* 40,800 years. As the dates relate to the calcite that has grown on the art, the underlying stencil and circle are older than these dates.

obtained were totally unexpected: at El Castillo, a red circle was more than 40,800 years old and a hand stencil dated to at least 37,300 years ago [122]. At Altamira, a minimum age of 22,000 years was obtained for a horse painting outlined by red dots on the ceiling of the polychrome chamber that young María Sanz de Sautuola had discovered back in 1879 [123]. Another minimum age of 35,600 years came from an abstract, claviform (club-like) symbol [124]. Similarly ancient ages were corroborated at Tito Bustillo, where red pigment was found to be more than 29,600 but less than 35,500 years old.

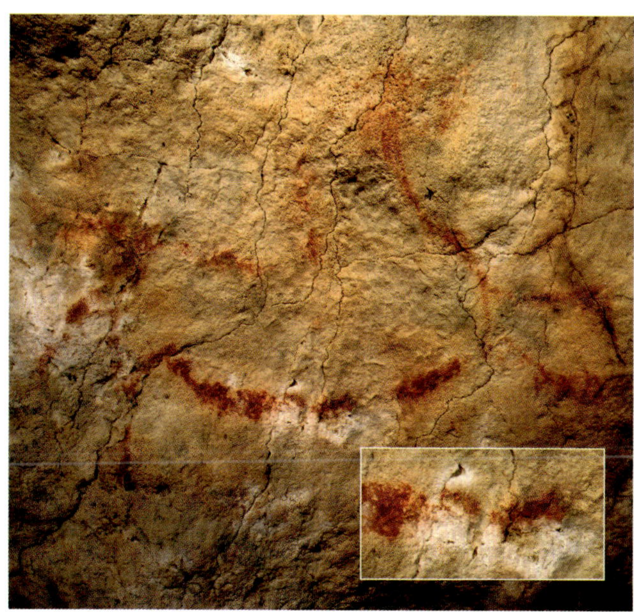

123. Painting of a horse outlined by red dots, Altamira, Cantabrian Spain. U-series dating has revealed a minimum age of 22,000 years for the horse. The inset shows the sampled area.

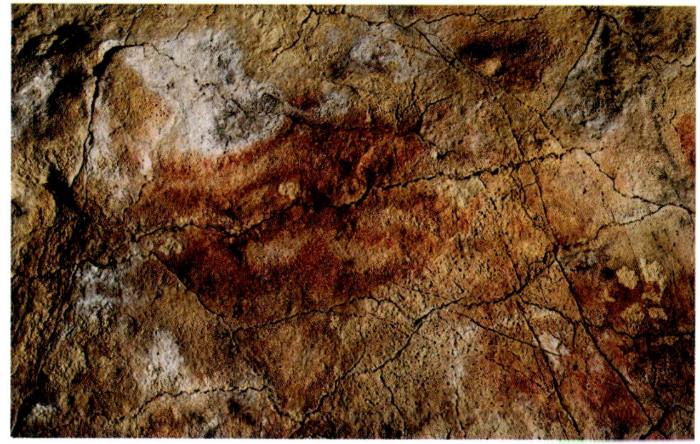

124. Red claviform-like symbols, Altamira. A U-series date obtained from the calcite overlying the upper of the two paintings gave a minimum age of c. 35,600 years for the art.

Not all archaeologists accept these results, because of concerns that what was dated does not entirely relate to the age of the calcite that overlies the art (see Chapter 3 for more details of the methodological issues relating to U-series dating).[4] But while the jury is out, the work has raised questions about what we really know of the antiquity of Ice Age art in Europe: we may know more than we did in 1879, when Sanz de Sautuola announced that Altamira's paintings were Palaeolithic, but we still cannot neatly fit the age of Western Europe's artworks into the culture-historical pigeonholes better constructed for the stone tools, the Châtelperronian, Aurignacian and so on. And as Altamira, and Chauvet Cave (see below), have well taught us, there remain many surprises ahead, with artworks continuing to be found older than initially thought.

In northern Spain, the oldest reported ages for excavated archaeological deposits with biologically modern human remains come from the cave of Morín, carbon dated to 36,590 ± 770 BP. This translates to around 41,000 years ago when the carbon dates are converted to calendar ages.[5] But there were also Neanderthals in parts of Spain around 40,000 years ago, leading the Portuguese scholar João Zilhão to question whether the earliest art at El Castillo was made by modern humans or their Neanderthal cousins,[6] although there is no evidence from anywhere in Europe or further afield that Neanderthals could make such art. The timing of the earliest art, as evidenced by decorated portable objects and on-wall depictions, corresponds with the arrival of biologically and cognitively modern humans into Western Europe around 45,000 years ago, without any traces of such artworks demonstrably associated with Neanderthals anywhere. The new dates that Pike and his colleagues reported for rock art in northern Spain are entirely consistent with this picture.

Dating the art of Chauvet Cave

Around the time of the earliest paintings and stencils in Spain, Chauvet Cave was also decorated with artworks. The site is located 800 km (500 miles) east of El Castillo in the Massif Central of south-central France. Its discovery in 1994 (see Chapter 2) created great excitement, as this massive cave revealed a variety of artistic conventions curiously not falling neatly into any single phase of the Upper Palaeolithic. The art closest to the original entrance of the cave tends to be in red, and it is more sparse than that deeper in the cave, where most of the art is in black [33]. Some red art is also found in the deeper chamber, and here it tends to lie underneath the black art. Are these signs of two phases of artistic activity, or of a structuring of the cave into zones where different activities took place within a single phase? At first, it was thought that there were numerous hints of two phases: clusters of large red dots were combined to form shapes [32], reminiscent of Solutrean or Gravettian art elsewhere, such as two horses at Pech Merle further to the west but still in France [125]. Similarly, at Chauvet Cave yellow pigment was used to paint the heads of small horses, a colour then thought to be typically but not exclusively used during the Solutrean; in addition the belly-lines of mammoths were arched, and aurochs were erroneously thought to have S-shaped horns akin to those of Solutrean caves elsewhere in France. However, ideas about the features of artworks in different phases of the Upper Palaeolithic have changed since then, and in any case other features also pointed to a later dating, as some of the techniques used to

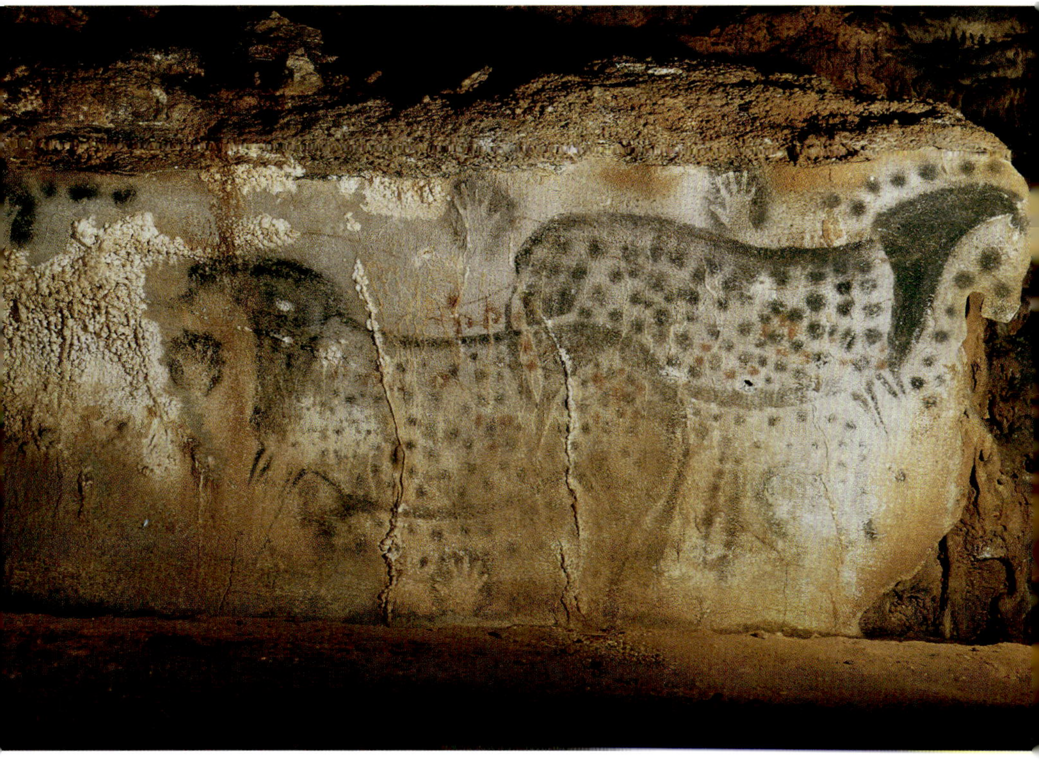

125. The Gravettian spotted horses deep in the cave of Pech Merle, France. A carbon date on the black charcoal pigment from the right-hand horse indicates that it was painted *c.* 28,700 years ago.

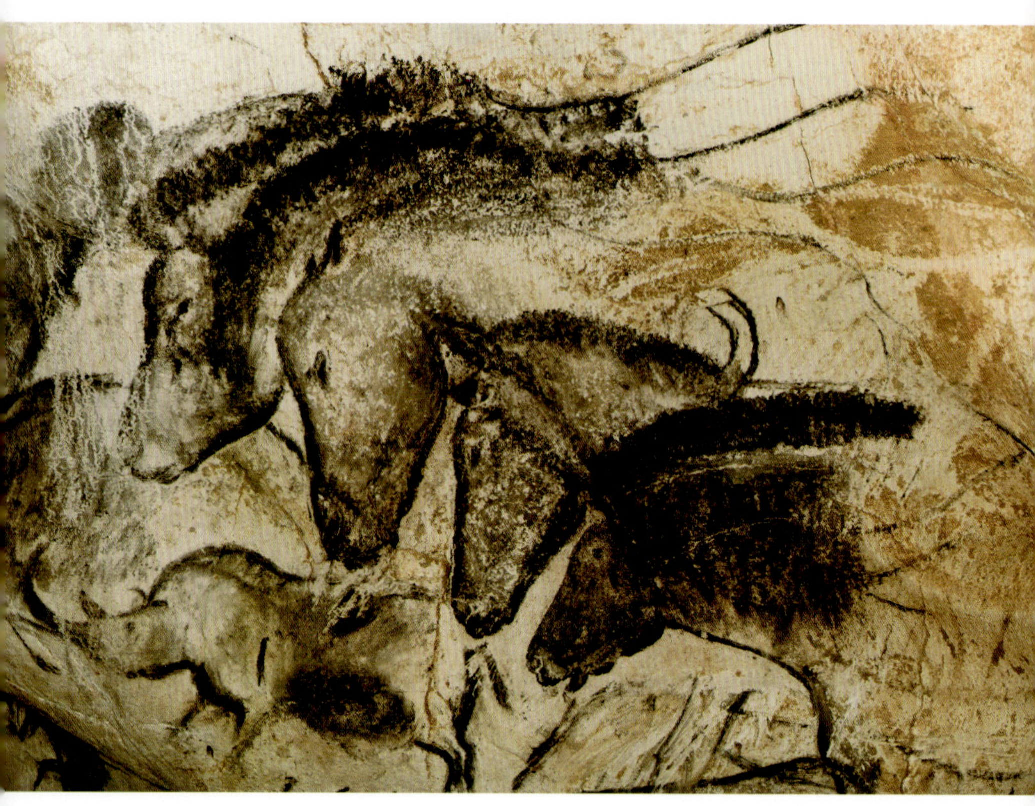

126. (above) Overlapping horses on the Panel of the Horses, Chauvet Cave. Do they represent a herd, or the movement of a single animal? The rock wall was scraped clean, creating a white surface before the horses were painted in black charcoal.

127. (opposite above) Pride of lions, Lion Panel, Chauvet Cave. The rock wall was scraped clean before painting, and then a thin line was scraped immediately around the edge of some lions' heads to more sharply define them.

128. (opposite below) Crash of rhinoceroses, Chauvet Cave. Their varied angles, overlaps that hide parts of more distant animals, and concertinaed horns create a scene with depth.

make the art were thought to have been unknown prior to the Magdalenian, the final phase of the Upper Palaeolithic in France. Examples include a pronounced sense of perspective among the animals depicted, with numerous overlapping outlines giving an impression of herds or movement [126, 127]. Background fauna are partially hidden by those in the foreground, giving a sense of depth to the scene [128]. This effect is accentuated by the decorative technique used: the rock wall was scraped to make a clean white background prior to painting, thereby combining engraving and painting techniques to create a well-defined, pronounced white outline that served to sharply demarcate the animal from what lies around it, further heightening the sense of depth, such as in the Panel of the Horses [126] and parts of the Lion Panel [127].[7] Unusual for Upper Palaeolithic cave art anywhere in Europe is the use of shading, and perhaps even of chiaroscuro, the management of light and dark spaces to create shadows, enabling the artist to further refine a sense of curvature and depth as well as details of the animal's coat.[8]

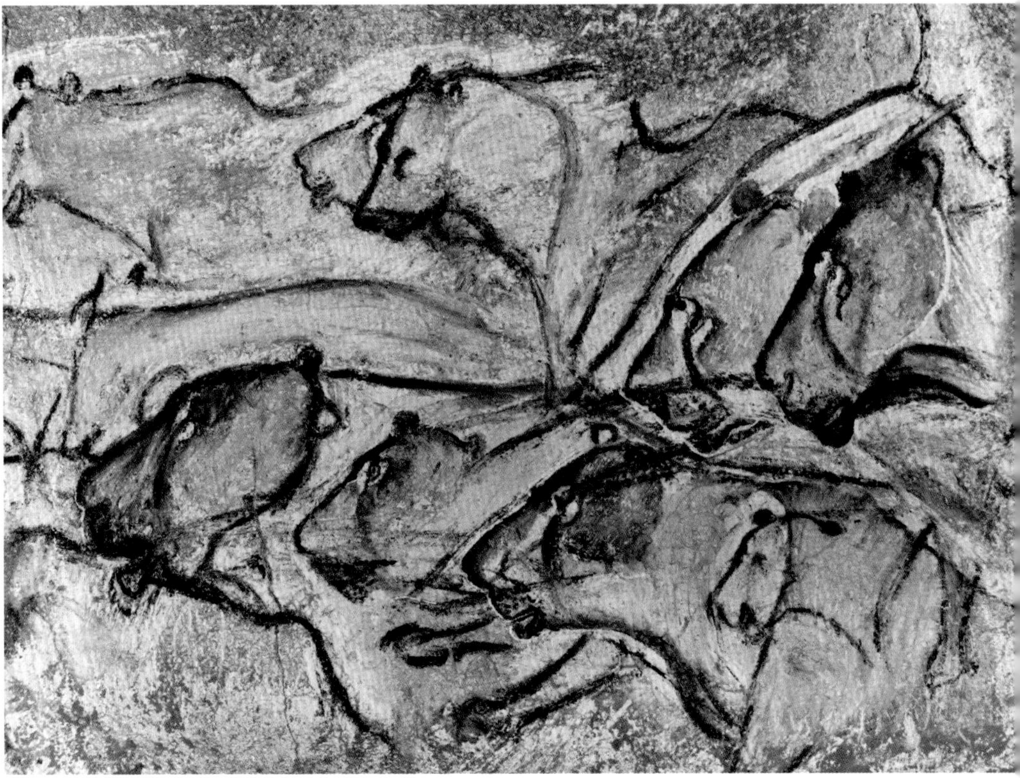

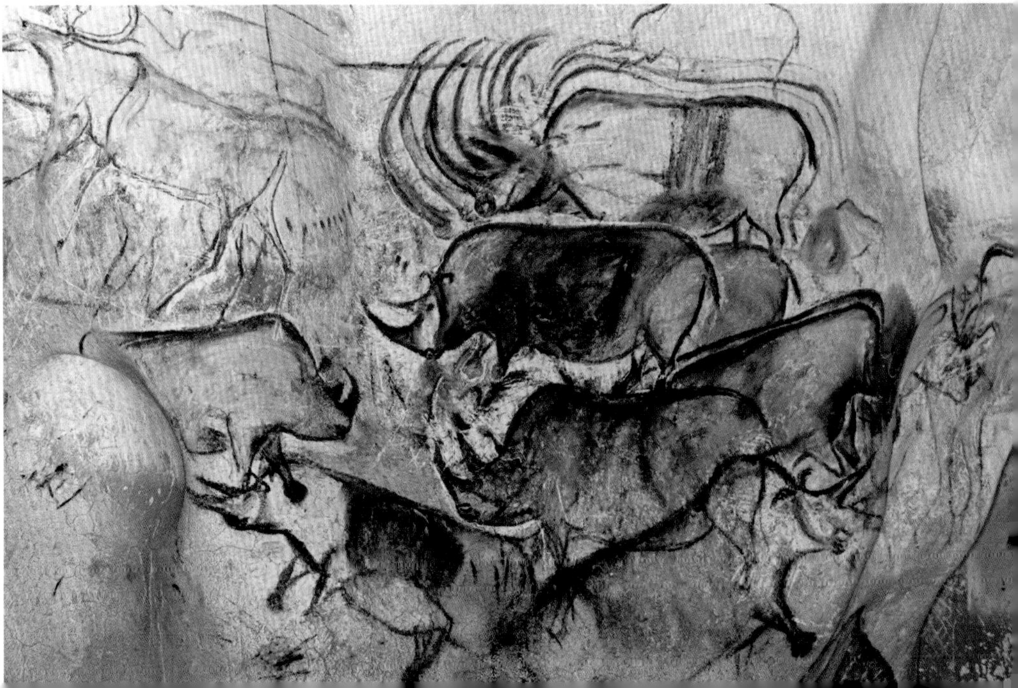

Given the mixed chronological hints offered by the artistic conventions at Chauvet Cave, the art was originally thought to have been made over a long period of time or, more likely, in two phases, the Solutrean and early Magdalenian, because the images employed artistic conventions sometimes found at other Solutrean and Magdalenian sites.

The first four carbon dates obtained for Chauvet Cave's charcoal paintings blew expectations out of the water. This was not Magdalenian art at all, nor was it Solutrean, but something much older, dating to as early as the Aurignacian. Those initial results obtained directly on two painted rhinoceroses and a large bison (one rhinoceros was dated twice) revealed carbon dates of 32,410 ± 720 BP, 30,790 ± 600 BP, 30,940 ± 610 BP and 30,340 ± 570 BP, once calibrated meaning that they had been painted some 36,000 to 35,000 years ago. Three carbon dates obtained on two different torch marks smeared on rock walls revealed ages of 26,980 ± 410 BP, 26,980 ± 420 BP and 26,120 ± 400 BP, calibrating to around 31,000 years ago. The existence of two phases of human presence and on-wall depictions, separated by 4,000 to 5,000 years, was confirmed (during those early years of research at Chauvet Cave, two other, slightly younger carbon dates were obtained suggesting the presence of a third phase, but these were later shown to be a laboratory error).

For nearly twenty years these dates remained the oldest for cave art anywhere in the world, and yet the paintings were not rudimentary, as many argued should have been expected of the oldest art, but instead arguably the most precise, delicate and aesthetically composed artworks known from any cave or rockshelter. For some cave art specialists this simply could not be so, because more than 100 years of Spanish, French and other European Upper Palaeolithic cave art research had revealed what was surely a secure sequence of artistic conventions, with only Solutrean and Magdalenian art achieving the kinds of artistic heights demonstrated by the carbon-dated motifs from Chauvet Cave. The Chauvet Cave carbon dates were either wrong, or they may have correctly dated the charcoal on the walls but not the art made by it, or they would bring doubt and chaos into what we thought we knew about the evolution of art styles in Europe. For them, these should have progressed through time from simple to increasingly more complex artworks (a symptom of thinking of European art as the earliest in the world, as if they tracked the progress of humanity's artistic evolution). And there was a further problem. Large pieces of charcoal lay on the floor in a number of

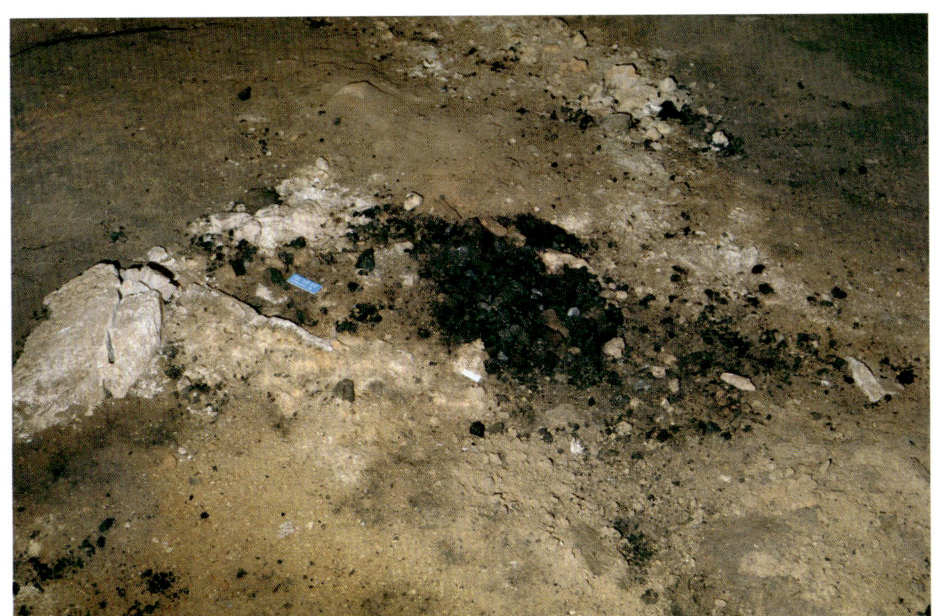

chambers at Chauvet Cave, such as the Megaloceros Gallery [129]. In the words of Jean Clottes,[9] Director of Chauvet Cave's scientific investigations at the time, charcoal lay 'in great quantity and in an excellent state of conservation', and that charcoal piled up on the cave's floor gave a carbon date of 29,000 + 410 BP, 'very close to that obtained for the paintings' from the early phase. How do we know that people during the second, later phase didn't pick up that older charcoal to make paintings, so that what has been dated to 36,000–35,000 years ago was in effect painted 31,000 years ago during the later phase? The question is perhaps academic, because either way the art is much older than anything else previously known, but in archaeology we aim to understand as much about the past as we can, and with as much certainty as possible. Accurate dating is fundamental to our ability to write a reliable history of the past and of the art.

Let us not forget that the majority of the black paintings, and arguably all of the most complex and magnificent painted friezes, occur in the deeper sections and recesses of Chauvet Cave. People could not have made those paintings unless they carried torches when traversing the pitch-dark cave. The implication is that during the early phase, as with the later one, people would have brought with them ample sources of light, presumably producing charcoal in the process. It is also significant that people did not camp in the cave itself; the dump or cache of charcoal from the early phase was associated with activities other than campfires, the most logical explanation being the production of charcoal for artworks given their abundance on the walls. We can thus assume that 36,000 to 35,000 years ago, people had contemporaneous charcoal with them when they painted the apparently oldest, black friezes. Artworks could theoretically have been made using legacy or ancient charcoal from the cave floor, but a simpler and more plausible scenario is that the first entry into the cave was in order to paint, so that the floor debris and art date from the same time. It seems implausible that people would have ventured into the deepest recesses of the cave around 36,000 years ago simply to dump large amounts of charcoal near the walls without using that charcoal at all. Nor does it make sense that a few thousand years later, accomplished artists ventured into those deep recesses, miraculously found charcoal on the ground and so decided to paint artistic masterworks (another alternative, that a large amount of old charcoal was brought into the cave at the time of the painting, also does not make sense, as artists would have had to have access to substantial caches of clean 5,000-year-old charcoal – and all of an identical age that they then piled into different parts of the cave).

The argument for the art being of a younger age than revealed by the carbon dates has been championed by Paul Pettitt and Paul Bahn, who make a number of apt observations from the evidence available to them.[10] Firstly, they agree with the Chauvet Cave research team that there appear to be two phases of art, with the earlier phase represented by less complex imagery, including abstract marks and animal designs depicted in simple outline, among these red and black bears closer to the entrance chamber. All of the more detailed, black imagery, such as the lions found deeper in the cave, they argue, dates to a later phase.

Secondly, the cave walls contain extensive evidence of cave bear claw marks, scratches made when those animals lived in the cave. But, they pointed out, such claw marks only occur over bare wall and over what appeared to be the older art, such as red abstract and outlined animal motifs, never above the more complex motifs of the more impressive black friezes that have been dated to 36,000–35,000 years ago [33]. As cave bears became extinct across the region some 26,000 years ago, so it was then thought, the latter art must be more recent than this, for it would be unreasonable to think that cave bears chose to avoid scratching the most beautiful and detailed art galleries of the cave, but not the more simple designs, an argument one would have to make to claim that the more complex panels were older than 26,000 years old and thus contemporaneous with cave bears. They conclude, therefore, that all of Chauvet Cave's most complex compositions, mostly in black, are Gravettian, Solutrean or early Magdalenian in age, in other words, dating to sometime between 26,000 and 17,000 years ago, a conclusion supported by the fact that Upper Palaeolithic paintings exhibiting the kinds of anatomical detail, sense of depth and movement found at Chauvet Cave are elsewhere exclusively found during the Solutrean and Magdalenian.

There are, however, considerably more scientific results from Chauvet Cave than those cited by Pettitt and Bahn, although many of these were not available to them at the time.[11] Over the past fifteen years, first under the directorship of Jean Clottes and then, upon his retirement in 2002, Jean-Michel Geneste, the Chauvet Cave research team has obtained 261 carbon dates directly on the art, on charcoal torch marks on the walls and speleothems [130], on pieces of charcoal lying on the floor, and on cave bear and other animal bones [131]. Additionally, there are now luminescence ages on hearths, U-series dates on speleothems, some of which contain charcoal torch marks that have also been independently carbon dated, and cosmogenic dates on rock to

130. Charcoal torch marks on the wall in the Candle Gallery, Chauvet Cave. Here the torch marks have been carbon dated to 31,000–29,000 years ago.

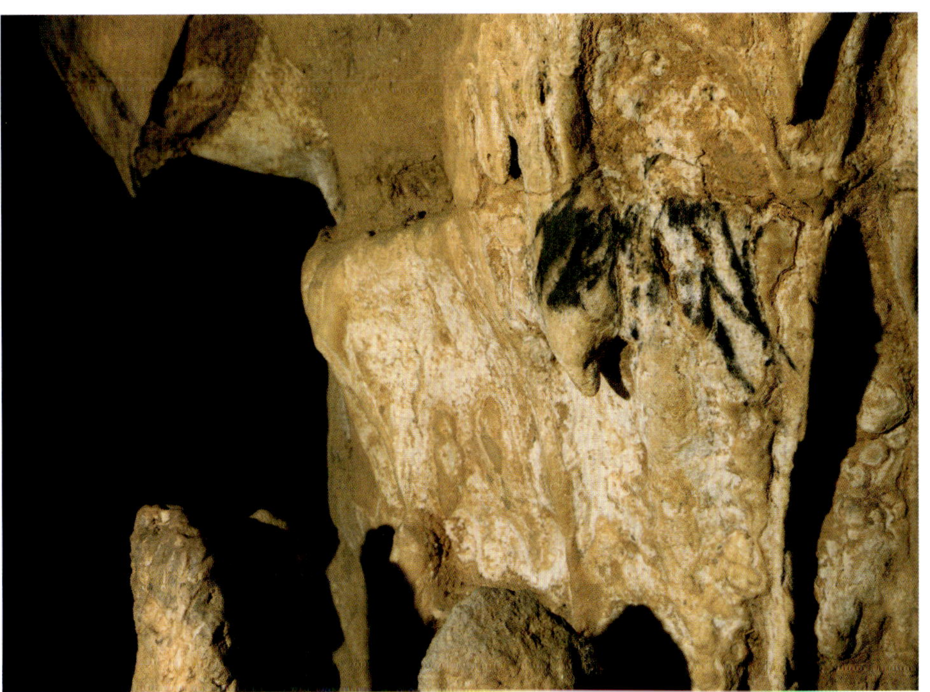

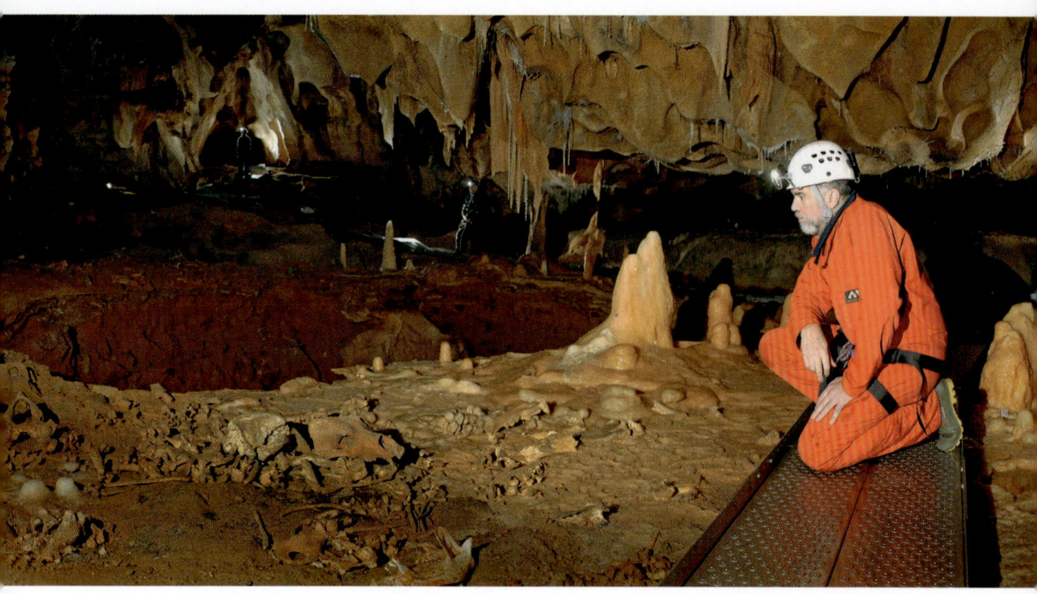

131. Geomorphologist Jean-Jacques Delannoy examines cave bear bones on the floor of the Hillaire Chamber, Chauvet Cave.

determine when the cave entrance collapsed (see Chapter 3 for explanation of some of these methods). The totality of the dates associated with the actions of people fall into two age groups, conclusively indicating that the cave was frequented during two distinctive phases, one dating between 37,000 and 33,500 years ago, the other between 31,000 and 29,000 years ago.

Three further comments can be made regarding the new set of results. Firstly, the only known Upper Palaeolithic entrance to the cave began to close 29,000 years ago, when a series of cliff collapses dumped tonnes of rock over it, completely sealing the cave to human entry by 21,500 ± 1,000 years ago.[12] Any art within the cave must therefore be greater than c. 21,000 years old. Secondly, twenty-one animal images and fourteen charcoal torch marks have now been carbon-dated, rather than the eight carbon dates from six images available to Pettitt and Bahn at the time of their critiques. There are now also 160 carbon dates on charcoal pieces from the ground surface, adding considerably to our understanding of temporal relationships between on-wall artworks and dumped or cached charcoal on the ground. These results consistently reveal ages of 37,000 to 33,500 years ago for the dated artworks, including the complex paintings of the Lion Panel; only four carbon dates obtained directly from three animal images are from the later phase dated between 31,000 and 29,000 years ago. Two clear phases of activity are also evident from the pieces of charcoal on the ground, corresponding in age with the two phases of art and torch marks evident from the on-wall carbon dates. Those fragments of charcoal closest to complex artworks, such as the brushed horse in the Megaloceros Gallery [132], date to the first phase, as does the brushed horse itself. Thirdly, cave bear claw and rub marks are not only found on the simpler, usually more linear artworks nearer the entrance chamber, but also over numerous black paintings from the entrance to the depths of the cave. We also now know that cave bears were present at Chauvet Cave from 48,000 years ago until they became extinct 33,000 years ago, not 26,000 years ago as previously thought. This latter conclusion can now be made following the carbon dating of thirty-three cave bear bones lying on the surface across the cave. And it is comforting to note that none of the carbon dates now available for on-wall images, charcoal on the ground or the bones of large animals are younger than the age of the final collapse of the cliff that closed the only known Upper Palaeolithic entrance of the cave some 21,000 years ago, giving extra confidence to the overall dating of human and animal entries, and to the science involved. All in all, a now much expanded database of carbon dates continues to be consistent with the initial results, that at Chauvet Cave the magnificent

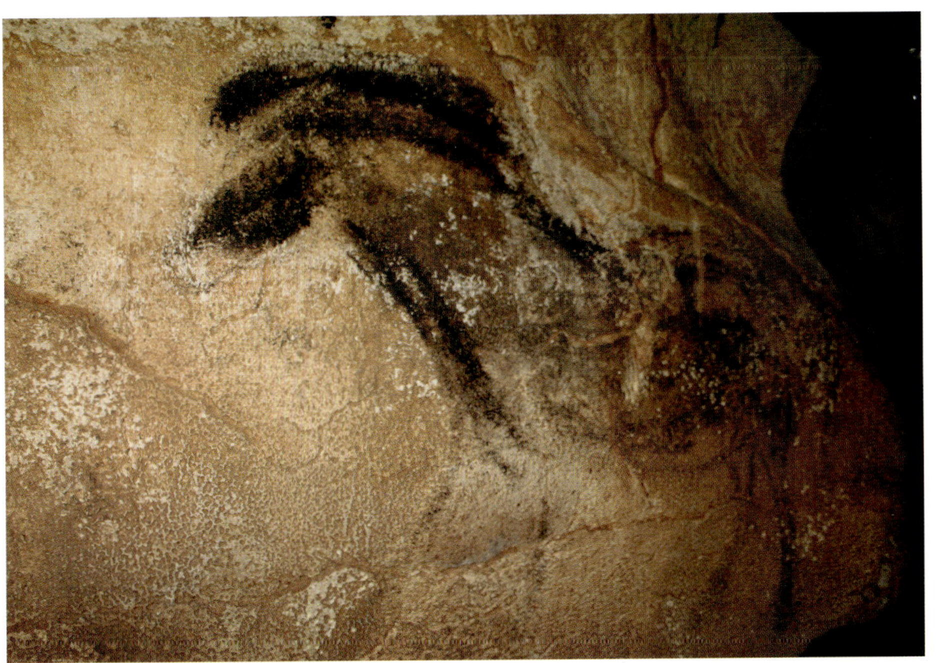

galleries of predominantly black zoomorphic paintings, including friezes of rhinoceroses and lions showing movement and shaded details in their coats and faces, are indeed of the Aurignacian, dating back to between 37,000 and 33,500 years ago.

Was the art meant to be seen?

For over a century, Western Europe's Ice Age art has stood among the world's greatest artistic works. 'The Sistine Chapel of Prehistory' is how the Abbé Henri Breuil, France's foremost prehistorian of the time, labelled Lascaux in the wake of its discovery. Despite its deep underground setting and prehistoric context, Upper Palaeolithic cave art has come to be known as a refined achievement, albeit one of great age. Yet it remains as much an intriguing curio of ancient times as an exemplar of fine art.

Unlike the works of the Renaissance, for example, Europe's Palaeolithic images raise an unusual question for a visual art: were they meant to be seen at all? This may at first appear to be a strange question, for what makes an image able to be appreciated, what makes it a work of visual communication and aesthetic appeal, is its ability to be seen. Yet there is more to visual art than its appreciation in public display, be it on canvas, on a rock surface, or as a portable object.

We have come to know the Ice Age art of Europe for its magnificent galleries of painted bison, reindeer, woolly mammoths and other such creatures of ancient times. Sometimes these animals are painted in isolation, such as the red cave bear near the entrance of Chauvet Cave. At other times there are entire pantheons of creatures, as if marching in unison in a common direction, swimming across a body of water [133] or confronting

133. The 'swimming' stags of Lascaux.

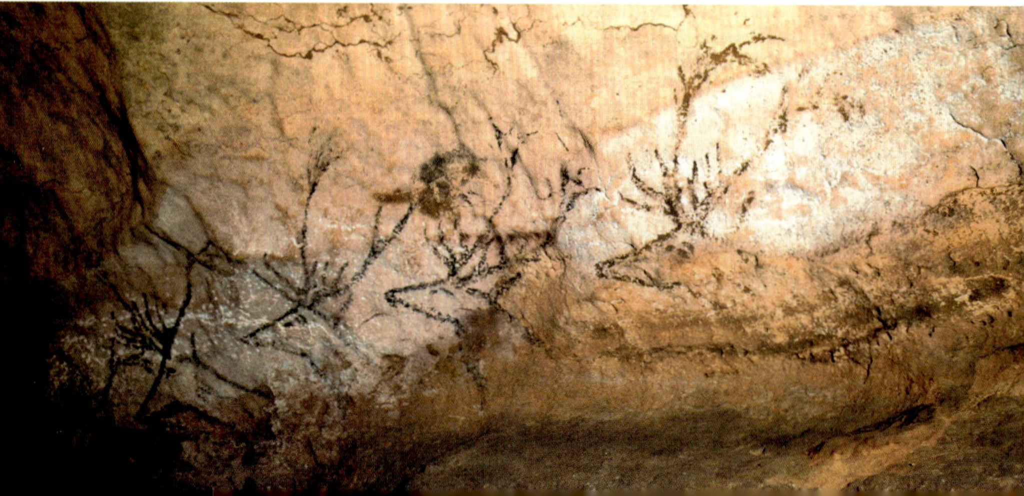

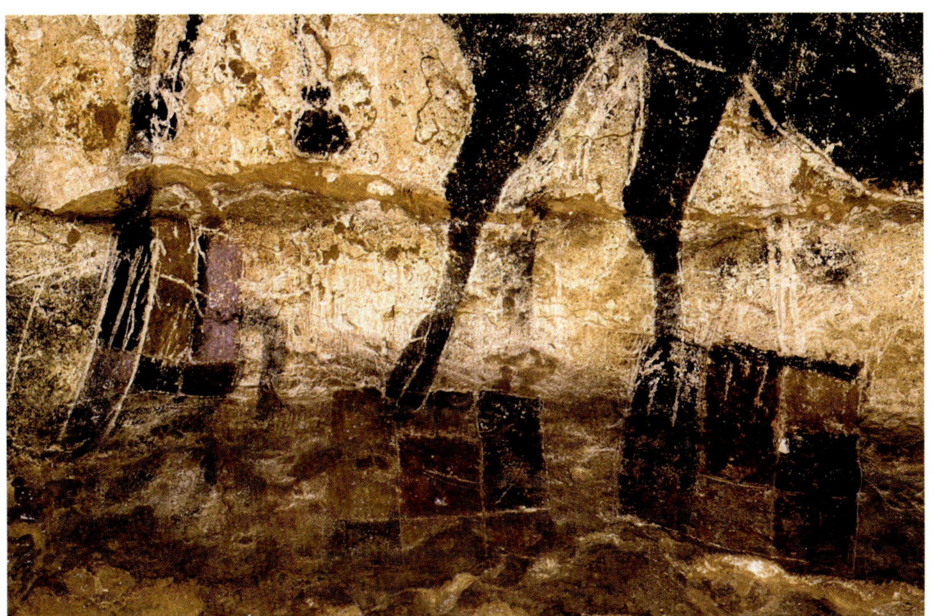

134. The curious, multicoloured 'blazons' beneath the large cow's hooves, Lascaux.

each other in opposing herds. There are abstract signs also, such as P-shaped claviforms that are largely restricted to the contiguous region from Cantabrian Spain eastwards to the Pyrenees, Dordogne and Ariège regions of France, suggesting that they may have been the exclusive cultural expression of a network of interacting groups. Claviforms date largely to the Magdalenian and are only found on cave walls, never on mobiliary art.[13] The stylized bird-shaped aviforms [149] and the heart-shaped cordiforms are rarer and even more geographically restricted. Hut-shaped tectiforms are more restricted again, occurring mostly in the Dordogne region of southwestern France, where they appear to have been made over more than 10,000 years from the Gravettian to the Magdalenian. At Lascaux there are beautiful rectilinear patchwork patterns painted under the hooves of a large cow [134]. Their compartmentalization in colour fields of yellow, grey, purple and red catches the eye like a work of more modern art, a Palaeolithic abstract expressionism in the mould of Mark Rothko, Barnett Newman or Theo van Doesburg perhaps. What they might mean is largely conjectural, although the fact that they are so closely associated with the painted cow indicates a worldly connection. Working with a team of chemists and archaeologists, Emilie Chalmin, herself a chemist at the Université de Savoie Mont Blanc in the French Alps, has worked out that the patchwork paintings were prepared to attain carefully prescribed colour palettes. Furthermore, the multicoloured 'blazons' associated with this one scene contain in their patches the full range of colours used in all the paintings at Lascaux, as if in these abstract forms the entire plethora of artworks was somehow connected: the ensemble of paintings are united in this one spot, perhaps meaning that all the artists and what they could paint, or the artists' varied social affiliations, were here unified. Are we seeing here an ordering of Upper Palaeolithic artworks as imagery with social associations, perhaps special animals that people could relate to, their coloured patchwork designs symbols of those associations? We cannot be certain, but such connections between the colours, the fauna and the abstract signs are suggestive.

Aggregation sites

The social significance of Europe's Ice Age art received a new twist in 1980 when Meg Conkey of the University of California, Berkeley, added another important clue as to the use of the caves.[14] She knew that the entrances of some caves contain abundant evidence of human presence including food remains, as plainly evident in the huge numbers of animal bones left behind after meals. At Altamira and many other large caves, there is also ample evidence of artistic activity nearby. At La Garma, there are tens or even hundreds of thousands of animal bones near the cave entrance of Magdalenian times [135], but deeper

135. At La Garma in northern Spain, extraordinary numbers of broken animal bones 'litter' the floor near the cave's Upper Palaeolithic entrance. Should they be seen as a Magdalenian rubbish heap, or as a cache of bones waiting to be used?

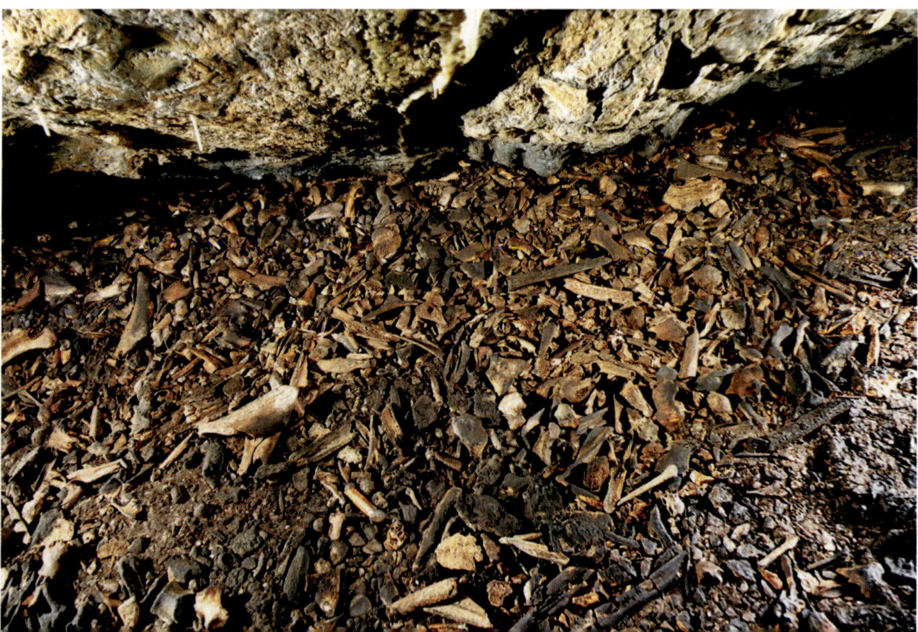

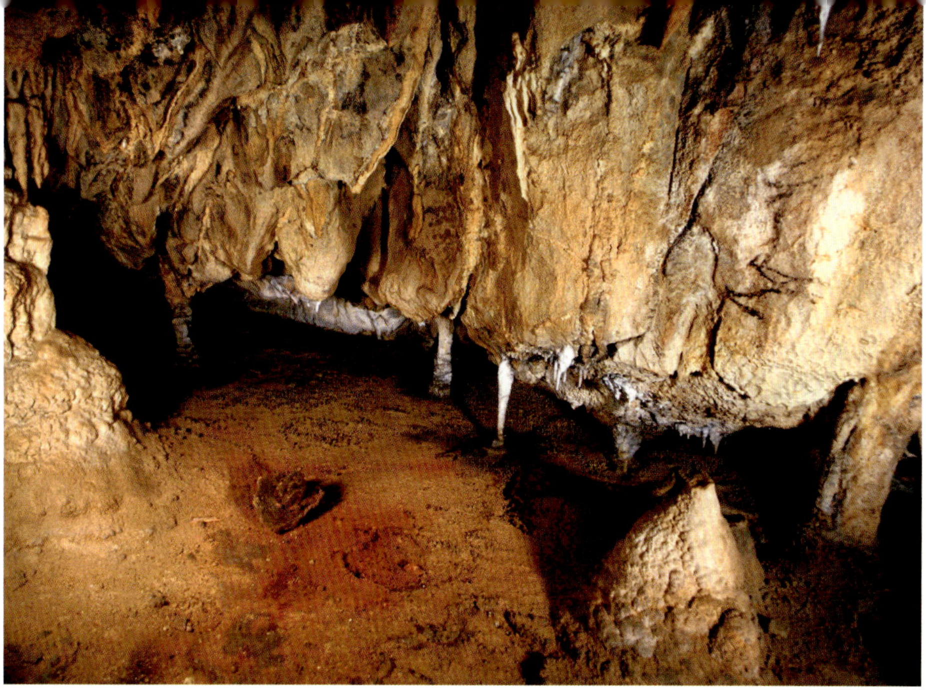

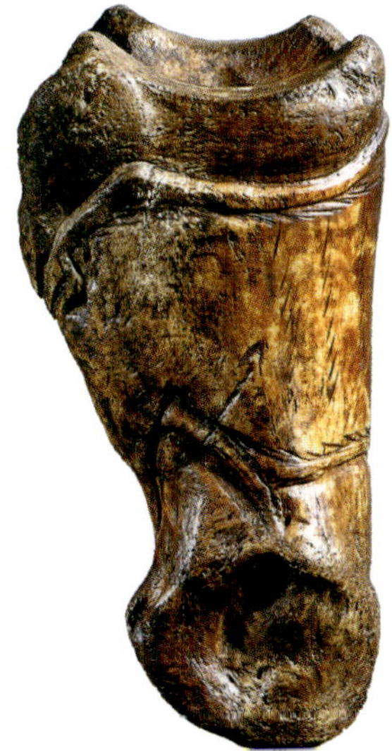
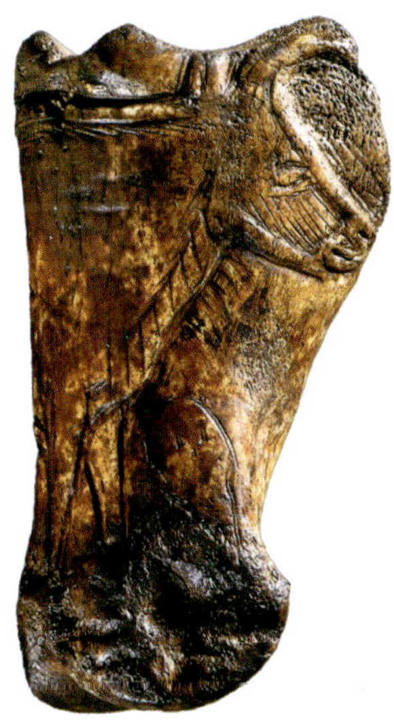

137. Phalange of an aurochs (extinct wild cattle, *Bos primigenius*) from La Garma, intricately carved with an aurochs bull during Magdalenian times. A human-shape and arrow design are also Incised on the bone.

136. Red ochre processing floor deep in the cave of La Garma, northern Spain.

inside there is no such evidence for the mass consumption of animals, although there we find the results of much artistic activity, including the manufacture of red pigment [136] and carvings of intricate naturalistic faunal designs on animal bones [137]. Conkey hypothesized that such culturally rich locations were where people had assembled from more distant lands, aggregation sites that

were also places of special significance where social relationships
could be renewed and nurtured, where mates could be found,
objects exchanged, ideas passed on, and social tensions resolved,
temporarily patched or aggravated. These were sites not only
of individual and group activity, but also of social performance.
Such sites by necessity were found in locales with favourable
ecologies where food could be obtained in sufficient quantities
to sustain large social gatherings. Because of this they tended
to be located in areas of seasonal plenty. The art was a form
of social marking: sometimes emblems of cultural style to be
broadly seen, sometimes by-products of more secretive rituals
by which societies made sense of the life-forces that animated
their world.

Cougnac

This connection of place-marking, public or restricted viewing
and social performance takes a curious turn in the Dordogne
region of southwestern France and in the deep caves of the
Pyrenees. At Cougnac near the village of Gourdon in the
Dordogne – a small cave but for many one of the most beautiful
in Europe, discovered in 1952 and opened to the public just two
years later – hundreds of red and black artworks decorate three
subterranean chambers.[15]

The cave extends some 200 m (650 ft) into the rock [138].
The entrance begins as a shallow overhang that leads into a long
corridor devoid of art, labelled the Main Gallery. Soon the Lower
Gallery splits off to the right. Back along the Main Gallery, the
passage divides into two chambers in a region of total darkness.

138. Plan of the cave of Cougnac,
France.

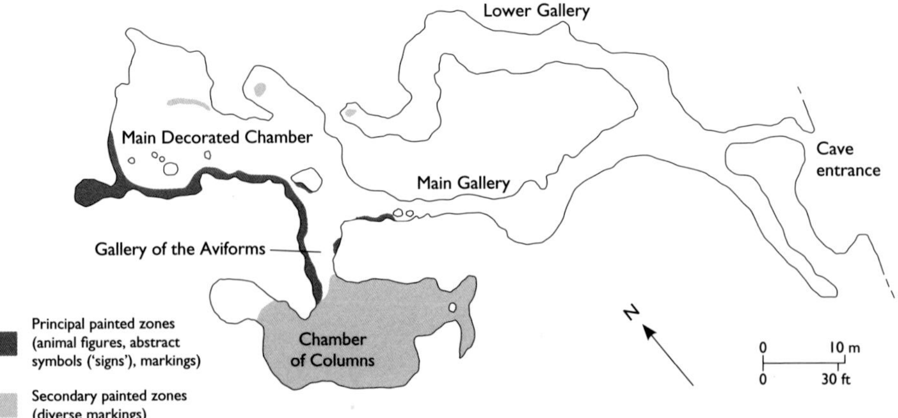

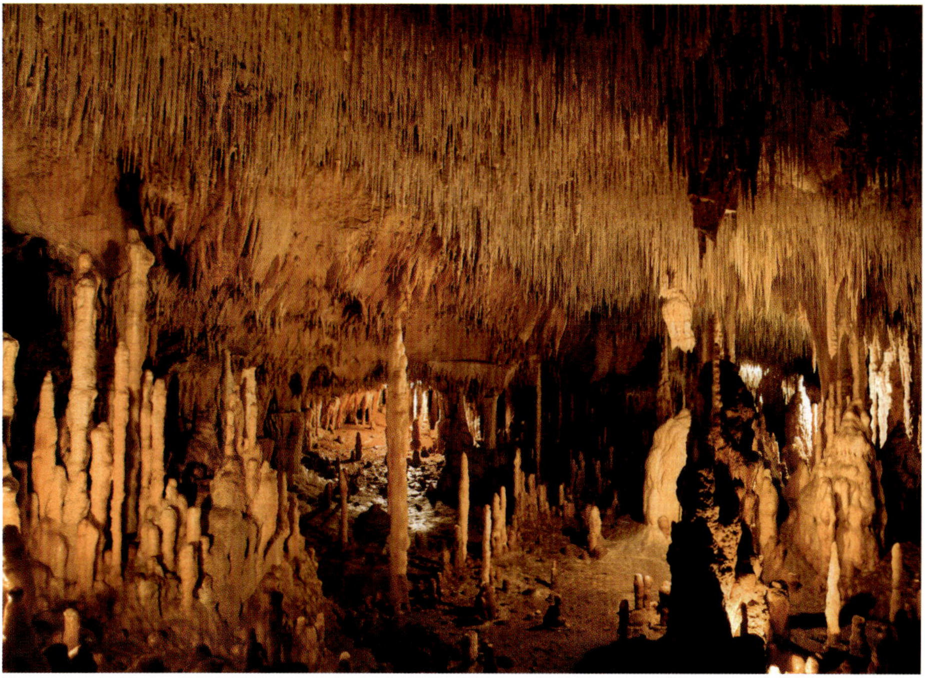

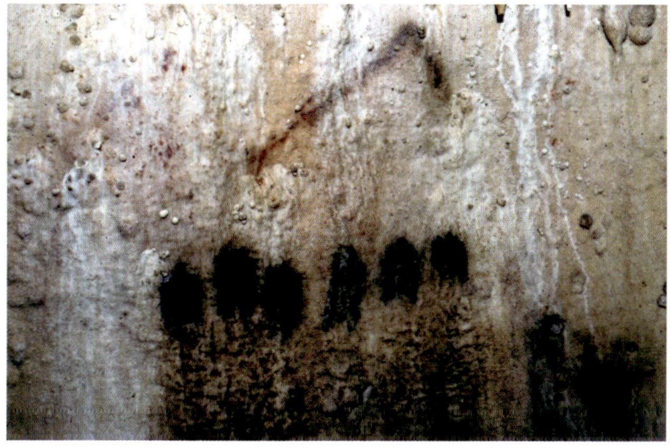

139. The cave of Cougnac opens up into a number of chambers and passageways richly ornate with 'forests' of speleothems.

Here the Main Decorated Chamber lies more or less straight ahead, the Chamber of Columns separating out to the left [139]. It is at this junction, where the corridor splits, that the first artworks are found, two red dots some 60 m (200 ft) from the cave's entrance. A few metres further on, cave bear scratch marks appear on the wall, a red ochre stain covering some of the scratches; then some black finger marks and abstract designs [140].

140. Red abstract linear design above black finger marks on the wall at the entrance of the Main Decorated Chamber, Cougnac. The finger marks consist of the three middle fingers of the same left hand, pressed twice side-by-side. The same three fingers were pressed another four times nearby.

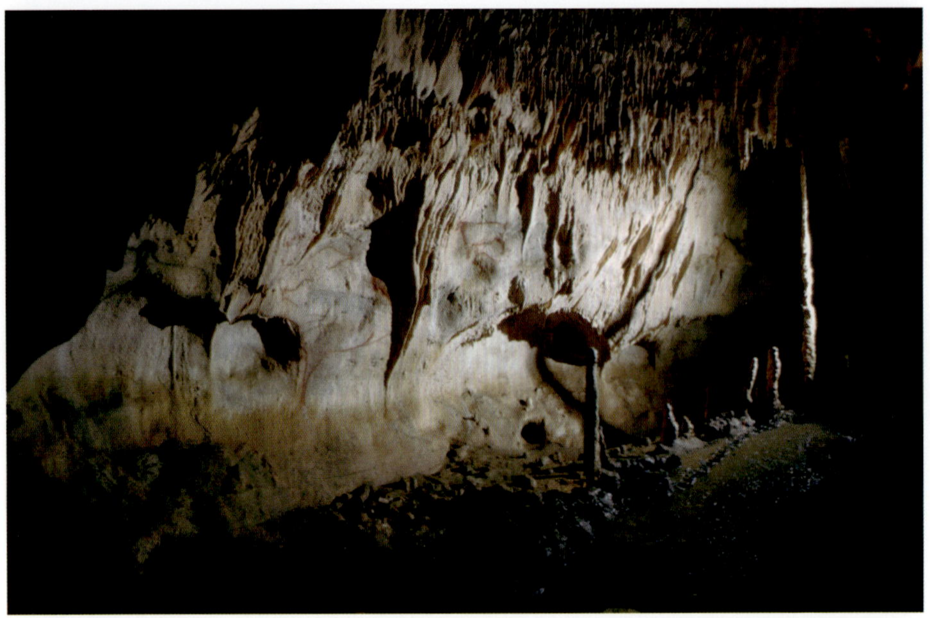

141. Long painted frieze along the left-hand wall of the Main Decorated Chamber, Cougnac.

142. Painted black lines define two ghostly shapes, their outlines guided by natural concretions on the left-hand wall shortly past the entrance of the Main Decorated Chamber, Cougnac. The shape of a third head is painted in black nearby.

Then the corridor opens up into the Main Decorated Chamber [141]. In the words of Michel Lorblanchet, the archaeologist who has studied the cave in greatest detail, this is the 'coeur du sanctuaire', the heart of the sanctuary. Here are found some forty paintings of animals plus many abstract designs. The animal images are often large and easy to see, and many make use of the natural configuration of the wall to help shape them. There are also the upper parts of three ghostly human figures, parts painted in black, two of which have their torsos and legs shaped by natural concretions on the wall [142]. Not far away is a black stag and, slightly further along, the wall is covered with red ochre. Numerous rock shawls and stalactites were also intentionally broken during the Ice Age, and many of these breaks are covered in red ochre stains. A cache of red ochre was found at floor level near the entrance of the chamber. During Upper Palaeolithic times, people had repeatedly dipped the palms of their hands into the wet ochre and rubbed them onto the walls of the chamber [143]. A similar ritual had also taken place with black pigment, except that only the fingers were covered with black and thence pressed or rubbed onto the walls. The sizes of those finger markings indicate that adults were responsible for them. Limited numbers of animal bones on the ground, some with cut marks, suggest limited consumption of meat over periods totalling a few days at the most; food

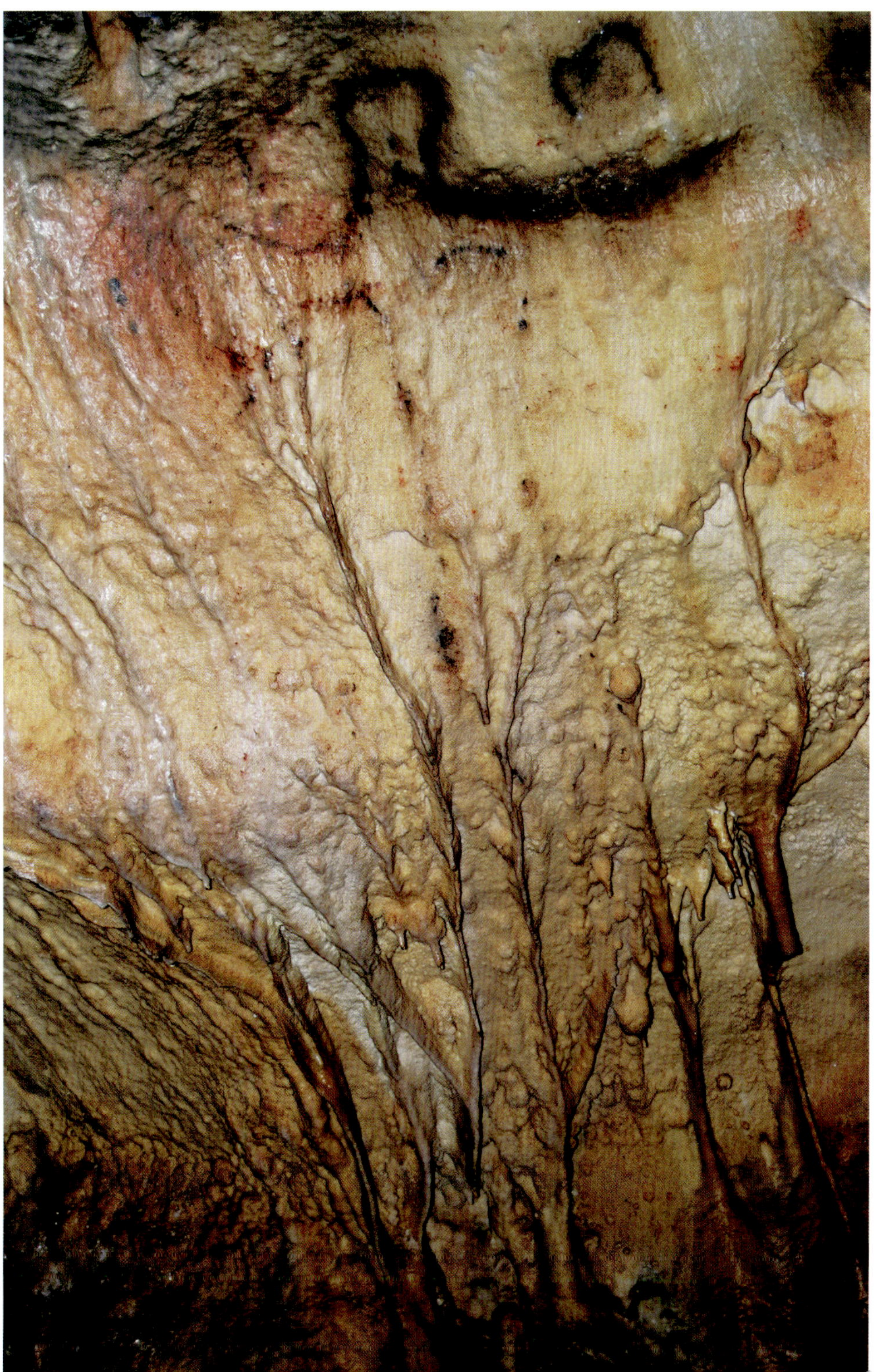

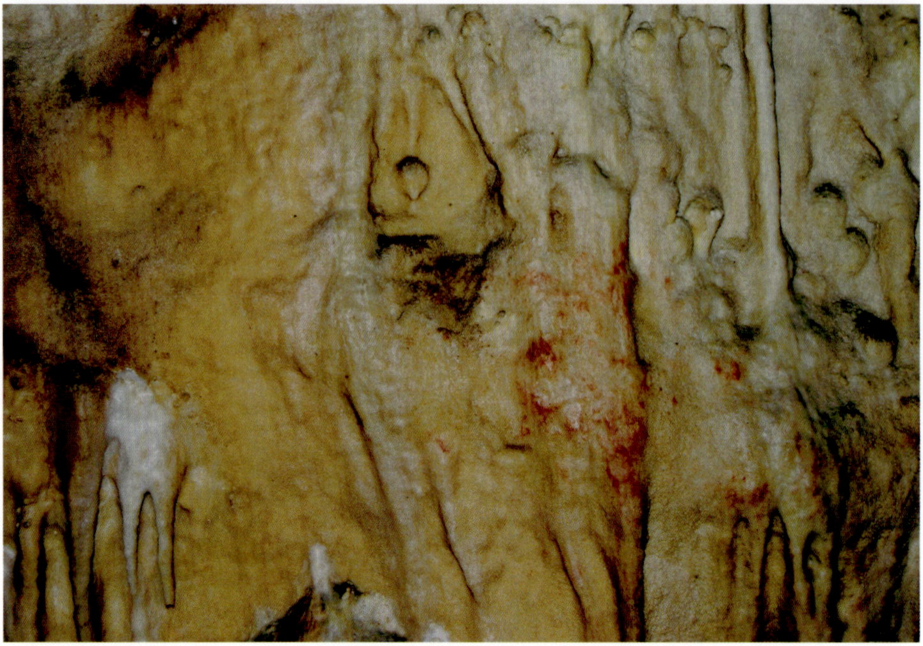

143. (above) Red marks at
Cougnac made by rubbing the
palms of hands dipped in wet
ochre onto the wall. The marks
shown here occur about one
metre further into the Main
Decorated Chamber than the two
ghostly figures shown in ill. 142.

144. (right) Lamp used to burn
the oil produced from animal fat.
It was found at the entrance of
the Main Decorated Chamber,
Cougnac.

145. (opposite above) Female
(above) and male (below) ibexes
to the right of a small ibex,
the first three in the panel of
ibexes along the Main Decorated
Chamber, Cougnac.

146. (opposite below) Large ibex,
the furthest along the panel of
ibexes in the Main Decorated
Chamber, Cougnac. Viewed from
the opposite side of the chamber,
on each side it is framed by a
dripstone column covered with
red ochre.

consumption had not been a major activity inside the cave. On the
ground, a stone lamp was found near the entrance, revealing how
the dark Main Decorated Chamber had been artificially lit [144].

On the flattest sections of the wall, along the southern side of
the Main Decorated Chamber, there are close to thirty exquisite
paintings of ibexes, elks and woolly mammoths along with many
abstract marks. Each species is found in its own section of the wall,
separated from the others as if different parts of the cave belonged
to individual animals. Closest to the entrance of the chamber are
the elks [148], then, progressing 3 or 4 m (10 to 13 ft) along the
wall, come the ibexes [145, 146], and another 6 m (20 ft) after
the last ibex the woolly mammoths appear. More pigment stains
and finger marks occur low down on the wall, and now we find

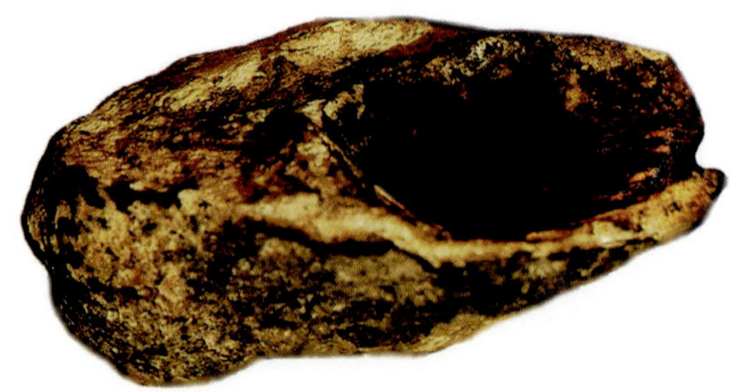

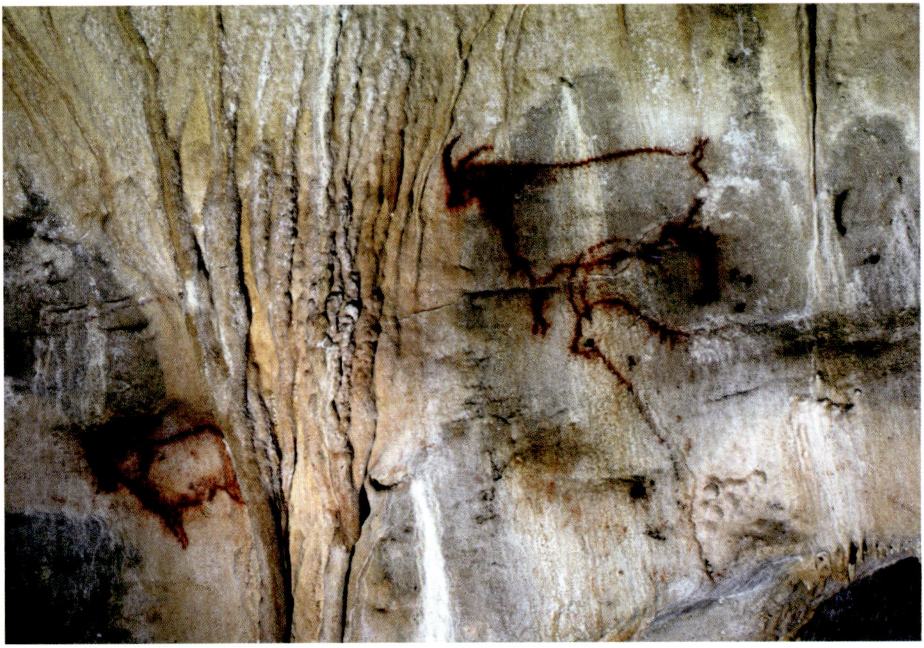

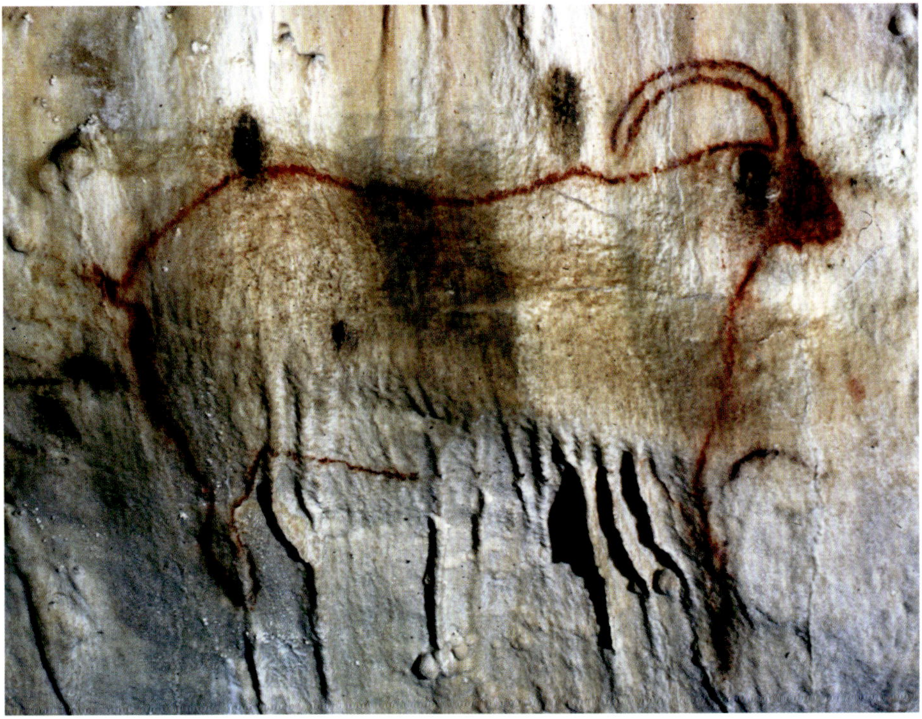

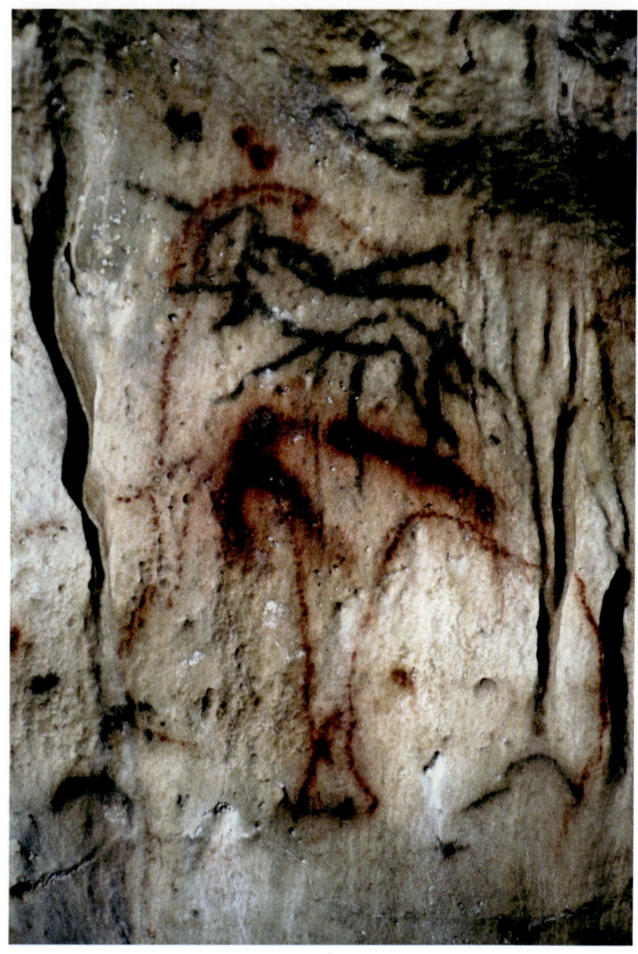

broken concretions of rock once attached to the ceiling or walls. Originally those concretions would have echoed a ringing sound when tapped, signalling that their breakage probably took place in the making of sound. One large male ibex [146] was carefully positioned on the wall; when viewed from the opposite side of the chamber it becomes neatly framed by a dripstone column on either side, each one covered with red ochre. But other concretions once stood here, having been removed in antiquity, presumably so as to improve the view of the ibex. At ground level in the vicinity of the viewing point large numbers of thin calcite concretions were broken, snapped pieces littering the chamber floor. Up on the wall and hanging down from the ceiling, shawls and stalactites are scarred with impact marks, having been hit, it is thought, to make sound. Here are distinctive signs of performance and restricted group viewings of the art that seem to have involved the production of sound as rocky shawls and stalactites were tapped in an echoing underground cavity, creating a form of prehistoric chamber music.

The woolly mammoth panel also holds special interest, for here, among the lines of a giant animal, is a painted anthropomorph – a person, or at least something of human shape – with seven spears sticking into his or her body [147]. Two other such speared anthropomorphs are painted elsewhere in the cave, one among the elks [148]. These paintings have long been known as the 'wounded men', but in truth we have no idea whether they were men or women, as no breasts, genitalia or any other features that could identify their sex are shown. A stylized depiction of ibex horns occurs nearby, immediately behind the mammoths and speared anthropomorph. All around this complex scene are fourteen black and one red paired finger markings, and eleven black dots. More finger markings and dots surround the panel slightly further out.

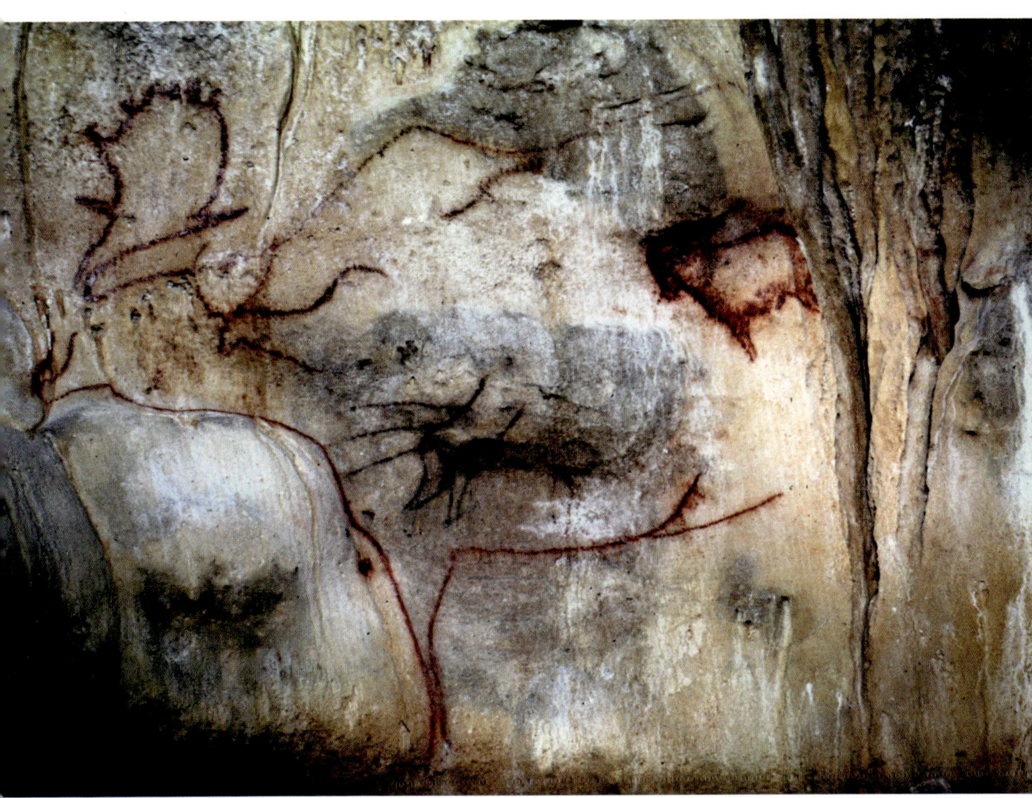

148. Speared anthropomorph in the panel of elks, before the panel of ibexes, Main Decorated Chamber, Cougnac.

At the foot of the painted frieze that features the elks, the ground shows signs of much human activity such as the preparation of paint, and treadage and crushing of objects such as small patches of ochre dating back to Upper Palaeolithic times. We know that this treadage took place so far back in time because the ground has a thin lamina of redeposited calcium carbonate, and a few metres away on the floor closer to the entrance a reindeer bone is coated with a similar layer of calcium carbonate. The coated bone was carbon dated to Magdalenian times, so anything below that mineral crust must date to the Magdalenian or older.

The cave of Cougnac contains other decorated chambers, such as the Gallery of the Aviforms that connects the Main Decorated Chamber with the Chamber of Columns. Here are found four sets of red abstract motifs covered by a thin layer of calcite, on top of which are ten black aviform and six other abstract designs [149]. The separation of the two colours by naturally redeposited calcite indicates that some time elapsed between the two phases of painting. What the aviforms represent is uncertain, but the fact that they are repeatedly found both at Cougnac and in other Upper Palaeolithic caves of Western Europe indicates that they were a socially recognized motif of the time. The Chamber of Columns nearby is richly covered with

149. Abstract black aviform designs, Gallery of the Aviforms, Cougnac.

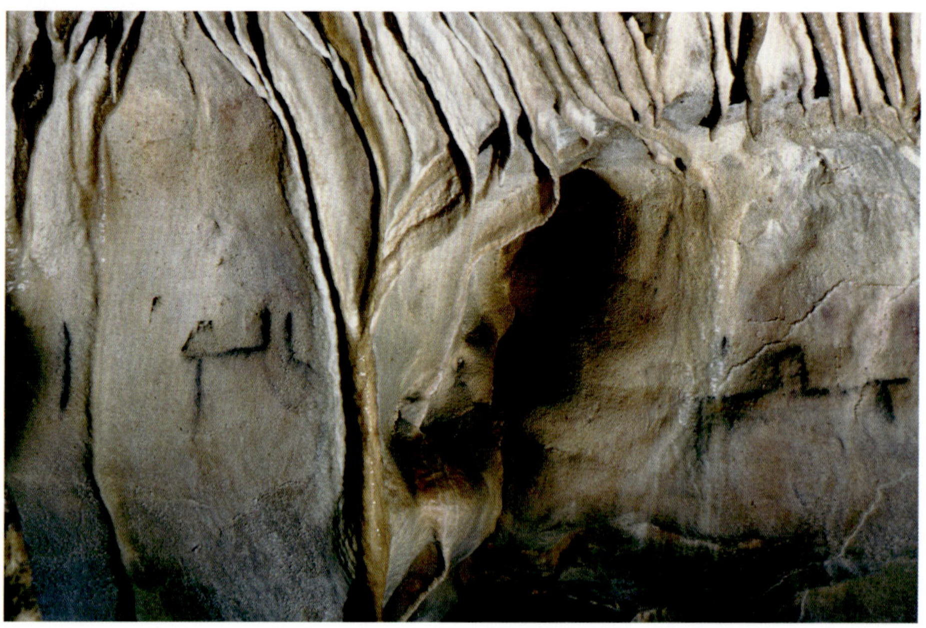

stalagmites, stalactites and other concretions. The walls and many
of these concretions have been marked with red and black marks,
but here there is a total absence of animal and human figures.
A total of 205 abstract marks are found in this chamber, 116
of which are red and 89 black. Here at least eleven concretions
were broken or otherwise damaged by people.

It is clear from the paintings and other traces of human
activity that Cougnac was alive not only with the actions of
people, but with the presence of animals on and in the rock.
Human engagements in the deep, dark space of the cave are
intriguing: here are found animals that take shape along rock walls
in a combination of natural concretions and painted red or black
lines. At the entrance of chambers, palms of hands were dipped
in red ochre and fingers smeared with black pigment, and then
pressed against rock walls to leave distinctive marks. Animals
were neatly arranged along rock walls, their viewing intentionally
and carefully choreographed. Depictions were made of repeatedly
speared humans or human-like creatures, and rocky concretions
were tapped to make a ringing sound, it appears. This is the
stuff of rituals that simultaneously separated and bridged the
world of human society outside and the hidden nebulous world
inside. Those rituals gave sense to both worlds by connecting
them through composed human actions. At Cougnac only some
members of society appear to have participated in the rituals, for
there are no signs of children, of those too young to have been
initiated into the deeper secrets of the inner world. The art was
not just to be seen by anyone. It formed part of an inner sanctum
of knowledge, of an inner life, one that needed to be performed.

Some of the art at Cougnac dates back to about 28,000 years
ago; other artworks are younger, around 17,000 years old.
We know this because carbon dating has been done directly
on two of the elks painted in black charcoal (the older paintings)
and on two finger impressions (the younger paintings), and we
can assume that other artworks that cannot be dated, the red
paintings, date to either one or the other of these two periods
because of their stylistic similarities. A further carbon date on
a reindeer bone lying on the floor is comparable in age to that
of the later phase of art. These dates indicate that during the
Gravettian people painted animal scenes across the walls of the
Main Decorated Chamber, but it was more than 10,000 years
later that subsequent, early Magdalenian peoples undertook the
rituals that saw them dip their fingers into paint and touch the
walls to make finger marks. The pre-existing animal paintings

must have drawn these later visitors to interact with the cave in a new way through rituals that made sense of what was already there. What Cougnac signals to us today is that what artworks mean is not fixed for all times; foundations were set for future engagements that were not necessarily like those at the start. Meanings change through time. If we want to understand the art, we need to differentiate its components and date them individually, and to look beyond it, to other things, to what else occurs nearby that may not be art but that may give us clues as to why individual motifs were put there in the first place, and how the existing configuration was subsequently used. At any point in time, a given art site was not simply the completed whole that we see today, but was rather continuously in the making through the way that people engaged with it.

Tuc d'Audoubert

This same theme of orchestrated performance deep under the ground is also found at the wondrous site of Tuc d'Audoubert in the Pyrenees. The site has been owned and carefully maintained by the family of Count Bégouën since 1893, with numerous spectacular archaeological discoveries ever since, including the clay bison discovered in 1912; their exceptional efforts to look after the site have been instrumental to its ongoing preservation. Here a network of interconnected passageways winds for hundreds of metres through the rock. The tunnels are rather narrow in places, sometimes requiring crawling on hands and knees. Like Cougnac, without lamps the action takes place in pitch-black darkness.

The entrance of Tuc d'Audoubert is spectacular, being the exit point of the River Volp that runs deep below ground under the entire length of the cave network [150]. Today the cave is entered by boat, from which a pebble beach then welcomes the visitor. The path into the cave continues through a pebble-lined creek-bed. Following a series of climbs and descents, narrow passageways and open chambers perched some 3 m (10 ft) above the flowing waters of the Volp are well decorated with artworks. A long upper passageway can here be reached; it, too, is covered with art on the walls. But at the very end of the long, narrow tunnel, positioned on the floor near the centre of the chamber, lie two bison modelled in clay, awe-inspiring and unlike anything ever seen before [151]. Adjacent to the Gallery of the Clay Bison is the Chamber of Heels, a slightly lower, open space with hollows in the clay floor. They were formed when sculptors mined for

150. The entrance of Tuc d'Audoubert as seen from inside the cave looking out. It is from this point that the cave is entered by boat.

151. The clay bison, sculpted during Magdalenian times deep in the cave, Tuc d'Audoubert.

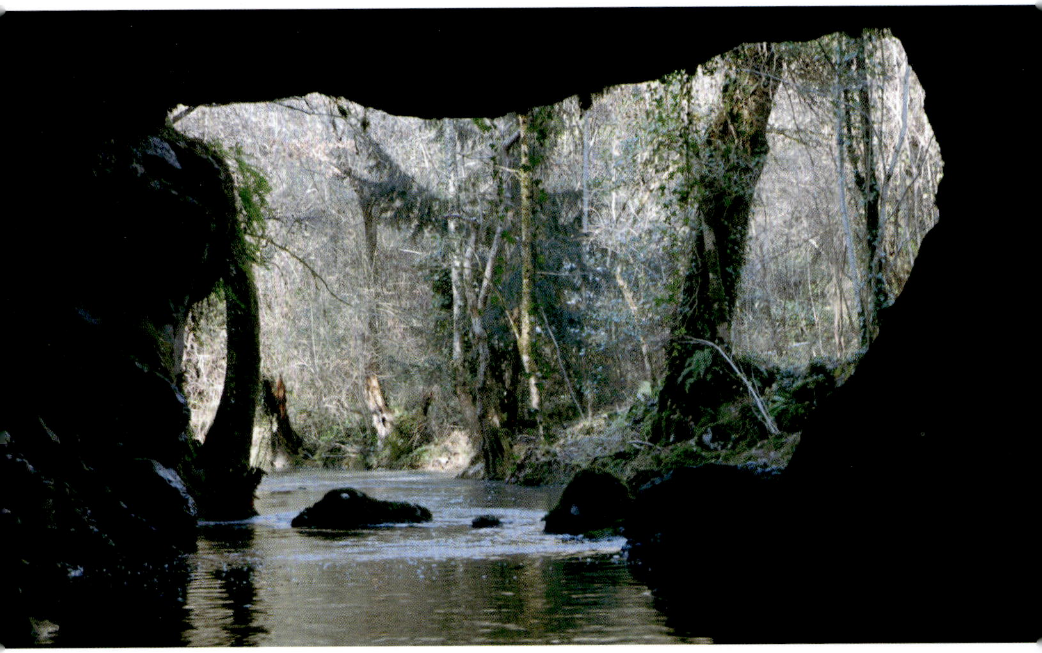

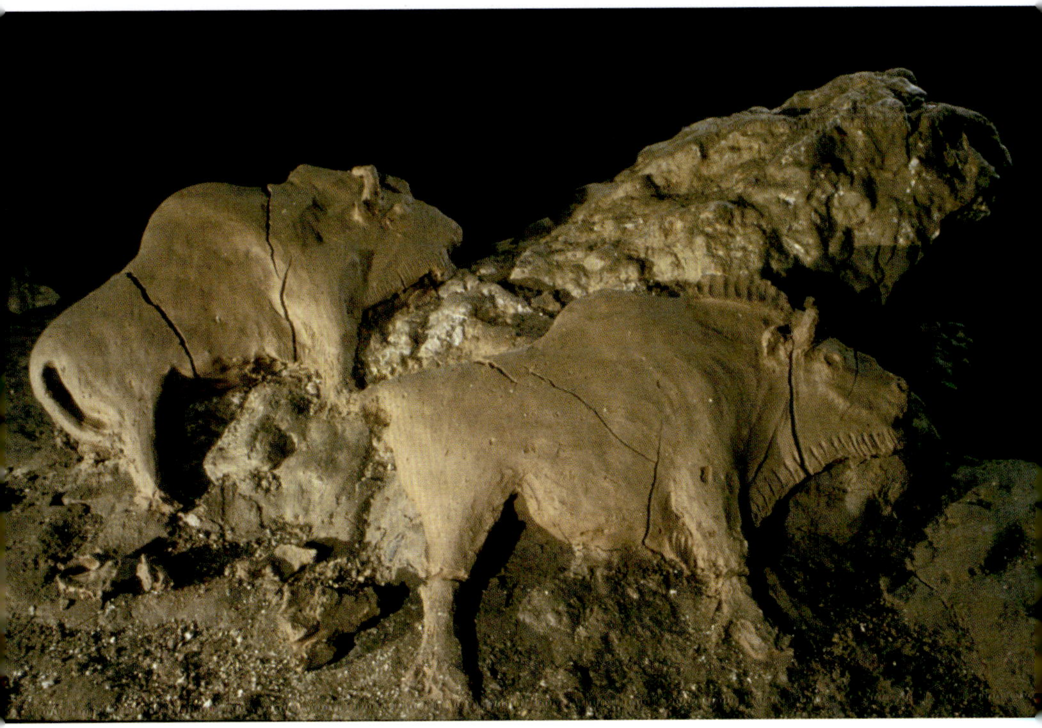

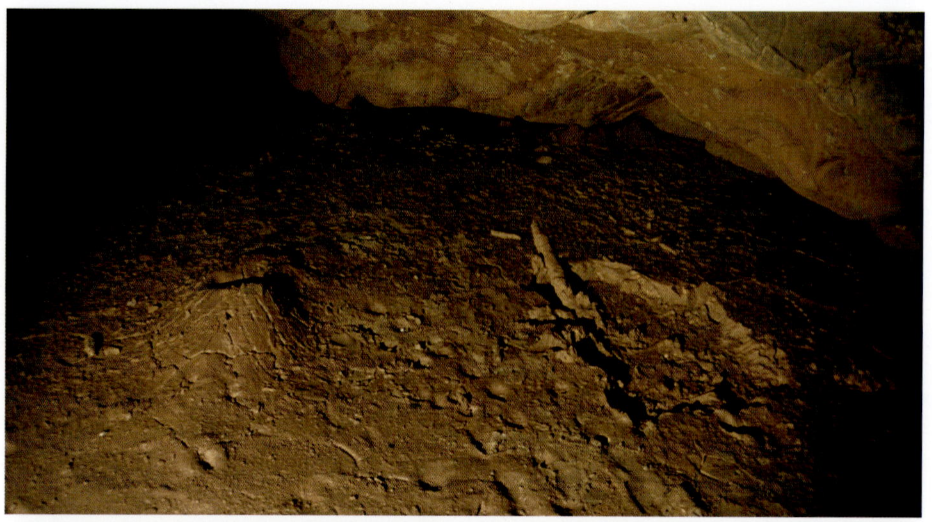

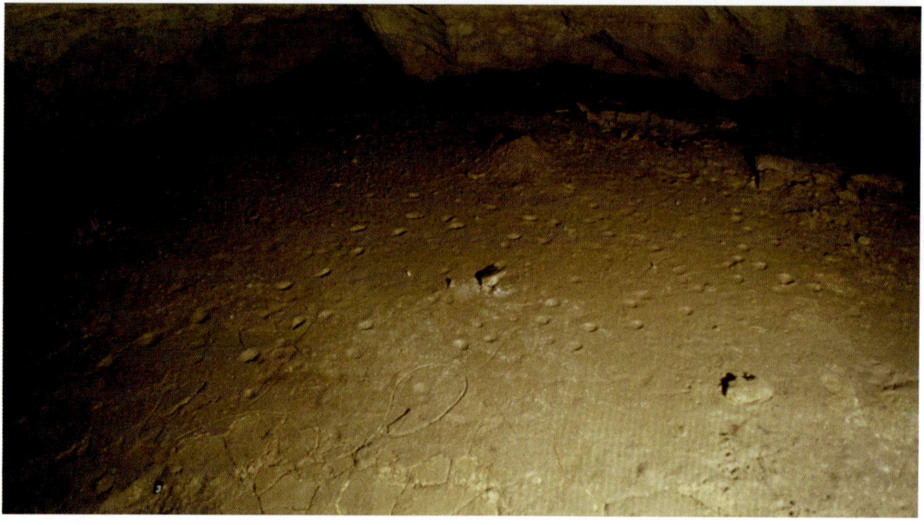

152. (top) In the Chamber of Heels at Tuc d'Audoubert, the clay floor retains evidence of the extraction of clay. Here a 52-cm-long (20.5 in.) broken stalactite lies on the edge of the depression, evidence of the extraction tool used during Magdalenian times.

153. (above) Impressions made by the heels of human feet, Tuc d'Audoubert.

clay for their creations [152]. There are also many traces of the handling or shaping of clay, such as long skinny clay 'sausages', by-products of artistic creations. As if that wasn't enough, our imagination cannot help but wonder in an altogether different yet complementary way, for here too are found 183 impressions of the balls of human heels [153] and myriad shallow impressions of fingertips pressed into the clay floor; such fingertip impressions occur in other parts of the site also, such as in the Gallery of Prints [154]. The heel prints show that those who walked this space did

174

so on the heels of their feet, carefully avoiding placing the flat of their feet on the ground, although in the Gallery of Little Feet that precedes the Gallery of the Clay Bison and the Chamber of Heels complete footprints of one or more children are clearly evident [155]. The size of the heel imprints in the Chamber of Heels indicates that they were not made by adults but by youths, probably adolescents. On the floor also are numerous abstract lines impressed or incised into the clay, many made into series of well-defined aligned dots (one of these has a combination of a curvilinear line of circular impressions and shallow dragged lines that together make an image of a deer[16] or bison [156]).

Like at Cougnac, the long pathway into the deepest, pitch-black recesses of Tuc d'Audoubert, richly decorated with artworks and other signs of human activity dating back 17,000 to 16,000 years ago, alerts us that what we see concerns not just decorations fixed on walls or installed on the ground. What we see in the art and imprints in the clay are the products of choreographed actions involving youths walking on the balls of their feet and pressing their fingertips into the clay along long and sometimes narrow corridors deep underground, leading to sculpted clay bison that were never meant to be seen by the broader populace of the outside world. These were rituals along passageways that were, we think, literally rites of passage for youths approaching adulthood. The art was not just to be seen, but to be performed.

This sense of performance in the caves of the Pyrenees is emphasized by a range of enigmatic images of part-human,

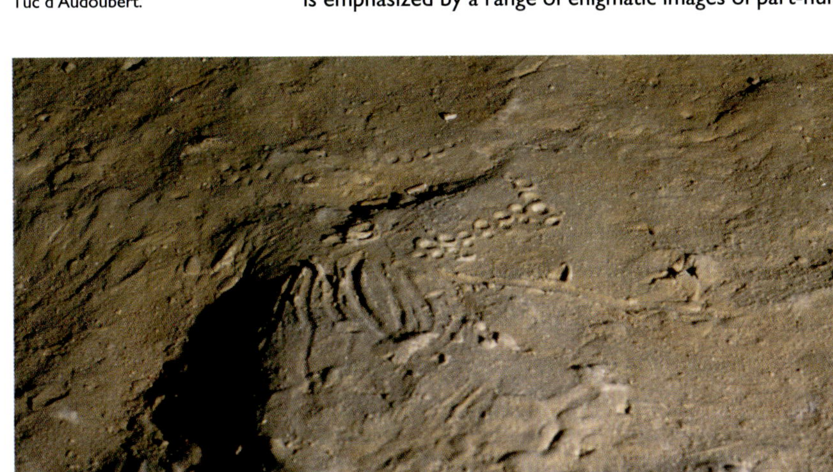

154. Dragged lines and fingertip impressions on the clay floor of the Gallery of Prints, Tuc d'Audoubert.

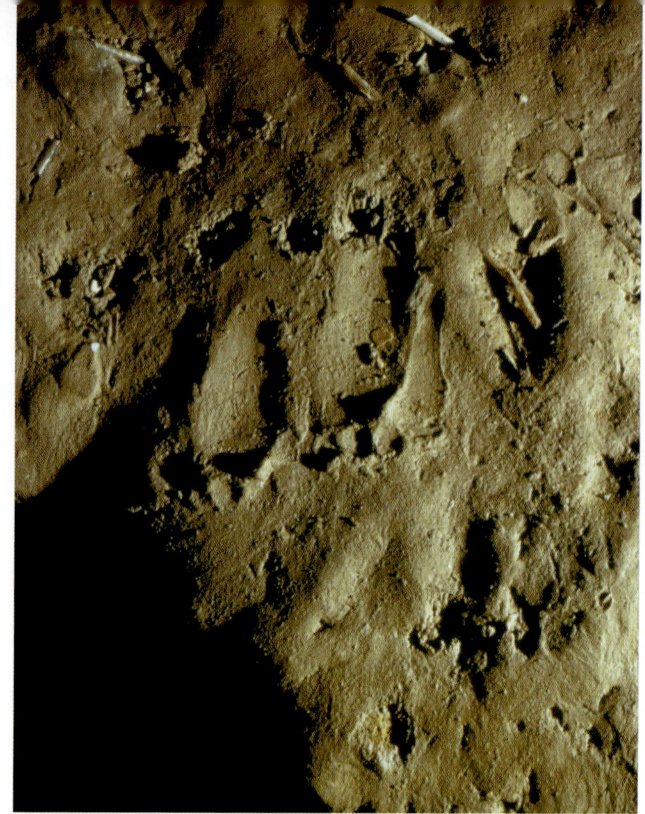

155. Footprints of a child who during Magdalenian times had slipped on the clay floor, as they halted repositioning their foot to avoid falling. Gallery of Little Feet, Tuc d'Audoubert.

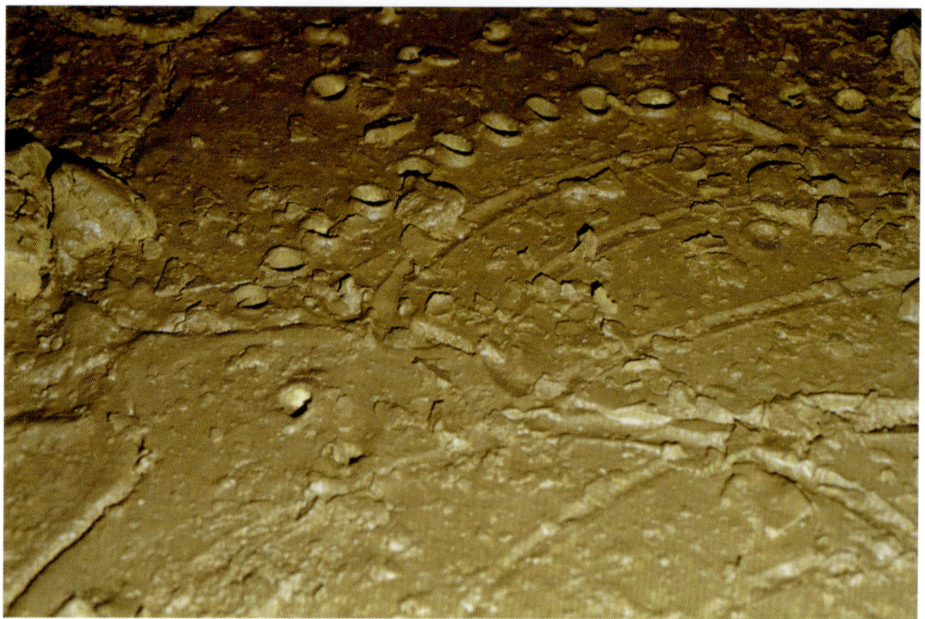

156. Curvilinear alignment of fingertip impressions and dragged lines, Chamber of Heels, Tuc d'Audoubert.

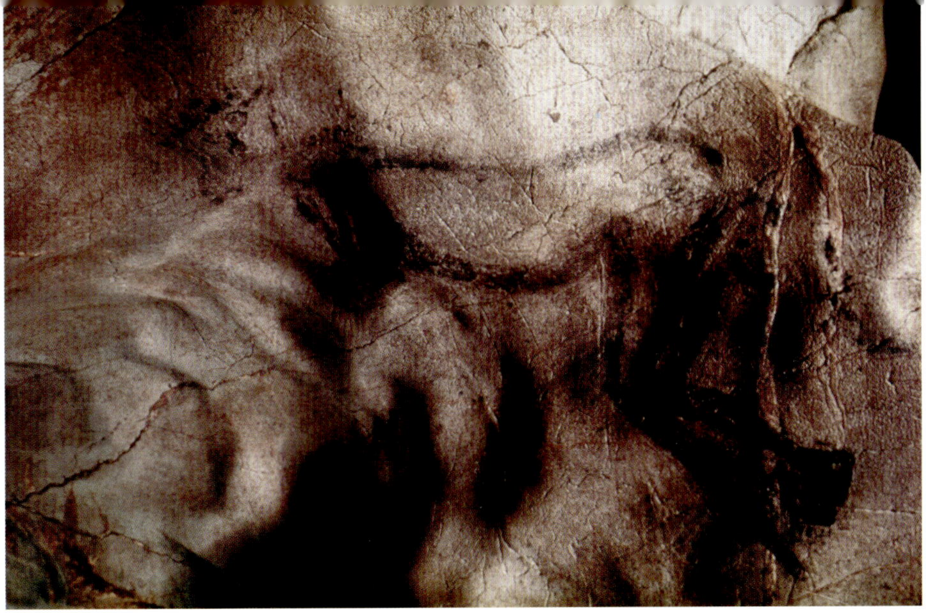

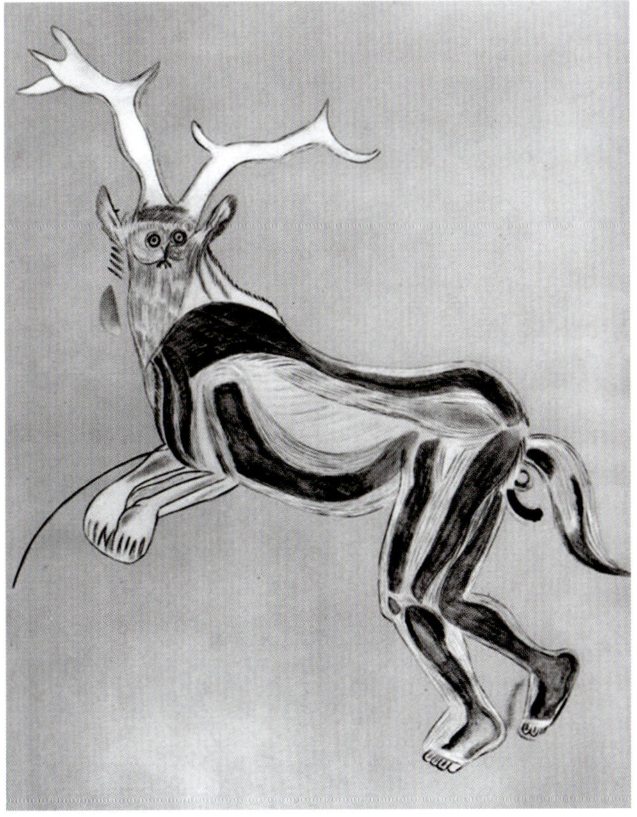

157. (above) Engraved and partly painted compound deer-human figure popularly known as 'The Sorcerer', Les Trois-Frères, France. (right) 'The Sorcerer', as recorded by the Abbé Henri Breuil in the 1920s.

158. Complex engraved panel
containing the bison-human motif
at Les Trois-Frères.

159. The 'bird-man' panel
of Lascaux.

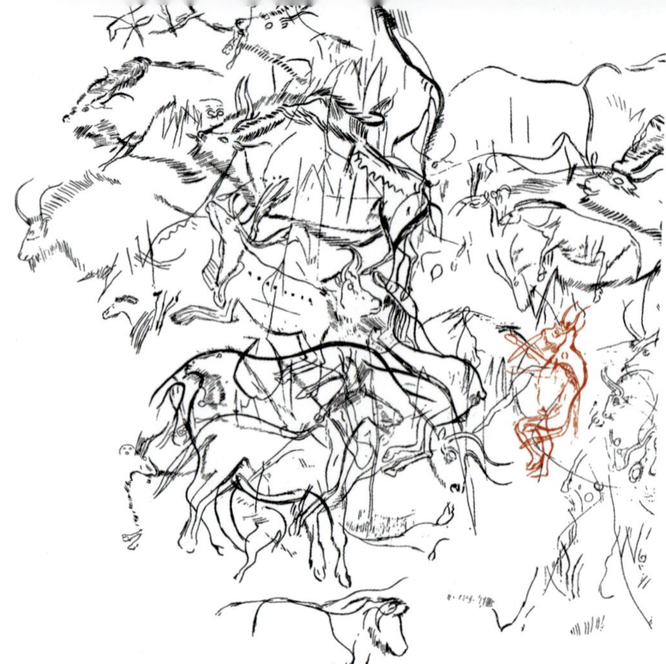

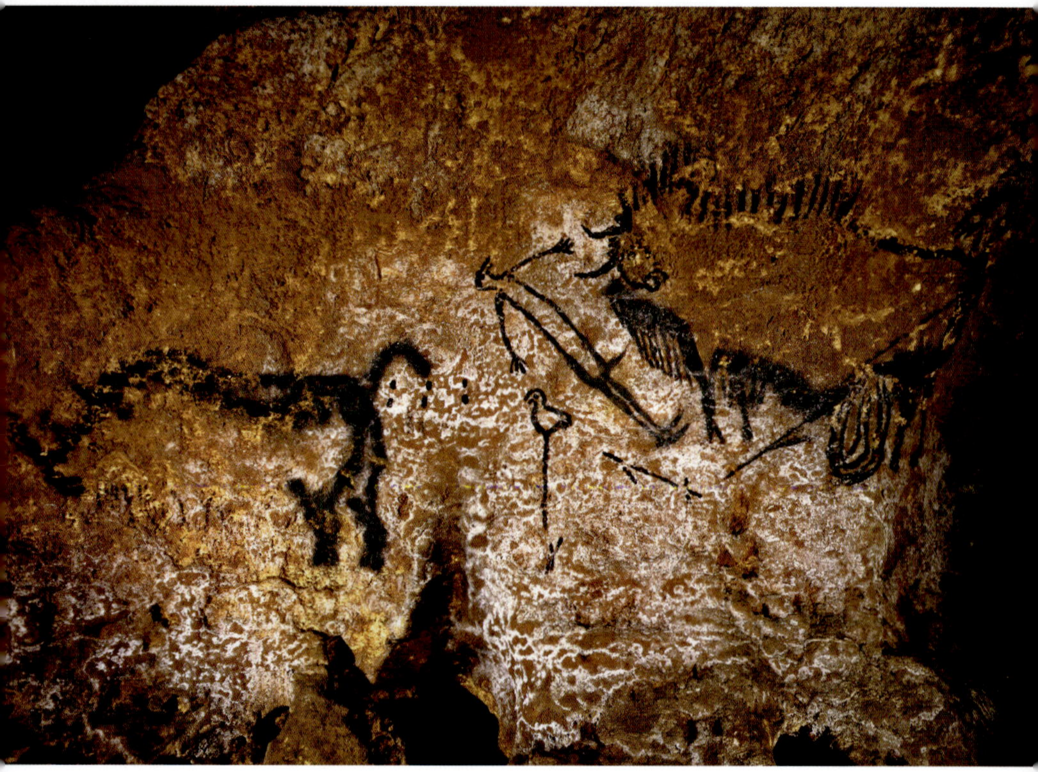

part-animal beings. These are found in a number of Magdalenian caves of Western Europe, and include the engraved and painted deer-human figure often referred to as 'The Sorcerer' (whose precise lineworks are now faded and thus disputed by some scholars) [157] and bison-human engraving at Les Trois-Frères near Tuc d'Audoubert [158], and the 'bird-man' (which has a bird's head and man's body) of Lascaux in the Dordogne to the east [159]. Are these examples of rituals, religious performances that involved people wearing masks and, in the case of the 'bird-man' of Lascaux, associated with a kind of bird wand, close to 14,000 years ago? Are they artistic expressions of the mutability of species – of hybrids with a mix of animal and human bodies (and presumably facilities) – as may have been a belief at the time? Or rather, are they expressions of something else again, such as the communion between species deep underground, where worlds meet in liminal spaces at the interstices of cosmic layers (see Chapter 7 for such a belief during more recent times, in another part of the world)? To properly know such things we would need access to the cosmology of the artists; we would need a deeper understanding of their world views than that which we can retrieve from the art today. But what we can reasonably deduce is that the Pyrenean art of the Magdalenian signals performances of a world in which people and animals are somehow closely entwined, and where recesses deep under the surface of the earth appear to be places where some kind of intimate communion can take place.

Les Combarelles

The question of whether the art was to be seen takes an altogether different tack at Les Combarelles, 35 km (22 miles) to the northwest of Cougnac. Les Combarelles was a key site that soon after its discovery in 1901 had convinced prehistorians of the Upper Palaeolithic antiquity of artworks, because here engravings had become covered with a thin layer of calcite, indicating that they were very old. Émile Rivière and Henri Breuil's conviction of the great age of the artworks of Les Combarelles had paved the way for Émile Cartailhac to finally accept and formally announce in 1902 that Altamira's paintings were indeed Ice Age art (see Chapter 2).

To the casual observer today, the artworks of Les Combarelles can seem rather unimpressive. Here we do not find stunning paintings of ibexes or bison or woolly mammoths

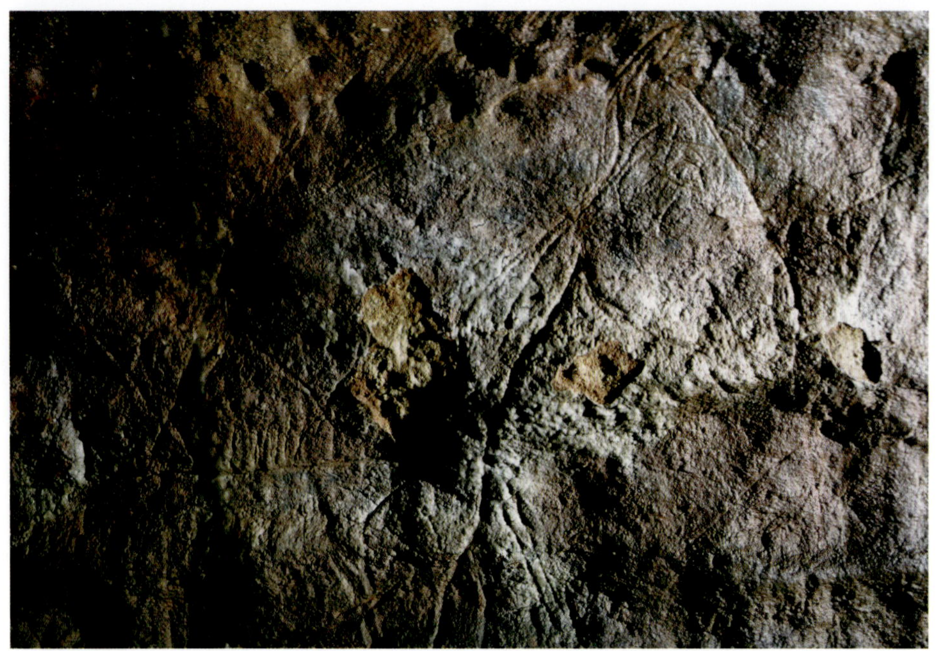

160. Intricately engraved horse, Les Combarelles, France.

such as those at Chauvet Cave, nor magnificent multicoloured depictions of abstract patchwork designs such as those beneath the hooves of the large cow at Lascaux. Rather we have incisions, and often very faint ones at that. Sometimes the thin, shallow lines of the engravings make recognizable shapes, including masterly depictions of horses and lions, and many of these are clearly akin in style to the more remarkable paintings of those same fauna found in other Ice Age caves. A horse with expressive facial features and details of the mane may be faint and hard to see [160], but it is exquisite nonetheless. Yet often the recognizable shapes are lost in a forest of squiggly lines, like fine spaghetti splattered on a canvas, figurative masterpieces awaiting to be extracted from the confusing mass [161]. But who was the onlooker, we may ask? These fine incisions were not done in large, open underground art galleries, but along narrow pitch-black corridors *c.* 1 m (3 ft) wide and high, sometimes less [162]. The long corridor of Les Combarelles extends for 240 m (790 ft) into the heart of the rock – with most of the art only appearing more than 160 m (525 ft) from the entrance – and 14,000 to 12,000 years ago during late Magdalenian times much of it would have been accessed on hands and knees, or lying flat along the narrowest sections (today the floor level has been deepened,

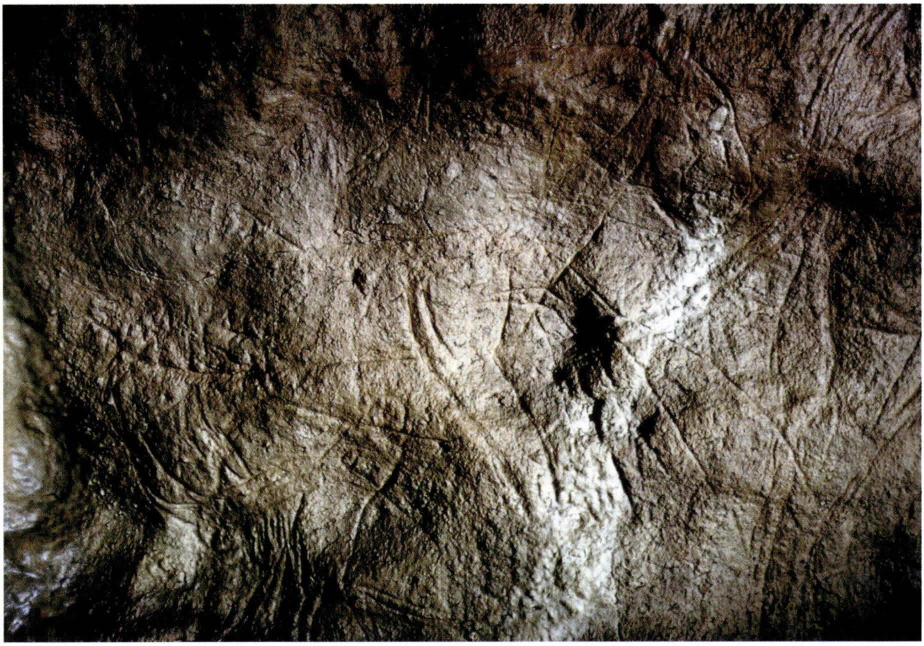

161. Engraved lion amid a mass
of finely engraved curvilinear
lines, Les Combarelles. The eye
is delineated by a small rock
naturally embedded in the wall,
indicating that the entire figure
must have been conceptualized
in advance around the rock.

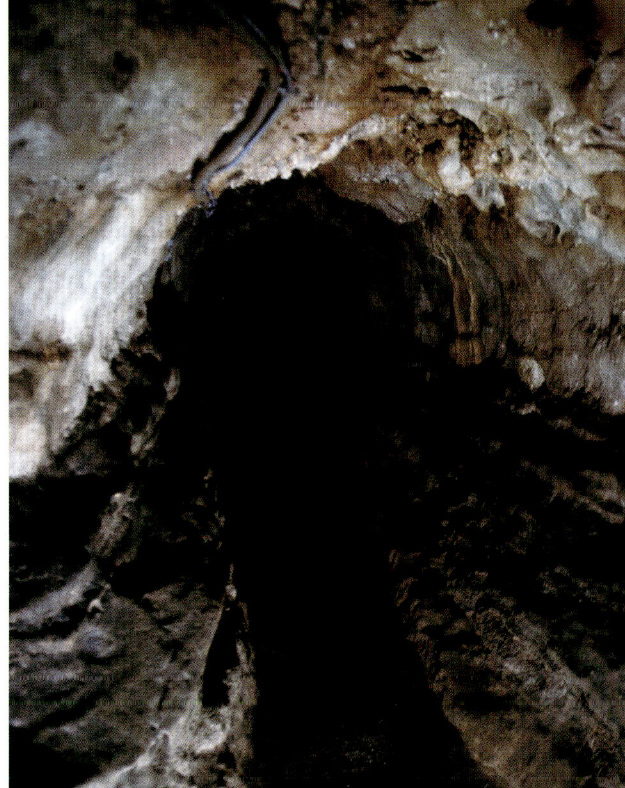

162. The long, narrow corridor
deep into the rock at Les
Combarelles, where the walls are
covered with hundreds of thin and
shallow engravings. The floor was
lowered during the 1940s to allow
visitor access.

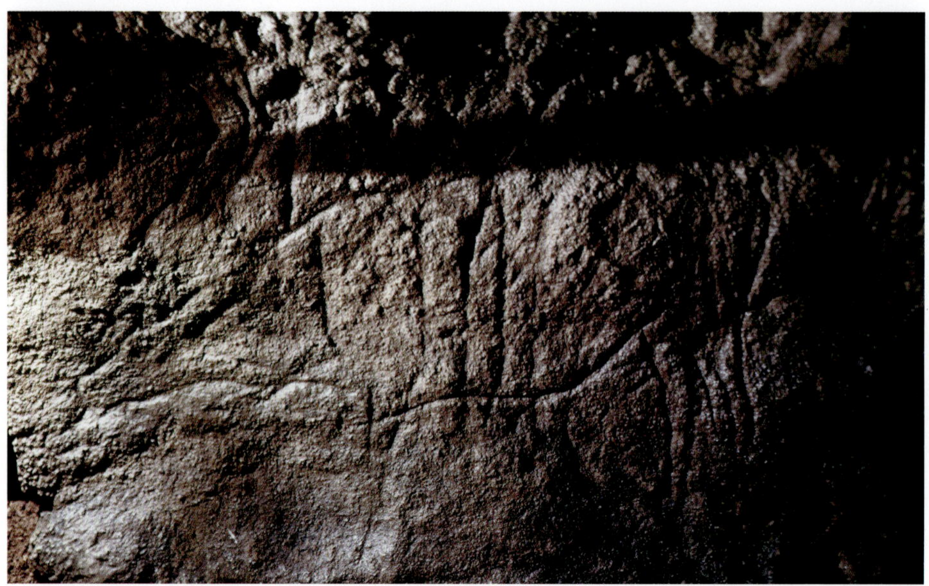

163. 'The drinking reindeer', Les Combarelles's most celebrated artwork. During Magdalenian times, the reindeer was engraved with its protruding tongue extended to an opening where water naturally exudes from the rock.

enlarging the height from floor to ceiling to allow easier access for tourists). Although some of the artworks can be clearly seen, such as a reindeer with lowered head drinking water that once emanated from a crack in the rock [163], the only way of finding much of the more than 600 artworks would have been to carefully look on the walls, oil lamp in hand, one person at a time and face almost pressed against the rock in the narrow space. Here the art was never meant for public display; once made it may not even have been meant to be seen at all. So why was the art made in the first place? Many engravings were clearly skilfully done by master artists. Was this a place where communion was made with enigmatic life forces in liminal spaces, places somewhere between the known physical world and the unknown spirit world? These are pure, imaginative wonderings. We will probably never know, but what we do know is that only a privileged (or burdened?) few would have entered those dark corridors and seen the art.

How were the paints made?

Europe's Ice Age artists employed a number of techniques to give body and colour to paintings. One that we see time and again is the enhancement of natural shapes already configured by the walls. At Pech Merle, two polka-dotted horses are framed by the natural shape of the rock, in particular the right-hand horse whose muzzle is naturally shaped like the outline of a horse's head [125]. At Cougnac, the torsos and legs of two human shapes were defined by natural concretions on the rock wall when their painted heads were added, giving meaning to the whole in the process [142]. The swimming stags of Lascaux [133] and drinking reindeer of Les Combarelles [163] are further examples, but there are many more from numerous caves across Europe (and a similar technique was often used for portable objects too). Is it simply that the artist enhanced an already existing shape to make a nice depiction? Or rather did they think that the animal, or the animal's spirit, lay there in the cave somewhere between the world of the living and the world of the spirits, and that it was the artist's job to help bridge the two worlds, to give this bridge currency in their own physical world? A similar kind of logic occurs among many peoples of more recent times (and more generally, perhaps this task of connecting worlds is found in the job of the 'priest' in all religions, in modern Western society included): among the Keipte Kuyumen clan of the upper Kikori River in Papua New Guinea, stone tool-makers don't just flake the rock to make a tool, but rather extract tools that are already present, embedded in the rock; and in rites of the Catholic church, the body and blood of Christ come to life in godly communion through the priest's blessing of a wafer biscuit and glass of wine.

Niaux

Whatever the motive may have been, the artists nevertheless needed to bring shapes to the walls, be it by chipping away at the rock or rubbing or cutting it to make an engraving, or by adding pigment such as in a painting. But how did Ice Age artists make the paints used on rock walls such as those of Lascaux, Cougnac and Pech Merle?[17] Investigations at the cave of Niaux provide a useful example.[18]

Niaux is a complex network of cave entrances interconnected by underground tunnels in the French Pyrenees [164]. Some of these tunnels were traversed by Upper Palaeolithic peoples, others not, and for practical purposes the unfrequented tunnels divide the used cave chambers into distinct archaeological sites.

The paintings of Niaux were first discovered in 1906, and have been studied by a Who's Who of cave art research ever since. The most celebrated chamber is the Salon Noir, which dates to the Magdalenian, close to 15,500 years ago. Here black, largely outlined, naturalistic paintings of bison (some with spears sticking

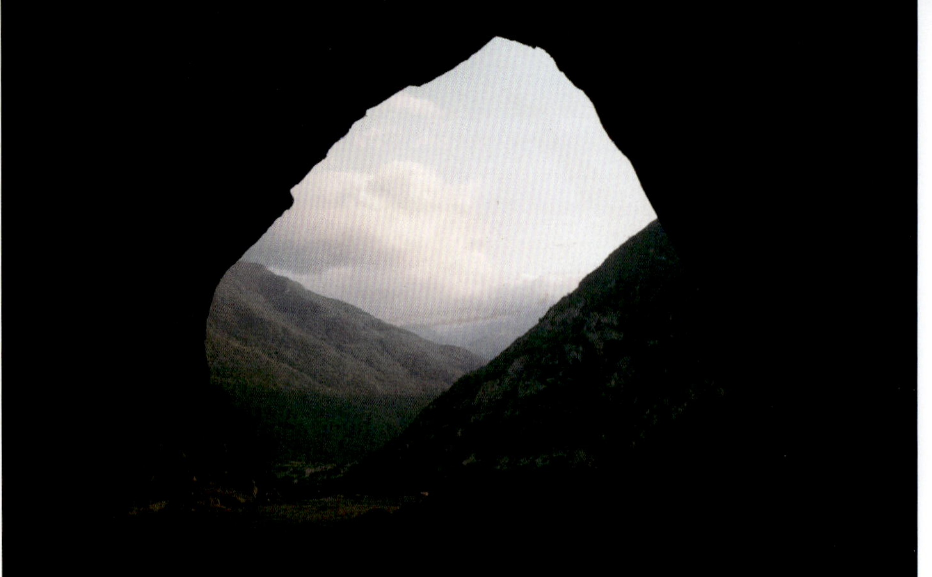

164. Entrance to the cave of
Niaux, French Pyrenees.

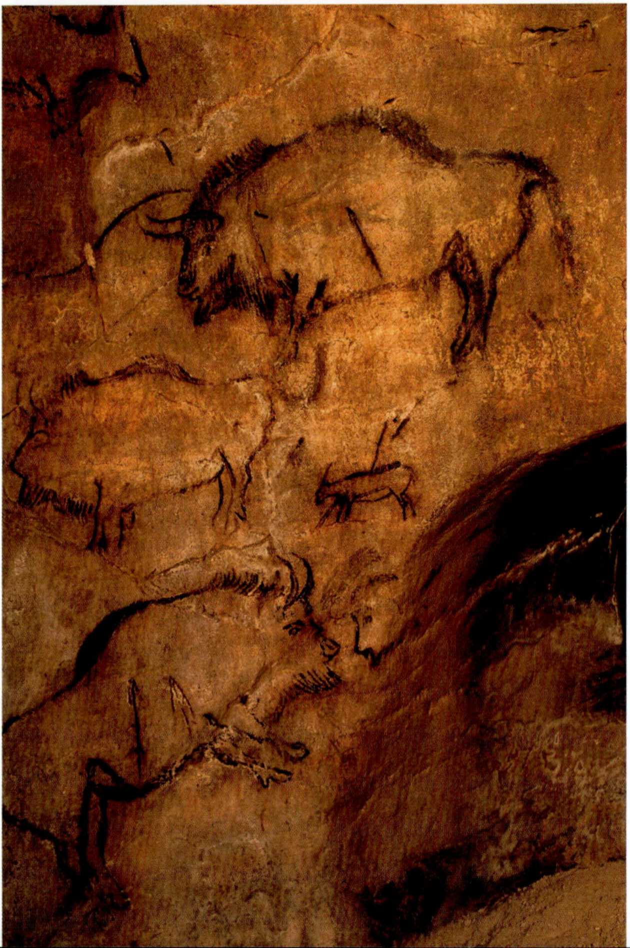

165. Speared bison, Salon Noir,
Niaux.

out of their bodies [165]), ibexes [166] and other fauna testify to the mastery of Upper Palaeolithic artists and evoke the chase of hunting parties so long ago. Whether the speared bison represent an actual or ritual hunt, or both, is unknown, but the massive, cathedral-like Salon Noir chamber appears to have been a focal point in the Niaux complex, a place of gatherings, perhaps by communities, perhaps by noted individuals such as leaders, elders, ritual specialists or artists who had the skill to depict, recall and connect with the painted fauna [167].

In an attempt to determine whether the Niaux paintings were all done at about the same time, or at different times over an extended period, the chemistry of the paintings was analysed in some detail. The aim was to determine the recipes used to make the paints, understanding that the knowledge of how to mix ingredients to make a 'pot' of paint requires training and social communication between individuals, from teacher to pupil, and across generations. There is a wide choice of ingredients that can be used to make a paint: black can be obtained from manganese as well as from charcoal, for instance, and various compounds could be used as extenders. These are components that do not alter the colour of the paint, but that enhance its quality in one way or another. For example, they could improve the paint's ability to adhere onto the wall (as with a binder), or facilitate the paint's application to a surface, or increase the density of the paint, making it less translucent. The particular set of ingredients that Palaeolithic artists chose to create a paint pot becomes their signature recipe, enabling researchers to determine whether the artworks on a wall were made following a single formula shared by all the artists, implying a narrow time frame, for as with 'style', paint recipes change with time, or, alternatively, by following different recipes, implying multiple artists each with their own, distinctive knowledge and skills. The latter option could imply a single artistic event involving multiple artists, or multiple painting events separated by more or less long periods of time.

Michel Menu and Philippe Walter analysed both red and black paintings of the Salon Noir, Réseau Clastres and other chambers. They used a raft of techniques to distinguish the different components of paintworks, including a scanning electron microscope coupled with an X-ray detector, X-ray diffraction (to identify mineral structures), and proton-induced X-ray emission (to identify the frequency of individual elements). They found that at Niaux four very particular yet complex paint recipes were used, differing principally in their incorporated extenders. One

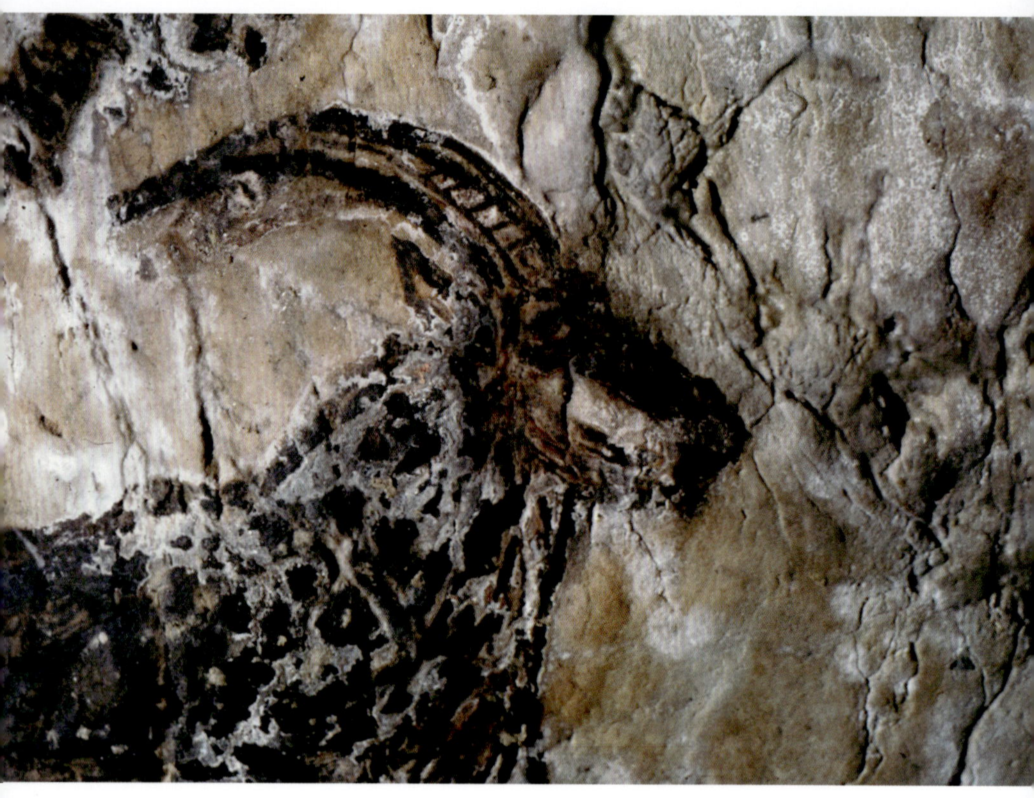

166. Naturalistic ibex in the Salon Noir, Niaux.

167. Finely depicted bison with pronounced beard and throat mane, Salon Noir, Niaux.

group of paintings used talcum powder, another a mixture of baryte and potassium feldspar, another just potassium feldspar, and yet another potassium feldspar mixed with biotite (the latter improving adhesion and limiting cracking once dry). The black of the paintings consisted either of manganese dioxide, charcoal or a combination of both. Each of the above minerals is locally available, but none of those paint recipes occurs naturally: they must have been mixed by people.

In the Salon Noir, at the main, cathedral-like entrance chamber of the Niaux site complex, by far the majority of paintings were made by mixing manganese dioxide with charcoal, but this was not so elsewhere at Niaux. The Salon Noir artworks were made by first outlining with charcoal crayons, and then elaborating with paint consisting of manganese oxide mixed with potassium feldspar and biotite. However, sometimes the paint contained rutile with alumina-silicates, sometimes albite, indicating that while the base formula remained the same, its mineral contents varied, signalling multiple raw material sources for those components. Despite

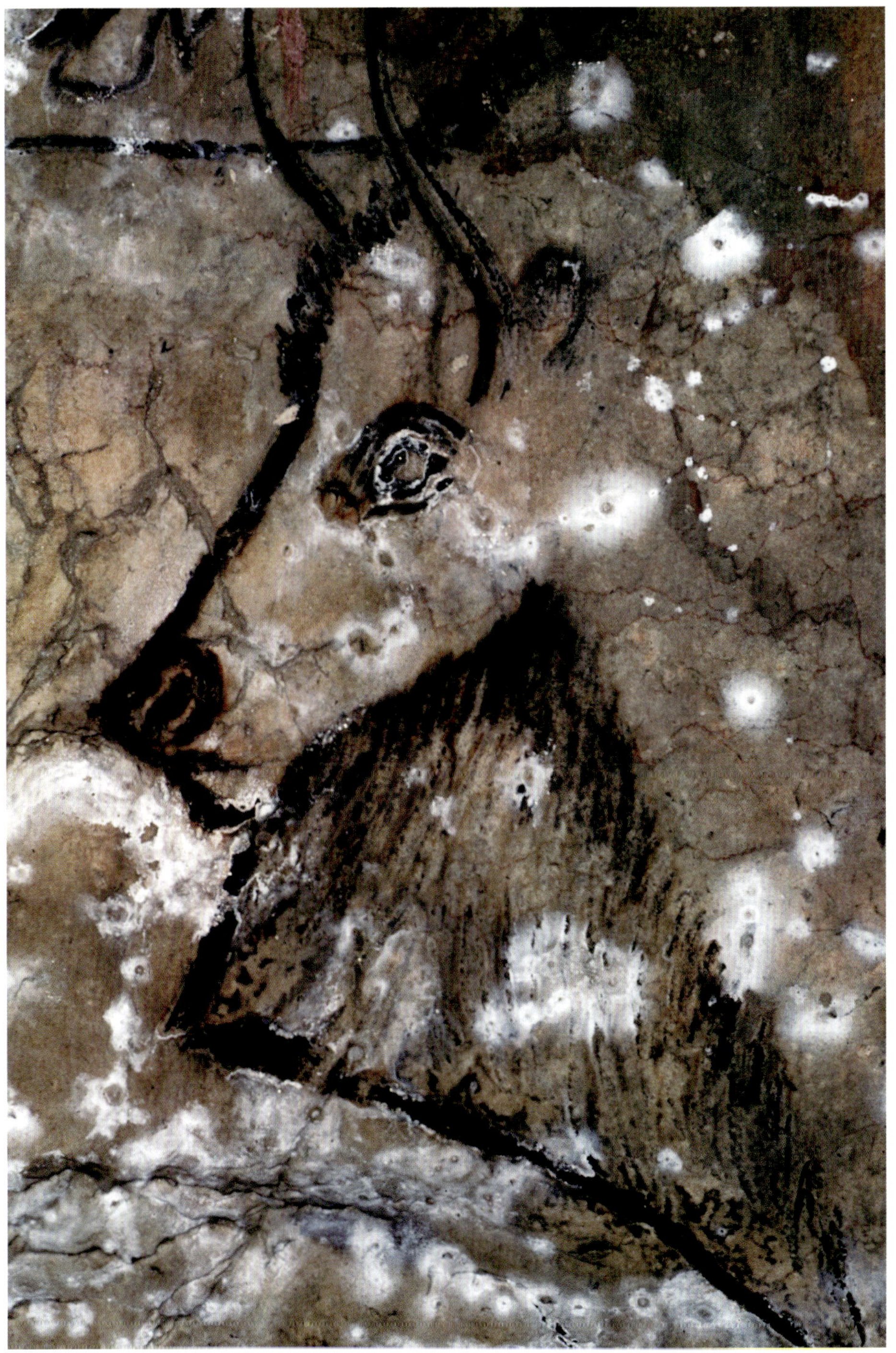

this variability, the Salon Noir black paints followed an essentially uniform formula, especially when compared with the paintings of other chambers where the recipes used were noticeably different, and where, unlike at the Salon Noir, painting did not begin with an outline sketch. Because of these differences, indicating variability in the way people manufactured paints as well as variability in methods of depiction, Jean Clottes, Michel Menu and Philippe Walter concluded that the Niaux paintings were not all done over a single, short-lived phase of cultural activity, but rather over a more extended period of time. A particular paint recipe is in effect a 'fingerprint' of the know-how of a particular group of individuals from a particular time, allowing researchers to use that recipe as a temporal marker for the art. The Salon Noir paintings were done with careful planning, but those elsewhere, including in the deepest recesses of the cave complex, were more quickly made, more spontaneous. The Salon Noir had a more communal expression (although apparently more as a 'sanctuary' than a habitation site), even if that expression involved restrictions of one kind or another.

Did cave painting suddenly begin 40,000 years ago?

For 100 years, debates over the origins of art have tended to revolve around the Ice Age of Europe, not so much because this is where the earliest art could be shown to exist, but simply because specialists were at hand to study it in demonstrably ancient settings. Yet the earliest evidence of modern humans anywhere in Europe dates to sometime between 45,000 and 43,000 years ago at Grotta del Cavallo in Italy,[19] between 42,000 and 38,000 years ago at Peştera cu Oase in Romania,[20] and is suggested to be between 44,000 and 41,000 years ago by association with extinct fauna at Kent's Cavern in England.[21] Is it significant, we might wonder, that all of these earliest traces of modern humans and on-wall art in Europe are found in caves, where temperate conditions with good potential for the preservation of bone and marks on walls are found?

One question that continues to be asked by professional archaeologists is why it is that all of a sudden, around 40,000 years ago, we find the first examples of artworks on walls. Is this a sign that *Homo sapiens* became cognitively modern only then, more than 100,000 years after the species had become biologically modern? The art that we see from around 40,000 to 35,000 years ago is not just an isolated painting, nor is it rudimentary in design, but rather comes to us as fully blown galleries of figurative motifs executed with great dexterity, as if all of a sudden the artist's hand, and the human mind, had bloomed. This may be so for Europe, where modern humans first arrived around the time of the earliest artworks on cave walls, but does this also truly reflect the situation elsewhere around the globe?

The apparent blossoming of art around 40,000 years ago has been given the label the 'human revolution'. And yet, looks can be deceiving. First of all, European cave paintings emerged after a slow evolution of more rudimentary symbolic expression over hundreds of thousands of years in Africa and Southeast Asia, as evident from the c. 500,000-year-old Trinil engraved shell, the 101,000–85,000-year-old Klasies River Cave 1 and 100,000–75,000-year-old Blombos Cave paint-making toolkits and engraved ochres, and the 65,000–55,000-year-old Diepkloof engraved ostrich eggshell, for example. Secondly, the sudden burgeoning of cave art in Western Europe appeared well away in space and time from the pathway of early human migrations out of Africa eastwards into Asia. While there are no known traditions of figurative painting between Africa and Southeast Asia dating to more than 40,000 years ago, by the time people left Africa they clearly knew how to paint. So why would the human mind evolve in European backwaters rather than at the forefront of the migration route?

The Ice Age art of Europe is found mostly in deep caves where paintings are well protected from the elements. What if earlier art occurred elsewhere – in Africa or Asia, let's say – not in caves but rather in more open settings on rock faces or boulders subject to erosion from the forces of wind, water and the like? João Zilhão has argued another possibility: that people started marking with artworks the landscape in which they lived as a way of marking territory, and that this only became necessary when human populations grew to such a level that competition between groups had reached critical levels. As the 100,000-year-old paint-making toolkits of Blombos Cave in South Africa show well, painted artworks were clearly made well before the Spanish and French painted caves of the Ice Age, but there are no signs of the artworks themselves. A bridge not yet crossed is what happened between the time of abstract lineworks such as those found in South Africa from about 100,000 to 55,000 years ago, and the first signs of figurative art that signal the arrival of modern humans in Europe, around 45,000 to 40,000 years ago. Is it simply that earlier figurative art exists but has not yet been found?

Under the sea: Cosquer Cave

One rather unusual but spectacular example of how cave art may today be hidden from view comes from Cosquer Cave in southern France.[22] In 1985, Henri Cosquer was diving along the coast off Marseille when he spotted the entrance to an underwater cavern 37 m (55 ft) below the surface of the Mediterranean Sea [168]. The entrance gave way to an upward-sloping tunnel some 175 m (575 ft) long, eventually leading to a large and only partly submerged chamber whose lower half is below sea level, the upper half an open cavity [169]. What Cosquer saw when he emerged out of the water remains unprecedented in the archives

168. Cape Morgiou at the tip of the Calanque de Morgiou near Marseille, France, where Cosquer Cave was found 37 m (55 ft) below the Mediterranean Sea.

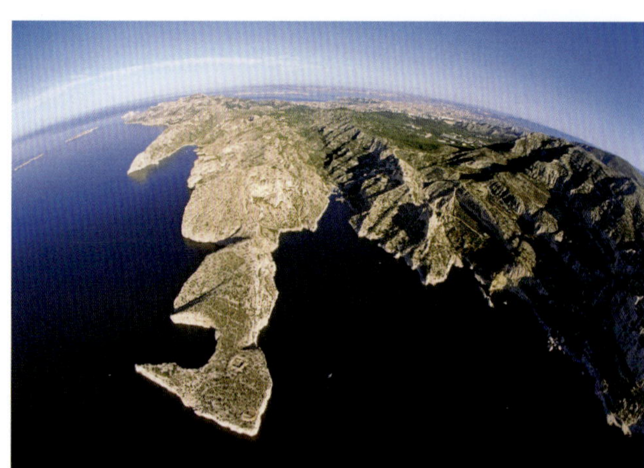

169. Profile view of Cosquer Cave, its lower half submerged beneath the Mediterranean, its upper half above the water line like an air bubble trapped in the rock.

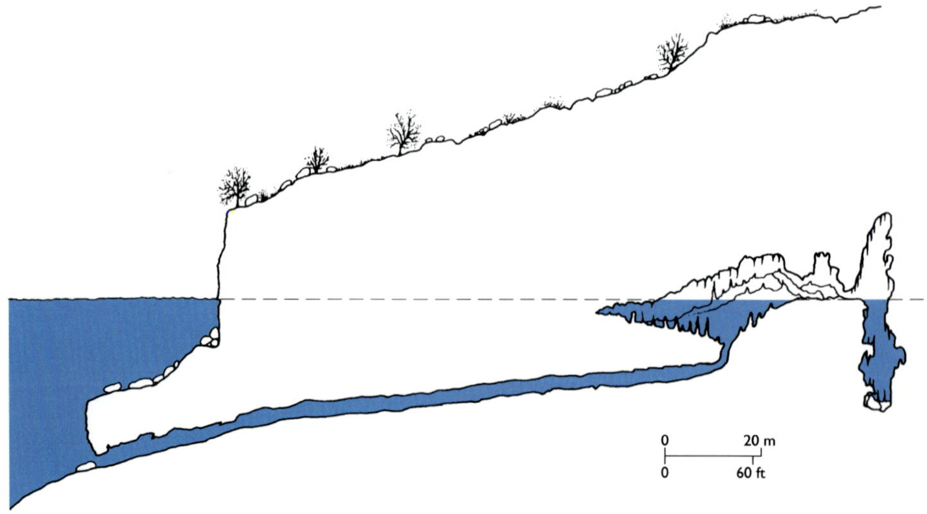

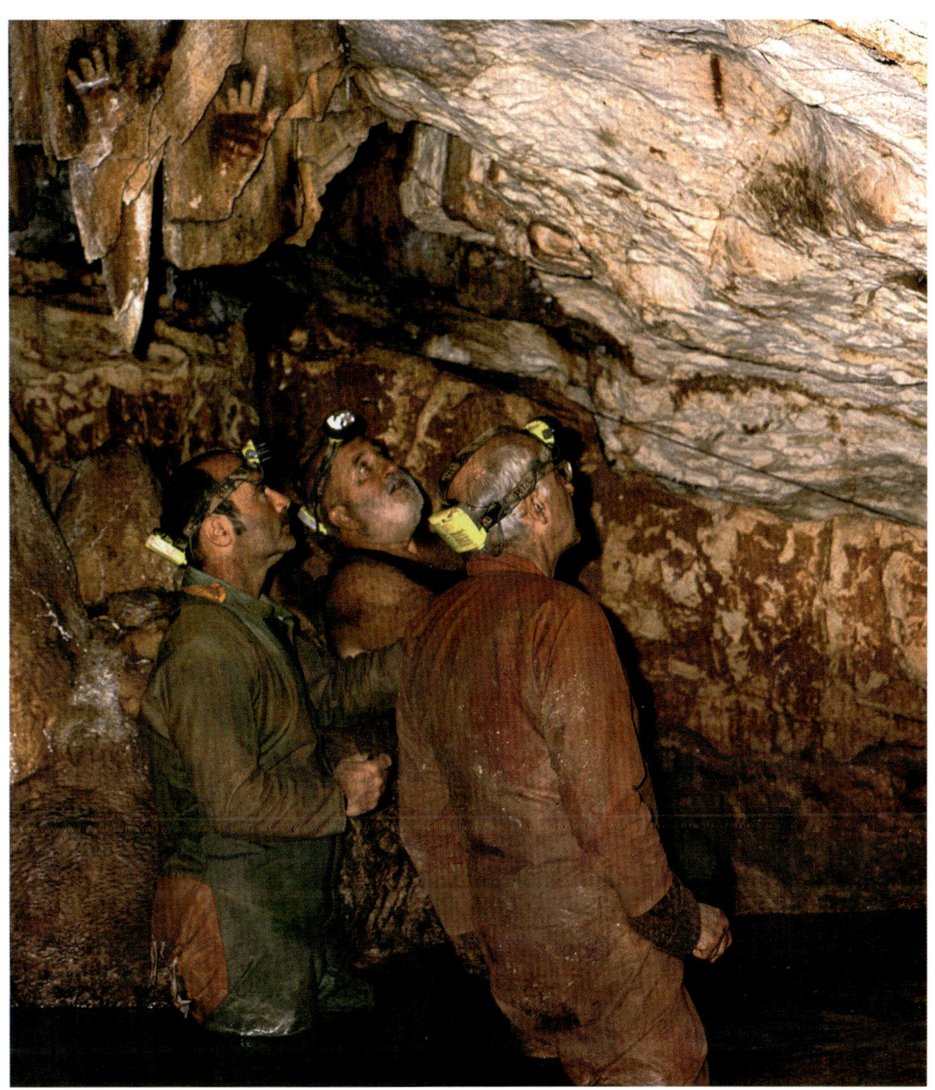

170. Luc Vanrell, Jean Courtin and Jean Clottes examine artworks on the ceiling of Cosquer Cave, Ice Age hand stencils perching overhead.

of archaeological research anywhere in the world: a stunning cavern eerily covered with stalagmites and stalactites from floor to roof, many of the former jutting out of the submerged floor. Within this underground air bubble, on those parts of the walls above the water level, dozens of paintings, stencils and engravings decorate the walls [170]: three beautifully shaded black horses [171], little penguin-like 'auks' [172] that have been long-extinct in this part of the world, in all some 150 Ice Age artworks from a period when the Mediterranean was tens of metres lower

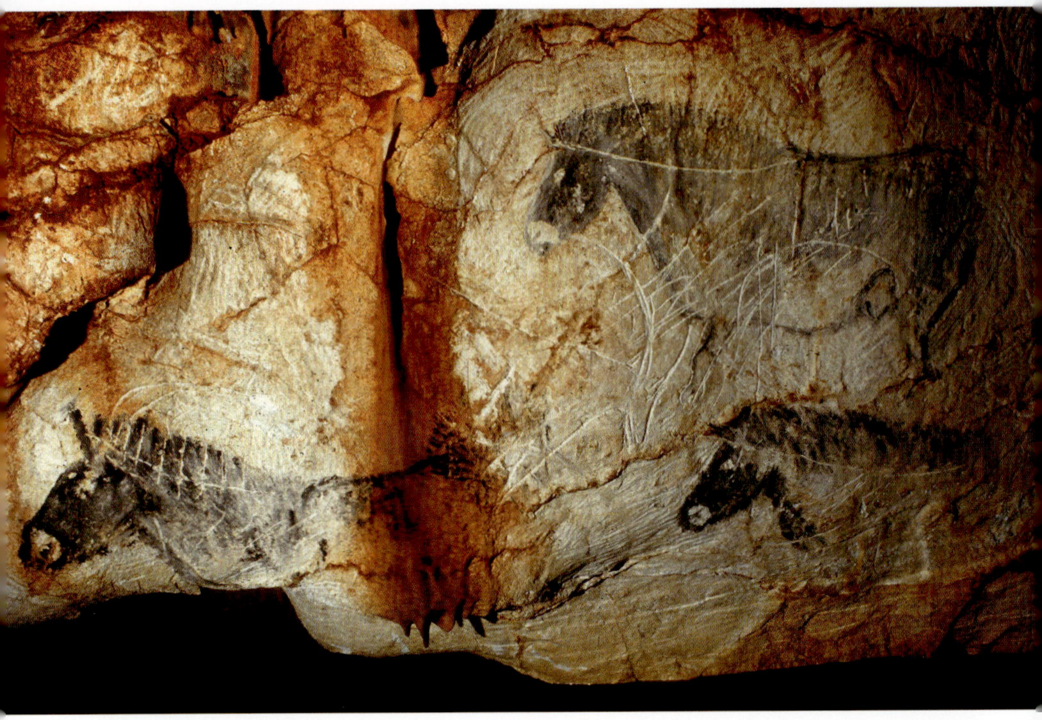

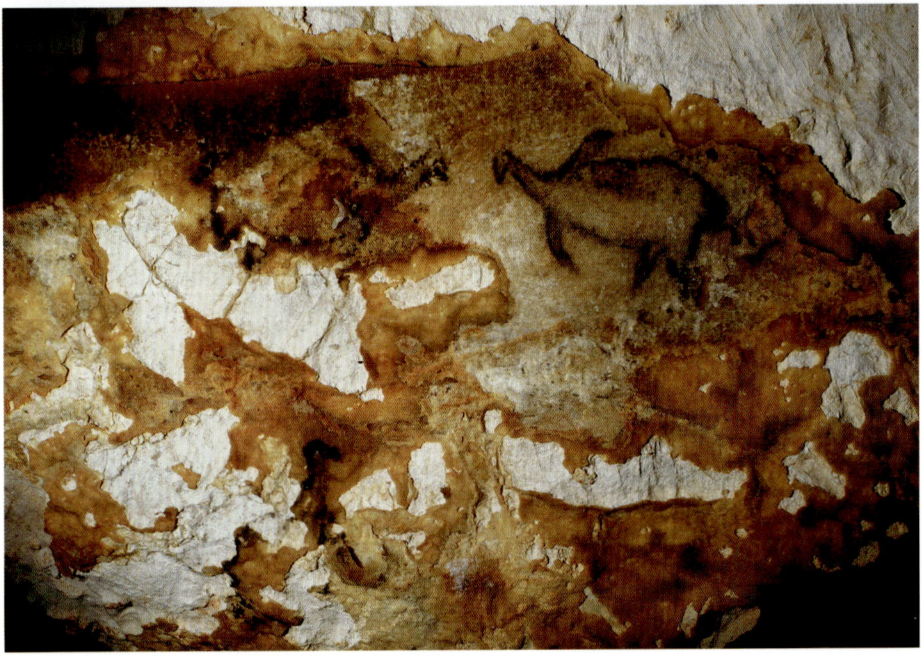

171. Three beautifully shaded horses perched only a few tens of centimetres above the still waters of the Mediterranean Sea inside Cosquer Cave.

172. Penguin-like 'auks', still clearly visible on the disintegrating wall surface, Cosquer Cave.

than it currently is and the cave accessible. In those parts of the cave now submerged, the art has been entirely destroyed. As sea levels rose following the melting of ice sheets at the end of the Ice Age, the entrance to Cosquer Cave was sealed by rising waters, and the art was also sealed in an air pocket inside the rock. But Cosquer Cave was not alone: the fate of rock art lying on ancient plains near the sea would have been similar wherever it occurred below today's sea levels. Very few now-submerged coastal plains have been investigated for prehistoric art, yet Ice Age caves, and rock art, almost certainly abound around the world, waiting to be discovered.

Art hidden under layers of rock

Rather than being lost beneath the sea, some art is hidden under thin layers of redeposited mineral 'skin' on rock walls. The network of fourteen cave and rockshelter sites at Arcy-sur-Cure, along the River Cure in central-eastern France, has been known for more than 150 years, with the first archaeological excavations beginning in 1860. Here traces of Neanderthals have been unearthed at the Grotte de l'Hyène, along with later modern humans in a combined cultural sequence spanning some 300,000 years.

In 1946, three young speleologists exploring local caves found sixteen Magdalenian engravings in the Grotte du Cheval, including that of a horse [173]. This was the first Palaeolithic cave art discovered north of the Loire River. The engravings were found deep in the cave, some 70 m (230 ft) along a narrow corridor. The cavers knew from the outset that the art was of great antiquity, because among the engravings were depictions of woolly mammoths, extinct since the Ice Age.

Over the course of the nineteenth and twentieth centuries, visitors had frequented the local caves to explore their geological wonders. At Grande Grotte, the 'large cave' near the Grotte du Cheval, a narrow, 500 m-long (1,650 ft) bifurcated corridor extends deep into the rock. At first the visitors had come with candles and various kinds of torches that left sooty marks on the walls and ceilings. And worse, graffiti came to be abundantly written onto those same rock surfaces. By the 1970s the damaged walls had become an eyesore, and so the decision was made to wash them clean. The process began in 1976, with pressurized jets of chlorinated water aimed at the walls of the Grande Grotte. What had been soot-stained, graffiti-ridden corridor walls now

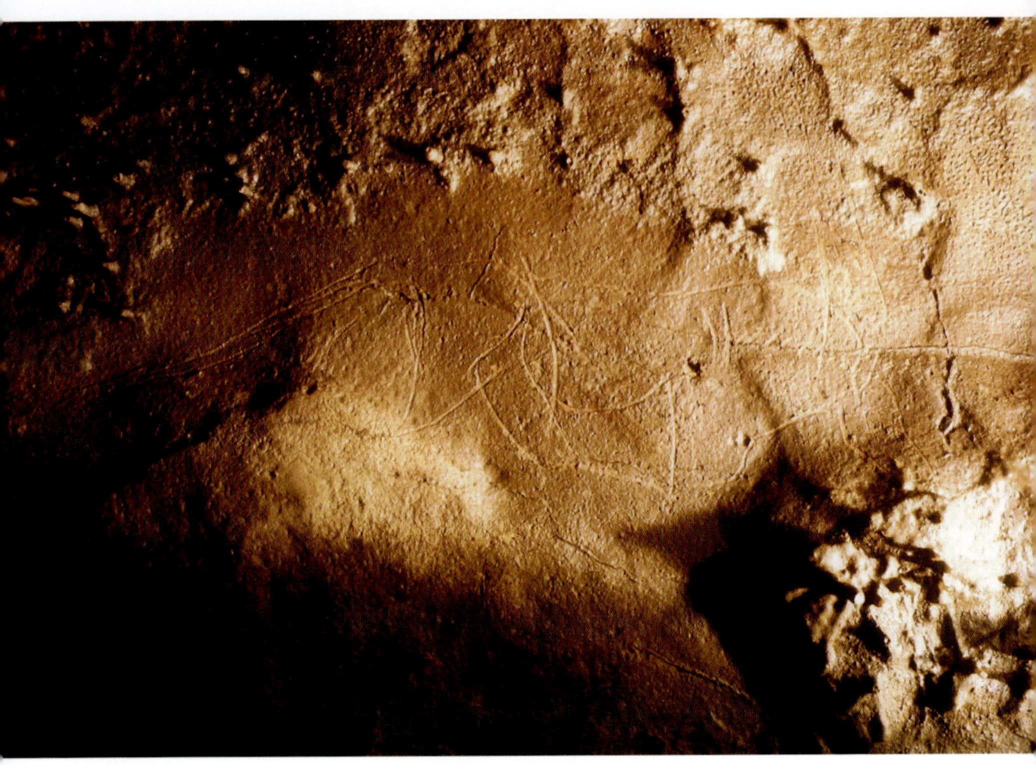

became clean, sparkling white rock surfaces, the dark accretions jettisoned forever. Some 80 per cent of the surface area of the rock was cleaned in this way.

Soon something else became evident: the rock walls had not featured the accumulated soot and graffiti of recent visitors alone, for they also were the canvas for ancient artworks that had been obstructed both by thin skins of redeposited calcite, and in places by the subsequent layers of recent soot. In the process of cleaning the walls, ancient art had also been forever removed (we know this because in some places, the ancient mineral skins were only partially removed, and here remnant traces of pigment survived).

It was in 1990 that the first of many ancient rock paintings began to be seen on the walls of the Grande Grotte, when archaeologist Pierre Guilloré discovered a painting of a black ibex near the terminal end of the cave, in an area where the walls had only been partially cleaned [174]. Here beneath the thinned mineral concretions, painted lines showed through, evidence that something more may lie beneath the rock surface elsewhere in the cave. Dominique Baffier and Michel Girard then commenced their own study of the cave – Baffier studying the art that remained on the walls, Girard the archaeological deposits on the ground. The uncleaned walls were photographed under infrared and ultraviolet light to reveal traces of more than 180 prehistoric artworks partially or entirely covered by calcite. We now know that the art under that carbonate mineral coating had been made some 28,000 to 27,000 years ago.[23] Through time, dissolved limestone particles had seeped through the rock, only to be redeposited as calcite on the wall and ceiling surfaces as the moisture evaporated. Much of the art became covered by the calcite, a soft mineral skin that effectively laminated the art, eventually hiding it from view. But the art survived beneath, protected from surface damage. For us in the late twentieth century, the challenge was to now see properly what lay beneath the accretions.

It is thought that the rock surface at the Grande Grotte was dry when the paintings were done, because the art occurs beneath but not over the redeposited calcite, which requires humidity to form. Sometimes that calcite was several millimetres thick, and in some places even a few centimetres. It had formed a mineral veil both on horizontal ceilings and vertical walls, especially near natural cracks in the rock where water

174. The first painting to be seen in the Grande Grotte by Pierre Guilloré in 1990, of a black ibex deep in the cave. Here the calcite coating is relatively thick, so the jets of chlorinated water did not entirely remove the calcite – and the art beneath – when the walls were cleaned.

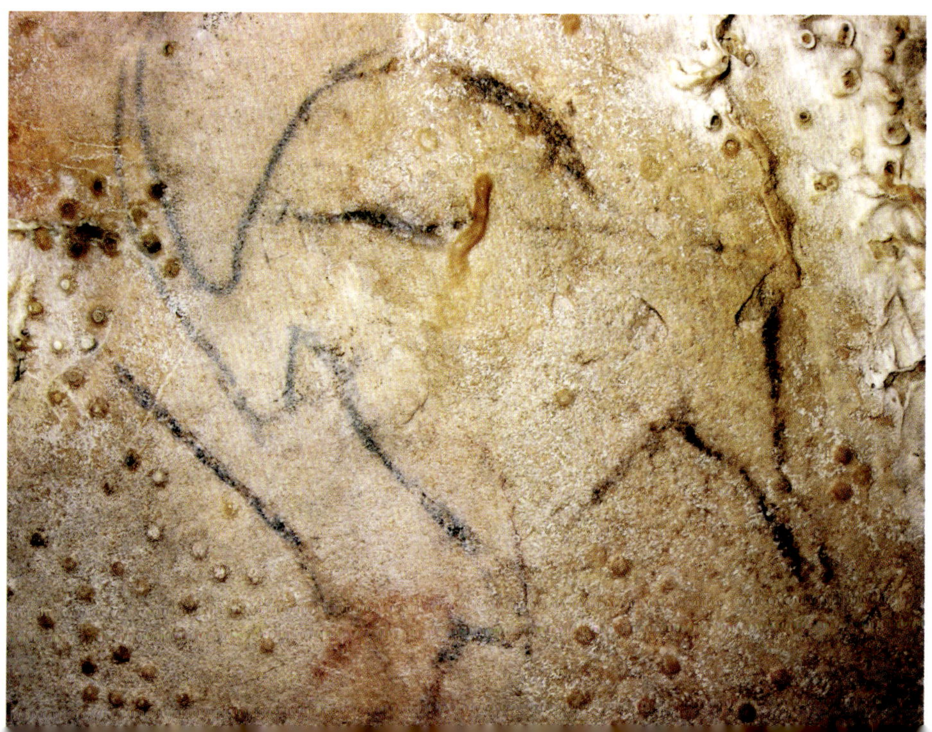

preferrentially seeped out of the rock. By 1990, when Guilloré and, soon after, Baffier and Girard examined the site, traces of pigment could be seen between, and sometimes penetrating through, areas where the calcite had 'grown'.

There are actually two layers of calcite superimposed on each other, not just one, and this soon came to be an important factor in deciding how to conserve the underlying art. The lowermost calcite layer, the one that immediately covers the paintings, is yellowish and translucent. It formed during the Ice Age, reaffirming the great antiquity of the underlying (and therefore older) art. The second and more recent deposit overlies the first calcite layer, and it is itself Holocene in age (less than 11,700 years old). This latter layer is white and opaque, and it is this layer that today hides the rock paintings from view. Baffier and Girard realized that the two layers were not stuck to each other, but like pages of a book could be neatly separated out, giving them a way of both exposing the art for viewing (by removing enough of the opaque layer on top) and also protecting it (by keeping the underlying transparent layer).

The work of peeling away the overlying layer of calcite and thus uncovering the paintings was first undertaken by specialist cave art conservator Eudald Guillamet in 1997 [175].

175. Eudald Guillamet removing with a diamond-studded bronze drill the upper, opaque layer of calcite that covers a red woolly mammoth in the Grande Grotte.

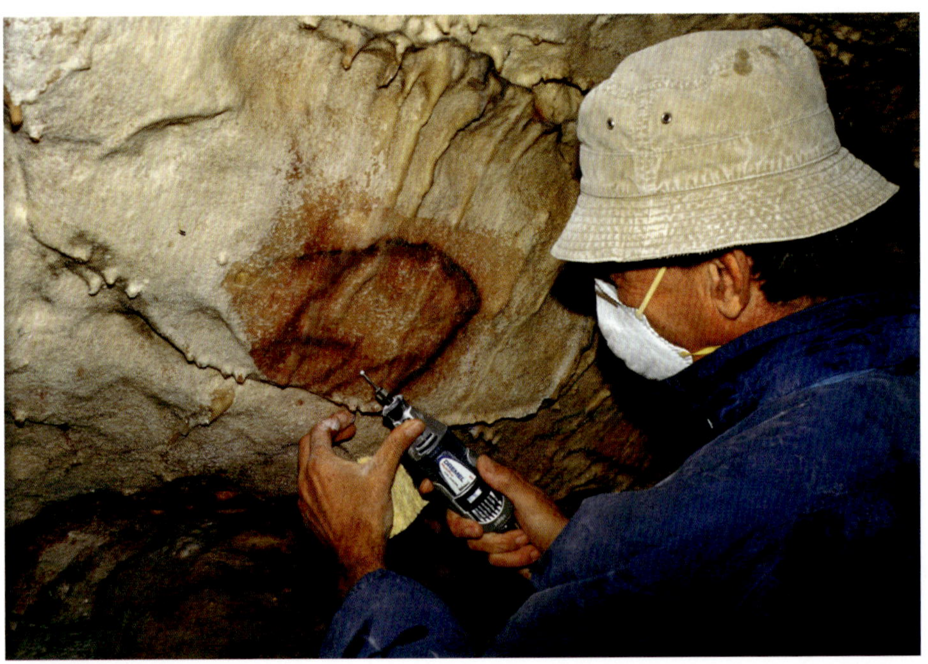

176. The first woolly mammoth discovered by abrading away the overlying calcite with a diamond-studded bronze drill in the Grande Grotte, 1997. (above) Wall surface prior to conservation work. (below) After removing most of the upper layer of calcite.

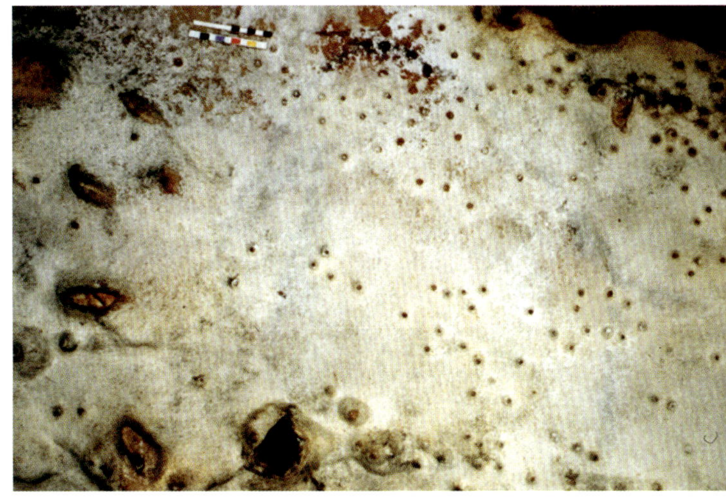

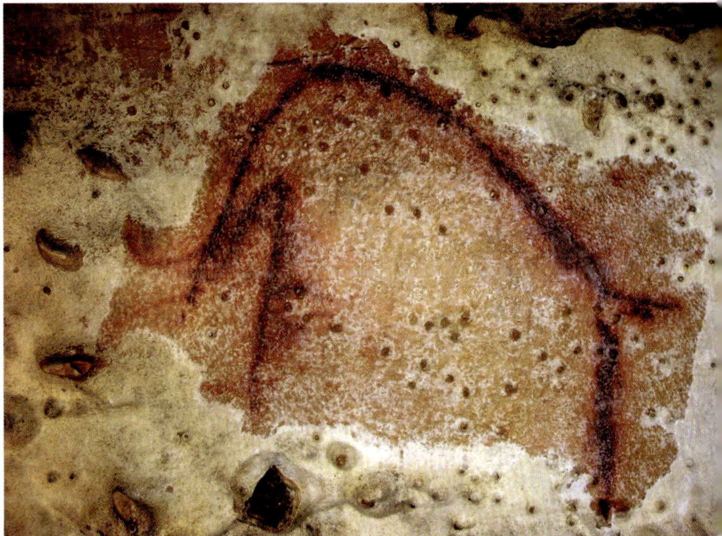

His meticulous work involved thinning the white, opaque calcite layer by mechanical abrasion with a diamond-studded bronze drill. This layer was sufficiently thinned to remove its opacity, keeping the translucent calcite layer beneath intact. The transparency of the remnant calcite layers allowed the paintings to be clearly seen with the naked eye [176, 177, 178].

The first mammoth painting was revealed on the ceiling of the Grande Grotte in 1997, the initial year of Guillamet's work [176]. Another subsequently found is immense, measuring 1.6 m (5 ft 3 in.)

177. Conservators Eudald
Guillamet and Laura Ballester
working on the western wall
of the Grande Grotte.

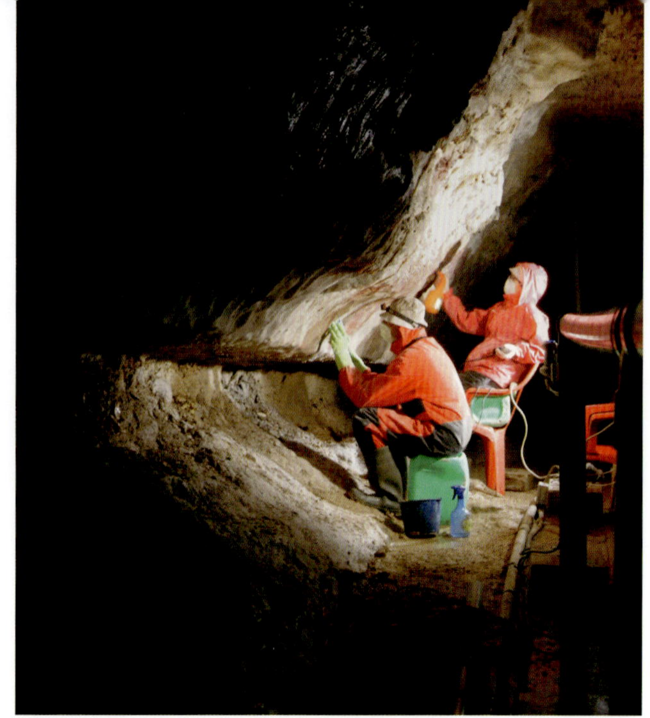

178. (below and opposite)
Sequence of photographs showing
the gradual uncovering of a large
woolly mammoth on the wall of
the Grande Grotte.

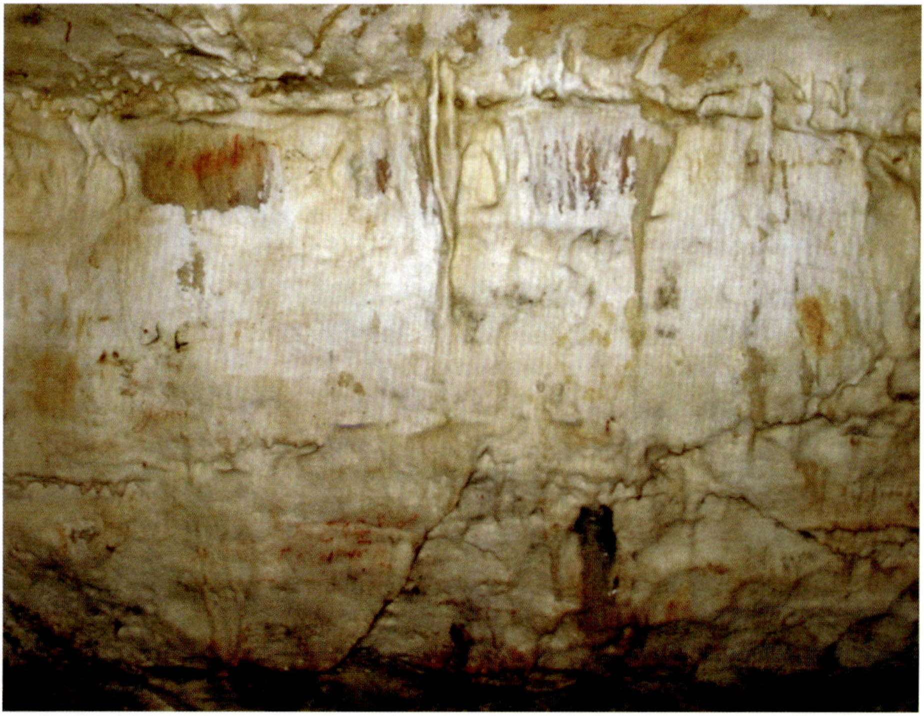

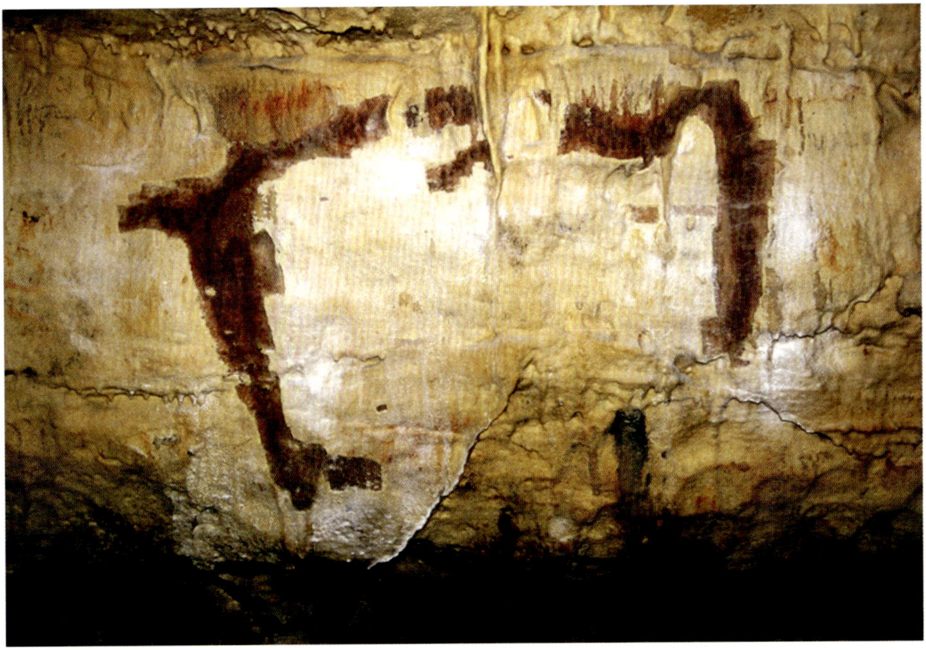

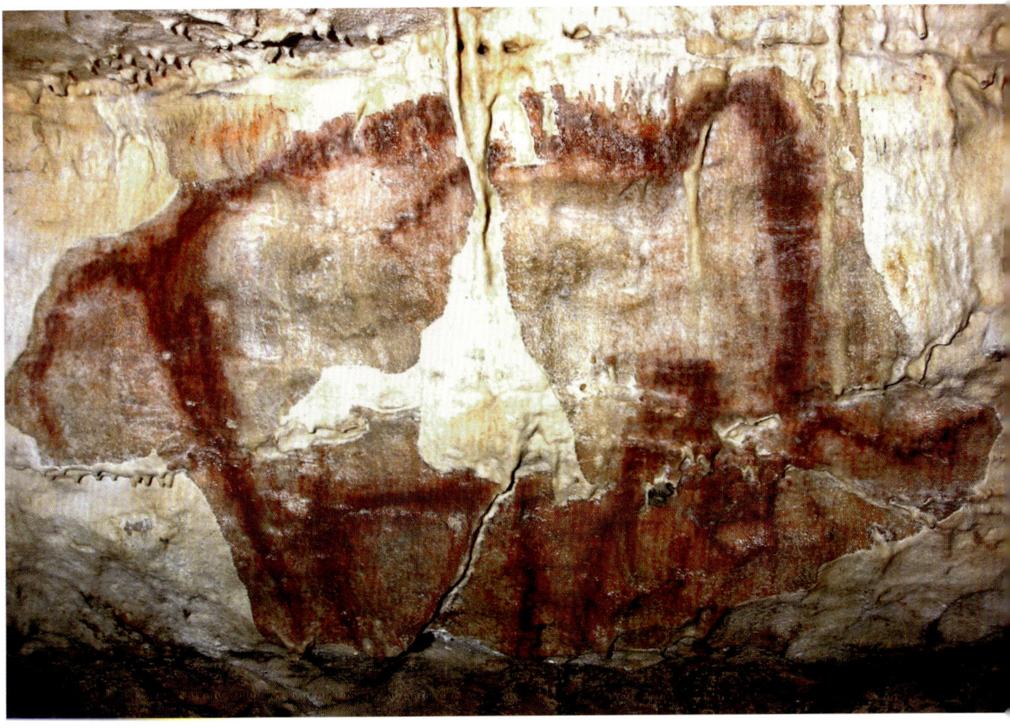

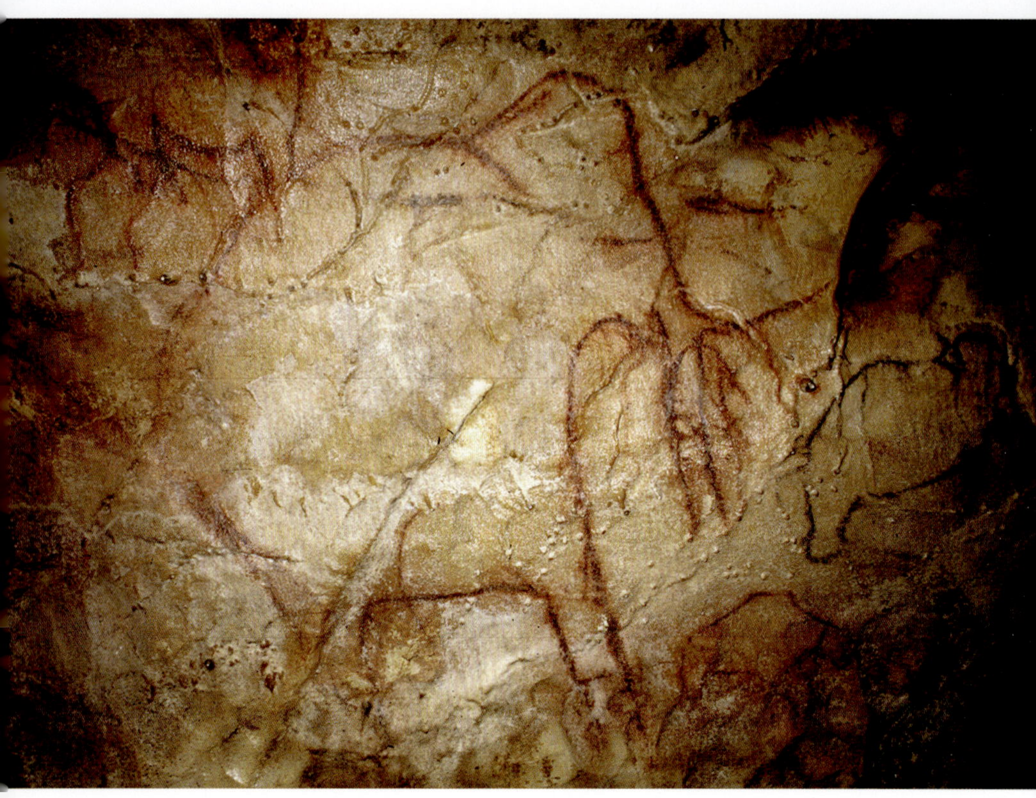

long and larger in execution than most other known paintings of
the species [179]. It is flanked on each side by a painted bear. These
Arcy-sur-Cure discoveries are spectacular, and perhaps even more
so because they were so unexpected when first noticed. And they
flag to us now that many other paintings have probably suffered the
same fate, awaiting discovery both in known and unknown caves
where walls are covered with calcite.

The Ice Age art of Western Europe is instructive in that it tells
us that the first Europeans already knew how to make magnificent
galleries of figurative art when they arrived. It also alerts us to
the fact that cave art was not necessarily done everywhere,
but instead probably took place among peoples who shared
cultures of deep cave exploration and ritual engagement. These
are archaeological hotspots from our present-day perspective,
not so much because they are where art was first done on
rock canvasses, but because they are well-protected locations
that have served to preserve the art over vast periods of time.

Elsewhere, where rock surfaces are not as well protected,
the paintings have eroded away and walls have broken up over
the ages, removing with each successive phase of collapse any
remaining art; and in some cases redeposited calcite and other
similar rocky skins have covered the art, making it invisible to the
naked eye. Along coastal plains ancient sites now lie deep under
the sea. But as Blombos Cave and other early African sites make
abundantly clear, early humans knew how to make visual symbols
long before the Ice Age art of Europe. And so too did people
continue to make art long after the climate warmed.

Chapter 7:   Beyond the European Ice Age

Only a few parts of the world have cave art dated to the Ice Age. This paucity is due to a combination of factors, chief among these being that only in some regions did the ancients venture deep into the recesses of caves, where rock surfaces have remained well protected from the elements and therefore been preserved over many thousands of years.

In Africa, the earliest figurative images date to the Ice Age. They consist of four schist plaquettes (or tablets) buried deep underground at Apollo 11 Cave, in southern Namibia. Each features a painted animal or part of one, for most of the flat pieces of rock have long ago snapped across the painted images. One has a zebra, its black stripes showing clearly over a white body [180], another depicts a rhinoceros drawn in black outline, probably over a white wash [181], and two conjoining pieces are of the hindquarters and head and torso of a four-legged animal thought to be either a wild cat such as a lion (because of the shape of the head), or a kind of antelope (because there are two painted lines that seem to emanate from the head) [182]. Another

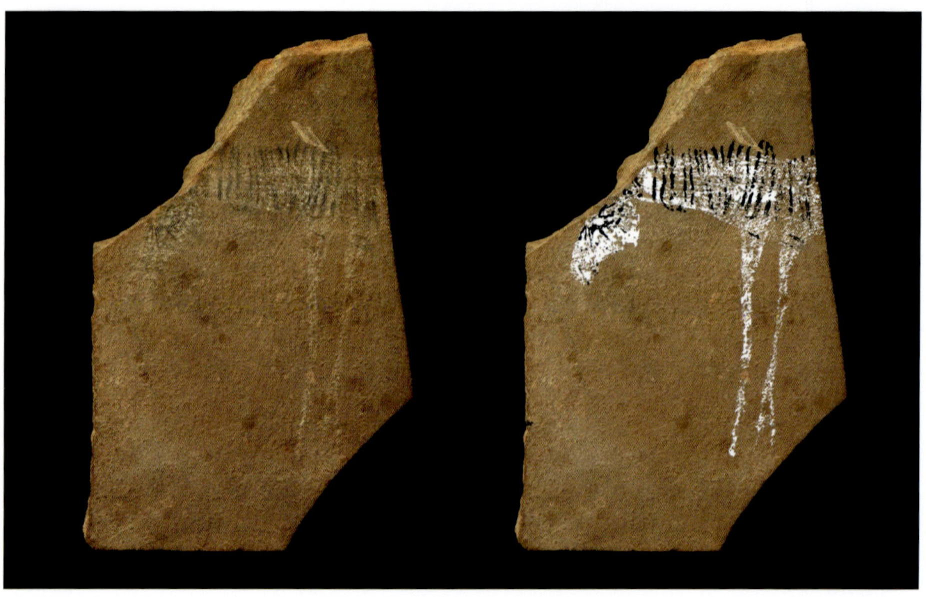

180. Fragment of a broken schist plaquette with a painted zebra excavated from Apollo 11 Cave, Namibia, c. 30,000 years old; (left) original photograph; (right) after digital enhancement to bring out the painting.

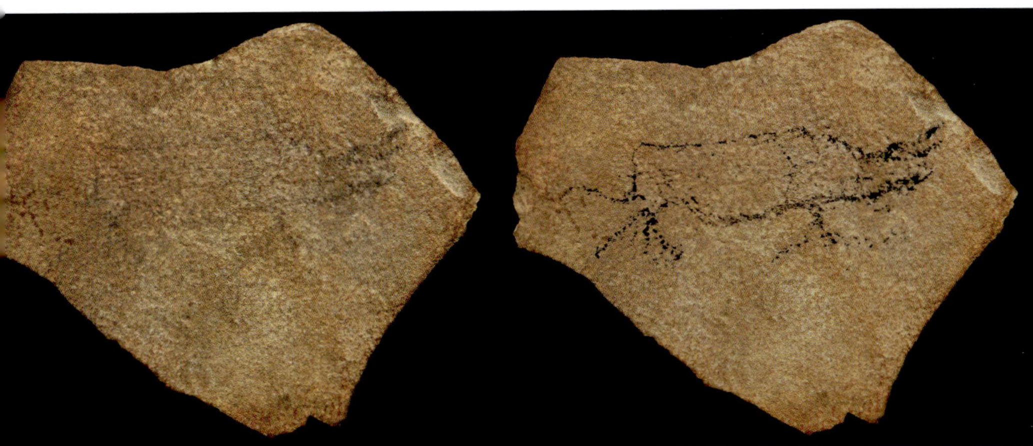

181. Black-outlined rhinoceros on a schist plaquette excavated from a *c.* 30,000-year-old layer at Apollo 11 Cave, showing both the original (left) and digitally enhanced (right) photograph.

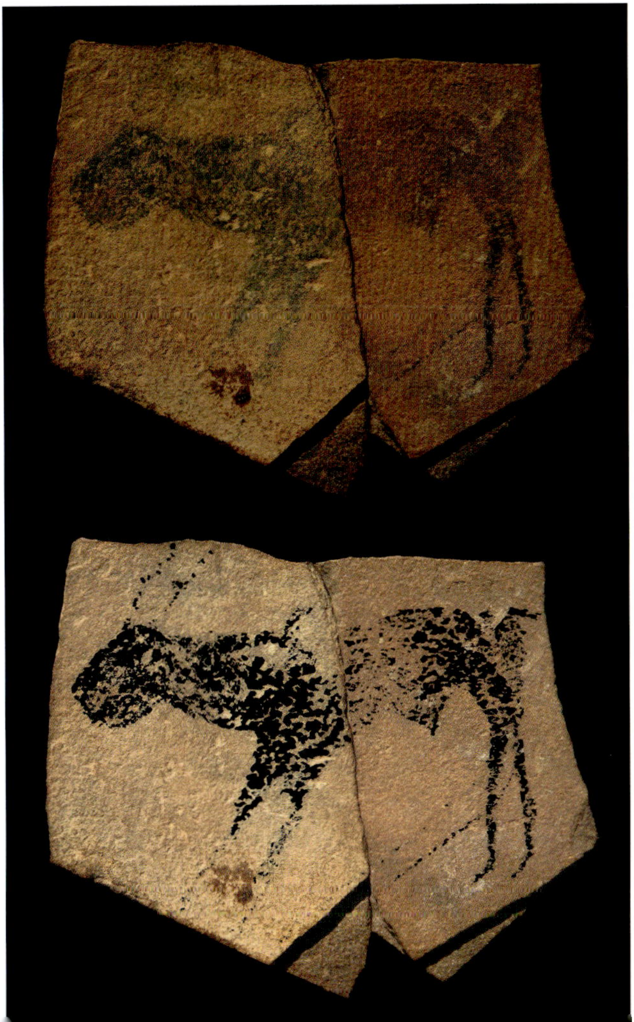

182. Two conjoining fragments of a schist plaquette excavated from a *c.* 30,000-year-old layer at Apollo 11 Cave, showing both the original (above) and digitally enhanced (below) photograph. It contains a painting of an animal that may be a wild cat or antelope.

three plaquettes from the same buried level – and therefore dating to the same period of time – have faded paintings or drawings of indeterminate forms. They all date to about 30,000 years ago.[1]

In Australia, I would estimate that there are somewhere between 150,000 and 250,000 rock art sites, with only a tiny fraction of these being true caves or particularly deep rockshelters. We know that art was practised there from the earliest arrival of people on the Australian continent, shortly before 50,000 years ago, because fragments of imported ochre have been found in archaeological deposits dating that far back at Madjebebe (aka Malakunanja II) and Nauwalabila I in Arnhem Land, and there is a rock slab with traces of ochre dating to sometime between 37,000 and 50,000 years ago at Carpenter's Gap in the Kimberley region (see Chapter 5). But the oldest dated actual image in Australia is many thousands of years younger. It is not a full design but on a tiny rock that fell from the ceiling in the well-protected site of Nawarla Gabarnmang, already described in earlier chapters. That 3-cm-long (1 in.) piece of rock has charcoal lineworks painted or drawn on one surface, representing a small, broken section of an originally larger motif. It is not possible to determine what was depicted, as the excavated piece is too small to tell, but it dates back some 27,000 years [39].

Along the coastal plains of southern Australia on the opposite side of the continent to Arnhem Land, during the peak of the Ice Age, Aboriginal people dragged their fingers, and sticks, into the soft 'moonmilk' that coats the surfaces of the walls of limestone caves beneath the Nullarbor Plain [183, 184]. Here there is Ice Age art deep in the caves – at Koonalda Cave, c. 22,000-year-old charcoal from ancient fireplaces is associated with 'finger fluting' on the walls of the Art Passage[2] – but this is one of the very few places in Australia where people ventured far into caves, and therefore where underground cave art has been found.

Further to the south again, on the walls of Ballawinne Cave, a limestone cavern near the shores of the Maxwell River in Tasmania's dense beech rainforest, hand stencils are partly covered with redeposited calcite. One of the hand stencils has the first joint of the middle finger missing, perhaps a sign of ritual mutilation far back in the past (a number of Aboriginal groups across Australia ritually removed parts of their fingers during the early ethnographic period of the late 1700s and 1800s).

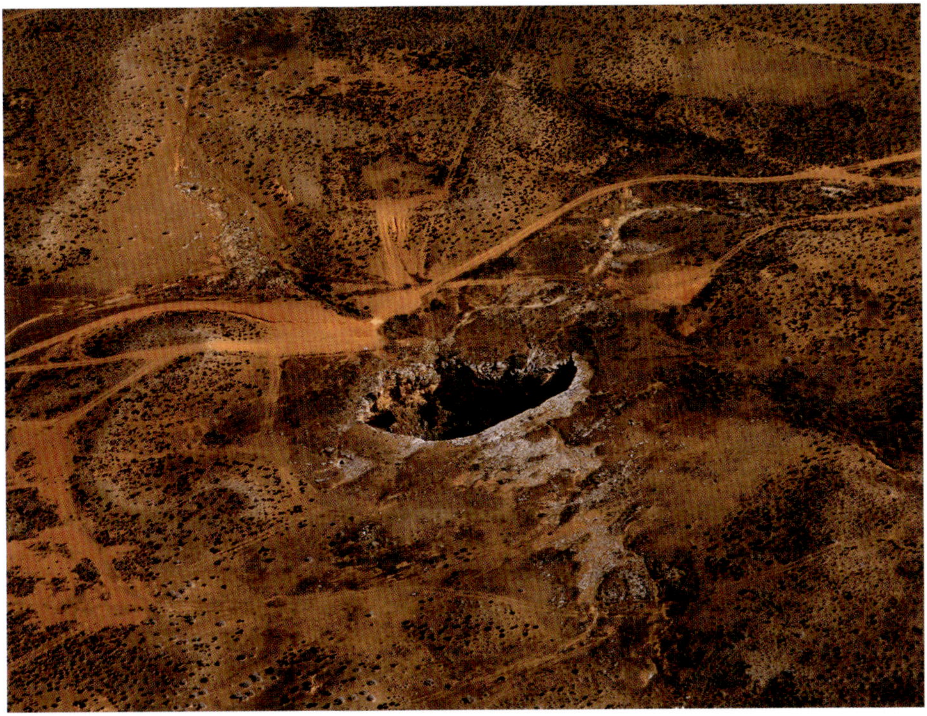

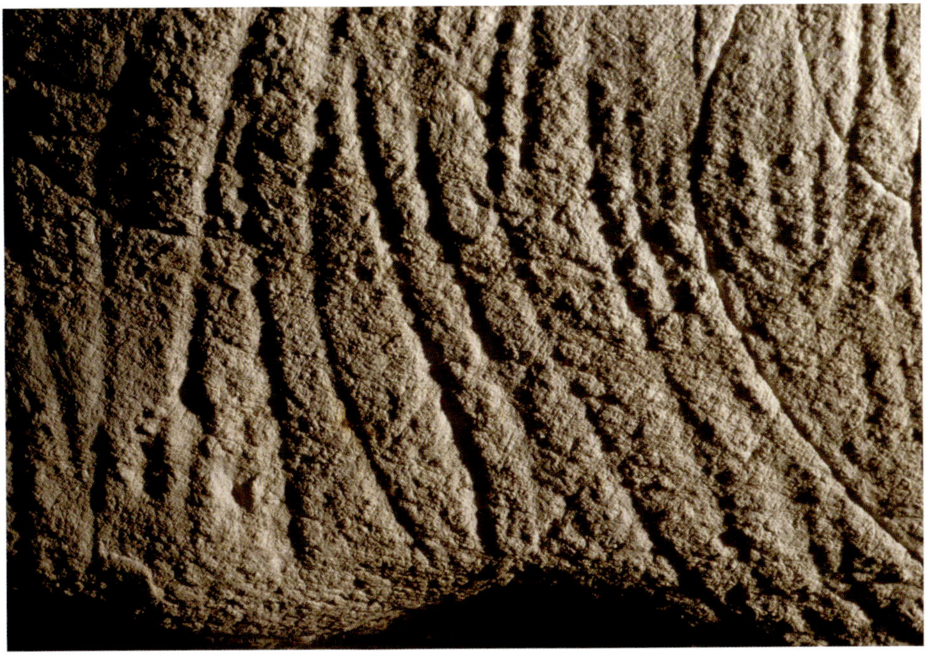

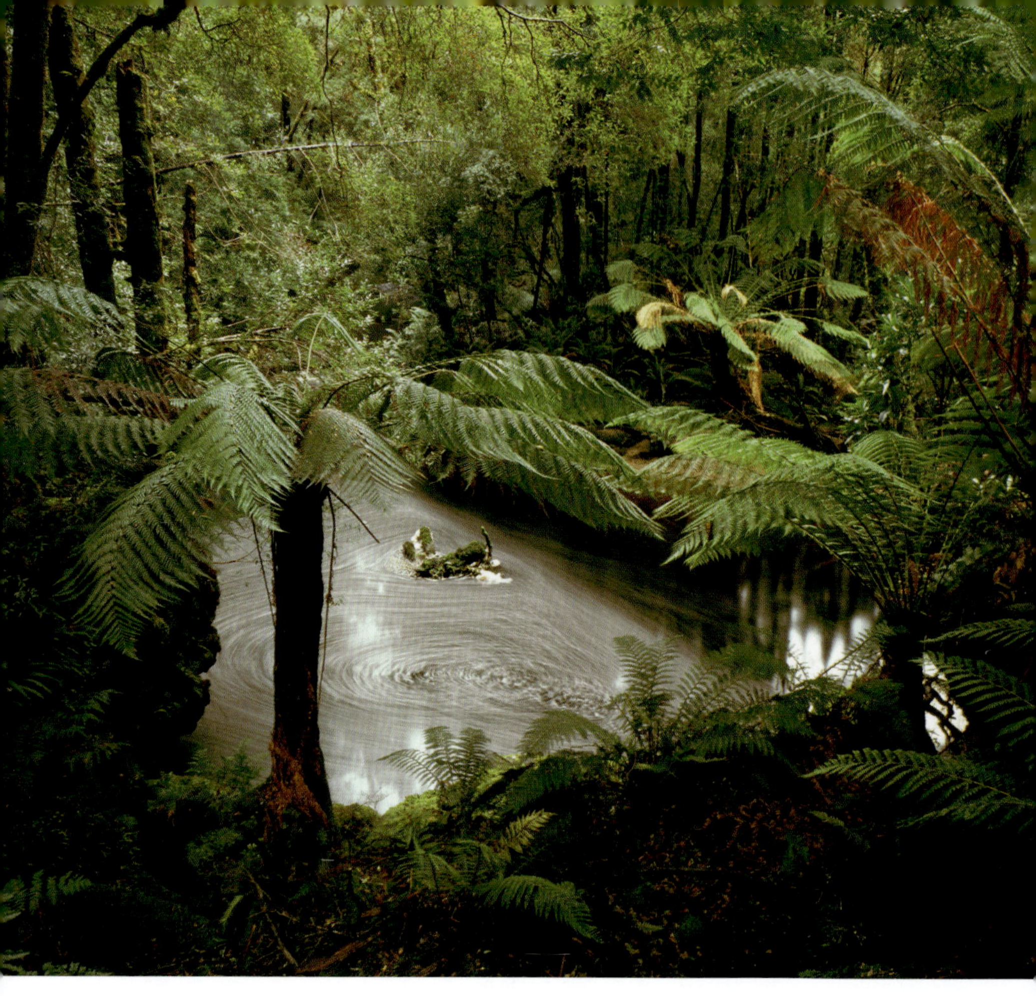

185. Dense temperate rainforest in Tasmania's southwest. In the 1980s, limestone caves with rich archaeological deposits began to be found in the rainforest, carbon dates revealing that Aboriginal people occupied them during the Ice Age, between 40,000 and 13,000 years ago, when the regional vegetation was more open. Two of the caves have hand stencils thought to date to the period of occupation.

Some 85 km (50 miles) away is Wargata Mina in the Cracroft Valley, also in the midst of Tasmania's dense temperate rainforest [185]. Here, too, hand stencils are partly covered with speleothems, redeposited calcite. The overgrowing mineral deposit is thought to be more than 12,000 years old, because of the environmental conditions required for its growth, and as the hand stencils lie beneath the calcite, the art is likely to be older than that. All the buried archaeological deposits of the region date to between 40,000 and 13,000 years ago, a time when regional mountain tops were covered with ice, and lowland to montane plains and valleys were open vegetation with patches of grassland and scrub rather than rainforest. Tasmania's dense temperate rainforests contain few food resources and are almost impenetrable, so it is very unlikely that the art could date to the time of the rainforest.

In Australia there are other clues that very old art may survive on rock walls, although such art remains undated. Across the 1,400-km-long (875 miles) region spanning from the Kimberley to Arnhem Land – comparable in distance to the area from northern Spain, where Altamira is found, to France's Massif Central, which contains Chauvet Cave – enigmatic human figures and associated fauna are painted in fine lines in thousands of rockshelters. Here the rock is extremely hard, usually quartzite, and sometimes the paint has penetrated into the rock, and a very thin mineral layer now coats the art, protecting it. What is striking about the art's distribution across the landscape is that it occurs on both sides of the Joseph Bonaparte Gulf (named by the famed French explorer Nicholas Baudin in 1803, one year before Joseph's brother Napoleon was crowned Emperor of France) [186]. The Gulf became inundated when sea levels rose at the end of the Ice Age, meaning that comparable artworks found on either side of it most probably developed before the sea had risen. On the Kimberley side to the west of the Gulf are found what we now know as Gwion paintings, curious human shapes richly decorated with accoutrements such as feather or hair tassels, elaborate headgear, hand-propelled spears and boomerangs [187, 188]. Hundreds of kilometres to the east, in Arnhem Land, we find what archaeologists call Dynamic Figures, similar in style to the Gwion figures of the Kimberley, the musculature of the legs often well defined, and again richly attired with tassels, headdresses, hand-propelled spears and boomerangs [189]. In Arnhem Land boomerangs are entirely unknown as hunting or fighting weapons during

186. Painted Gwion motifs of the Kimberley and Dynamic Figures of Arnhem Land on either side of the Joseph Bonaparte Gulf, northern Australia.

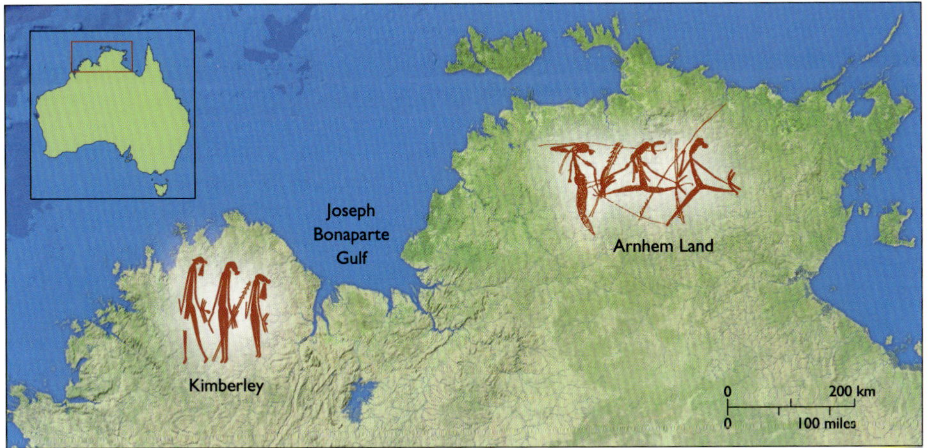

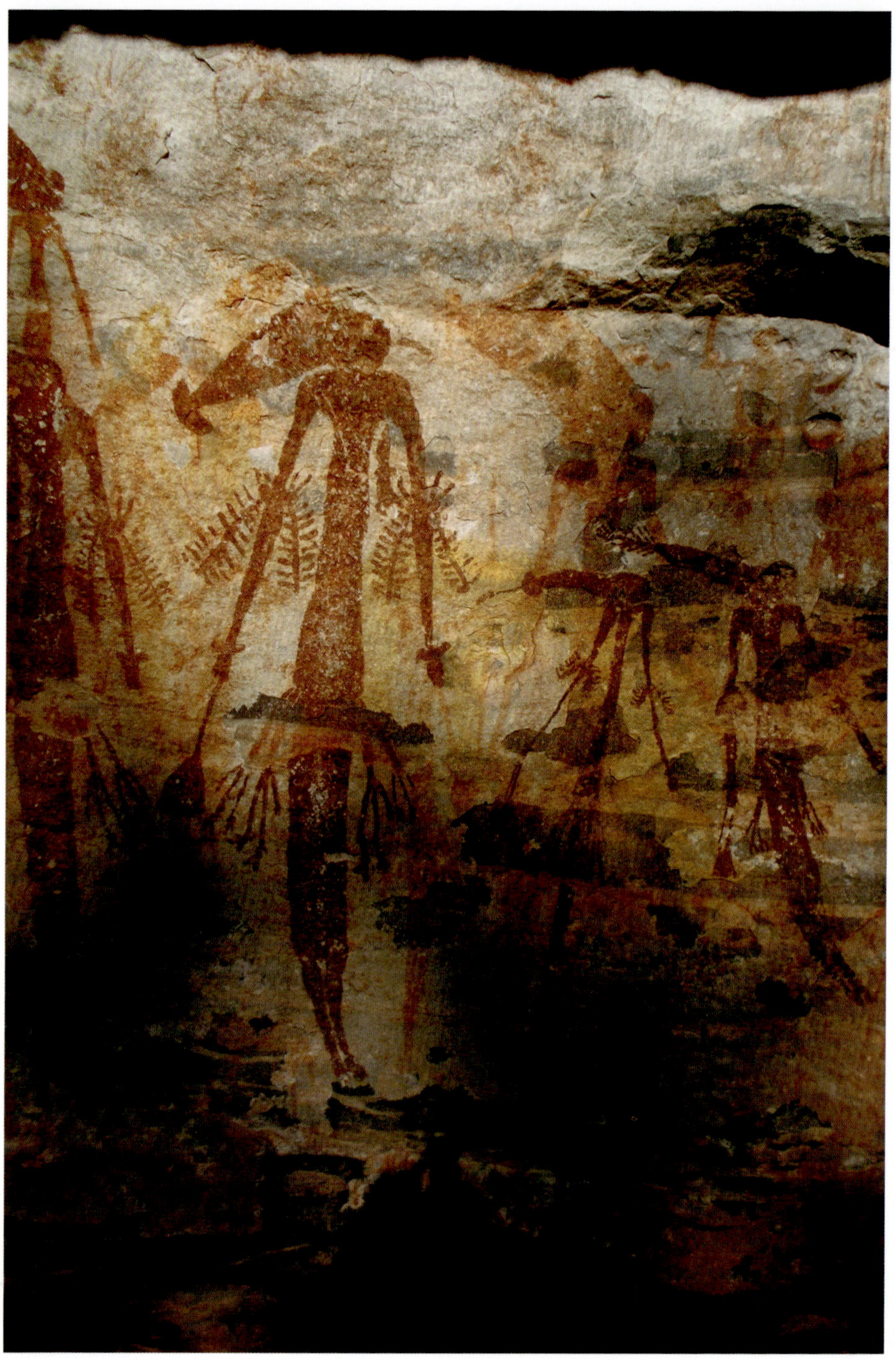

187. (opposite) Guyon (Gwion) rock paintings of human figures decorated with tassels, arm bands and sporting elaborate headdresses in Kwini Country, East Kimberley region, northern Australia.

188. (right) Guyon (Gwion) paintings in a shallow but well-protected rockshelter in Kwini Country, East Kimberley region, northern Australia.

189. (below) Dynamic Figures high up on the Arnhem Land plateau, Jawoyn Country, northern Australia.

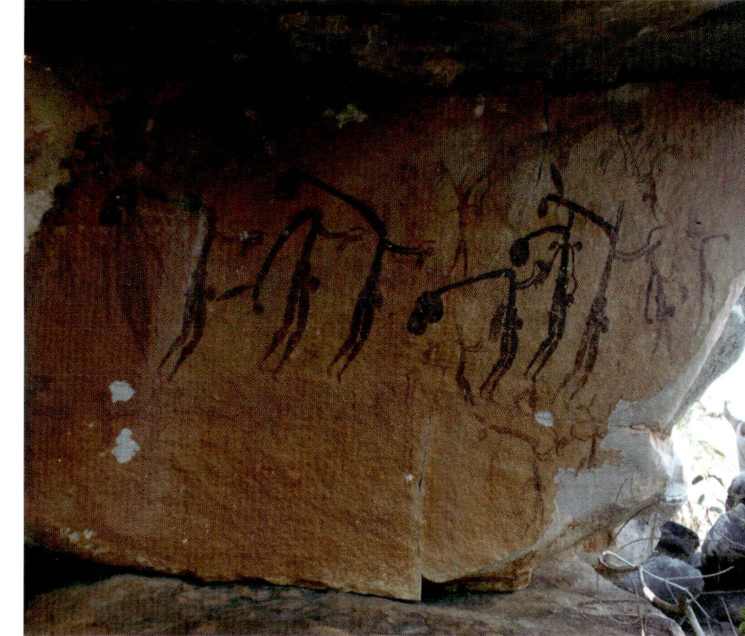

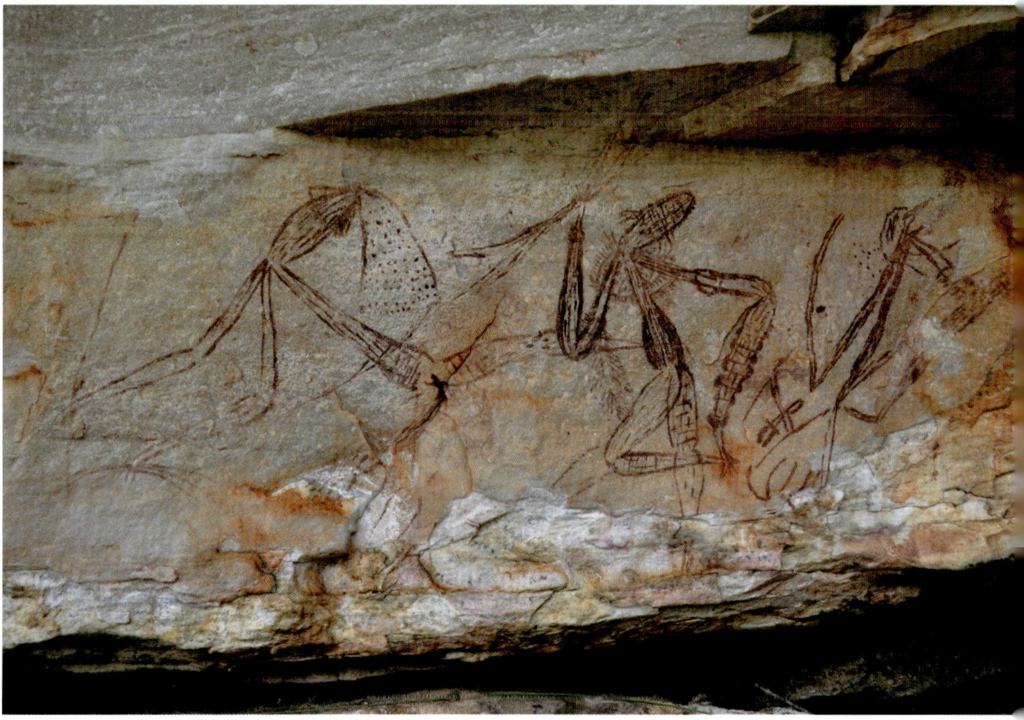

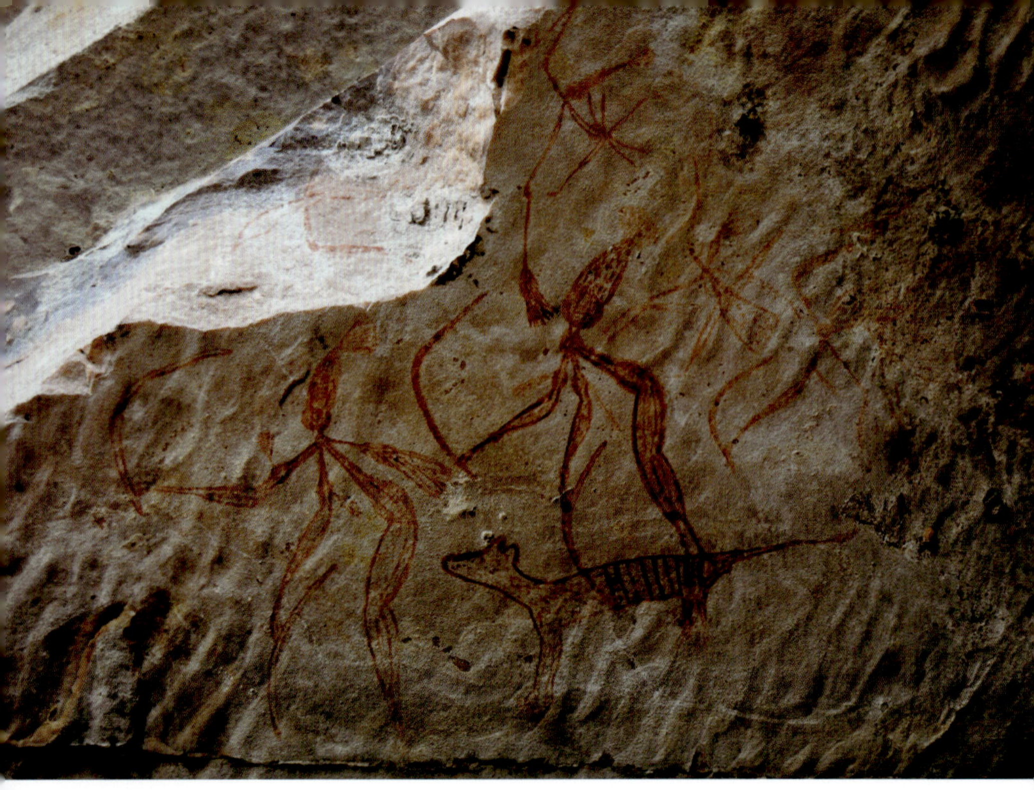

190. Dynamic Figures wielding boomerangs on the Arnhem Land plateau, Jawoyn Country. They are accompanied by a thylacine ('Tasmanian tiger'), a marsupial animal that became extinct across mainland Australia sometime between 4,000 and 3,500 years ago. The scene signals a symbiotic relationship, perhaps even a degree of domestication. The art allows us to consider a past that we would not otherwise be aware of.

more recent times (in the 1800s they were used as clapsticks to make music), but in the Dynamic Figure paintings they are carried in-hand while hunting or on the run, or tucked into thin, presumably hair, belts around the waist.

Curiously, in Arnhem Land some Dynamic Figures are closely associated with Tasmanian tigers, four-legged marsupial animals that became extinct on the Australian mainland sometime between 4,000 and 3,500 years ago, around the same time that the dingo, the Australian 'native' dog, first arrived on the continent. This artistic association between Tasmanian tigers and Dynamic Figures confirms that the latter must be older than 3,500 years in age. It also brings to mind some kind of symbiotic relationship between the Aboriginal peoples of the time and the Tasmanian tiger. Could this kind of 'marsupial dog' [190] – biologically not a dog at all, and socially a normally timid animal – have developed a close association with humans in this part of the continent? Could they even have been to some degree domesticated, thousands of years before any known domesticates in Australia? We do not know the answers, but the questions challenge us to think outside what we know, outside our comfort

191. Wandjina in the traditional country of the Woddordda Aboriginal people. This site was first recorded in 1838 by the European explorer George Grey during his journey through the Kimberley. Contemporary Woddordda explain that Grey did not understand that Wandjina are their spirit-ancestors, powerful sentient creator-beings who transformed themselves into paintings during the era of creation called Lalai, 'the Dreaming'. Woddordda stress that at Wandjina sites it is important to observe cultural protocols that show respect for the Wandjina, and that it is the community's duty to periodically renew the paintings to maintain their brightness.

zone, and to question what we think we know about what people did so long ago. Although it set the foundations for how we are now, the past was culturally different, and through the imagery that was made thousands of years ago, the art helps us think in new ways about those differences, to some degree free from the traditionally imposed conceptual lens (and restrictions) of historical and ethnographic comparisons.

Across the Kimberley and Arnhem Land, the Gwion and Dynamic Figures share common attributes presumably dating back to the Ice Age when the two regions were connected by a land bridge. In both regions the art of boomerang wielders gave way to paintings of people who carried hooked sticks that were used to propel spears (some of these are depicted attached to the ends of spears ready for launching). When the Joseph Bonaparte Gulf began to form after post-glacial sea level rises, art styles started to further diverge across the two regions, an observation first made by rock art specialist and historian Darrell Lewis in the 1980s.[3] Eventually, the art developed into strongly regionalized forms, such as the Wandjina of the Kimberley [191], the X-ray designs of Arnhem Land [49, 192] and complex figurative designs in Wardaman Country in between [193], indicating that by the time those styles had developed, the more

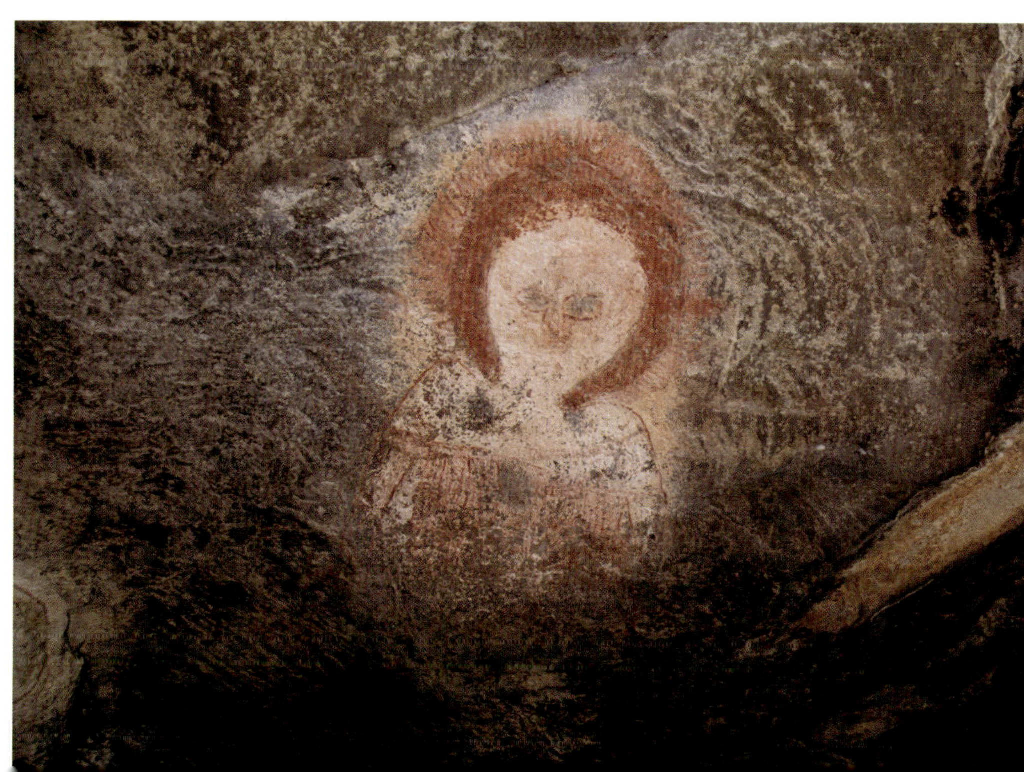

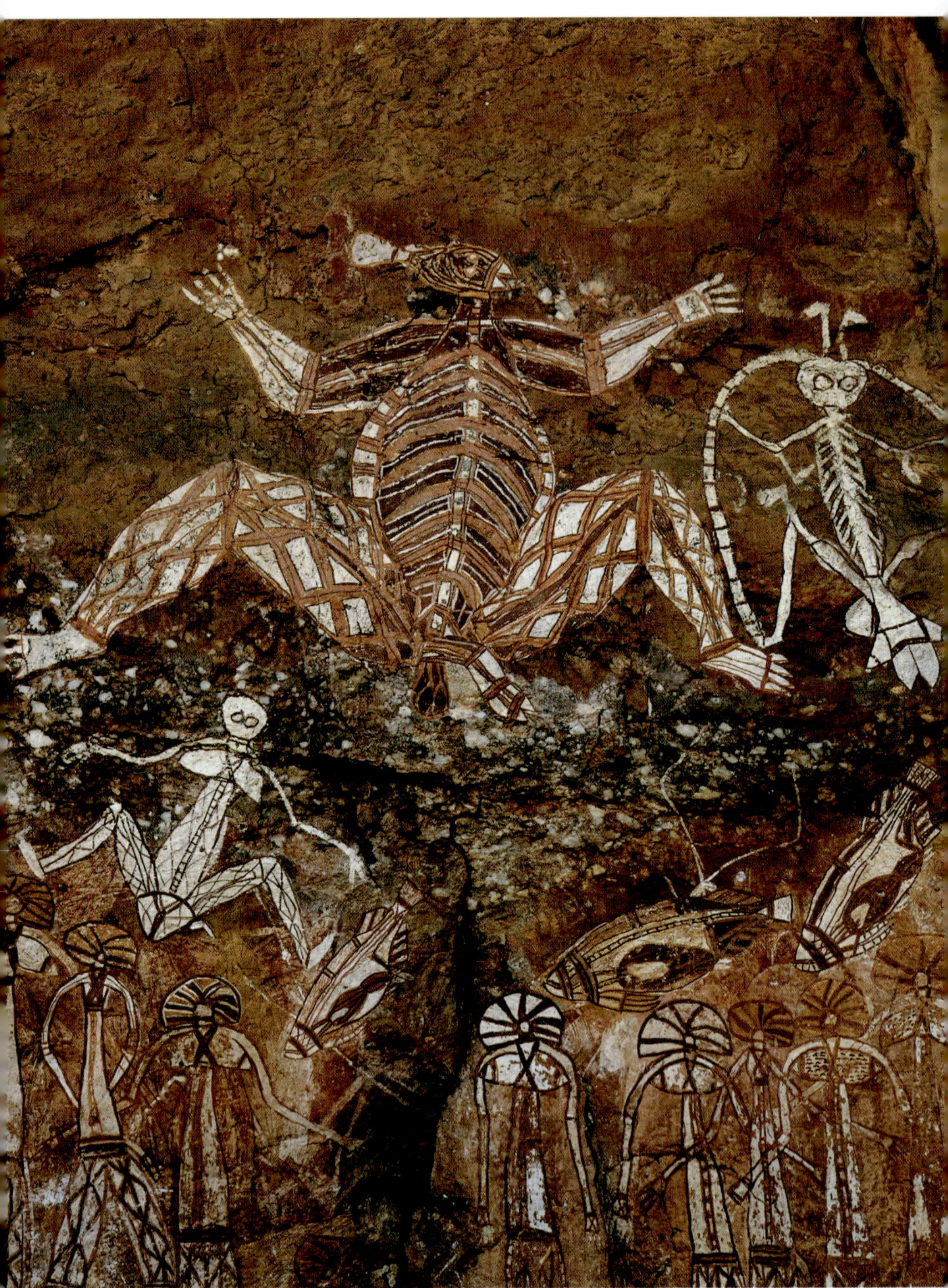

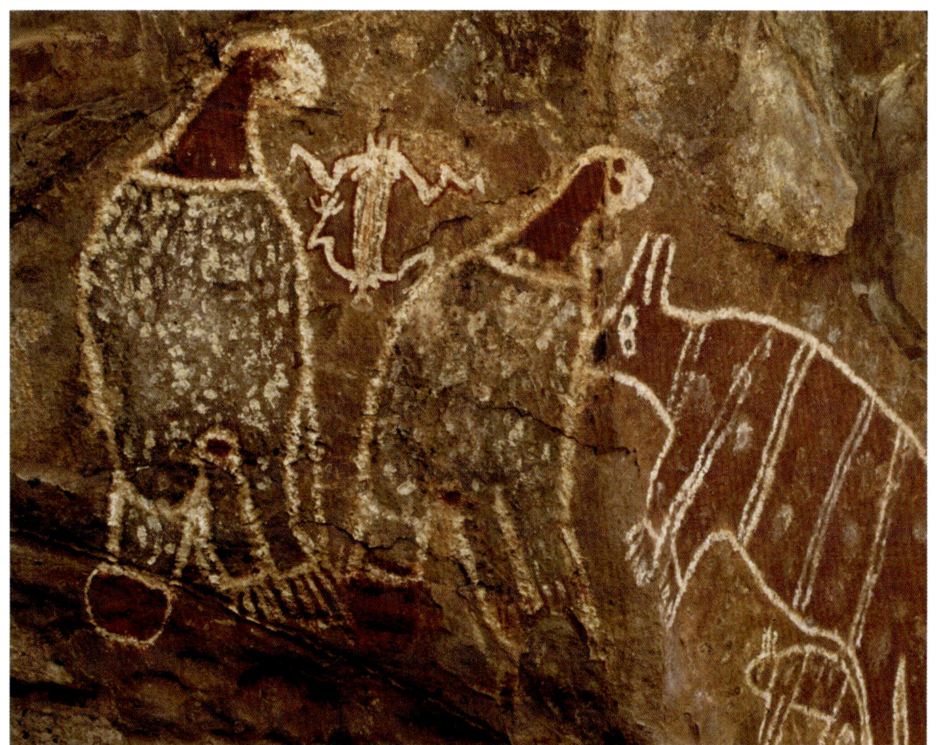

193. (above) *Buwarraja* (Dreaming) *gornbu* (hawks) at the site of Garnawala in Wardaman Country, half-way between the Kimberley and Arnhem Land.

192. (opposite) X-ray rock paintings at Burrungkuy, in Arnhem Land's Kakadu National Park, northern Australia. Traditional Owner Jeff Lee says of this and other rock paintings on his ancestral lands: 'Rock art is very important to me. It reminds me of the ancestors and respect for the cultural laws that we live by'.

or less united physical and cultural landscape that had bridged the exposed plains between the Kimberley and Arnhem Land during the Ice Age was now severed.

After the Ice Age

It is only in a few places in the world that detailed study of ancient rock surfaces in well-protected caves and rockshelters with deep overhanging roofs has been carried out. In some regions still devoid of scientific study, people may nonetheless have entered caves long ago in the past, and here there could be much more Ice Age art waiting to be discovered. A case in point is Sulawesi, one of Indonesia's 18,000 islands, where in 2014 Maxime Aubert and fellow archaeologists decided to try U-series dating on rock accretions that had built up over cave paintings in the limestone pinnacles of the Maros district (see Chapter 3). In some cases the concretions over the art were shown to have formed close to 40,000 years ago, and so the underlying paintings must be older.

Much more common is the art that was made after the end of the Ice Age. One simple reason for this is that this art is younger, and therefore it is more likely to have survived. In addition, global populations multiplied after the end of the Ice Age as temperatures warmed and biomass increased, and it is likely that these growing populations led people to increasingly mark their territories through socially recognizable imagery. The artworks functioned as aesthetic expressions of culture as people reinforced their social identity within their territories or in the places where they went or lived.

The proliferation of artworks following the Ice Age saw the development of new and highly regionalized art styles across all continents (artistic regionalism also existed during earlier times). In Europe, Upper Palaeolithic figurative and abstract designs ceased to be depicted on the walls of caves and rockshelters, making way for new kinds of post-glacial artworks such as Azilian painted pebbles immediately following the Magdalenian [194]; Mesolithic, Neolithic and Metal Age depictions then followed as agriculture, pastoralism and long-term settlements became established. Rather than in the dark chambers of deep caves, most artworks were now made near the entrances of sites in association with human habitation, agricultural fields,

194. Azilian pebbles from Mas-d'Azil, Ariège region of France. The Azilian is an archaeological period of Western Europe, in particular Spain and France, that immediately followed the Magdalenian at the end of the Upper Palaeolithic. It dates to *c.* 12,000 years ago.

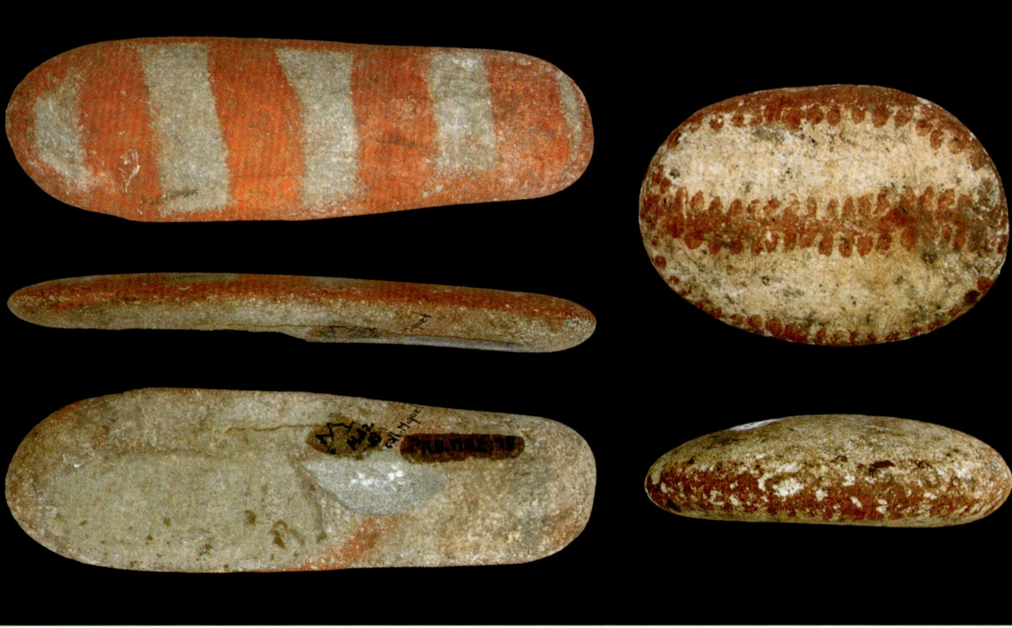

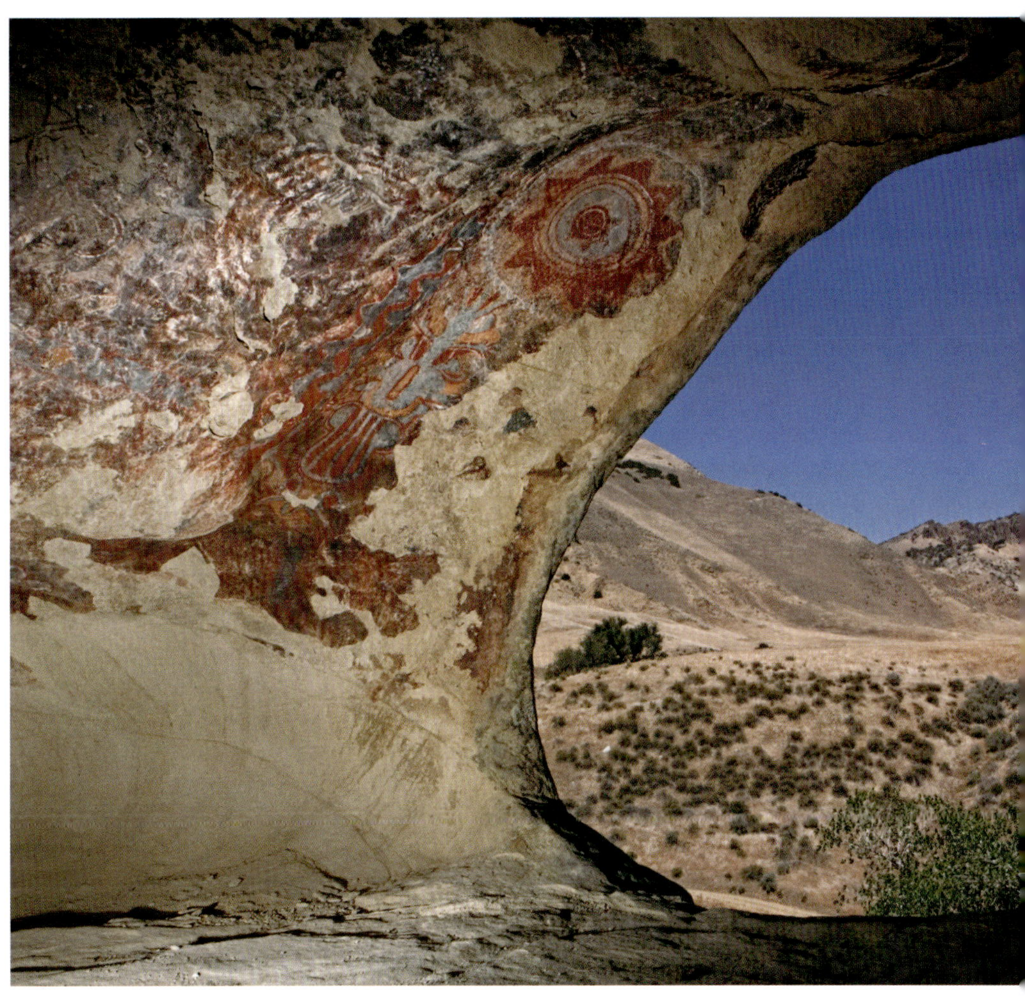

paths of communication, animal pens and ritual activities.
In North America new regional styles developed, such as
the Chumash art of southern California with its rich and often
polychrome geometric patterns consisting of diamond shapes,
zigzags, shield-like designs and related forms [195]; or the
engravings of bighorn sheep (*Ovis canadensis*) and other fauna,
humans (sometimes with elaborate body decoration) and items
of material culture, such as near Moab in Utah [196].[4] Many
other rock art styles developed in North America, mostly
during the past 7,000 years. These individual styles became highly
differentiated from each other, suggesting fundamental cultural
differences between territorial groups and social networks

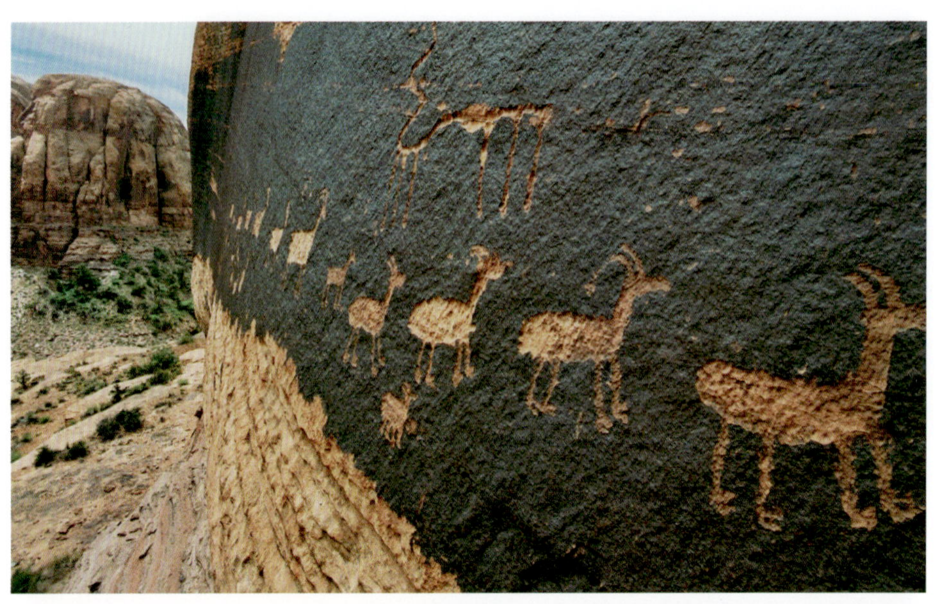

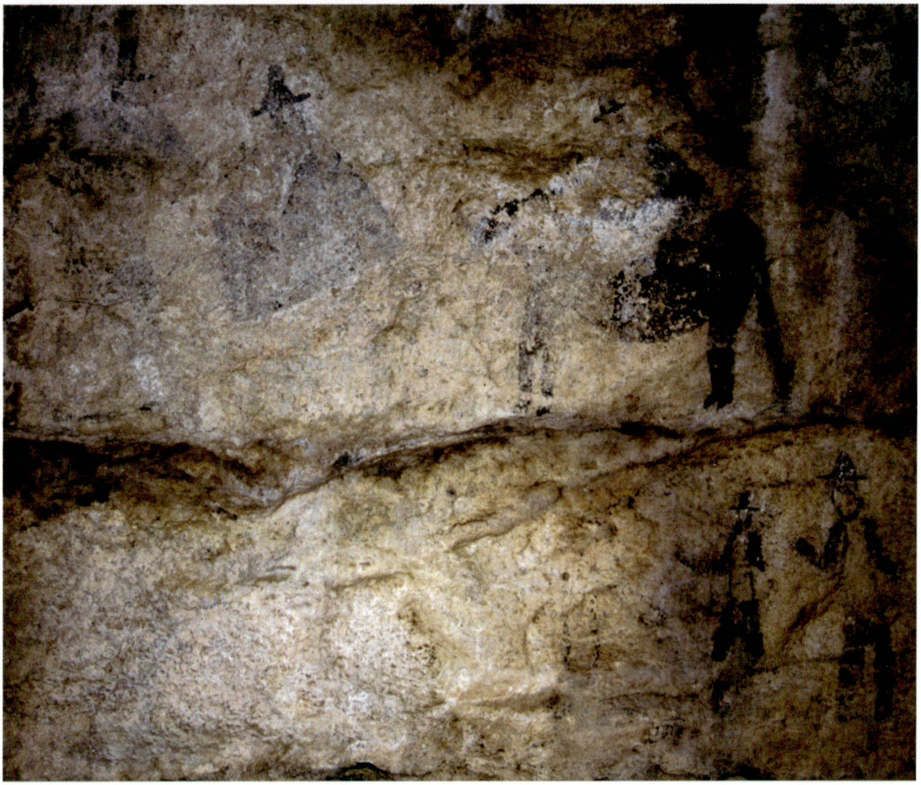

196. (opposite above) Moab art, Utah, USA. The Moab region contains many rock art styles thought to span some 7,000 years, although the exact age of the art is not yet well understood. One of these art styles features engravings of bighorn sheep, thought to have been made mainly during the Ancestral Puebloan (Anasazi) period, and probably dating within the last c. 2,000 years.

197. (opposite below) Paintings of people on horses wearing tall, felt-like hats. Manzano Mountains, New Mexico, USA.

of alliance and information exchange. High up in the beautiful Manzano Mountains that rise up some 3,000 m (10,000 ft) above sea level in western New Mexico, a secluded rockshelter has faded paintings of people on horses. They wear tall, felt-like hats, and robes reminiscent of sixteenth- or seventeenth-century Spanish missionaries and travellers, tantalizing signs of early European intrusions (Spanish settlers first arrived in New Mexico in 1598) [197].

In Australia, the past 6,000 years in particular saw the development of distinctive artistic expressions across much of the continent. In the southeast region of Cape York Peninsula, for example, rich traditions of figurative art consisting of human figures and animals began to take shape at various times between 6,000 and 2,000 years ago [198], such as the echidna-anthropomorph compound beings ('therianthropes', part-animal, part-human figures) of the Koolburra Plateau; 'Quinkan' and other kinds of spirit-beings of Laura; moth/butterfly depictions and zoomorphs with crescent heads of coastal Princess

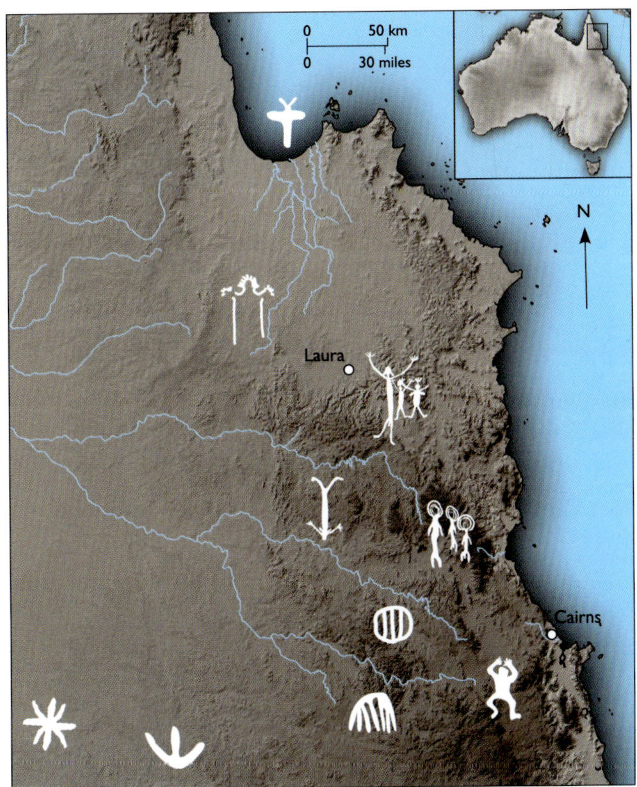

198. (right) Southeast Cape York Peninsula, northern Australia. Here mid to late Holocene paintings, in some regions beginning c. 6,000 years ago but mostly dating to the last 2,000 years, become highly regionalized, suggesting increasing symbolic (artistic) differentiation during that time.

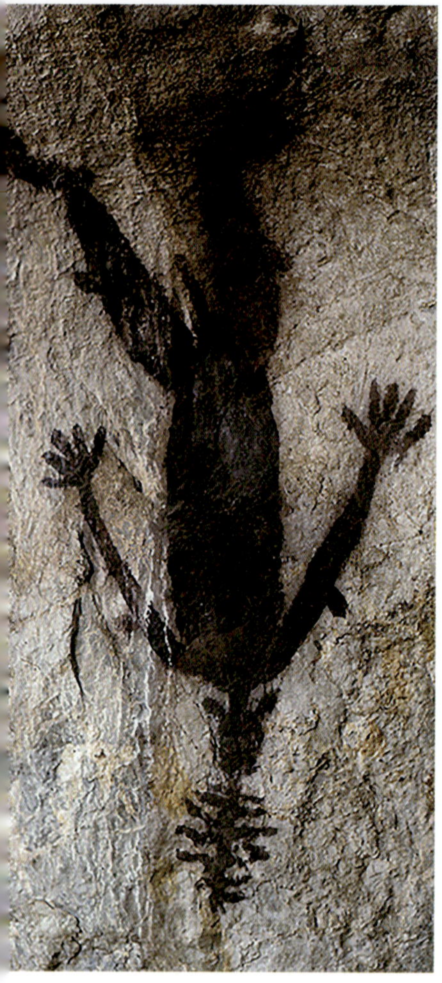

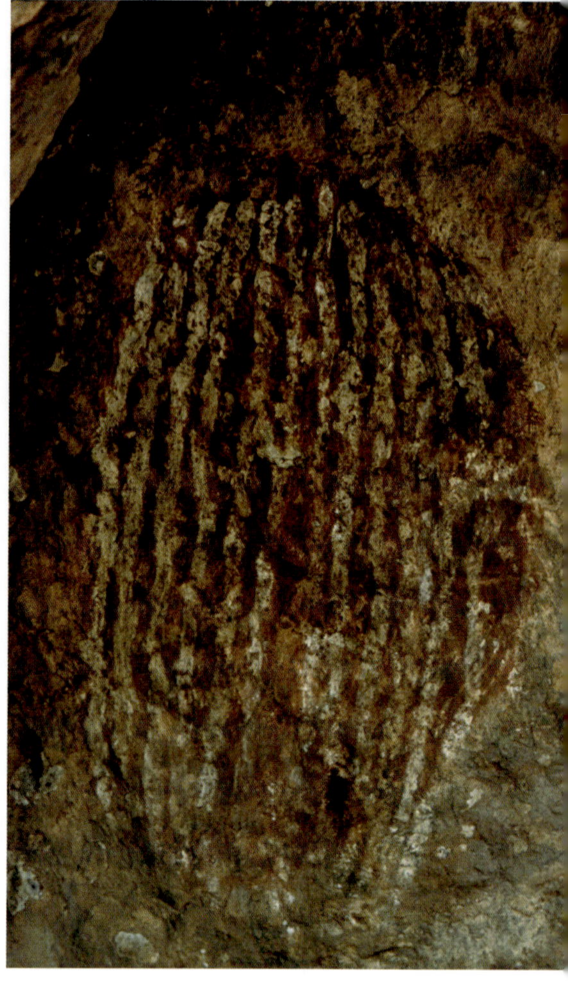

199. (above left) Upside-down male anthropomorph at Mitchell River Cave, a type of image common in the late Holocene cave art of the Mitchell-Palmer region of southeast Cape York Peninsula. It is thought to date within the last 2,000 years, and probably much more recently.

200. (above right) Abstract late Holocene art of the Chillagoe region, southeast Cape York Peninsula.

Charlotte Bay and the Flinders Islands that may relate to clan totems or the onset of a new religious idea; anthropomorphic depictions of the Mitchell-Palmer limestone zone, many painted upside-down and probably relating to burial rites and cosmological beliefs about the afterlife [199]; and abstract designs of the Ngarrabullgan-Chillagoe region [200]. In Cape York Peninsula, the geographical patterning of those regionalized artistic traditions often approximates well the distribution of language groups of the ethnographic period dating to the 1800s and early 1900s, suggesting that the art's antiquity may to some degree be used to estimate when the distinctive, territorially restricted major language groups began to form.

The cave art of ethnography

As we get closer to our own time, we begin to approach the period for which there are written records about the art, a time of ethnography for which anthropological observations and direct testimony by Indigenous peoples exist. It is for this period that we can begin to speak of what the art meant to the people who made it and to the communities who used it, and in some places continue to use it. This is a special phase of cave art, because now we are privileged to hear the voices of people who can inform us about how the art fits into the world of their own experiences, cosmological beliefs and cultures.

Using ethnography to understand the art

Until anthropological documentation of ethnographic rock art began in earnest towards the end of the nineteenth century, there was an assumption by antiquarians and prehistorians that cave art generally had been made by 'primitive' peoples passing leisurely time between hunts. The art was little more than doodling, art for art's sake. But early ethnographic observations in Australia in particular showed that Indigenous peoples at the far ends of the earth (relative to Europe, which was then the self-proclaimed intellectual centre of the globe, the apogee of human achievement) painted rock walls as they communed with the spirit world. A classic example came from the works of the pioneering anthropologists Baldwin Spencer (originally a zoologist) and postmaster Frank Gillen, who together documented the painting of rock walls among Indigenous Australian desert peoples. They noted that Aboriginal people made paintings in sacred places such as shallow caves or secluded gorges [201]. The paintings were created with charcoal and natural earth pigments in hues of red, yellow, white and black, on rare occasions with human blood allowed to flow over them.

In some parts of Australia, the art consists of figurative depictions of animals and abstract designs associated with the totems of animal or plant species. Those depictions were used in sacred ritual performances to ensure the continuation of the earth's abundance, as 'increase' or, more correctly, 'maintenance' ceremonies that saw the represented species multiply along totemic songlines that represent geographical extensions of those species' spiritual sources (the expression 'songlines' relates to the journeys taken by ancestral spirit-beings during the creative era of

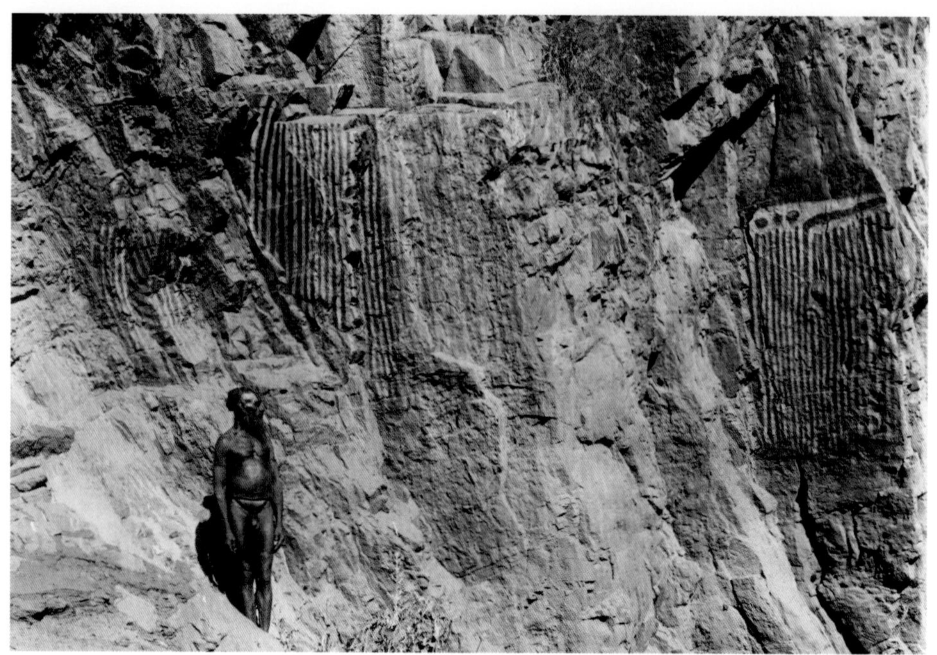

201. Emily Gap, MacDonnell Ranges, central Australia. This photograph was taken by Frank Gillen in 1896. It shows Irrapmwe Peltharre, an Arrernte man and elder of the Utnerrengatye ('emu bush caterpillar') Dreaming. Utnerrengatye created important geological features during the creative era of the Dreaming; here it is depicted along with two other Dreaming beings (Ayepearenye, the 'elephant grub', and Alkngiltye, the 'tar vine caterpillar') on the rocks at Emily Gap.

the Dreaming (see below); those journeys are now geographical pathways along which can be found important locations where the spirit-beings (or parts of them) emanated from and returned into the earth, forming key locales where social order and the earth's fecundity must be nurtured through sacred knowledge, ritual and song.

Prehistorians in Europe adopted the Australian ethnographic accounts as inspiration for understanding the art of Europe as expressions of 'hunting magic'. However, in reality neither the region of Europe nor the concept of 'hunting magic' had anything to do with Aboriginal cultures. European commentators of the day saw Australian Aboriginal totemic performances as rituals aimed at the proliferation of animals and plants as sources of food, for Aboriginal peoples were widely conceived as being close to nature, devoid of real religion and the higher orders of human achievement: they were usually relegated to little more than hunters and gatherers essentially concerned with subsistence. It seemed logical at the time, then, to associate Aboriginal peoples of the nineteenth century with European Ice Age peoples who were also hunters, but this was a function of Western prejudices that erroneously saw the 'races' of the world ordered in a ladder of evolution, with Aboriginal peoples

220

(along with ancient humans, such as Ice Age hunters) at the bottom. In one text, published in 1920, the 'Wiltshire Englishman (Gros Propriétaire)' (the English landed gentry) is positioned at the very apex of the evolutionary ladder, with the 'Wiltshire farmer' immediately below, followed progressively down by a further arrangement of British types; then, immediately above Neanderthals, come the 'Portuguese Government officials' and 'Portuguese "inactifs"'. Below the Neanderthals are various other Portuguese, Scottish and Irish categories. Then a number of extinct fossil hominids are listed, with Aboriginal people tucked in among them, until, at the bottom rung, we have the gorilla![5] Such evolutionary formulations – called 'appropriated pasts' by archaeologist Ian McNiven and historian Lynette Russell, aptly, given their revelations of the prejudices involved, in a book published by AltaMira Press[6] – are imaginations that reveal deep-seated preconceptions, and although in retrospect those now-blatant biases may make us shake our heads and laugh, they have had serious consequences for social attitudes towards Indigenous cultures and groups.[7]

Nevertheless, what those early observations of Australian Aboriginal art-making did announce was that the art was not simply mindless doodlings, but rather an integral expression of culture. The art of cultures other than those of the West could now be seen to function, and to have functioned, within the intellectual realm of those lifeworlds. Artistic expressions do not relate simply to environmental conditions, nor do they relate to generic concepts of 'hunting and gathering'. It makes little or no sense whatsoever to assume that one group of people's artworks are to be understood by reference to another group's simply because they, too, hunt and gather items of food (after all, we cannot meaningfully understand our own cultural expressions and creativity by reducing ourselves to 'food buyers'). People make sense of their world in many ways other than through generic methods of obtaining food. This is the stuff of culture, and reducing artistic practices to notions of 'hunters and gatherers' is entirely inappropriate when trying to understand the social, intellectual and creative life of artists and the societies in which they operate. To understand the art, we need rather to understand cosmologies – existential and religious beliefs and practices – and how places, social structures and imagery all operate within a people's world views. It is thus not appropriate to directly apply the meanings of artworks from one part of the world – Aboriginal Australia, for example – to another, such as Europe, unless the two share or shared philosophies of life and explanatory frameworks. Furthermore, in the Australia of nineteenth-century ethnography, there are close to 500 different language groups (the exact number is difficult to ascertain with good precision, as they varied in their degree of distinction), each with their own beliefs and expressions, making it even more problematic and entirely inappropriate to apply a generic 'Aboriginal culture' to the period of ethnography. And within any given region, the meaning of the art changed through time. Australian Aboriginal cultures saw major transformations over the past 50,000 years, making the application of a stereotypical ethnographic Aboriginal culture to that of Ice Age Europe highly problematic.

Naj Tunich, Guatemala

The message that art relates to more than material depictions, always implicating how people relate to the world at large, is evident in cave art across the world, including in the Mesoamerican world of the Maya, where some fifty caves with art have been found.[8] The art of deep caves is not common in the Americas, and in central America it is pretty much limited to Maya art, with only one other period being represented, the cave of Juxtlahuaca in Mexico that contains Olmec-style art ('Olmec' refers to an earlier culture that thrived in the Veracruz and Tabasco states of Mexico between 3,500 and 2,400 years ago; it had wide cultural influences and eventually gave rise to later Mesoamerican cultures such as those of the Maya, in the first millennium AD, and the Aztecs, in the fourteenth to sixteenth centuries AD).[9]

In 1979 Maya studies were developing academically and in the popular imagination, with tales of a fallen civilization, temples overgrown with dense rainforest that blanketed bas-relief artworks on their walls, great staircases carved with glyphic descriptions of long-dead kings, such as at Copan in Honduras, and stories of bloodletting and ritual cannibalism. With the decipherment of Maya glyphs, this was a rare example of a distant culture whose thoughts could be known through the very words and images of its ancient people. But then the deep decorated cave of Naj Tunich was found, opening a hitherto unknown doorway into how the Maya expressed their beliefs in hidden places.

Naj Tunich is the grandest decorated cave in all of Mesoamerica. It lies hidden amid the natural limestone grottos of the municipality of Poptún in Guatemala [2]. In the local Mayan language of Mopan, still widely spoken today across the region, '*naj tunich*' means 'stone house', signalling that the cave operated as some kind of special house (many cave names mean 'stone house' in Mayan languages, such as *na'ch'en* in Jacaltec, and *ochoch pek* in Kekchi). It is, in effect, a centre of worship, and has been so for a very long time. The cave has many artworks that penetrate deep into underground tunnels and more open chambers. Some of these artworks are paintings (including writings) [3], others are handprints, while others again are incised petroglyphs. The paintings are of special significance for understanding what took place in the cave. The glyphs are fashioned in a professional hand that has the fine, compact whip-like manner of Late Classic Maya vase paintings. Andrea Stone, the archaeologist from the University of Wisconsin–Milwaukee who recorded the art, points out that the calligraphic scripts document the use of the cave as a pilgrimage shrine by elites from far and wide (much of our knowledge of Naj Tunich stems from her research in the 1980s; the following details come largely from this source[10]). One ruler from the important Classic Maya city of Caracol in Belize [202], located some 60 km (40 miles) away, is mentioned in the art.[11] No such important cave art site is known closer to Caracol, testimony that this was no ordinary cave.

202. Part of the ancient Maya city of Caracol, Belize.

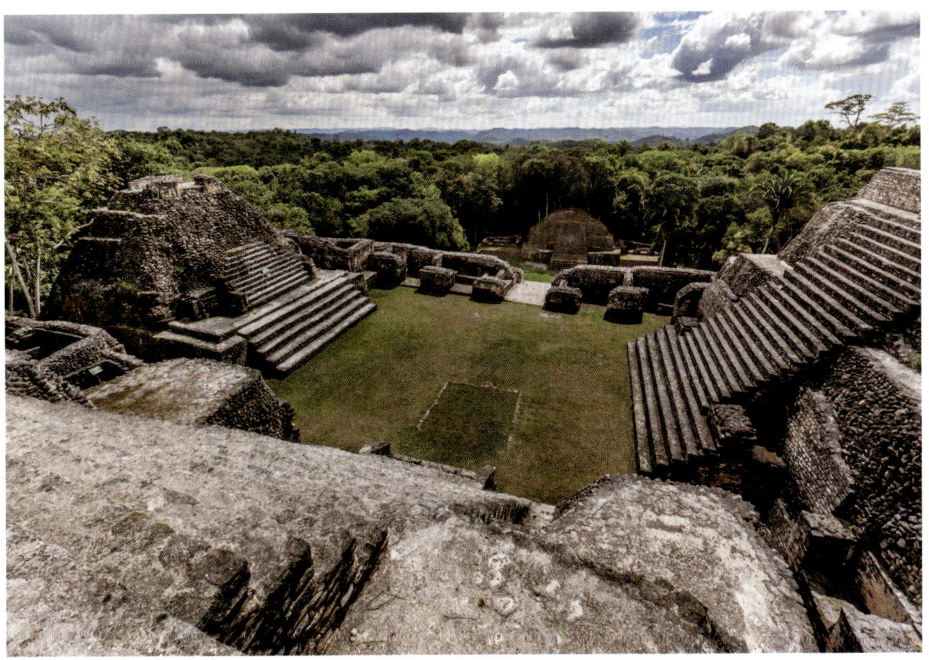

In order to understand what makes Naj Tunich so important as an underground shrine, we need to understand more of Maya culture, for it is in that culture that the art attains its significance. Such information has come from a number of sources: the archaeology that reveals other kinds of material culture from the Maya past, such as ritual offerings, forms of decoration, domestic residences, religious edifices and the like; glyphic writings on stone stele [203], monumental stairways [204] and architecture walls that recount tales of past rulers and special happenings; ancient codices (folded bark-paper books) that document in considerable detail specifics of Maya thought and practice [205]; historical and ethnographic texts dating back from the first Spanish incursions in the early 1500s; and more recent oral traditions from living Maya, millions of whom still live today on ancient Maya lands spread across southern Mexico to Belize, Guatemala, Honduras and beyond.

Among both ancient and modern Maya, in common with other Mesoamerican cultures past and present, caves hold a special place as sacred geography in the landscape. Caves relate to the world of gods and spirits in a number of ways: as the inside of corporeal beings, as godly residences, and as containers that house both powerful beings and their special powers. Mountains and caves are exceptional topographic features that lie beyond the ordinary world of people: they are the realms of the gods and of extraordinary creatures who animate the world with powers of life and death. Yahval Balamil, for example, the earth god of the Tzotzil Maya of Zinacantán in the mountains of Chiapas in southern

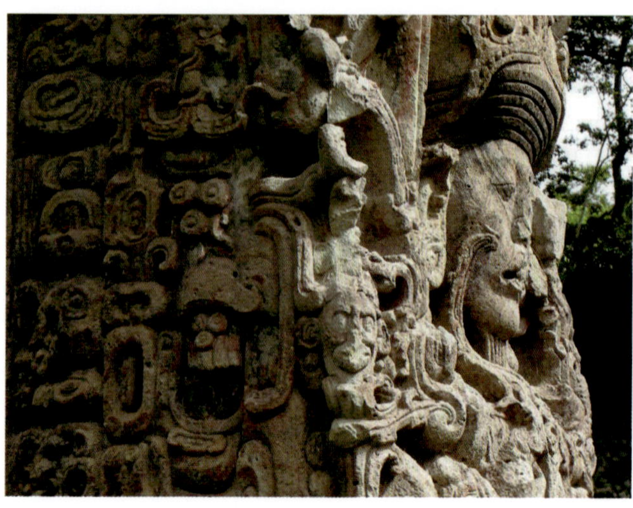

203. Stela B at the ancient Maya city of Copan, Honduras, portraying Waxaklaju'n U B'aah K'awiil ('18 Rabbit'), the city's thirteenth ruler. The carved glyphs identify 22 August AD 731 as the day the stela was commissioned for. They also tell of Waxaklaju'n U B'aah K'awiil supplicating his patron god by burning incense and offering blood to renew the world and its fertility.

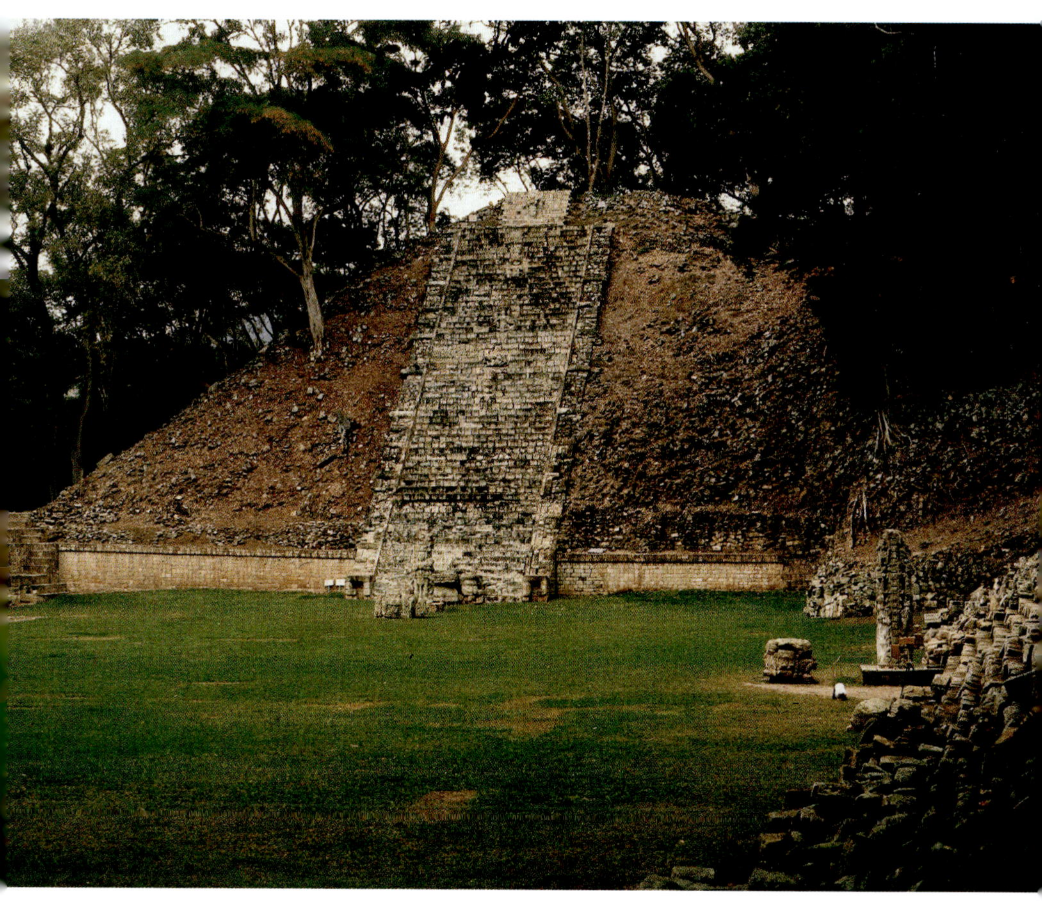

Mexico, resides in a cave. He controls the rain and the earth's bounty, much like the earth lord Niwan Pukuh for the nearby Tojolobal who also live in parts of Chiapas; or Tzultaca of highland Guatemala. Propitiatory rites allow local groups to tap into these preternatural forces to ensure the earth produces for the living.

Individual caves are often the home of particular deities invested with specific kinds of powers. Saki C'Oxol, a Quiché deity, for example, is renowned for his ability to spread material wealth. Caves are portals, cosmic strata through which the world of people and the power of deities and the spirit-world are bridged, and people enter caves to petition the gods and to expunge malignant objects and forces from the earth. Having come through a cave, objects undergo a kind of transformation that sees them purified as they travel between cosmic layers. Among the Maya, a cave is a site of passage between states of

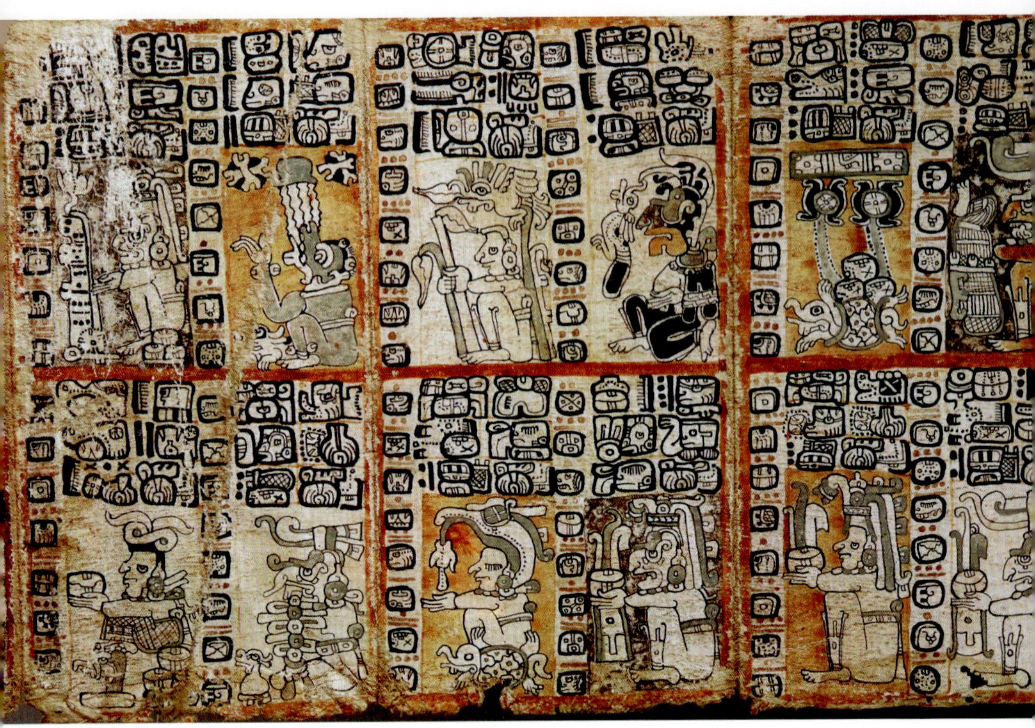

existence. It comes as no surprise to find that a grave is a kind
of cave in which the dead are sent on their way to the afterlife,
and that sometimes caves themselves are made repositories of
the dead. And given that gods who control the rain tend to reside
in caves – rain being associated with the power of life and growth,
such as to give growth to the all-important maize that the Maya
depend on for survival – it is into caves that people go to placate
the gods in ritual pilgrimages and supplications.

The art and other traces of human activity in the cave
of Naj Tunich need to be understood within this Maya logic.
To understand this body of cave art means to understand what
caves stand for generally in the Maya world, as houses of powerful
deities and life-giving forces, and of dangerous cave monsters.
The art, architecture and portable objects found at Naj Tunich
speak of these forces, and of the ritual appeals made to the gods.
Deep underground inside the rock, artworks decorate the walls
and ritual structures such as a stone altar [206], and portable
objects such as smashed plates, ceramic jars and torches, 'litter'
the floor [207], although these are purposeful deposits that
cannot be likened to discarded piles of rubbish.

206. Stone altar in the Maya cave site of Naj Tunich, Guatemala.

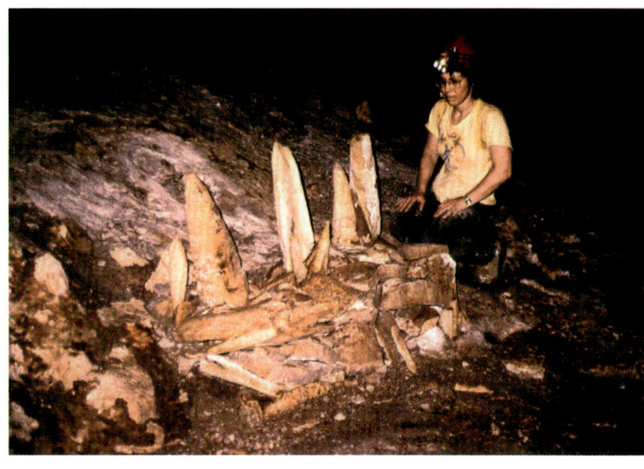

207. Broken ceramics in 'the balcony' at Naj Tunich. The cave contains large numbers of sherds from broken vessels, many still retaining traces of copal incense, commonly used in Maya rituals.

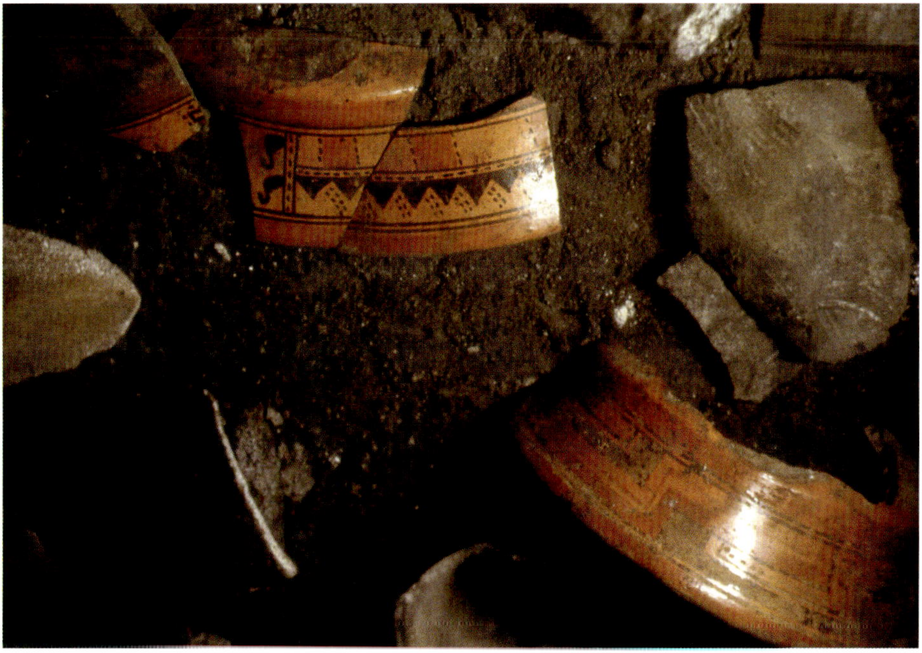

The art was made by a large number of artists, and the figurative paintings were produced in ritual. Andrea Stone writes that 'This was a time when Maya cave ritual was an event of high drama, when it moved to the rhythms of music, dance, and the cries of human sacrifice'. In the art of Naj Tunich there are more than sixty paintings of people, many partial representations of the head only, along with deities in human form. Those anthropomorphic figures are well attired with accessories that reveal aspects of their social status. They are all clothed in unassuming garments largely restricted to loincloths, hipcloths and headwraps, none with footwear [208]. Jewelry is also worn, including a 'cloth ear ornament … associated with sacrificial rites, both of captives and lords', and some of the jewelry depicted in the art was recovered in the cave, such as jade and ceramic earflares, and a 'drooping-mouth' pendant

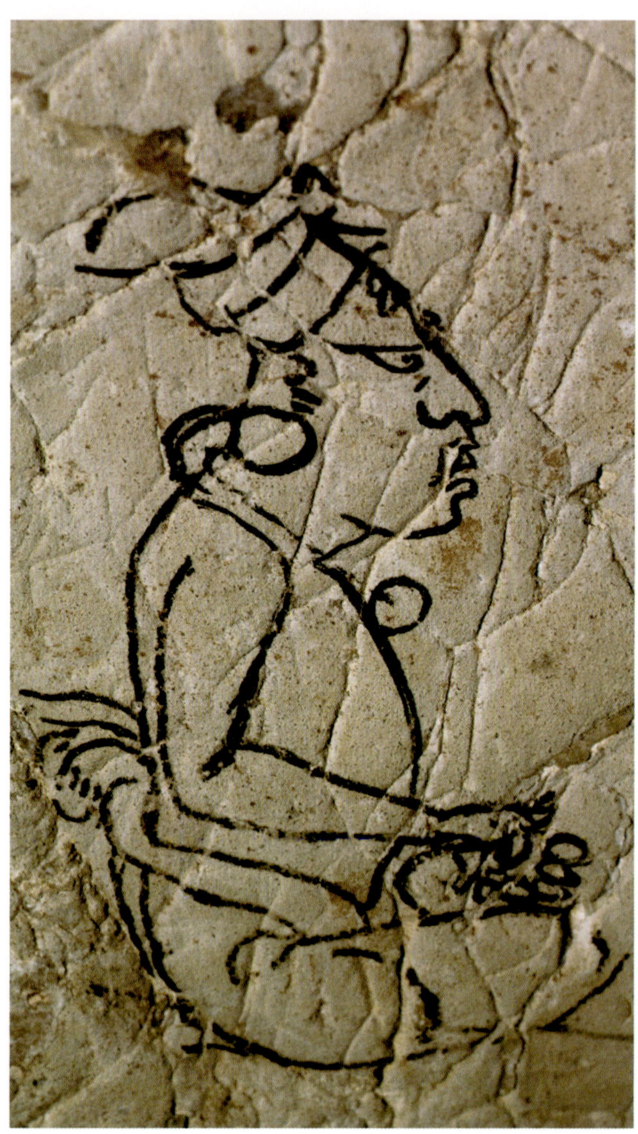

208. Drawing 72, Naj Tunich, a figure sitting attired with cloth headwrap and ear and pendant jewelry.

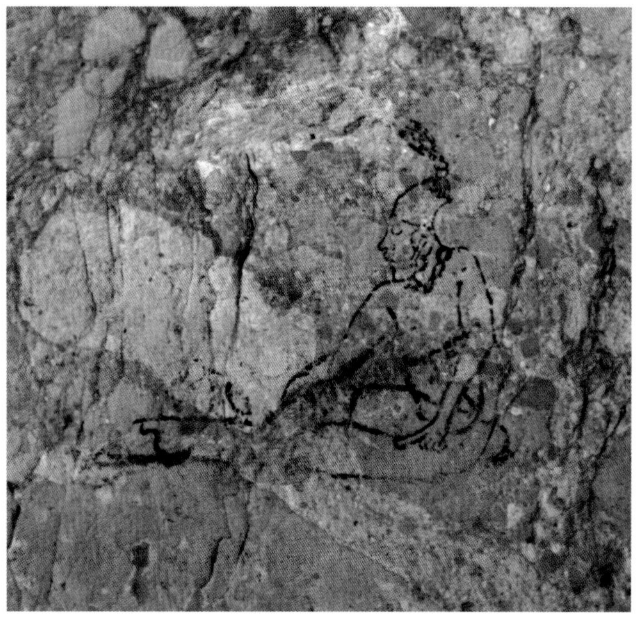

209. Drawing 63 at Naj Tunich, showing a person sitting in front of a flat-bottomed dish of a kind used by the Classic Maya to burn incense. Smoke rises from the dish. Such ceramics were found aplenty within the cave, many containing traces of copal incense.

found among votive offerings. 'At Naj Tunich ... the cloth headwrap seems to be a general form of ceremonial attire', stripped of its variable folds that elsewhere point to the social rank of the wearer [208]. Individually and in its totality, the garments and accoutrements worn by the painted individuals at Naj Tunich all suggest ritual wear, of a kind we know of from Maya ethnography and iconography.

Ritual performances are also depicted. In Drawing 63 a human figure sits in front of a flat-bottomed ceramic vessel of a type used by the Maya to burn incense [209]. Smoke rises from the vessel, signalling the progress of ritual. Drawings 27 and 40 each depict a group of three musicians, reminiscent of the number of musicians painted on regional ceramic vases [210]. The figure in Drawing 71 is attired with a face-mask in the shape of a bat and a headdress shaped like a deer, and shakes a rattle in one hand while wearing a choker around his neck, a telltale mark of ritual performers. Drawing 11 is of a seated figure holding a human head with unkempt hair; in Maya culture dishevelled hair marks a person of lower rank, such as a war captive.

Eight of the nineteen human skeletons found lying on the ground at Naj Tunich bear the physical marks of ritual sacrifice. The glyphic writings show scripts associating deities with special

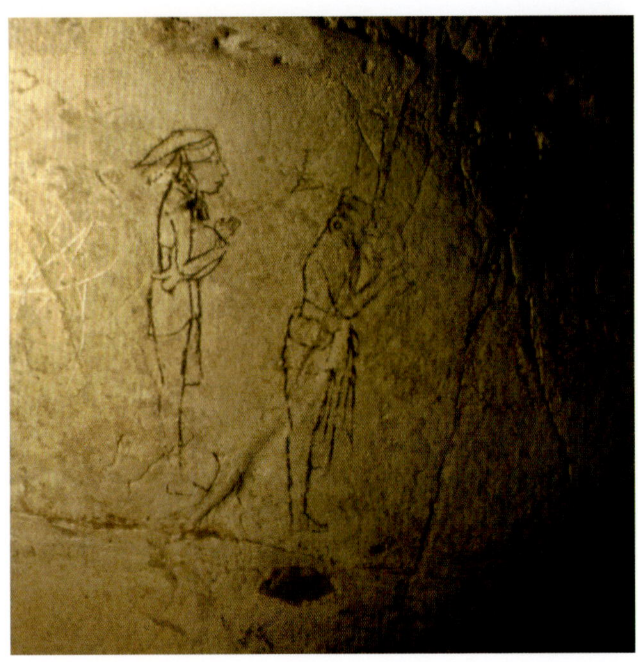

dates in the Maya calendar. 'Text and image suggest that a ritual decapitation was performed at Naj Tunich as part of a *k'atun* anniversary celebration, an event that occurred only three days before the beginning of the Uayeb and eight days before the New Year', writes Andrea Stone (the Madrid Codex also has images of a ritual decapitation of a shrouded victim as part of the Uayeb New Year rites). Another painting, Drawing 18, depicts God N – 'the Maya's stereotypical lecherous old man' – in sexual congress with the Maya Moon Goddess ('the patroness of the month called ch'en in Yucatec, a word ... meaning "cave" or "well" in a number of Mayan languages. Her abode is also a cave'; the sex of the Maya Moon Goddess is not evident in the Naj Tunich paintings, an important lesson when trying to identify what an artist meant purely from the imagery) [211]. But the pairing of God N with the Moon Goddess in Maya thought is also a pairing of the hideous, often deformed old man with a young woman, a common theme in Maya ritual performances.

Other, less active figures in Naj Tunich are depicted in the same attire as their more active counterparts. Drawing 22 is a beautifully rendered depiction of a person sitting cross-legged in front of a conch shell [212]. Similar sitting postures are also found elsewhere in Naj Tunich.

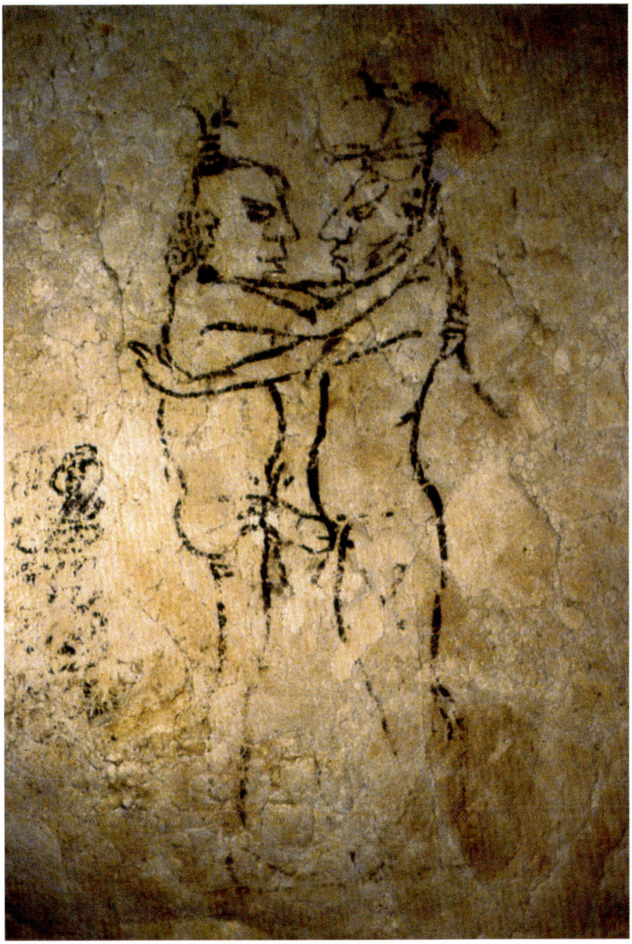

211. Drawing 18, depicting God N
in sexual congress with the Maya
Moon Goddess, Naj Tunich.

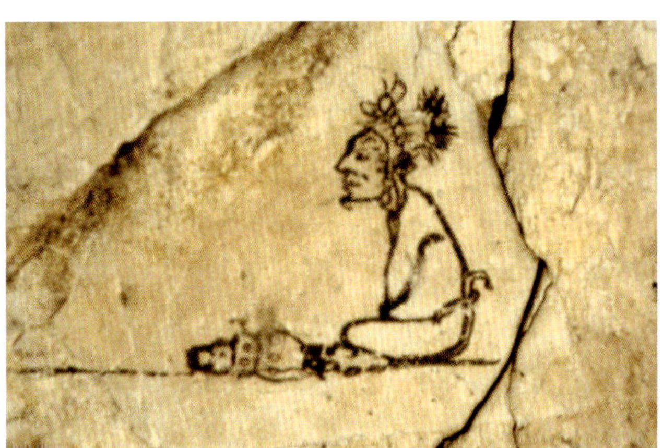

212. Drawing 22, a figure sitting in
front of a conch shell, Naj Tunich.

213. Drawing 87, the Hero Twins, Hunahpu and Xbalanque, Naj Tunich.

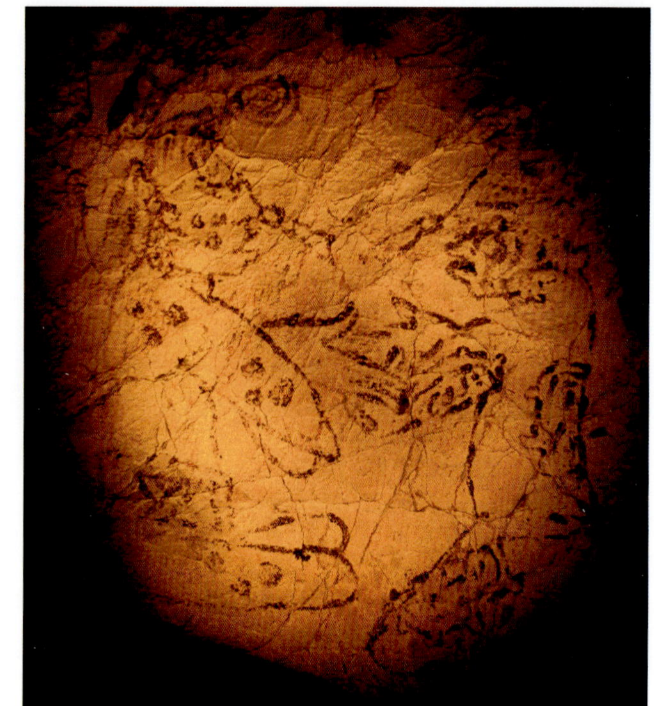

214. Drawing 21, Hunahpu wearing a jaguar skin in a ballgame scene, Naj Tunich.

215. Drawing 83, the Dwarf, Naj Tunich.

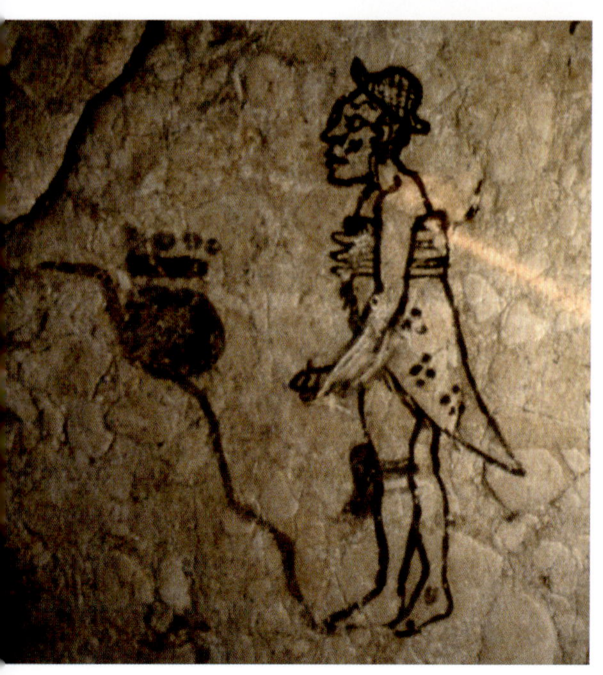

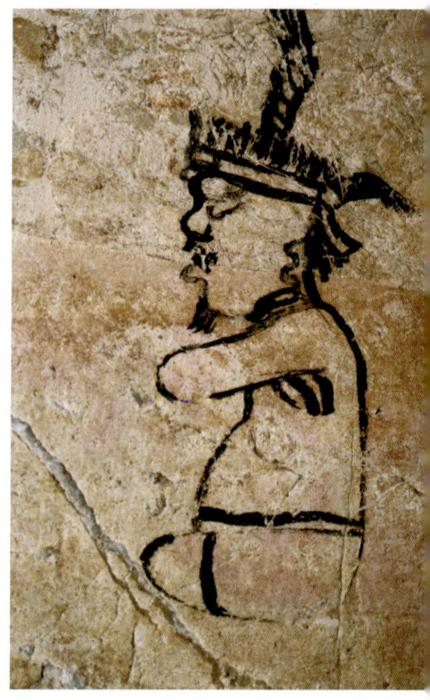

Deities are also represented. Drawing 87 is of the Hero Twins or Headband Gods, Hunahpu and Xbalanque [213], both mentioned in the Popol Vuh, the sacred Maya text. Drawing 21 is a depiction of Hunahpu wearing a jaguar skin around his waist; he is the blowgun hunter depicted here in a ballgame scene [214]. Four ballgame scenes are represented at Naj Tunich. Drawing 83, the Dwarf [215], is thought to be, according to Andrea Stone, 'a denizen of the underworld', because of his unusual attire and because among the Maya there is a widespread belief 'that dwarves live in the subterranean world', often inhabiting 'woods and caves'. Such dwarves often have special powers over the weather and animals.

There are many other depictions at Naj Tunich that reference ritual performances and godly beings, all signalling the art as a space of performance relating to how Maya artists understood the world to operate, and the actions required by the living to ensure the healthy continuation of the world.

Yalo and Apialo, Vanuatu

That cave art is made meaningful by how people engage with it is made abundantly clear at two caves on the island of Malekula in the South Pacific island nation of Vanuatu. Here the caves are steeped in the power of *kastom*, the traditions and spirit-forces that have been passed down from ancient times and that can often be traced back to a time prior to the first coming of Europeans in the 1600s. The two caves are located in the neighbourhood of two adjacent cultural groups: the site of Yalo is in Small Nambas territory, and Apialo in Big Nambas (a '*nambas*' is a penis sheath, a traditional item of attire that men wore, the two groups wearing slightly different forms that helped differentiate them through their material culture). In both languages, the cave names Yalo and Apialo mean 'place of the spirits', for here could be found the walking dead, not in the flesh but in spirit form, living in their new recluse after death.

Archaeologist Meredith Wilson and a team of researchers, including Jimmyson Sanhambath, the chief of Apialo, and Pita Dan Senembe, the chief of Yalo, together with their communities, have studied the caves and the art. They point out that the two caves are centres 'from which connecting pathways run out to other important places'.[12] The caves are connected physically by the land that simultaneously separates and bridges them, in life through the rites of passage that give them both a common meaning gradually learnt over time (Small Nambas and Big Nambas individuals spent much of their life undertaking grade-taking ceremonies that prepared them for death), and in death through the spirits who head home into the caves. Both Yalo and Apialo are microcosms of the world of the living, but spaces for the dead. Yalo contains physical structures that mirror those found in local villages, such as a *nakamal* or men's house, and a *nasara* or dancing ground. Within the cave those structures are for the spirits of the dead who continue to perform their everyday lives in spirit form. Today people can sometimes hear those spirit-performances as they walk past Yalo while running their daily affairs, especially when the spirit of the newly deceased enters the cave for the first time, welcomed by the spirits already there. Yalo and Apialo are the shape of the afterworld.

One phenomenon common to this part of the world is that during life, community members need to learn to make a particular kind of drawing, often made in sand by dragging a finger until the design is completed. It is important that the living memorize the exact twists and turns of the design, for in death they will be required to reproduce the image in all its intricacies. At Yalo, in the cave of the dead, there is a painting of such a design [216], and nearby a spirit 'watcher' guards the entrance of the cave. Failure to complete the drawing after death will see the spirit of the newly dead devoured by the guardian, their spirit gone forever.

At both Yalo and Apialo, the caves have multiple entrances: a main one at ground level, the entrance that people walk through today (and from which they need to announce their coming to the spirits, by blowing through a small hole in the rock) [217]; and a large, circular opening in the ceiling, through which a large tree grows from the floor of the cave high up past its roof (Apialo has two trees) [218]. Soon after death, the spirit enters the cave through one of the two entrances, their manner of death determining which of the two: a person who died a violent death enters the cave through the hole in the roof and down the trunk of the tree, while someone who died a more normal death enters through the main entrance. Signs of new spirit arrivals can be seen through the blood that trickles down the tree in the form of red sap.

At Yalo there is a third, smaller entrance to the side of the main opening, also at ground level but of much lower reach and thus more difficult to access. Here, just inside this low entrance, is where the guardian 'watcher' stands, alerted to the arrival of a new spirit through a flash of light. 'The watchman greets the spirit

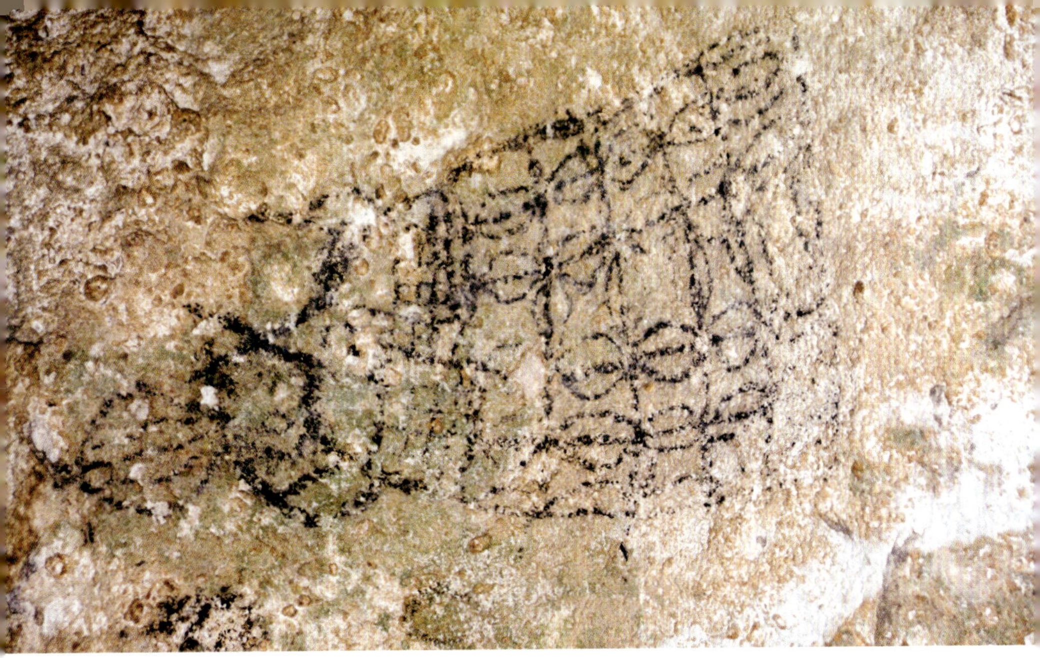

216. Intricate curvilinear design,
Yalo, Vanuatu. Such designs were
finger-drawn in the sand during
life, and reproduced by the spirit
of the deceased after death.

217. Chief Pita Dan Senembe
blows into a hole in the wall at
the main entrance of Yalo, to
announce to the spirits the coming
of people into the cave.

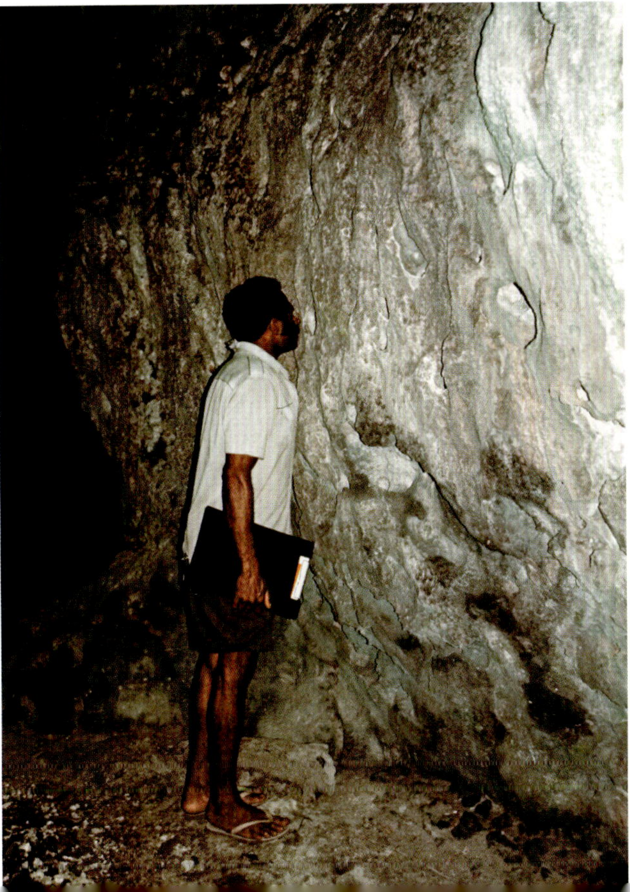

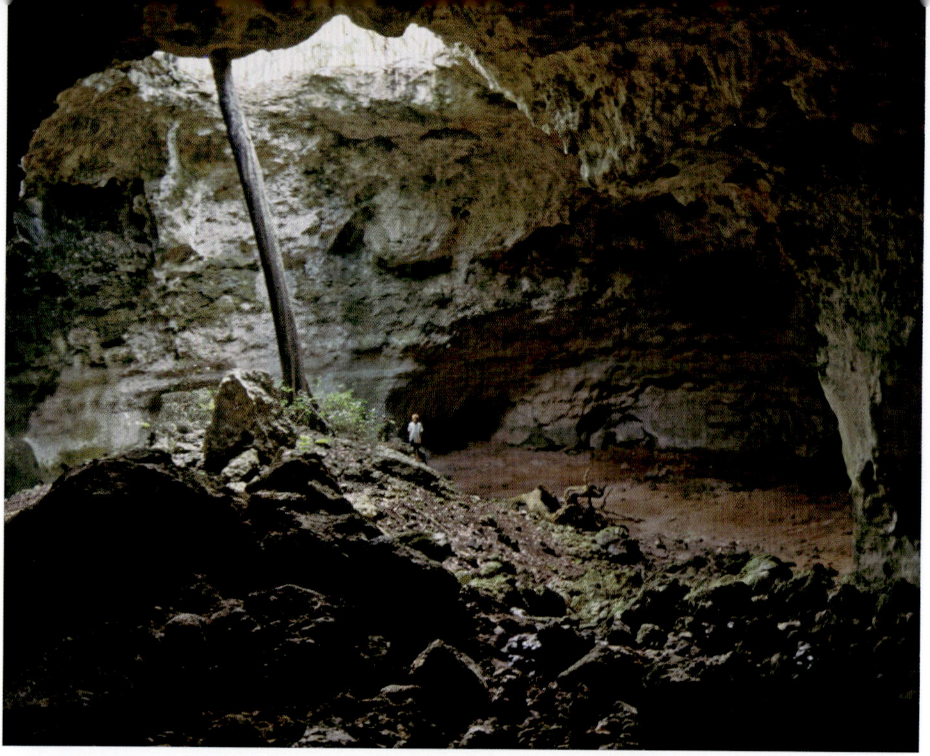

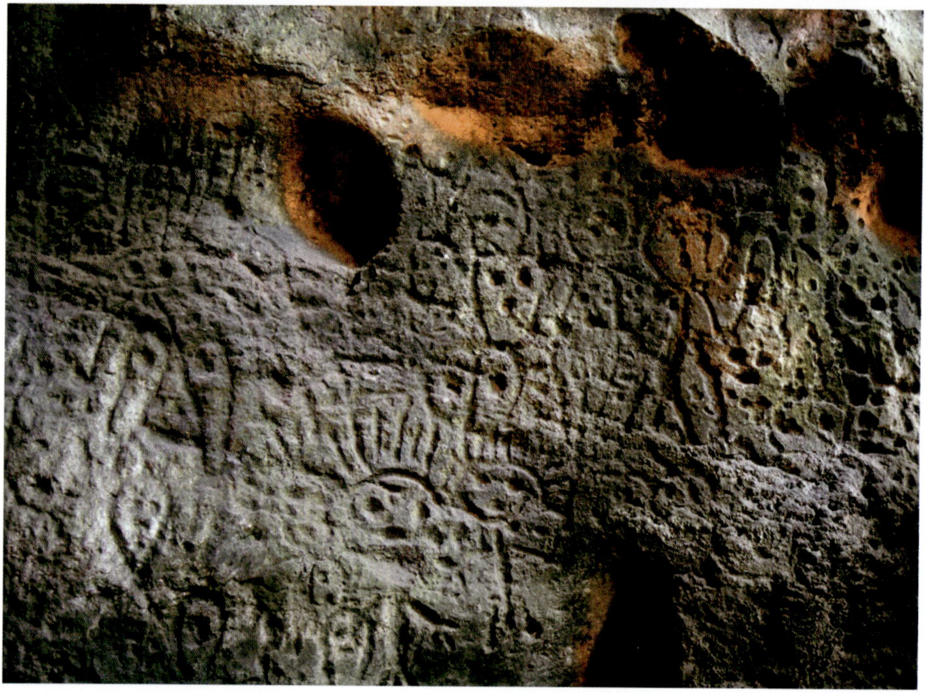

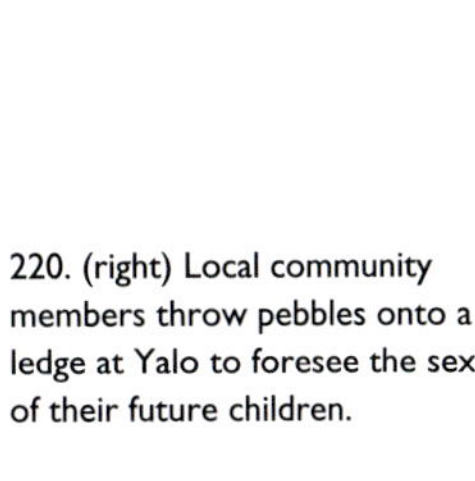

218. (opposite above) The main chamber in the cave of Yalo, showing the entrance through the roof where the spirits of community members who have died a violent death enter down the trunk of the tree.

219. (opposite below) Engraved faces at Yalo, self-portraits made by spirits of the deceased who live in the cave.

220. (right) Local community members throw pebbles onto a ledge at Yalo to foresee the sex of their future children.

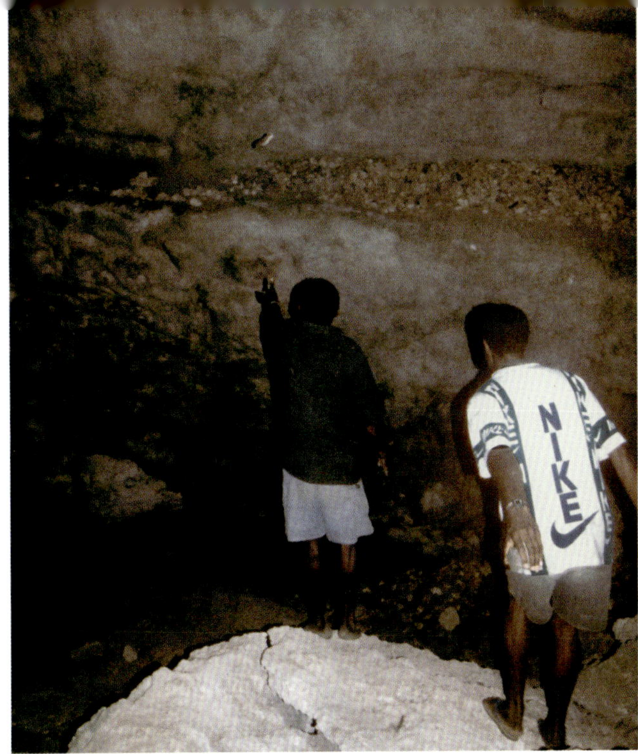

and deposits him/her in a receptacle in the rock in another part of the cave', write Wilson and her co-researchers.[13] That receptacle is a cupule-like hollow in the cave wall, and through time the spirits engrave their faces into the wall, self-portraits in the land of the dead [219].

People come from far and wide to Yalo and Apialo, where deceased family members can still be visited long after death, their footprints seen on the ground after a spirit-dance, and their faces on the walls, with the knowledge of their continued existence in the sanctity of the cave. People visit for other reasons too: there is a ledge high up along the wall in one of Yalo's corridors. Here expecting parents, or simply curious individuals, throw a rock with their non-preferred hand to determine whether they will have a daughter or a son: if the stone lands on the ledge, it will be a boy, if it does not, a girl. Thousands of small stones, all thrown by human hand, can today be seen on the ledge and nearby floor below [220]. Near the secondary, spirit entrance where the 'watcher' stands, the living also test themselves, in the past prior to battle especially. Here the ceiling suddenly dips to close to ground level, but there is enough space to crouch beneath and thereby exit the cave [221]. People would test their mettle by

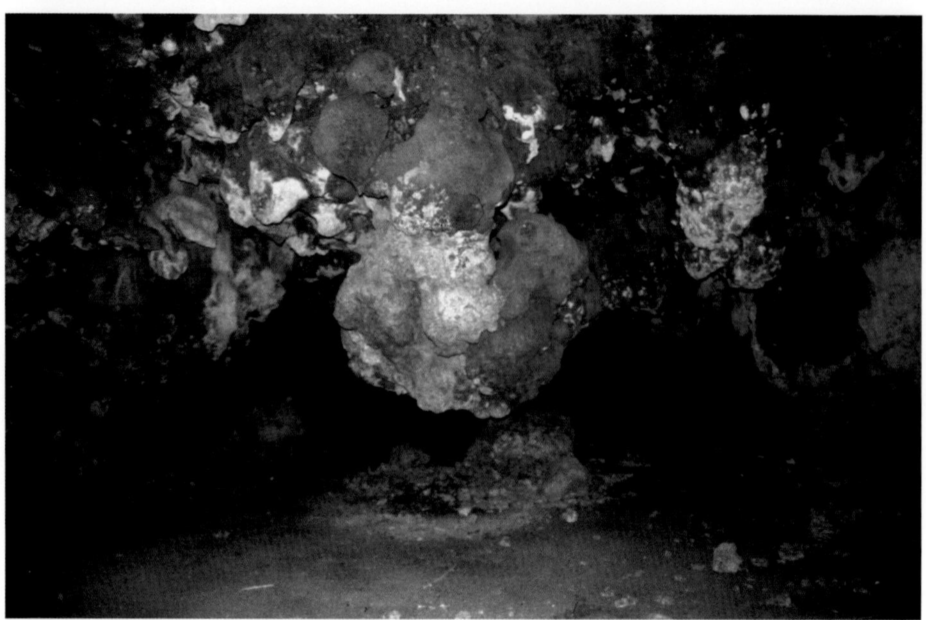

221. The dipping ceiling at Yalo, where warriors tested their mettle prior to battle.

trying to crawl below the dipping ceiling. If their backs touched the rock, they would not survive in battle, but if they passed through untouched their safety would be assured. However, the feat was not entirely under their control, for the rock would find a means of touching them if this was their fate.

Yalo and Apialo are eerily beautiful caves, rich in detail both in their physical configurations and in the art that adorns their varied nooks and crannies. And yet we have to go beyond that physical display to really appreciate the art, for its meaning lies in how it operates in local society today. The art is active for the living, participating in how community members see the workings of the world, how they connect to each other, to their ancestors, and to the land in which they dwell. Yalo and Apialo, and the art that adorns them, allow people to maintain connections with their ancestors and to negotiate their lives in the knowledge that one day they, too, will join them; the caves and the art guide towards that coming future.

X-ray art of northern Australia

In Aboriginal Australian ethnography, key to understanding local art are the deeply meaningful notions of the 'Dreaming' and 'Country'. The Dreaming relates to the creative events of ancestral forces that shaped the earth, giving the land, water and skies an ontological and physical topography in which descendant Aboriginal populations can live. The Dreaming is a timeless past-present-future where, rather than when, Aboriginal groups are given their laws, territories, languages, dances and varied cultural expressions by ancestral spirit-forces. Those territories are known as 'Country', a term that articulates not only the physical place today, but also the legacy of all that went on beforehand within that landscape. That legacy continues to live on in the present and into the future, both in the life of descendant populations and places that have inherited their present states from the ancestors, and in the ancestral spirit-beings who may not now be visible but who nevertheless continue to reside within Country, metamorphosed into the landscape. Those ancestral beings communicate with and guide the living through the landscape, or, if the law of the land is not adequately followed, they may take away mindful reference points so that the living become lost.

An excellent example of the fundamental importance of the Dreaming and Country in the making of northern Australian Aboriginal art is found in the works of social anthropologist Luke Taylor.[14] Taylor studied the X-ray art of the peoples of Arnhem Land, an art style commonly depicted in bark paintings [222] and in caves and rockshelters of the region's lowlands and plateaux [49]. Here X-ray artists 'see the inside', not just of the animals depicted in the imagery, but of human society and social relationships that are also symbolically expressed through the art. X-ray art reveals both 'outside' appearances commonly grasped by onlookers, such as the shape of animal parts, and more esoteric 'inside' knowledge that is gradually and ritually learnt by clan members as they attain progressively higher levels of knowledge about the workings of the world. Those higher orders of cultural knowledge speak of interactions between the physical realm and less visible lifeforces, as well as the existential structure of relations between individuals and social groupings, and life and death.

In Arnhem Land X-ray images typically depict internal organs such as the liver, heart and backbone, items not usually seen from the outside. These elements, and the depictions as a whole, are painted in a range of colours and through the application of varied conventions such as cross-hatching, herringbone patterns and parallel lines. But those colours and patterned lineworks are more than physical traits: they express a logic of social structure and belonging that connects back to local Dreamings and Country.

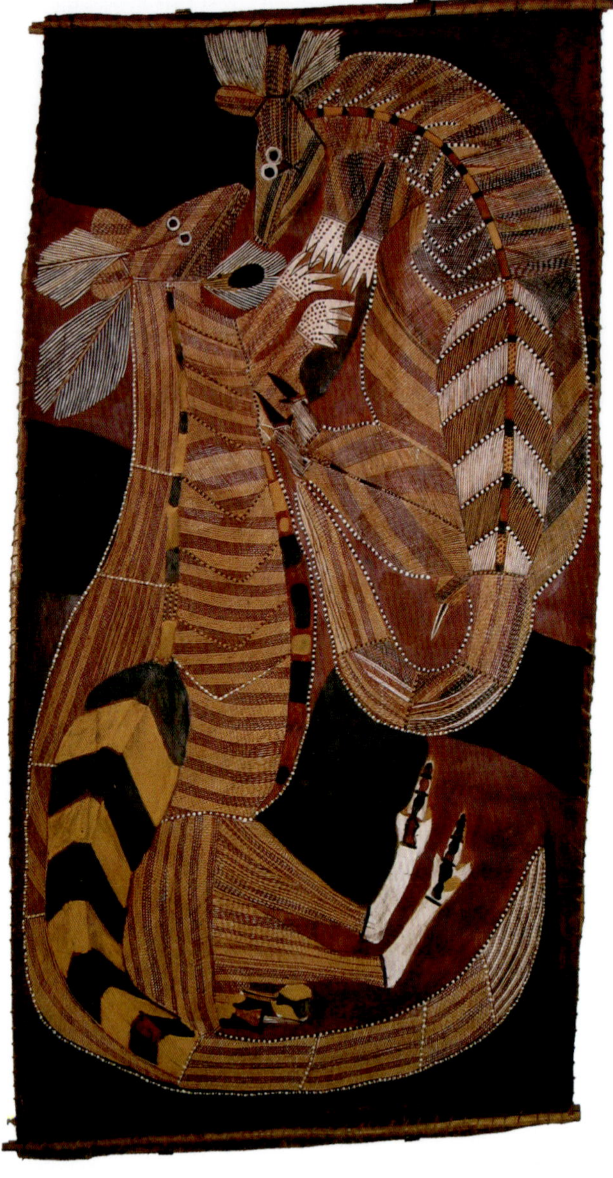

222. Bark painting, *Two Wallabies, Barrk*, 1979, by Peter Marralwanga (Arnhem Land, Australia). The image shows finely cross-hatched 'inside' details (*rarrk*) of the *djang* creator-beings; both the internal details, and the creator-beings, relate to higher-order knowledge of the workings of the world. This knowledge is gained through increasing levels of initiation, given by socially appropriate kin.

The peoples of Arnhem Land divide themselves into two major social groups that anthropologists call 'moieties' (from the French word *moitié*, meaning 'half'): Yirridjdja and Duwa. Each moiety consists of a set of clans who trace back their ancestry to an apical ancestor, with individual affiliation passed down from parent to child. Those clan and moiety affiliations enable each person to map out their own relationships with specific ancestral beings, and know how to behave with other people from each of the clans and with parts of the landscape. By belonging to a particular clan and moiety, a person can work out their territorial rights, managerial obligations to Country, and roles in cycles of initiation and other ritual performances. Members of a particular moiety will own particular tracts of land (owners are called *gidjan*), and will be responsible for looking after lands of the opposite moiety as guardians (called *junggayi*), society and landscape thereby achieving a working whole through complementary relations between the two moieties. As everyone (and many things) belongs to either one moiety or the other, the whole of society is implicated.

It is through ritual performances that lifeforces are rejuvenated, allowing the earth's fecundity, and society itself, to survive, and each moiety has a complementary role to play in the totality of social obligations towards those successful performances. Local Aboriginal people call these moieties and clans their 'skin', signalling how they intimately express social identity and personal being. The moieties are shared across language groups, enabling peoples to recognize and connect socially both within and across territories, for the living landscape is more than just one's own territory.

X-ray paintings express this divided yet paired social structure and the lifeforces in which it operates. The painted animals depict more than physical fauna – animals capable of being hunted and consumed – for they are also *djang*, the originary creator-beings who emerged from the earth (i.e. from Country) in the Dreaming. Depending on their clan affiliation, individual members of society will have spiritual (and therefore existential) connections with particular animal species, and those connections require ritual communion. The *djang* can be seen in X-ray art, not just as 'outside' depictions but as living essences. The 'inside' is further evident in the colours used, and in the choice of pattern: each colour is the charge of one moiety or the other, with light colours such as white and yellow being the province of Yirridjdja, and the dark colours such as red and black, Duwa. Similarly, individual patterns create senses of shade or glow, cross-hatched patterns (called *rarrk*) worn by the *djang* creator-beings. The patterns are imbued with the power of the *djang* and were passed on to the clans, who now engage with them during ritual performances. 'The production of *rarrk* designs on the initiate's body is a way of communicating this power to humans', writes Luke Taylor, and signals a means by which initiates acquire knowledge of the 'inside', ancestral knowledge that emanates from the creator-beings.[15] Tallness is associated with Yirridjdja, and shortness with Duwa, so that, for example, long-necked turtles are associated with Yirridjdja and short-necked turtles with Duwa.

X-ray art dominates many rockshelters across the northern half of the Arnhem Land plateau, where it is thought to date only to the past 3,000 years. Towards its southern limits, it only dates to the past 400 years or so, suggesting a southern expansion of artistic influence over relatively recent times (see Chapter 3). The implication is that the ethnographically known Arnhem Land social structures began to be expressed symbolically on fixed rock surfaces across the landscape during this period, heightening an assertion of territoriality in the process. Here the art signals an aesthetic expression of cosmology and social order that implicates entangled patterns of land ownership, custodial responsibilities, social connectivities and ritual obligations. Those cultural ways relate specifically to this region, and to a particular period in the history of Arnhem Land societies.

The canary in the mine

Through ethnography we learn that cave art is more than decoration; it concerns the ways that the world operates. As Jane Young has written in relation to the Zuni art of New Mexico, 'Rock art depictions in particular have the power to evoke the past, they serve as vehicles that bind together past and present, linking the ancestors and the myth time to contemporary Zuni life'.[16] Cave art reflects the culture of the artist in more ways than descriptions of lineworks and filled-in spaces permit us to explain. It speaks of the strength of ongoing and enduring connections between people, places, the ancestors and other spirit forms. In doing so cave art expresses the well-being of society, reminding us of our responsibilities to others and to the land itself. Archaeologist Liam Brady and social anthropologist John Bradley have worked with community members across a number of continents, pointing out a recurring theme in how Indigenous peoples relate to rock art both in Australia and beyond. In Yanyuwa Country in the Gulf of Carpentaria to the east of Arnhem Land, Aboriginal people recognize owners (*ngimirringki*) and managers (*jungkayi*) of Country, much like their counterparts do in Arnhem Land (see above). Here the contemporary *li-Anthawirrayarra*, the

Sea Rangers, promote 'caring for Country', the passing down of knowledge and the fulfilment of Law – the maintaining of obligations and respectful treatment of the land rich in its spiritual powers, as handed down at the beginning of time – to younger generations. Caring for Country involves ensuring that appropriate community members continue to visit their ancestral places, to look after it by burning the grass, performing even small rituals of connection, passing on knowledge. Such visits to Country are not simply visits to the land and waters; they are visits to the ancestors themselves and to the spirit-beings who have gone into the ground. The rock art articulates those connections, its state a measure of the health and well-being of the land and people as a living whole. When they visit rock art sites, individuals call out to the old people in recognition of what went on before them, announcing that today there is a continued, or renewed, cognisance of the salience of the land [223]. As Liam Brady and John Bradley note, here 'the fading

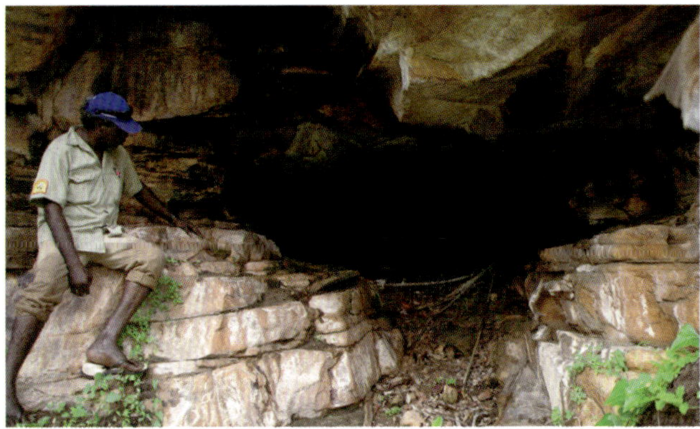

223. Leonard Norman at the entrance of site Limiyimiyila 1 (top), and participating in the recording of art site Limiyimiyila 2 (bottom), Black Craggy Island, Yanyuwa Country.

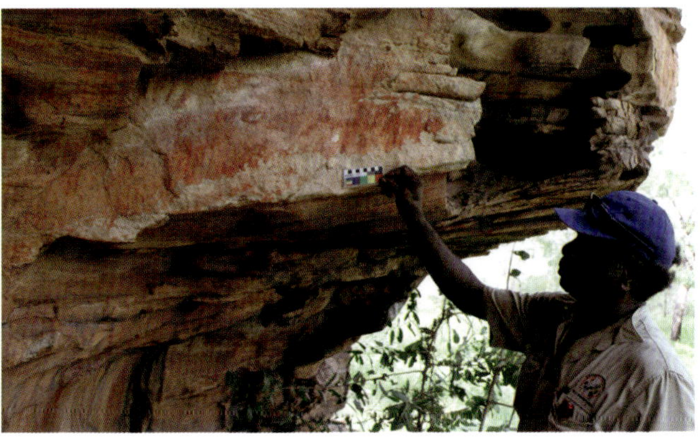

or deterioration of many images in country is directly linked to
its kin dying, the health of the Yanyuwa community, or even the
present generation's lack of engagement with that country…
at another level they provide unique insight into the potential
of rock art in contributing to Yanyuwa social well-being'.[17] The
art announces to the people the state of relationships between
people – between land owners and managers, for example, and
elders and youths – and between people and their deceased
human and non-human kin. Implicated in this relationship is the
agency of the old people or spirits who have the ability to 'take
away' the paintings if they see that the community is unhealthy
or that too many old people are dying, or that not enough people
are coming onto Country to care for it. If Country isn't healthy
then the art isn't healthy; and when strangers intrude onto sites,
the spirits take away the paintings and make them 'weak'.

Conclusion

There are lessons to be learnt about how people relate to cave
art as a living expression of culture, and of life itself. The art of
the 'other' enables us to rethink ourselves: thinking of people
with different cultural practices to our own as 'others' forces us
to think of ourselves as 'others' also – as 'other others' – for we
are all somehow different to each other. It is by embracing these
differences that we can come to recognize each other as a united
yet varied biological and social species, a species to which we
can all trace ancestral connections deep in the heart of Blombos
Cave, for example, where artists left behind their early paint-
making palettes so long ago. Our artworks since those early times
speak to this perfectly, for across the world we can see with our
own eyes a long history that ultimately goes back to a common
ancestry from which we all stem. We may have diverged as our
ancestors populated the earth, but have recombined in copious
entangled ways ever since. Sometimes our ancestors went their
own way; at other times their paths connected and reconnected.
What makes cave art so special in world archaeology is that it
represents the aesthetic sensitivities and symbolic actions of these
entangled paths and pasts, and in this cave art gives us clues as to
the cognitive energies and cultural practices of people in particular
places at particular times in the past.

    There is a voyeurism about the study of cave art: like the
space travel of science fiction or journeys into the remotest
corners of the earth, cave art allows us to wander into both

our own and other worlds, to explore a realm of otherness
by contemplating the makings of the creative minds of distant
peoples, of other times. It affords us a doorway through which
we may walk into the past, often of others, separated from
us by long geographical distances or deep expanses of time,
or both; other worlds that we do not quite understand due
to fundamental cultural differences, yet that somehow feel at
home in that we, too, share creative, artistic urges and interests.
Finding out about cave art is finding out about ourselves by
finding out about things beyond ourselves, through what other
humans do or did, but that are essentially familiar. Cave art
reminds us of the varied cultural ways in which people live out
their lives, but ultimately we are all connected, and therefore
we somehow relate to other ways of doing, to other ways of
painting and representing the world. We explore connections
with peoples and times beyond those of our own everyday
experience. And through cave art we wonder about our
differences as much as about our similarities. All this while
in reality the art of other peoples usually speaks of cultures
different to ours, of inspirations and motivations other than our
own, and of communities and creative rights to which we can
claim no attachments beyond that common humanity.

Notes

Chapter 1

1   p. 28 in Smith, C. 1992. The articulation of style and social structure in Australian Aboriginal art. *Australian Aboriginal Studies* 1992(1):28–34.
2   The French philosopher Jean-Paul Sartre had previously developed such a dual method of historical investigation in an essay he published in 1957. It was eventually further developed in his book *Questions de Méthode* (Éditions Gallimard, Paris), translated in English in 1963 as *Search for a Method* (Alfred A. Knopf, New York).
3   Taçon, P. S. C. and C. Chippindale 1998. An archaeology of rock-art through informed methods and formal methods. In C. Chippindale and P. S. C. Taçon (eds), *The Archaeology of Rock-Art*, pp. 1–10. Cambridge University Press, Cambridge.
4   Eco, U. 1994. *The Limits of Interpretation*. Indiana University Press, Bloomington.
5   Young, M. J. 1988. *Signs From the Ancestors: Zuni Cultural Symbolism and Perceptions of Rock Art*. University of New Mexico Press, Albuquerque.
    Merlan, F. 1989. The interpretive framework of Wardaman rock art: A preliminary report. *Australian Aboriginal Studies* 1989(2):14–24.
6   For a useful discussion of how during ethnographic times artworks articulate connections between Aboriginal people, Country and the spirit-beings who dwell within, see Caruana, W. 2012. *Aboriginal Art* (3rd ed.). Thames & Hudson, London.
7   For example, see Layton, R. 1991. *The Anthropology of Art*. Cambridge University Press, Cambridge.
8   Christian, D. 2004. *Maps of Time: An Introduction to Big History*. University of California Press, Berkeley.
9   An interesting recent book on this topic is Brady, L. M. and P. S. C. Taçon (eds) 2016. *Relating to Rock Art in the Contemporary World: Navigating Symbolism, Meaning and Significance*. University Press of Colorado, Boulder.

Chapter 2

1   p. 762 in Chen Zhao Fu 2001. Asia. In D. S. Whitley (ed.), *Handbook of Rock Art Research*, pp. 760–85. AltaMira Press, Walnut Creek.
2   For one account of nineteenth- and early twentieth-century struggles to make sense of Palaeolithic art, see Moro Abadía, O. 2015. The reception of Palaeolithic art at the turn of the twentieth century: Between archaeology and art history. *Journal of Art Historiography* 12/OMA1. https://arthistoriography.files.wordpress.com/2015/06/moro-abadia.pdf
3   Bahn, P. 1998. *Prehistoric Art*. Cambridge University Press, Cambridge.
    Bahn, P. and J. Vertut 1997. *Journey Through the Ice Age*. Weidenfeld & Nicolson, London.
4   Saura Ramos, P. A. (ed.) 1998. *The Cave of Altamira*. Harry N. Abrams, New York.
5   Cartailhac, É. 1880. *Congrès International d'Anthropologie et d'Archéologie Préhistoriques: Rapport sur la Session de Lisbonne*. Eugene Boban, Paris. http://gallica.bnf.fr/ark:/12148/bpt6k6542057x/f7.image (see in particular the dismissive reporting on p. 76).
6   Siret, L. 1913. *Questions de Chronologie et d'Ethnographie Ibériques*. Geuthner, Paris.
7   Harlé, É. 1881. La grotte d'Altamira, près de Santander (Espagne). *Matériaux pour l'Histoire Primitive et Naturelle de l'Homme* (second series), 16(12):275–83. http://gallica.bnf.fr/ark:/12148/bpt6k4453295/f4.image
8   Rivière, É. 1896. La Grotte de la Mouthe. *Comptes Rendus Hebdomadaires des Séances de l'Académie des Sciences* 123:543–46.
9   Rivière, É. 1897. La grotte de la Mouthe (Dordogne). *Bulletins de la Société d'Anthropologie de Paris* 8:302–29.
10 'ma conviction était faite: *les gravures de La Mouthe étaient des gravures préhistoriques*'. Rivière, É. 1897. La grotte de la Mouthe (Dordogne). *Bulletins de la Société d'Anthropologie de Paris* 8, p. 314.
11 Lawson, A. J. 2012. *Painted Caves: Palaeolithic Rock Art in Western Europe*. Oxford University Press, Oxford.
12 See the reports by Émile Rivière referenced in Notes 8 and 9.
13 'Bref, nous croyons pouvoir dire, sans être démenti par aucun d'eux, que l'antiquité paléolithique de tous les dessins gravés et peints des trois grottes de La Mouthe, de Font-de-Gaume et des Combarelles ne laisse désormais aucun doute dans l'esprit de nos Collègues'. In É. Rivière 1902. Excursion de la section aux Eyzies. *Association Française pour l'Avancement des Sciences. Montauban* 1, p. 272.
14 'Il resort de tout ce qu'ils ont observé que *nous n'avons plus aucune raison de suspecter l'antiquité des peintures d'Altamira. … Il faut s'incliner devant la réalité d'un fait, et, je dois pour ce qui me concerne, faire amende honorable à M. de Sautuola.'* In E. Cartailhac 1902, Les cavernes ornées de dessins, La Grotte d'Altamira (Espagne): Mea culpa d'un sceptique. *L'Anthropologie* 13, p. 354.
15 Cartailhac, É. & H. Breuil 1903. Les peintures préhistoriques de la grotte d'Altamira à Santillane (Espagne). *Comptes Rendus des Séances de l'Académie des Inscriptions et Belles-Lettres* 46:256–65.
16 Aujoulat, N. 2004. *Lascaux: Le Geste, l'Espace et le Temps*. Seuil, Paris.
17 Delluc, B. and G. Delluc 2003. *Lascaux Retrouvé*. Pilote 24, Périgueux.
    Thaon-Coty 1940. Les figures peintes de la Grotte de Lascaux. *Le Figaro* 1 Novembre 1940:1–2.
18 Many published accounts of the discovery of Lascaux speak of four youths and their dog Robot who was said to have fallen into a hole in the ground and thus needed rescuing, causing the discovery of the cave and its art. However, as explained by those four youths many years later, the dog did not fall down into the deep depression needing to be rescued, but was rather a member of a larger party of youths exploring and playing through the woods a few days before the discovery of the cave. The testimonies of a number of the youths have recently been listed and analysed in Brigitte and Gilles Delluc's book *Lascaux Retrouvé*, see pp. 291–311 in particular.
19 Bastian, F., V. Jurado, A. Nováková, C. Alabouvette and C. Saiz-Jimenez 2010. The microbiology of Lascaux Cave. *Microbiology* 156:644–52. doi: 10.1099/mic.0.036160-0
20 Malraux, A. 1967. *Antimémoires*. Gallimard, Paris.
21 Chauvet, J.-M., E. Brunel Deschamps, C. Hillaire, J. Clottes and P. Bahn 1996. *Chauvet Cave: The Discovery of the World's Oldest Paintings*. Thames & Hudson, London. Quote is from pp. 36–40.
22 See note 21.
23 See note 21.
24 Clottes, J. (ed.) 2001. *La Grotte Chauvet: L'Art des Origines*. Seuil, Paris.
25 For a good discussion of the Australian Aboriginal notion of 'Country', see also Sutton, P. 1995. *Country: Aboriginal Boundaries*

and Land Ownership in Australia. Aboriginal History Inc., Canberra.

Chapter 3

1 Huguet, D. and S. Compoint (ed.) 2015. *La Caverne du Pont d'Arc.* Actes Sud Beaux Arts, Paris.
2 David, B., J.-J. Delannoy, R. Gunn, E. Chalmin, G. Castets, F. Petchey, K. Aplin, M. O'Farrell, I. Moffat, J. Mialanes, J.-M. Geneste, B. Barker, B. Sadier, M. Katherine, M. Manataki and U. Pietrzak in press. Dating painted Panel E1 at Nawarla Gabarnmang, central Arnhem Land plateau. In B. David, P. Taçon, J.-J. Delannoy and J.-M. Geneste (eds), *The Archaeology of Rock Art in Western Arnhem Land, Northern Australia.* Terra Australis, ANU Press, Canberra.
  Gunn, R., B. David, J.-J. Delannoy and M. Katherine in press. The past 500 years of rock art at Nawarla Gabarnmang, central Arnhem Land plateau. In B. David, P. Taçon, J.-J. Delannoy and J.-M. Geneste (eds), *The Archaeology of Rock Art in Western Arnhem Land, Northern Australia.* Terra Australis, ANU Press, Canberra.
3 Delannoy, J.-J., B. David, J.-M. Geneste, M. Katherine, B. Sadier and R. Gunn in press. Engineers of the Arnhem Land plateau: Evidence for the origins and transformation of sheltered spaces at Nawarla Gabarnmang. In B. David, P. Taçon, J.-J. Delannoy and J.-M. Geneste (eds), *The Archaeology of Rock Art in Western Arnhem Land, Northern Australia.* Terra Australis, ANU Press, Canberra.
4 David, B., B. Barker, F. Petchey, J.-J. Delannoy, J.-M. Geneste, C. Rowe, M. Eccleston, L. Lamb and R. Whear 2013. A 28,000 year old excavated painted rock from Nawarla Gabarnmang, northern Australia. *Journal of Archaeological Science* 41:1–9.
  David, B., B. Barker, J.-J. Delannoy, J.-M. Geneste, F. Petchey and L. Lamb 2014. Dessin ou peinture Pléistocène au charbon en Australie du nord/A Pleistocene drawing or painting from northern Australia. *International Newsletter on Rock Art (INORA)* 69:18–22.
5 Lymer, K. 2015. Image processing and visualisation of rock art laser scans from Loups's Hill, County Durham. *Digital Applications in Archaeology and Cultural Heritage.* doi: 10.1016/j.daach.2015.01.002i
6 David, B., I. J. McNiven and J. Brayer 2003. Colourful past. *British Archaeology* 73:14–15.
  David, B., J. Brayer, I. J. McNiven

and A. Watchman 2001. Why digital enhancement of rock paintings works: Rescaling and saturating colours. *Antiquity* 75:781–92.
7 Cerrillo-Cuenca, E. and M. Sepúlveda 2015. An assessment of methods for the digital enhancement of rock paintings: The rock art from the precordillera of Arica (Chile) as a case study. *Journal of Archaeological Science* 55:197–208.
  Domingo, I., B. Carrión, S. Blanco and J. L. Lerma 2015. Evaluating conventional and advanced visible image enhancement solutions to produce digital tracings at el Carche rock art shelter. *Digital Applications in Archaeology and Cultural Heritage.* doi: 10.1016/j.daach.2015.01.001
  Mark, R. and E. Billo 2002. Application of digital image enhancement in rock art recording. *American Indian Rock Art* 28:121–28.
8 David, B., I. J. McNiven, L. Manas, J. Manas, S. Savage, J. Crouch, G. Neliman and L. Brady 2004. Goba of Mua: Archaeology working with oral tradition. *Antiquity* 78:158–72.
9 Brady, L., B. David, L. Manas and Mualgal (Torres Strait Islanders) Corporation 2003. Commemorating and teaching cultural awareness on Mua Island, Torres Strait. *Australian Journal of Indigenous Education* 31:41–49.
10 Wilson, M., J. Sanhambath, P. Senembe, B. David, N. Hall, and M. Abong 2000. 'Tufala kev blong devil': People and spirits in North West Malakula, Vanuatu – implications for management. *Conservation and Management of Archaeological Sites* 4:151–66.
11 See note 2.
12 Harris, E. C. 1979. *Principles of Archaeological Stratigraphy.* Academic Press, London.
  For an early application of Harris Matrices to rock art, see Chippindale, C., J. de Jongh, J. Flood and S. Rufolo 2000. Stratigraphy, Harris matrices and relative dating of Australian rock-art. *Antiquity* 74:285–86. doi: 10.1017/S0003598X00059275
13 See note 2.
14 Roberts, R. G. and Z. Jacobs 2008. Dating in landscape archaeology. In B. David and J. Thomas (eds), *Handbook of Landscape Archaeology,* pp. 347–64. Left Coast Press, Walnut Creek.
15 Wilson, M., M. Spriggs and E. Lawson 2001. Dating the rock art of Vanuatu: AMS radiocarbon determinations from abandoned mud-wasp nests and charcoal

pigment found in superimposition. *Rock Art Research* 18:24–31.
16 For an account of Lapita, see Kirch, P. V. 1996. *The Lapita Peoples: Ancestors of the Oceanic World.* Blackwell, Cambridge.
17 See note 15.
18 Watchman, A. L. and N. Cole 1993. Accelerator radiocarbon dating of plant-fibre binders in rock paintings from north-eastern Australia. *Antiquity* 67:355–58.
19 Watchman, A. L., B. David, I. J. McNiven and J. M. Flood 2000. Micro-archaeology of engraved and painted rock surface crusts at Yiwarlarlay (the Lightning Brothers site), Northern Territory, Australia. *Journal of Archaeological Science* 27:315–25.
20 Watchman, A. L., S. O'Connor and R. Jones 2005. Dating oxalate minerals 20–45 ka. *Journal of Archaeological Science* 32:369–74.
21 Roberts, R. G., G. Walsh, A. Murray, J. Olley, R. Jones, M. Morwood, C. Tuniz, E. Lawson, M. Macphail, D. Bowdery and I. Naumann 1997. Luminescence dating of rock art and past environments using mud-wasp nests in northern Australia. *Nature* 387:696–99.
22 See note 21.
23 Aubert, M., S. O'Connor, M. McCulloch, G. Mortimer, A. Watchman and M. Richer-LaFlèche 2006. Uranium-series dating rock art in East Timor. *Journal of Archaeological Science* 34:991–96.
24 Taçon, P. S. C., M. Aubert, L. Gang, Y. Decong, L. Hong, S. K. May, S. Fallon, J. Xueping, D. Curnoe and A. I. R. Herries 2012. Uranium-series age estimates for rock art in southwest China. *Journal of Archaeological Science* 39:492–99. doi: 10.1016/j.jas.2011.10.004
25 Pike, A. W. G., D. L. Hoffmann, M. García-Diez, P. B. Pettitt, J. Alcolea, R. De Balbín, C. González-Sainz, C. de las Heras, J. A. Lasheras, R. Montes and J. Zilhão 2012. U-series dating of Paleolithic art in 11 caves in Spain. *Science* 336:1409–13.
26 Aubert, M., A. Brumm, M. Ramli, T. Sutikna, E. W. Saptomo, B. Hakim, M. J. Morwood, G. D. van den Bergh, L. Kinsley and A. Dosseto 2014. Pleistocene cave art from Sulawesi, Indonesia. *Nature* 514:223–27.
27 Cheng, H., R. L. Edwards, J. Hoff, C. D. Gallup, D. A. Richards and Y. Asmerom 2000. The half-lives of uranium-234 and thorium-230. *Chemical Geology* 169:17–33.
28 Bednarik, R. 2002. The dating of rock art: A critique. *Journal*

of Archaeological Science 29:1213–33. http://www.idealibrary.com

29 See note 23.

30 See note 24.

31 See note 26.

32 Smith, M. A., B. Fankhauser and M. Jercher 1998. The changing provenance of red ochre at Puritjarra rockshelter, Central Australia: Late Pleistocene to present. Proceedings of the Prehistoric Society 64:275–92.

33 Smith, M. A. and S. Pell 1997. Oxygen-isotope ratios in quartz as indicators of the provenance of archeological ochres. Journal of Archaeological Science 24:773–78.

34 Mooney, S. D., C. Geiss and M. A. Smith 2003. The use of mineral magnetic parameters to characterize archaeological ochres. Journal of Archaeological Science 30:511–23.

Chapter 4

1 Mellars, P. A. and C. B. Stringer 1989. The Human Revolution: Behavioural and Biological Perspectives on the Origins of Modern Humans. Edinburgh University Press, Edinburgh.

2 McBrearty, S. and A. S. Brooks 2000. The revolution that wasn't: A new interpretation of the origin of modern human behavior. Journal of Human Evolution 39:453–563.

3 'Les espèces sont choisies non commes bonnes à manger, mais comme bonnes à penser'. See C. Lévi-Strauss 1962. La Pensée Sauvage. Librairie Plon, Paris, p. 128.

4 Harmand, S., J. E. Lewis, C. S. Feibel, C. J. Lepre, S. Prat, A. Lenoble, X. Boës, R. L. Quinn, M. Brenet, A. Arroyo, N. Taylor, S. Clément, G. Daver, J.-P. Brugal, L. Leakey, R. A. Mortlock, J. D. Wright, S. Lokorodi, C. Kirwa, D. V. Kent and H. Roche 2015. 3.3-million-year-old stone tools from Lomekwi 3, West Turkana, Kenya. Nature 521:310–15.

5 J. M. Parés, L. Arnold, M. Duval, M. Demuro, A. Pérez-González, J. M. Bermúdez de Castro, E. Carbonell, J. L. Arsuaga 2013. Reassessing the age of Atapuerca-TD6 (Spain): New paleomagnetic results. Journal of Archaeological Science 40:4586–95.

6 Morwood, M. J., R. P. Soejono, R. G. Roberts, T. Sutikna, C. S. M. Turney, K. E. Westaway, W. J. Rink, J.-X., Zhao, G. D. van den Bergh, Rokus Awe Due, D. R. Hobbs, M. W. Moore, M. I. Bird and L. K. Fifield 2004. Archaeology and age of a new hominin from Flores in eastern Indonesia.

Nature 431:1087–91. doi: 10.1038/nature02956

Van Oosterzee, P. and M. Morwood. A New Human: The Startling Discovery and Strange Story of the 'Hobbits' of Flores, Indonesia. Collins, London.

7 Sutikna, T., M. W. Tocheri, M. J. Morwood, Saptomo, E. W., Jatmiko, R. Due Awe, S. Wasisto, K. E. Westaway, M. Aubert, B. Li, J.-X. Zhao, M. Storey, B. V. Alloway, M. W. Morley, H. J. M. Meijer, G. D. van den Bergh, R. Grün, A. Dosseto, A. Brumm, W. L. Jungers and R. G. Roberts 2016. Revised stratigraphy and chronology for Homo floresiensis at Liang Bua in Indonesia. Nature 532:366–69.

8 Wood, R. E., C. Barroso-Ruíz, M. Caparrós, J. F. J. Pardo, B. G. Santos and T. F. G. Higham 2013. Radiocarbon dating casts doubt on the late chronology of the Middle to Upper Palaeolithic transition in southern Iberia. Proceedings of the National Academy of Sciences USA 110:2781–86.

For a great read on Neanderthals, see Papagianni, D. and M. A. Morse 2013. The Neanderthals Rediscovered: How Modern Science is Rewriting Their Story. Thames & Hudson, London.

9 Meltzer, D. J. 2013. The human colonization of the Americas: Archaeology. In I. Ness (ed.), The Encyclopedia of Global Human Migration, pp. 1–9. Wiley-Blackwell, Hoboken. doi: 10.1002/9781444351071. wbeghm808

10 Green, R. E., J. Krause, S. E. Ptak, A. W. Briggs, M. T. Ronan, J. F. Simons, L. Du, M. Egholm, J. M. Rothberg, M. Paunovic and S. Pääbo 2006. Analysis of one million base pairs of Neanderthal DNA. Nature 444 (7117):330–36.

Noonan, J. P., G. Coop, S. Kudaravalli, D. Smith, J. Krause, J. Alessi, F. Chen, D. Platt, S. Pääbo, J. K. Pritchard and E. M. Rubin 2006. Sequencing and analysis of Neanderthal genomic DNA. Science 314 (5802):1113–18.

11 See note 10.

12 Neves, A. G. M. and M. Serva 2012. Extremely rare interbreeding events can explain Neanderthal DNA in living humans. PLoS ONE 7(10): e47076. doi: 10.1371/journal.pone.0047076

13 Fu, Q., M. Hajdinjak, O. T. Moldovan, S. Constantin, S. Mallick, P. Skoglund, N. Patterson, N. Rohland, I. Lazaridis, B. Nickel, B. Viola, K. Prüfer, M. Meyer, J. Kelso, D. Reich and S. Pääbo 2015.

An early modern human from Romania with a recent Neanderthal ancestor. Nature 524 (7564): 216–19.

14 Mendez, F. L., G. D. Poznik, S. Castellano and C. D, Bustamante 2016. The divergence of Neandertal and modern human Y Chromosomes. American Journal of Human Genetics 98:728–34.

15 Reich, D, R. E. Green, M. Kircher, J. Krause, N. Patterson, E. Y. Durand, B. Viola, A. W. Briggs, U. Stenzel, P. L. F. Johnson, T. Maricic, J. M. Good, T. Marques-Bonet, C. Alkan, Q. Fu, S. Mallick, H. Li, M. Meyer, E. E. Eichler, M. Stoneking, M. Richards, S. Talamo, M. V. Shunkov, A. P. Derevianko, J.-J. Hublin, J. Kelso, M. Slatkin and S. Pääbo 2010. Genetic history of an archaic hominin group from Denisova Cave in Siberia. Nature 468 (7327):1053–60.

16 For an account of the development of the notion of the 'Acheulean', see Sackett, J. 2014.Boucher de Perthes and the discovery of human antiquity. Bulletin of the History of Archaeology 24(2):1–11. doi: 10.5334/bha.242

17 Bednarik, R. G. 2005. Middle Pleistocene beads and symbolism. Anthropos 100: 537–52.

Rigaud, S., F. D'Errico, M. Vanhaeren and C. Neumann 2009. Critical reassessment of putative Acheulean Porosphaera globularis beads. Journal of Archaeological Science 36:25–34.

18 Bednarik, R. G. 2003. A figurine from the African Acheulian. Current Anthropology 44:405–13.

19 Rincon, P. 2003. 'Oldest sculpture' found in Morocco. BBC News 23 May. http://news.bbc.co.uk/2/hi/science/nature/3047383.stm

20 Goren-Inbar, N. 1986. A figurine from the Acheulian site of Berekhat Ram. Mitekufat Haeven: Journal of the Israel Prehistoric Society 19:7–12.

21 Marshack, A. 1997. The Berekhat Ram figurine: A late Acheulian carving from the Middle East. Antiquity 71(272):327–37. doi: 10.1017/S0003598X00084957

22 d'Errico, F. and A. Nowell 2000. A new look at the Berekhat Ram figurine: Implications for the origins of symbolism. Cambridge Archaeological Journal 10:123–67. doi: 10.1017/S0959774300000056

23 Dart, R. A. 1974. The waterworn Australopithecine pebble of many faces from Makapansgat. South African Journal of Science 70:167–69.

24 Bednarik, R. G. 1998. The 'australopithecine' cobble from Makapansgat, South Africa. South African Archaeological Bulletin 53:4–8.

25 Joordens, J. C. A., F. d'Errico, F. P. Wesselingh, S. Munro, J. de Vos, J. Wallinga, C. Ankjærgaard, T. Reimann, J. R. Wijbrans, K. F. Kuiper, H. J. Mücher, H. Coqueugniot, V. Prié, I. Joosten, B. van Os, A. S. Schulp, M. Panuel, V. van der Haas, W. Lustenhouwer, J. J. G. Reijmer and W. Roebroeks 2015. *Homo erectus* at Trinil on Java used shells for tool production and engraving. *Nature* 518:228–31. doi: 10.1038/nature13962

26 Barham, L. S. 2002. Systematic pigment use in the Middle Pleistocene of south-central Africa. *Current Anthropology* 43:181–90.

27 Gargett, R. H. 1989. Grave shortcomings: The evidence for Neandertal burial. *Current Anthropology* 30:157–90.

28 Pettitt, P. 2011. *The Palaeolithic Origins of Human Burial.* Routledge, Abingdon.

29 Fiacconi, M. and C. O. Hunt 2015. Pollen taphonomy at Shanidar Cave (Kurdish Iraq): An initial evaluation. *Review of Palaeobotany and Palynology* 223:87–93.

30 Trinkaus, E. 1983. *The Shanidar Neanderthals.* Academic Press, New York.

31 Rendu, W., C. Beauval, I. Crevecoeur, P. Bayle, A. Balzeau, T. Bismuth, L. Bourguignon, G. Delfour, J.-F. Faivre, F. Lacrampe-Cuyaubère, C. Tavormina, D. Todisco, A. Turq and B. Maureille 2014. Evidence supporting an intentional Neandertal burial at La Chapelle-aux-Saints. *Proceedings of the National Academy of Sciences USA* 111:81–86.

32 See note 28.

33 Chazan, M. and L. K. Horwitz 2009. Milestones in the development of symbolic behavior: A case study from Wonderwerk Cave, South Africa. *World Archaeology* 41: 521–39.

34 Roebroeks, W., M. J. Sier, T. K. Nielsen, D. De Loecker, J. M. Parés, C. E. S. Arps and H. J. Mücher 2012. Use of red ochre by early Neandertals. *Proceedings of the National Academy of Sciences USA* 109:1889–94.

35 Soressi, M., W. Rendu, J.-P. Texier, É. C. Loïc Daulny, F. D'Errico, V. Laroulandie, B. Maureille, M. Niclot, S. Schwortz and A.-M. Tillier 2008. Pech-de-l'Azé I (Dordogne, France): Nouveau regard sur un gisement moustérien de tradition acheuléenne connu depuis le XIX siècle. In J. Jaubert, J.-G. Bordes and I. Ortega (eds), *Les Sociétés Paléolithiques d'un Grand Sud-Ouest: Nouveaux Gisements, Nouvelles Méthodes, Nouveaux Résultats: Actes des Journées Décentralisées de la SPF des 24–25 novembre 2006.* Société Préhistorique française, pp. 95–132. Mémoire XLVII de la Société Préhistorique Française, Paris.

36 For a counter-view, see Bednarik, R. G. 2006. The Middle Paleolithic engravings from Oldisleben, Germany. *Anthropologie* 44(2): 113–21.
Mania, D. and U. Mania 1988. Deliberate engravings on bone artefacts of *Homo erectus. Rock Art Research* 5:91–107.

37 Soressi, M. and F. d'Errico 2007. Pigments, gravures, parures: Les comportements symboliques controversies des Néandertaliens. In B. Vandermeersch and B. Maureille (eds), *Les Néandertaliens: Biologie et Cultures*, pp. 297–309. Documents Préhistoriques 23. Éditions de CTHS, Paris.

38 Jaubert, J., S. Verheyden, D. Genty, M. Soulier, H. Cheng, D. Blamart, C. Burlet, H. Camus, S. Delaby, D. Deldicque, R. L. Edwards, C. Ferrier, F. Lacrampe-Cuyaubère, F. Lévêque, F. Maksud, P. Mora, X. Muth, É. Régnier, J.-N. Rouzaud and F. Santos 2016. Early Neanderthal constructions deep in Bruniquel Cave in southwestern France. *Nature.* doi: 10.1038/nature18291

39 Peresani, M., I. Fiore, M. Gala, M. Romandini and A. Tagliacozzo 2011. Late Neandertals and the intentional removal of feathers as evidenced from bird bone taphonomy at Fumane Cave 44 ky B.P., Italy. *Proceedings of the National Academy of Sciences USA* 108:3888–93.

40 Radovčić, D., A. O. Sršen, J. Radovčić and D. W. Frayer 2015. Evidence for Neandertal jewelry: Modified white-tailed eagle claws at Krapina. *Plos One* 10(3): e0119802. doi: 10.1371/journal.pone.0119802

Chapter 5

1 For further evidence of the expansion of early modern humans out of Africa via Arabia, see for example Armitage, S. J., S. A. Jasim, A. E. Marks, A. G. Parker, V. I. Usik and H.-P. Uerpmann 2011. The Southern Route 'Out of Africa': Evidence for an early expansion of modern humans into Arabia. *Science* 331:453–56.

2 Reyes-Centeno, H., M. Hubbe, T. Hanihara, C. Stringer and K. Harvati in press. Testing modern human out-of-Africa dispersal models and implications for modern human origins. *Journal of Human Evolution.* doi: 10.1016/j.jhevol.2015.06.008

3 Henshilwood, C. S., F. d'Errico, K. L. van Niekerk, Y. Coquinot, Z. Jacobs, S.-E. Lauritzen, M. Menu and R. García-Moreno 2011. A 100,000-year-old ochre-processing workshop at Blombos Cave, South Africa. *Science* 334: 219–22.

4 Jacobs, Z., R. G. Roberts, R. F. Galbraith, H. J. Deacon, R. Grün, A. Mackay, P. Mitchell, R. Vogelsang, L. Wadley 2008. Ages for the Middle Stone Age of southern Africa: Implications for human behavior and dispersal. *Science* 322:733–35.

5 Wadley, L., C. Sievers, M. Bamford, P. Goldberg, F. Berna and C. Miller 2011. Middle Stone Age bedding construction and settlement patterns at Sibudu, South Africa. *Science* 334:1388–91.

6 d'Ericco, F., R. G. Moreno and R. F. Rifkin 2012. Technological, elemental and colorimetric analysis of an engraved ochre fragment from the Middle Stone Age levels of Klasies River Cave 1, South Africa. *Journal of Archaeological Science* 39:942–52.

7 Henshilwood, C. S., F. d'Ericco and I. Watts 2009. Engraved ochres from the Middle Stone Age levels at Blombos Cave, South Africa. *Journal of Human Evolution* 57: 27–47.

8 Texier, P.-J., G. Porraz, J. Parkington, J.-P. Rigaud, C. Poggenpoel, C. Miller, C. Tribolo, C. Cartwright, A. Coudenneau, R. Klein, T. Steele and C. Verna 2010. A Howiesons Poort tradition of engraving ostrich eggshell containers dated to 60,000 years ago at Diepkloof Rock Shelter, South Africa. *Proceedings of the National Academy of Sciences of the United States of America* 107: 6180–85.
Texier, P.-J., G. Porraz, J. Parkington, J.-P. Rigaud, C. Poggenpoel and C. Tribolo 2013. The context, form and significance of the MSA engraved ostrich eggshell collection from Diepkloof Rock Shelter, Western Cape, South Africa. *Journal of Archaeological Science* 40:3412–31.
Henshilwood, C. S., K. L. van Niekerk, S. Wurz, A. Delagnes, S. Armitage, R. Rifkin, K. Douze, P. Keene, M. Haaland, J. Reynard, E. Discamps and S. Mienies 2014. Klipdrift Shelter, southern Cape, South Africa: Preliminary report on the Howiesons Poort levels. *Journal of Archaeological Science* 45:284–303.

9 Vogelsang, R., J. Richter, Z. Jacobs, B. Eichhorn, V. Linseele and R. G. Roberts 2010. New excavations of Middle Stone Age deposits at Apollo 11 Rockshelter, Namibia: Stratigraphy, archaeology,

chronology and past environments. *Journal of African Archaeology* 8:185–218.

10 Bednarik, R.G. 2015. The significance of the earliest beads. *Advances in Anthropology* 5:51–66. doi: 10.4236/aa.2015.52006

11 Hovers, E., B. Vandermeersch and O. Bar-Yosef 1997. A Middle Palaeolithic engraved artefact from Qafzeh Cave, Israel. *Rock Art Research* 14:79–87.

12 Hovers, E., S. Ilani, O. Bar-Yosef and B. Vandermeersch 2003. An early case of color symbolism: ochre use by modern humans in Qafzeh Cave. *Current Anthropology* 44:491–522.

13 Roberts, R. G., R. Jones, N. A. Spooner, M. J. Head, A. S. Murray and M. A. Smith 1994. The human colonisation of Australia: Optical dates of 53,000 and 60,000 years bracket human arrival at Deaf Adder Gorge, Northern Territory. *Quaternary Science Reviews* 13(5–7):575–83.

Clarkson, C., M. Smith, B. Marwick, R. Fullagar, L. A. Wallis, P. Faulkner, T. Manne, E. Hayes, R. G. Roberts, Z. Jacobs, X. Carah, K. M. Lowe, J. Matthews and S. A. Florin 2015. The archaeology, chronology and stratigraphy of Madjedbebe (Malakunanja II): A site in northern Australia with early occupation. *Journal of Human Evolution* 83:46–64.

14 O'Connor, S. and B. Fankhauser 2001. Art at 40,000 bp? One step closer: An ochre covered rock from Carpenter's Gap Shelter 1, Kimberley region, Western Australia. In A. Anderson, I. Lilley and S. O'Connor (eds), *Histories of Old Ages: Essays in Honour of Rhys Jones*, pp. 287–300. Pandanus Books, Australian National University, Canberra.

New carbon dates extending the original age determinations for Carpenter's Gap have recently been published; a useful article is Hiscock, P., S. O'Connor, J. Balme and T. Maloney 2016. World's earliest ground-edge axe production coincides with human colonisation of Australia. *Australian Archaeology* 82(1):2–11. doi: 10.1080/03122417.2016.1164379

For an interesting discussion of what the arrival of modern humans in Australia around 50,000 years ago means for global understandings of human evolution, see Balme, J., I. Davidson, J. McDonald, N. Stern and P. Veth 2009. Symbolic behaviour and the peopling of the southern arc route to Australia. *Quaternary International* 202:59–68.

Chapter 6

1 For a broad discussion of the history of the idea of ice ages, see Krüger, T. 2013. *Discovering the Ice Ages: International Reception and Consequences for a Historical Understanding of Climate*. Brill, Leiden.

For technical details of changes in ice cover during the Pleistocene, see for example EPICA community members 2004. Eight glacial cycles from an Antarctic ice core. *Nature* 429:623–28.

2 Nesbitt, S. 2001. Venus figurines of the Upper Paleothic. *Totem: The University of Western Ontario Journal of Anthropology* 9(1). http://ir.lib.uwo.ca/totem/vol9/iss1/6

Tringham, R. and M. Conkey 1998. Rethinking figurines: A critical view from archaeology of Gimbutas, the 'Goddess' and popular culture. In L. Goodison and C. Morris (eds), *Ancient Goddesses: The Myths and the Evidence*, pp. 22–45. British Museum Press, London.

3 Pike, A. W. G., D. L. Hoffmann, M. García-Diez, P. B. Pettitt, J. Alcolea, R. De Balbín, C. González-Sainz, C. de las Heras, J. A. Lasheras, R. Montes and J. Zilhão 2012. U-series dating of Paleolithic art in 11 caves in Spain. *Science* 336:1409–13.

4 Sauvet, G., R. Bourrillon, M. Conkey, C. Fritz, D. Garate, O. Rivero, G. Tosello and R. White 2015. Uranium–thorium dating method and Palaeolithic rock art. *Quaternary International*. doi:10.1016/j.quaint.2015.03.053

Pont-Branchu, E., M. Fontugne, V. Michel and H. Valladas 2015. Comment on: 'Uranium–thorium dating method and Palaeolithic rock art' by Sauvet et al. (2015, in press). *Quaternary International*. doi:10.1016/j.quaint.2015.10.015

5 Reimer, P. J., E. Bard, A. Bayliss, J. W. Beck, P. G. Blackwell, C. Bronk Ramsey, C. E. Buck, C. E., H. Cheng, R. L. Edwards, M. Friedrich, P. M. Grootes, T. P. Guilderson, H. Haflidason, I. Hajdas, C. Hatté, T. J. Heaton, D. L. Hoffmann, A. G. Hogg, K. A. Hughen, K. F. Kaiser, B. Kromer, S. W. Manning, M. Niu, R. W. Reimer, D. A. Richards, E. M. Scott, J. R. Southon, R. A. Staff, C. S. M. Turney and J. van der Plicht 2013. IntCal13 and Marine13 radiocarbon age calibration curves, 0–50,000 years cal BP. *Radiocarbon* 55(4):1869–87.

6 For a useful commentary, see Appenzeller, T. 2013. Old masters. *Nature* 497:302–04.

7 Clottes, J. 2001. Epilogue: Chauvet Cave today. In J.-M. Chauvet, E. Brunel-Deschamps and C. Hillaire, *Chauvet Cave: The Discovery of the World's Oldest Paintings*, pp. 89–127. Thames & Hudson, London.

8 Clottes, J. (ed.) 2001. *La Grotte Chauvet: L'Art des Origines*. Seuil, Paris.

9 See note 8.

10 Pettitt, P. and P. Bahn 2015. An alternative chronology for the art of Chauvet cave. *Antiquity* 89: 542–53.

11 Quiles, A., H. Valladas, H. Bocherens, E. Delqué-Količ, E. Kaltnecker, J. van der Plicht, J.-J. Delannoy, V. Feruglio, C. Fritz, J. Monney, M. Philippe, G. Tosello, J. Clottes and J.-M. Geneste 2016. A high-precision chronological model for the decorated Upper Paleolithic cave of Chauvet-Pont d'Arc, Ardèche, France. *Proceedings of the National Academy of Sciences of the USA* 113:4670–75.

12 Sadier, B., J.-J. Delannoy, L. Benedetti, D. L. Bourlès, S. Jaillet, J.-M. Geneste, A.-E. Lebatard and M. Arnold 2012. Further constraints on the Chauvet Cave artwork elaboration. *Proceedings of the National Academy of Sciences of USA* 109:8002–06.

13 Rappenglück, M. A. 2002. The claviform P-sign a time unit? Interpreting a Palaeolithic symbol. In *Istorija i kultura vostoka Asii*. Tom I: *Materialy meždunarodnoj naucnoj konferenzii Novosibirsk, 9-11 dekabrja 2002 g*, pp. 224–29. Institut archeologii i etnografii SO RAN, Novosbirisk.

14 Conkey, M. W. 1980. The identification of prehistoric hunter-gatherer aggregation sites: The case of Altamira. *Current Anthropology* 21:609–30.

15 Michel Lorblanchet has undertaken a masterful recording and analysis of Cougnac, published in detail in Lorblanchet, M. 2010. *Art Pariétal: Grottes Ornées du Quercy*. Éditions de Rouergue, Rodez. Many of the details of the layout of the site come from this book.

16 Bégouën, R., C. Fritz, G. Tosello, J. Clottes, A. Pastoors and F. Faist 2009. *Le Sanctuaire Secret des Bisons: Il y a 14,000 Ans, dans la Caverne du Tuc d'Audoubert*. Somogy Editions d'Art, Paris.

17 Lorblanchet, M., M. M. Labeau and J. L. Vernet 1988. Première etude des pigments des grottes ornées quercinoises. *Préhistoire Quercinoise* 3:79–94.

Lorblanchet, M., M. M. Labeau, J. L. Vernet, P. Fitte, H. Valladas, H. Cachier and M. Arnold 1990. Palaeolithic pigments in the Quercy, France. *Rock Art Research* 7:4–20.

Chalmin, E., M. Menu, M.-P. Pomiès, C. Vignaud, N. Aujoulat and J.-M. Geneste 2004. Les blasons de Lascaux. *L'Anthropologie* 108:571–92.

18 Clottes, J., M. Menu and P. Walter 1990. New light on the Niaux paintings. *Rock Art Research* 7: 21–26.

19 Benazzi, S., K. Douka, C. Fornai, C. C. Bauer, O. Kullmer, J. Svoboda, I. Pap, F. Mallegni, P. Bayle, M. Coquerelle, S. Condemi, A. Ronchitelli, K. Harvati and G. W. Weber 2011. Early dispersal of modern humans in Europe and implications for Neanderthal behavious. *Nature* 479:525–28.

20 Trinkaus, E., O. Moldovan, Ş. Milota, A. Bîlgăr, L. Sarcina, S. Athreya, S. E. Bailey, R. Rodrigo, G. Mircea, T. Higham, C. Bronk Ramsey and J. van der Plicht 2003. An early modern human from the Peştera cu Oase, Romania. *Proceedings of the National Academy of Sciences of USA* 100: 11,231–36.

21 Higham, T., T. Compton, C. Stringer, R. Jacobi, B. Shapiro, E. Trinkaus, B. Chandler, F. Gröning, C. Collins, S. Hillson, P. O'Higgins, C. FitzGerald and M. Fagan 2011. The earliest evidence for anatomically modern humans in northwestern Europe. *Nature* 479:521–24.

22 Clottes, J. and J. Courtin 1996. *The Cave Beneath the Sea: Paleolithic Images at Cosquer.* Harry N. Abrams, New York.

23 Baffier, D. and M. Girard 1998. *Les Cavernes d'Arcy-sur-Cure.* La Maison des Roches, Paris. Baffier, D. and M. Girard 2007. La Grande Grotte d'Arcy-sur-Cure. *Les Dossiers d'Archéologie* 324:74–85.

Chapter 7

1   Rifkin, R. F., C. S. Henshilwood and M. M. Haaland 2015. Late Pleistocene figurative art mobilier from Apollo II Cave, Karas Region, Southern Namibia. *South African Archaeological Bulletin* 70 (201): 113–23. Wendt, W. E. 1974. 'Art mobilier' from the Apollo II Cave, South West Africa: Africa's oldest dated works of art. *South African Archaeological Bulletin* 31 (121/122):5–11.

2   Flood, J. 1997. *Rock Art of the Dreamtime.* Angus and Robertson, Sydney.

3   Lewis, D. 1988. *The Rock Paintings of Arnhem Land, Australia: Social, Ecological and Material Culture Change in the Post-Glacial Period.* BAR International Series 415. British Archaeological Reports, Oxford.

4   Whitley, D. 1998. Finding rain in the desert: landscape, gender and far western North American rock-art. In C. Chippindale and P. S. C. Taçon (eds), *The Archaeology of Rock-Art*, pp. 11–29.

5   Elliott, G. F. S. 1920. *Prehistoric Man and His Story.* Seeley, Service and Co. Ltd., London.

6   McNiven, I. J. and L. Russell 2005. *Appropriated Pasts: Indigenous Peoples and the Colonial Culture of Archaeology.* AltaMira Press, Oxford.

7   Gould, S. J. 1981. *The Mismeasure of Man.* W. W. Norton and Company, New York.

8   Stone, A. 1997. Regional variation in Maya cave art. *Journal of Cave and Karst Studies* 59(1):33–42.

9   Gay, C. 1967. Oldest cave paintings in the New World. *Natural History* 76(4):28–35.

10 Stone, A. 1995. *Images from the Underworld: Naj Tunich and the Tradition of Maya Cave Painting.* University of Texas Press, Austin. The quotes in this section are from the above source. See also the writings of James E. Brady, in particular his unpublished doctoral dissertation, Brady, J. E. 1989. An Investigation of Maya Ritual Cave Use with Special Reference to Naj Tunich, Peten, Guatemala. University of California, Los Angeles. More easily accessible is the co-written illustrated article: Brady, J. E. and A. J. Stone 1986: Naj Tunich: Entrance to the Maya underworld. *Archaeology* 39(6): 18–25.

11 Chase, A. F. and D. Z. Chase 1987. *Investigations at the Classic Maya City of Caracol, Belize: 1985–1987.* Monograph 3. Pre-Columbian Art Research Institute, San Francisco.

12 Wilson, M., J. Sanhambath, P. D. Senembe, B. David, N. Hall and M. Abong 2000. 'Tufala kev blong devil': People and spirits in North West Malakula, Vanuatu – implications for management. *Conservation and Management of Archaeological Sites* 4:151–66.

13 Also of interest here is the work of social anthropologist Howard Morphy, in particular: Morphy, H. 1991. *Ancestral Connections: Art and an Aboriginal System of Knowledge.* The University of Chicago Press, Chicago.

14 Taylor, L. 1996. *Seeing the Inside: Bark Painting in Western Arnhem Land*, pp. 122–23. Clarendon Press, Oxford.

15 Young, J. 1988. *Signs from the Ancestors: Zuni Cultural Symbolism and Perceptions of Rock Art.* University of New Mexico Press, Albuquerque.

16 Brady, L. M. and J. J. Bradley 2016. 'That painting now is telling us something': Negotiating and apprehending contemporary meaning in Yanyuwa rock art, northern Australia. In L. M. Brady and P. S. C. Taçon (eds), *Relating to Rock Art in the Contemporary World: Navigating Symbolism, Meaning and Significance.* University Press of Colorado, Boulder.

List of illustrations

figurative art mobilier from Apollo 11, southern Namibia. *Expression: International Journal of Art, Archaeology and Conceptual Anthropology* 9:97–101, 2015. Image Enhancement Robert Gunn **183–185** Auscape/Getty Images **186** The late Grahame Walsh (for Gwion line drawings over Kimberley region); Darrell Lewis (for Dynamic Figures line drawings over Arnhem Land); Kara Rasmanis, Monash University (for base map) **187, 188** Images courtesy of traditional owner Ambrose Mungala Chalarimeri, Elder of the Kwini tribe **189, 190** Photos Bruno David. Reproduced with permission from Margaret Katherine, Jawoyn Elder

191 Photo Peter Veth, used with permission of the Dambimangari Traditional Owners **192** Photo N. Cirani/DeAgostini/The Art Archive. Permission by Jeff Lee, senior Traditional Owner Burrungkuy (Nourlangie Rock) Kakadu National Park **193** Photo Bruno David **194** Muséum de Toulouse. Photo Didier Descouens **195** Rich Reid/National Geographic Creative **196** Photo Jim Bouldin **197** Photo Bruno David **198** Map Julien Monney **199, 200** Photos Bruno David **201** Reproduced courtesy Museum Victoria, Melbourne **202** Patrick Endres/Design Pictures/SuperStock **203** Photo Talk2winik

204 Weltbild/Interfoto/akg-images **205** World History Archive/SuperStock **206** Photo George Veni **207** Photo James Brady **208** Wilbur E. Garrett/National Geographic/Getty Images **209–212** Photos James Brady **213** Stephen Alvarez/National Geographic Creative **214** Photo James Brady **215** Wilbur E. Garrett/National Geographic/Getty Images **216–221** Photos Meredith Wilson **222** Peter Marralwanga, *Two Wallabies, Barrk*, 1979 © Estate of the artist licensed by Aboriginal Artists Agency Ltd. Photo Luke Taylor **223** (above) Photo Liam M. Brady (below) Photo Amanda Kearney.

Acknowledgments

Writing this book has been an absolute pleasure, all the more so thanks to the many people who helped along the way. My deep gratitude to Chris Scarre for suggesting this book in the first place, and to all who gave much appreciated feedback on the good and bad of earlier drafts, and helped with images: Ken Aplin, Bryce Barker, Jean-Jacques Delannoy, Jean-Michel Geneste and Mike Hermes gave valuable advice on large parts of the book; and on specific sections, Maxime Aubert, Philip Batty, Valda Blundell, John Bradley, Liam Brady, Ambrose Chalarimeri, Emilie Chalmin, Richard Cosgrove, Carole Fritz, Michel Girard, Andy Gleadow, Robert 'ben' Gunn, Simon Haberle, Pauline Heaney, Christopher Henshilwood, Zenobia Jacobs, Margaret Katherine, Petro Keene, Peter Kershaw, Jeff Lee, Darrell Lewis, Ian McNiven, Jerome Mialanes, Maria Myers, Sue O'Connor, Gabrielle O'Loughlin, Sven Ouzman, Fiona Petchey, Alistair Pike, Martin Porr, Thomas Richards, Richard Roberts, Lynette Russell, Mike Smith, Chris Stringer, Traudl Tan, Luke Taylor, Gilles Tosello, Peter Veth, Alan Watchman, Meredith Wilson, Vicky Winton and Rachel Wood; and to the wonderful team at Thames & Hudson: Jen Moore, Ben Plumridge, Mark Sapwell, and Louise Thomas. The book benefitted also from Australian Research Council *Kimberley Visions* Linkage Grant LP150100490 and Centre of Excellence for Australian Biodiversity and Heritage Grant CE170100015; many thanks to the Kimberley Land Council and Balanggarra Aboriginal Corporation, and to project partners the universities of Western Australia, Melbourne and Monash, the Kimberley Foundation Australia, Dunkeld Pastoral and the Western Australian Department of Parks and Wildlife. Last but not least, thanks to the Monash Indigenous Centre at Monash University for their support.

portable objects 13, 18–19, 21, 24, 50–51, 85, 140–44, 202–4, *11, 18, 40, 92, 112, 113, 115–20, 137, 180–82*; versus fixed art 46
pottery: *see* ceramics
Poznik, David 91
Princess Charlotte Bay, Australia 217–18, *198*
Puritjarra, Australia 80–81, *65*

Qafzeh, Israel 118, 134

Ravidat, Marcel 27–28, *21, 23*
recording, of rock art 46–47, 48
representation: *see* symbolism
Rigaud, Solange 95–96
Riparo Bombrini, Italy 89
ritual 164, 171, 175, 179, 183, 226, 229–30, 233, *205, 206, 207, 209*
Rivière, Émile 23–24, 179
Roberts, Richard 74, *58*
Rochefoucauld, Count of La 27
rock pavements 13
Rouzaud, François 110–11
Russell, Lynette 221

Sadier, Benjamin 51
Sahul 137
Sanhambath, Jimmyson 233
Santillana del Mar, Spain 18
Sanz de Sautuola, Marcellino 18–19, 21, 22, 27, 145, 147, 148, *9, 11, 14*
Sanz de Sautuola, María 19, *12, 13*
semiotics, in rock art interpretation 9
Senembe, Peta Dan 233, *217*
shading, in cave art 150, 158, *126, 128*
shamanism, in rock art interpretation 9
Shanidar Cave, Iraq 104–5, *81*
Sibudu, South Africa 124
Smith, Claire 6
Smith, Mike 80, *65*
Solutrean 143, 149, 152, 155, *119*
songlines, in Aboriginal Australia 219–20
Soressi, Marie 108
spatial patterning of art 46, 81, 118, 137, 166–70, 185–88, 207, 217–18, *186, 198*
speared anthropomorphs 169, *147, 148*

speleothems, and cave art 24, 25, 75–78, 110–12, 145–46, 164, 168, 170–71, 179, 183, 191, 193–201, 213, *61, 64, 86, 87, 88, 89, 139, 142, 146, 175–80*
Spencer, Baldwin 219
St Acheul, France 94, *72*; *see also* Acheulean
Still Bay: *see* Middle Stone Age, southern Africa
Stone Age 119, 124–31, 138, *100*
stone altars 6
Stone, Andrea 223, 227, 230, 233
stone lamps 24, 166, *18, 144*
stratigraphy 24, 25
Stringer, Chris 82, *67*
Sunda 137
Swanscombe, England 94
symbolism 13–14, 82, 85–86, 126, 127–28, 130–31, 133, 143, 160, 170, 214, 242

Taçon, Paul 11
Tan-Tan 'figurine', Morocco 97, 105, *74*
Tasmanian 'tiger' 210, *190*
Tata, Hungary 108
Taylor, Luke 239, 241
tectiform 159
Temnata Cave, Bulgaria 108
Terra Amata, France 89, *70*
territorial marking, rock art as 214
Texler, Pierre-Jean 129–30
Thaon, Maurice 28
Three Gorges Dam, China 14
Timor Leste 75–78, *59*
Tito Bustillo, Spain 147
Torres Strait 54–58, *44–46*
totemism 9, 219
Trinil shell 100–1, 124, 189, *78*
Trinkaus, Erik 115
Tuc d'Audoubert, France 172–79, *150–56*
Turau Kula, Torres Strait (Australia) 55–58, *44–47*
Twin Rivers site, Zambia 101–2, 105, *79*
'two-way' historical research 10–11

Ulpunyali, Australia 81
Uma, Torres Strait (Australia) 55, 57

United Nations Educational, Scientific and Cultural Organization (UNESCO) 7
uranium-series (U-series) dating: *see* dating
Utah, USA 16, 215, *196*

Vanhaeren, Marian 95–96
'Venus' figurines 142–143, *116–18*
Villanova y Piera, Juan 21
Vindija Cave, Croatia 91
Virchow, Rudolf 21
visual codes: *see* symbolism
Volgu, France *119*

Walter, Philippe 185, 188
Wandjina paintings, Australia 74, 211, *57, 58, 191*
Wardaman Country, Australia 70, 193, 211, *55, 193*
Wargata Mina, Australia 206
wasp nests, dating cave art 68–69, 73–74, *57, 58*
Watchman, Alan 70, *72–73*
West Tofts, England 93, *71*
Whear, Ray 42
Wilgie Mia ochre mine, Australia *66*
Wilson, Meredith 55, 67–69, 233, 237
Woddordda Aboriginal people, Australia *191*
Wonderwerk Cave, South Africa 105
World Heritage List 7
World War II 27, *24, 115*
'wounded men': *see* speared anthropomorphs

X-ray art, Arnhem Land (Australia) 59–62, 211, 238–42, *48, 49, 50, 51, 212, 222*

Yalo, Vanuatu 58, 233–38, *216–21*
Yanyuwa Country, Australia 242, 244, *223*
Yiwarlarlay, Australia 70–73, *56*

Zafarraya, Spain 89
Zilhão, João 115, 148, 189
Zinacantán, Mexico 224
Zuni, USA 242